The JustMissional Church

Pursuing God's Path for Justice

Ronald P. Hesselgrave

To Kathi

Lifelong companion, confidant, and partner in ministry.

CONTENTS

Foreword

The church. What are the images that come to mind? We might think of a building with a steeple. Or a place where people gather for worship. Some might have negative images of abusive relationships with clergy. Many years ago when I was an undergraduate student at Texas A&M I thought the church was simply a place for me to go on Sunday. After all, my spiritual needs were met outside the church.

No matter the image many will agree that whatever the church is, it is certainly made up of people who have problems. Some might argue that the church itself has problems.   Indeed, we live in an imperfect world, with imperfect institutions run by imperfect people. Nevertheless those of us who have worked in the church, no matter the context, are increasingly aware of how dysfunctional and ineffective the church has been in fulfilling its mission to love God and love others.

Over the course of my career as a missionary, professor, and business entrepreneur the church has certainly exemplified the Reformation adage *ecclesia semper reformanda est*. In the 1980s the church was largely traditional. Sundays were still days of rest and people wore their best clothes to the service that generally lasted about an hour. By the end of the 1980s and going into the 1990s the church began to ask the question of how relevant it was in society. Church planting, although not new by any means, became focused on contextual forms while maintaining the meaning. Seeker services focused on bridging the cultural gap between the traditional Sunday service and contemporary culture. By the 2000s we talked about the emerging church and the ensuing theological challenges to some traditional doctrines that had an edge to them and did not fit in an increasingly pluralistic environment. Now we are into the missional church movement that sees God as active in the world carrying out his purpose as the church is invited to participate in his mission.

All along the journey of the past several decades the church has moved from an inward focus and soul saving to an outward focus on both the material and spiritual needs of people. I believe it has been a positive journey; one that is bearing fruit as people are learning that the church is concerned not only with one's personal salvation, but for the entire person. That is what *The JustMissional Church* is about.

Dr. Hesselgrave has written what is no doubt an important volume for those who want to continue the journey. *The JustMissional Church* is about the church rediscovering its call to justice. As Ron explains, justice is a far more rich concept than simply reducing it to the social gospel. It is at the core of God's character and should therefore characterize the church. As he says, the worship of God cannot be separated from acts of justice. Here is the challenge: "If our lives fail to reflect God's heart for justice and mercy our songs of praise are only noise in his ears, our offerings and religious observances are meaningless, and our most eloquent prayers are an affront to him." This is a must read for anyone concerned about the future of the church.

Michael T. Cooper, PhD
President, The Timothy Center for Sustainable Transformation, Inc.
Principal Partner, TCE Global Solutions, LLC
Editor of *Social Injustice: What Evangelicals Need to Know about the World*

Preface

Two words that one often finds in contemporary discussions regarding the role of the church in society are "justice" and "missional." The need for missional churches and communities is apparent from the stark reality that the church, especially in Western cultures, is not making any significant impact. The preoccupation with "attractional" churches as the preferred model of church planting has resulted in pockets of growth. But the church is in decline overall, and usually ends up mimicking culture rather than influencing it. The concept of "missional communities" highlights the role of the entire church in engaging and infiltrating culture with the gospel, without copying it. But I would contend that missional outreach alone is not enough. There is a growing recognition, given the blatent injustices, human slavery, and grinding poverty around the world, that the church must also manifest the justice of God's kingdom. At the same time, a concern for justice divorced from a witness to the gospel of the kingdom is not sufficient, nor is it biblical. What we need, then, is the integration of justice and mission in a way that forms what I would call JustMissional churches or communities.

This concept of the JustMissional church, which I will be developing throughout the course of this book, is rooted in the observation that *missiology* is closely bound up with *eccesiology*, or the doctrine of the church. Our understanding of mission shapes the church just as our understanding of the church influences our view of mission. Images of the church and mission abound. A brief internet search reveals the following adjectives that are used to describe the church: seeker-oriented, purpose-driven, externally focused, missional, emergent, multi-site, video-venue, cyber church, cell church, multi-service—and even the "cowboy" church. Similarly, missions is described in terms of tent making, indigenization, church growth through the homogeneous-unit principle, incarnational ministry, short-term mission, holistic mission, emerging mission, rapid-church-multiplication, business-as-mission, and the 10/40 window. These two internet searches are far from exhaustive.

What is revealing about most descriptions of church and mission is that emphasis is placed on missionary and church planting methods—that is, the functional *doing* dimension of church life and mission. This reflects the practical and pragmatic nature of Western, and particularly American, culture which focuses on activities, results, and accomplishments. Even innovative approaches to church planting are described as a different way of "doing" church. Likewise, the popularity of missions terminology that speaks of doing something (assignment, trip, methods, best practices, strategy, objectives, reach, mobilize, target, engage, spread the gospel, and so on.) reflects a concept of the church's mission as a "task" to be accomplished.[1]

Missionary methods and the accompanying activities are indeed important. After all, Jesus told his followers to "make disciples." And what is this mandate if it does not involve a task? We ought to be concerned about how we engage the world with the gospel. But, as Ken Baker rightly points out, if mission is seen *simply* as a task then the church is merely a "delivery mechanism" for the gospel. What is missing is the essential relational dimension, where the new divine and human relationship in Christ is lived out and "the imperative of kingdom character and community shapes God's people into the living gospel before the watching world."[2] Similarly, focusing on *functional* questions about "how to *do* church" or achieve the "right mixture" of programs and activities without first addressing *foundational* questions about the church's essential nature and identity is to put the cart before the horse and make "methods" the driving force behind all the church says and does. Since church-related programs and methods are often developed in response to a specific cultural context the danger is that church will be more reflective of the dominant cultural ethos than of what God has called it to be.

This was brought home to me in a visit that I made years ago to a local church as a missionary candidate. The church was very receptive to my appeal for support. But it was engaged in an extensive program to renovate and expand the church facilities. My heart sank as I heard the chairperson of the missions committee talk about the money that was being spent on a new entry way for the church. The installation of a new decorative door itself cost thousands of dollars. As a result, few resources were available to support new missionaries. My purpose in relating this story is not to engage in sour grapes. Nor is it simply to raise the issue of budgeting priorities. There is a more fundamental concern here. Within evangelical culture conversion in described almost exclusively in individualistic terms. We talk, for example, about "inviting Christ into one's heart." But it will be argued in this book that conversion has a horizontal or social dimension as well as vertical or spiritual dimension. "The issue here is that Christ intends to redeem humankind socially as well as individually. *The social redemption of humanity begins in the church.*"[3] In other words, redemption affects social structures and relationships. What, then, does it mean for the church to function as a redeemed community? As a corporate body how does it manifest the righteousness and justice of Christ's kingdom? What does this mean in practical terms for a church that is divided by class and race and when every night 1 out of 8 people in the world goes to bed hungry (WFP)? These are some questions that are the concern of this book.

This book is intended for laypersons interested in missions and the church's engagement with society as well as church pastors, leaders, missionary practitioners, and others engaged in Christian service. I realize, of course, that not everyone will have the same level of interest or familiarity with the issues treated here. Although I hope this book will also be of interest to academicians, I do not write as a biblical scholar and I have tried to avoid overly academic jargon as much as possible. For the reader who is interested, I have included more extensive definitions of terms, bibliographic references, and elaboration of my arguments in the endnotes which are located at the end of each chapter.

One author has compared writing a book to carpentry. Both involve little magic, and a lot of hard work and perseverance! This book, from its conception to completion, has been a long journey. I am grateful to both family and friends for their support, encouragement, and insights along the way. My father, Dr. David J. Hesselgrave; brother, Dennis Hesselgrave; Jim Baker; and others read portions of the manuscript and offered encouragement. Special thanks goes to Dr. Michael Cooper who gave valuable comments and insights on each chapter and to Lore Cooper who painstakingly edited the entire manuscript. I want to also thank Michael for graciously agreeing to write the foreword to this book. Lastly (but certainly not least!) I am indebted to my wife Kathi who has been my faithful and patient "sounding board" throughout the entire process.

Notes

[1] See Ken Baker, "Kingdom Mission—A Task to Finish? Recovering the Relational Narrative of Mission," (Unpublished paper read at the Southeast Regional conference of the Evangelical Missiological Society, March, 2012. http://www. edsmither.com/uploads/5/6/4/6/564614/baker_ems_2012.pdf
[2] Ibid.
[3] Craig A. Blaising and Darrell Bock, *Progressive Dispensationalism: An Up-To-Date Handbook of Contemporary Dispensational Thought* (Wheaton, IL: BridgePoint, 1993), p. 287.

Introduction

Stories are the stuff of life. Narrative is how we teach, explain, and entertain ourselves. Various types of stories shape us as much as we shape stories. In fact, our culture is permeated by the "power of story." It has become the dominant means by which we understand our world, ourselves, and each other.[1] Think, for example, of the summer and winter Olympics. For two weeks the eyes of over three billion people around the world are glued to television sets as they watch their nation's athletes compete for a medal. Throughout the history of the Olympic games there have been dramatic stories of remarkable human achievement—Jesse Owens conquering the world despite great physical and racial obstacles, the "miracle on ice" of the men's U.S. hockey team, the "perfect ten" of Nadia Comanici, and Michael Phelps winning the most medals in Olympic history. There are also inspirational stories—the Jamaican bobsled team, ski jumping's "Eddie the Eagle," and Oscar Blade Runner Pistorius, the first double amputee to compete in the Olympic Games. Finally, there are stories of tragedy, such as killing of Israeli athletes during the 1972 games in Munich. Each of these individual stories takes on additional significance and meaning in relation to the spirit of the Olympic movement as a whole.

But partial or incomplete stories can be misleading, even destructive. We observe this to our chagrin every time a new election cycle rolls around. Politicians are notorious for giving only part of the story in their campaign ads. Some of you may recall Paul Harvey's program *The Rest of the Story.* Beginning as a part of his newscasts during the Second World War and then premiering as its own series on the ABC Radio Networks on May 10, 1976, this popular program consisted of little known stories on a variety of subjects. Harvey would delay narrating key elements of the story until the very end (usually after a commercial break). Then, in his inimitable style, he would conclude with a variation on the tag line "and *now* you know the rest of the story. Good day!"

My contention in this book is that a large percentage of people in the Christian church today are taught only *part* of the story of God's "good news" of redemption in the Bible. Evangelicals are rightly concerned about personal redemption and regeneration through Christ's atonement on the cross. This is the part of the biblical story of redemption which is either ignored or downplayed by the more liberal mainline churches. Many evangelical churches, on the other hand, fail to see that personal regeneration is tied to God's broader kingdom purposes. They often have minimal impact on society because they either do not fully understand or fail to live out "the rest of the story" of God's concern for justice and mercy. Before delving into the theological context for this argument it is important to give a brief overview of the historical context—or the "story" of evangelical social involvement.

Evangelical Involvement in Social Justice

My concern in this section is to give a brief account of the evangelical heritage of social involvement in the 19th century and of changes that have occurred in the evangelical movement since then. This is important in providing an historical context for the issues that will be addressed throughout the course of this book. But, first, some clarification of terminology is needed. The following story is often used to illustrate the difference between justice and compassion:

Introduction

A man went to the river one day and noticed that someone was drowning in the middle of it. He quickly swam out to save the drowning person. He brought the person to safety and attempted to catch his breath. A short while later, the man noticed another person drowning in the river. He mustered up all of his strength and dove back into the river to save the second drowning victim. The second person was brought safely to shore. By this time, the man was exhausted and had a hard time breathing. Several minutes later, as he looked up, to his dismay, he noticed a third person floating down the river, crying for help. Once again, feeling he didn't have a choice, he dove into the water to save the third person. However, the man was so tired from having saved the first two victims that he wasn't able to continue swimming and he drowned.

The man's response to the drowning people was one of compassion . . . However, if [he] had driven up the road along the bend in the river, he would have noticed someone at a factory who was throwing people into the river. The abusive man was the source of the problem. If the compassionate man had intervened at the factory, that would have been an act of justice.[2]

We might say that while compassion is about helping people who are hurting, justice goes further to address the source or root causes of the problem.[3] As we will see, much of the debate among evangelicals over social involvement has had to do with whether the church should be involved in addressing issues of justice.

Nineteenth Century Missions and Revivalism

Two towering figures in the history of missions are William Carey and David Livingstone. The stories of both men have been an inspiration to thousands of Christians around the world. John Carey, a shoemaker turned missionary to India, is often credited with found-

15

ing the modern mission movement. Seven years after Carey's death (1834) David Livingstone arrived as a missionary in South Africa. Famous for his travels across the continent of Africa, Livingstone is often remembered as a great explorer. But he was first of all a missionary who had a burning desire to see the transformation of Africa through the gospel. We would do well to remember, however, that while these and other missionary pioneers were part of the enormous expansion of Christianity in the nineteenth century they did not concentrate on preaching the gospel to the exclusion of the social betterment of the indigenous peoples. Nor, as John Stott so aptly points out, was their social concern restricted to aid and relief, to the neglect of development and even sociopolitical activity.[4] Carey was so appalled by the practice of *Sati* in India, which involved burning the wife on the funeral pyre of her deceased husband, that he worked tirelessly to end the practice. Through cooperation with Hindus like Raja Ram Mohan Roy he put pressure on the British colonial government, which made *Sati* illegal in 1832. In recognition of his efforts for social reform and other improvements the Indian Government honored his memory with a postage stamp on the bicentennial anniversary of his arrival in India.[5] Similarly, Livingstone witnessed the great evils caused by the slave trade; and this "burned in his mind the conviction that the righting of this wrong was the greatest duty laid on Europe and the churches."[6] Carey and Livingston were not alone in their concern for social justice. As Pearce Beaver has argued, from the time of the apostles, social involvement in mission has not been limited to relief.

> The itinerating missionary carried with him a bag of medicine, new or better seeds and plants, and improved livestock. Nevius introduced the modern orchard industry in Shantung. The Basel missionaries revolutionized the economy of Ghana by introducing coffee and cocoa grown by families and individuals on their own land. James McKean transformed the life of Northern Thailand by eliminating its three major curses—smallpox, malaria, and leprosy. Wells and pure water of-

Introduction

ten came through the help of missionaries. Industrial schools were stressed through the nineteenth century, and industries were established. In addition, the missionaries were constantly the protectors of the native peoples against exploitation and injustice by government and commercial companies.[7]

Coinciding with the great missionary expansion there were the evangelical revivals in Britain and America. Donald Dayton, Timothy Smith, and others have documented that in the mid-nineteenth century social involvement was both the "child of evangelicalism and the twin sister of evangelism."[8] The Wesley's, Whitfield, and Finney all combined evangelistic fervor with a concern to address social problems and evils. John Wesley fought against slavery and for prison reform.[9] And Finney was convinced both that the gospel "releases a mighty impulse toward social reform" and that the church's neglect of social reform grieved the Holy Spirit and hindered true revival.[10] It is hard for us to comprehend the sheer inhumanity of the slave trade, which has been described as the greatest migration in human history. During the four hundred years of the slave trade (1444-1844) an estimated 40 million people were taken out of Africa. Some 20 million were brought to the New World. Millions died in the long voyage across the Atlantic Ocean. Those who survived were taken into captivity on farms and plantations.[11] According to Dayton, "The anti-slavery forces [in America] were drawn largely from the converts of Finney's revivals."[12]

The "Great Reversal"

Much has been written about what has been termed the "Great Reversal" in the attitudes of American evangelicals towards social involvement. In actuality, there were two distinct stages in this change of attitudes.[13] The first "preparatory" stage, which took place from 1865 to 1900, involved a diminishing of interest in the use of *political* means to promote the welfare of society, especially the poor and oppressed. The main reason for this shift was the transition from a postmillennial and Calvinistic vision of Christian culture to dispensational premillennialism.[14] In Calvinistic postmillennialism, Old Testament Israel was the model for political institutions. According to this view, which dominated American evangelicalism from the time of Puritanism to about the middle of the 19th century, "the Christian ideal was to introduce God's kingdom . . . not only in the lives of the regenerate elect, but means of civil laws that would both restrain evil and comprehensively transform culture according to God's will."[15] Charles Finney expressed this viewpoint when he stated that the Christian church was designed to work for the reform of individuals, communities and government "until the kingdom . . . shall be given to the people. . . [and] every form of iniquity shall be driven from the earth."[16] Jonathan Blanchard similarly envisioned "a perfect state of society" when "the Law of God is the Law of the Land."[17] Referring to the social effects of revivalism, Edward Beecher wrote in 1835 that the churches were "aroused as never before" to the belief that "a glorious advent of the kingdom of God" was near at hand. Christians were coming to see that their task was "not merely to preach the gospel to every creature, but to reorganize human society in accordance with the law of God. To abolish all corruptions in religion and all abuses in the social system and, so far as it has been erect on false principles, to take it down and erect it anew."[18]

Gradually, however, a growing emphasis on the New Testament "dispensation" of the Holy Spirit and its identification with the events of Pentecost led evangelicals to draw a clear distinction between the law and Spirit and the Old Testament and the New Testament. Within the dispensationalist movement a contrast was made between the present New Testament age of the Spirit and the previous Old Testament age of law. This involved a shift towards a more "private" and "pietistic" view of Christianity. As Marsden describes this view, "The Holy Spirit worked in the hearts of individuals and was known primarily through personal experience. Social action, still an important concern, was more in the province of private agencies. The kingdom was no longer viewed as a kingdom of laws; hence civil

law would not help its advance."[19]   It should be emphasized, however, that while premillennial dispensationalists in theory gave up the
Calvinist-Puritan Old Testament covenantal view of the advance of
the religious-political kingdom through the people of God they were
not entirely consistent in this regard. Many evangelicals with dispensationalist leanings promoted Sabbath legislation (despite its Old Testament origins), prohibition, and the idea of a "Christian civilization."
More significantly, revivalist evangelicalism still included those who
vigorously championed social concern, especially in the form of private charity.

The second stage of the "Great Reversal" dates from 1900 to 1930.
It was during this period that evangelicals virtually abandoned social
involvement altogether, or at least subordinated it to other concerns.
The most important factor in this sudden shift was the fundamentalist reaction to the rise of the liberal Social Gospel after 1900.[20]   This
reaction cannot be rightly understood unless we keep in mind that
evangelicals always viewed social involvement—whether expressed
individually or publicly, privately or politically—as an outgrowth of
individual regeneration through faith in Christ. The necessary first
step was repentance for sin and total dependence on God's grace.[21]
In the words of Samuel Schmucker, a Lutheran leader who was an
active supporter of the revivals, "Without holiness no one shall see
God. As all men are by nature and practice sinners; unless a man be
born again, be converted from sin to holiness, he cannot see the
kingdom of heaven."[22]   By contrast, the Social Gospel emphasized
social reform in a way that undercut the importance of eternal salvation through Christ's atonement for sins. This was evident from the
writings of Walter Rauschenbusch, the most popular spokesman for
the Social Gospel movement. In his first book, *Christianity and the
Social Crisis* (1907) he contrasted "the old evangel of the saved soul"
with "the new evangel of the Kingdom of God." "It is not a matter
of getting individuals into heaven," he argued, "but of transforming
the life on earth into the harmony of heaven."[23]   Rauschenbusch and
other proponents of the Social Gospel further implied that humans

can establish the kingdom of God by themselves. The kingdom of God was therefore equated with the progress of human civilization. With the growing dichotomy between the Social Gospel and the Revivalist Gospel "the position that one could have *both* revivalism and social action became increasingly cumbersome to defend."[24]

Recent Trends in Evangelical Social and Political Involvement

It is not possible here to give a detailed description of trends within the evangelical movement in the era that followed the 1920s. Suffice it to say that in the mid-decades of the twentieth century the more fundamentalist strains of evangelicalism avoided direct social and political involvement. The repeated mainline Protestant critique of fundamentalism was that its emphasis on personal conversion and "other worldliness" had caused it to become privatized and socially disengaged. Even the less militant "new evangelicals," who were defined by their support of Billy Graham, usually maintained the traditionally "pietist" position that churches and religious leaders should stay out of politics and confine themselves to more "spiritual" matters. The preaching of salvation of souls, especially, was viewed as the most effective response to social problems.[25] However, there were important exceptions to this pattern, most notably Carl F. H. Henry who challenged the overly pietistic tendencies of evangelicals and encouraged them to reclaim their heritage of social justice. In *The Uneasy Conscience of Modern Fundamentalism* (1947) he castigated fundamentalists for their retreat from social involvement and failure to "challenge the injustices of the totalitarianisms, the secularisms of modern education, the evils of racial hatred, the wrongs of current labor-management relations, the inadequate bases of international dealings."[26] For the most part, Henry's appeals seemed to fall on deaf ears. But gradually his message caught on as evangelical leaders once again began to grapple with the social implications of the gospel.

There are three developments within evangelicalism over the last fifty years or so that are worth mentioning. The first is the debate within

the evangelical community over the relationship between evangelism and social concern, which was sparked in large part by the International Congress on World Evangelization held in July 1974 in Lausanne, Switzerland. At that conference it was affirmed that "evangelism and socio-political involvement are both part of our Christian duty."[27] In the years following the Lausanne Congress there has been tension within the evangelical movement over the proper relationship between evangelism and social involvement, with some emphasizing evangelism and others urging a more "holistic" understanding of the gospel.

The second trend is the gradual suburbanization of churches since the 1950s and 1960s. This has been accompanied by the influences of large-scale religious marketing and "perplexing mixes of the spiritual and materialistic."[28] As Marsden points out, while evangelicals reject sexually permissive lifestyles as an essential part of the Christian life and are more generous than other religious groups "there are not many other material aspects of the American dream that most adherents are expected to give up. Rather, it is usually assumed, and sometimes advertised, that the comforts of the suburbs, ability to vacation in exotic places, and economic security may well be added benefits of 'seeking first the kingdom of God.'"[29]

The third development is the re-politicization of significant segments of evangelicalism since the 1970s. On the left, this can be seen in the "Chicago Declaration of Social Concern" (1973) and the emergence of the *Post American*, which developed into Sojourner Fellowship and *Sojourners Magazine*. Jim Wallis, the founder or Sojourners, has written numerous books that address racism, poverty, and the unequal distribution of wealth between the rich and poor. On the right, the resurgence of fundamentalism and conservative evangelicals as a political movement began with the founding of the Moral Majority by Jerry Falwell in 1980. Among conservative evangelicals concern for justice has been largely limited to abortion. Interestingly, the Supreme Court's legalization of abortion in 1973 did not at first spark an evangelical or fundamentalist reaction. It was not until the late 1970s that abortion became a leading evangelical concern.[30] Also, among conservative premillenialists there has also been a curious mixture of: (1) a keen interest in "end-times" scenarios; and (2) calls for a return to a "Christian American" which are more reminiscent of the postmillennial rhetoric of mid-nineteenth century evangelicalism.

The Bigger Picture

What can we conclude from this brief survey of evangelical attitudes towards justice and social involvement? The history of the Christian church reveals a mixture of divine and human factors. So, how can we discern what in the history of the church is truly the work of God's Spirit and what is not? How do we distinguish between the real forces for good and the powers of darkness disguised as angels of light? And how do we prevent culturally defined loves, allegiances and understandings from overwhelming our prior allegiance to God?[31]

In his recent book, *To Change the World: The Irony, Tragedy and Possibility of Christianity in the Late Modern World* (2010) James Davison Hunter points out that engaging the world and pursuing God's restorative purposes over all of life has been the dominant concern and rhetoric of Christian churches, ministries, and organizations, both liberal and conservative.[32] But, he argues, recent efforts to change culture have been flawed by the perspective that all we need is more individuals possessing the right values or "worldview" and, therefore, making better choices. This leads to the position in some faith communities that evangelism is the primary means of changing the world. "If people's hearts and minds are converted, they will have the right values, they will make the right choices and culture will change in turn."[33]

Since the 1980s this emphasis on choice has also predisposed Christians on both the left and the right to view *politics* as a means of changing the world. Bringing about the proper change requires that we get into office those who hold the right values or worldview and therefore make the right choices. Among those on the right the social vision is a right ordering of culture through politics and a "resacralization" of the social order. Those on the left emphasize the social vision of equality through politics. But on both ends of the political spectrum the presumption is "both that one can know God's specific plans in human history and that one possesses the power to realize those plans in human affairs."[34]

In Hunter's view the reliance on political power and social control as the overarching force for generating change is morally bankrupt and theologically suspect. What is needed, instead, is *"faithful presence . . . a recognition that the vocation of the church is to bear witness to and to be the embodiment of the coming Kingdom of God."*[35] Politics will never be the solution to the problems we face. The power we need is not power in the conventional sense, but "power to define reality in ways that sustain benevolence and justice."[36] In this light, the renewal of hearts and minds is an absolute precondition for a truly just and humane society. But change at the individual level alone is not enough. It must be accompanied by the mobilization of *networks* of elites and institutions that work together for a common purpose. This was the key to the success of the Reformation, the fight of Wesley, Wilberforce and other abolitionists against slavery, and dozens of other Christian movements throughout the history of the church. We must remember that

> Even Christ created a network of disciples (who, over time, became spiritual and cultural leaders). Though they originated on the periphery of the social world of that age, they moved to the provincial center of Jerusalem, and then, within a generation, to the center of the ancient world—Rome. They too created new institutions that not only articulated but embodied an alternative to the reigning ways of life of that time.[37]

Hunter's views on political engagement may strike some as being excessive. But his argument is a helpful corrective to current efforts to change culture through political means. As will be argued in the following chapters, while the church can and must speak out against more blatant forms of injustice we must also guard against an idolatrous mixing of the gospel and politics. Hunter's analysis is also important in pointing towards a broader and more comprehensive theological understanding of the church's mission than is often found among evangelicals. More specifically, Hunter's proposal is grounded within the over-arching story of Scripture and it calls us to locate our lives within this alternate story: "The entire biblical narrative centers around the shalom God intended and that he will, one day, restore. The details of the story, however, focus on the Fall, its consequences, and finally God's response to it."[38] This introduces what has generally been referred to as the "missional church"—setting the life and mission of God's people within the context of God's mission and connecting our understanding of God's grand narrative in Scripture to the church's specific mission.[39]

Reading the Bible as One Story

The Bible contains numerous stories, both inspirational and tragic, that describe the human condition. As Chris Wright states, the Bible is "not just a single narrative, like a river with only one channel. It is rather a complex mixture of all kinds of smaller narratives, many of them rather self-contained, with all kinds of other material embedded within them. But there is clearly a direction, a flow . . ."[40] This "direction and flow" of the Bible is the overarching story or "grand narrative" of redemption which takes place against the backdrop of creation and humanity's fall into sin. It is this "greatest story ever told" that gives the all-embracing perspective for understanding the collection of texts that constitute the canon of Scripture.[41] Furthermore, it is a story that describes the direction and flow of history itself. As such, it has universal validity. In Wright's words:

That the Old Testament tells a story needs no defense. My point is much greater however. The Old Testament tells its story as *the* story or, rather, as part of that ultimate and universal story that will ultimately embrace the whole of creation, time and humanity within its scope. In other words, in reading these texts we are invited to embrace a metanarrative, a grand narrative. And on this overarching story is based a worldview that, like all worldviews and metanarratives, claims to explain the way things are, how they have come to be so, and what they will ultimately be. . . It is a story that [is] a rendering of reality—an account of the universe we inhabit and of the new creation we are destined for. We live in a storied universe.[42]

Similarly, N.T. Wright has argued that worldviews are the grid through which humans perceive reality and "a story . . . is . . . the best way of talking about the world as it actually is." The Jewish story about the covenant God, the world and Israel is therefore the most natural way in which their worldview would find expression.[43]

Other theologians refer to the story of God's activity and presence in the world as a "theodrama" in which human beings have speaking and acting parts.[44] This does not in any way diminish the *content* of doctrine, but rather acknowledges the dramatic nature of doctrine itself. This drama of doctrine is rooted in Israel's history and reflects a worldview. The reader/believer participates in this historical process of creation and redemption and is spoken to in the text. So, the church itself is in the thick of drama. As Kevin Vanhoozer states, "It is the unique privilege and responsibility of the people of God to perform the Scriptures . . . Indeed the church constitutes a socially embodied, ongoing argument that claims God is good to and for humanity."[45] This does *not* mean that the church is the norm for theology, since tradition often becomes corrupted and practice becomes deformed. The church is not the *cradle* of theology but its *crucible—or the place where the community's understanding of faith is lived, tested, and reformed.*[46] In the words of Vanhoozer, "The task of theology is to enable hearers and doers of the gospel to respond and correspond to the prior Word and Act of God, and thus to be drawn into action."[47]

We are well aware of the danger of reading something without regard for the larger context. You are probably familiar with the story of the Bible student who decided to read the Bible as he was "led" by the Holy Spirit. Closing his eyes, he opened the Bible and let his index finger fall randomly on a section of the page. The verse to which his finger was pointing read "Then [Judas] went away and hanged himself" (Matt. 27:5). Repeating this procedure, the next words the student read were "Go and do likewise" (Luke 10:37). Humorous as it is, this story contains an uncomfortable truth about the average Christian's knowledge and use of Scripture. Many people in our churches have little awareness of the Bible as one story or how their personal stories and experiences are (or should be) grounded in this larger comprehensive and unfolding story of God's mission in the world. Christians (or would-be Christians) are increasingly accommodating themselves to the other competing stories which are shaped by forces of humanism, consumerism, statism, and religious pluralism largely because they do not know the master story of the Bible. This was impressed on me by a recent conversation that my wife Kathi and I had with an acquaintance who attends a local evangelical church. Somehow, the conversation drifted towards astrology. "Based on the Mayan calendar," she said, "there are people who are predicting the end of the world on December 21, 2012. I don't necessarily believe that, but I do think that the alignment of the stars on that date will have a physical impact." Part of the problem is that we have so chopped the Bible into bits or separate parts that we have lost the forest for the trees and the capacity to challenge other narratives that shape our culture. "The Bible bits are accommodated to the more all-embracing cultural story, and it becomes *that* story . . . that shapes our lives."[48]

This is not to say that there are not dangers in treating the Bible as one story. Recent novelized forms of the Bible such as the *100 Minute Bible*, which was written "for people who want easy access into the central Christian story," tend to downplay, distort and even ignore central teachings of Scripture.[49] Abridged versions of the Bible edit out non-narrative parts and reword the text in an attempt to make the Bible more palatable to the post-modern mindset. But "in pursuit of the larger story we've empowered ourselves to reorganize, distill, edit, and rewrite the actual Scriptures. We have failed to recognize that each of these activities not only interprets but also reduces Scripture."[50] In some cases, the concept of theology as story has been embraced by proponents of the emergent church who reject traditional doctrines of the faith.[51] Rob Bell complains in *Love Wins* that "[telling] a story about a God who inflicts unrelenting punishment on people because they didn't do, or say, or believe the correct things in a brief window of time called life isn't a very good story." And Brian McLaren's three-book fable series that offers a new vision of the Christian life makes almost no mention of original sin, creation-fall-redemption, the deity of Christ, God's holiness and sovereignty, the offense of the Cross, worship, justification and divine inspiration of the Bible.[52]

Reading the Bible as a narrative does not diminish in any way the importance of the other literary genres—prophecy, law, proverb, poetry, letters—that it contains. The non-narrative portions help us properly interpret the story of the Bible while the grand narrative illuminates and integrates the more didactic non-narrative parts. Relating the different genres of Scripture to each other in this way helps us to bridge the gap between theology and practice, orthodoxy and orthopraxis. Leslie Fields rightly states that narrative theology is important in "shift[ing] us from a disembodied hermeneutic of dissection and detachment . . ." The emphasis on story "connects us more tangibly to our common task: to live out the truth of God's Word in our world."[53] This, for example, is why Jesus taught with illustrative stories or parables. Jesus' parables shed light on some aspect of human behavior or experience for the purpose of conveying a spiritual or ethical principle that is to be embraced and lived out by the hearers. It is further significant that the earliest name for Christianity was the "Way" (Acts 9:2). To belong to a way was to follow it. This "way of life" is fundamentally "dramatic," involving speech and action on behalf of Jesus' truth and life.[54] "To be a Christian is to belong to Jesus' way, to be actively oriented and moving in the same direction as Jesus, toward the kingdom of God."[55]

One of the things that concerns me most is the way in which the cult of self-worship in our culture has crept into the church. As if the gospel is all about how to be happy, successful and "become a better you." In embracing the concept of story some evangelicals have described God's story in such a way that it simply affirms our own stories and makes them central. Eugene Peterson observes that "the 'text' that seems to be most in favor on the American landscape today is the sovereign self."[56] The group *A Call to an Ancient Evangelical Future* rightly argues that spirituality made independent from the story of God often leads to legalism, mere intellectual knowledge, an overly therapeutic culture, and a narcissistic preoccupation with one's own experience. It calls evangelicals to reject theological methods that "camouflage God's story or empty it of its cosmic and redemptive meaning"—to "recover the truth of God's Word as the story of the world, and to make it the centerpiece of evangelical life."[57]

Rightly understood, God's story embraces our individual stories and gives them direction. On the one hand, it conveys the truth of his sovereignty over creation and history. It's all about God and his glory, not ours. At the same time, it gives us a unique missional identity as his people who are called to participate in his redemptive mission—one which will culminate in the gathering of all nations to worship him and receive his covenantal blessings. Because of our cultural embrace of individualism, the Christian's sense of identity is often conceived only in personal and individualistic terms. As little children we are taught to sing the words "Jesus loves me this I know, for the Bible tells me so." This radically individualized notion of salvation continues into adulthood. As Michael Goheen has written, "In overemphasizing the benefits of the cross to the individual believer, we have mistakenly allowed its *communal* significance to be eclipsed."[58] Moreover, mission is itself a collective process. "Jesus sends a *community* on a mission to the nations. The whole of Jesus' ministry [was] to gather and form a people who will embody God's purposes for the sake of the world."[59]

The diagram below illustrates this collective nature of the church's mission:[60]

Figure 1. The Missional Church & God's Mission in the World

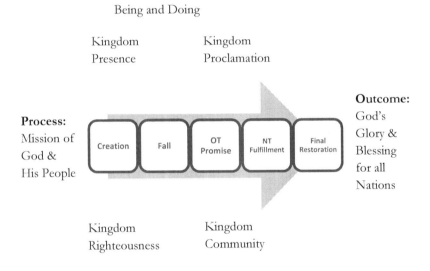

Mission is rooted in God's purposes for his creation. It begins with God's promise of redemption following humanity's fall into sin and his establishment of "a people" who will be a channel of blessing to the nations. It continues with the fulfillment of this promise through

Christ and his body, the church. The New Testament continually looks back to the Old Testament promise it fulfills. It also looks forward to the final restoration of God's purposes—the conclusion or final outcome of God's grand narrative when all nations will acknowledge him as Lord of all creation. The "overlap of the ages" in which we live is the time given for the witness of the church to the ends of the earth in obedience to Christ's command to "make disciples of all nations." It is important to see, however, that this process of making disciples does not just involve the multiplication of believers and churches among all peoples. It is also "a relational process which cultivates the character of the King toward, and within, 'community in Christ,' the interconnected life and identity of Christ-followers."[61] The witness of the church is therefore a kingdom witness—in the sense of both *missional outreach* through kingdom presence and proclamation (being and doing) in the world and *relational justice* extending from the community of believers (internal) to those in the outside world (external).

This view of mission provides the context for what I am calling the "JustMissional" church. As used in this book the term has a double meaning. On the one hand it means that the church should be "just missional" or "simply missional." Churches are intended to live as missional communities in their cultural context. They seek to live out the reality of God's restorative kingdom in a given place in order to transform its context and beyond.[62] Often, this involves doing away with complex systems and structures that only maintain buildings and programs and do not contribute to a simple disciple-making process that produces transformed lives, institutions, and communities. In another sense "JustMissional" means that the church lives out God's mandate for both mission and justice. Descriptions of the missional church often lack the dimension of justice. But I would contend that justice at least partly defines the motivation and goals of mission. Fulfillment of Christ's commission to "make disciples" necessarily involves a commitment to him as King and to his kingdom of just relationships.[63] As Tim Keller puts it, the missional church "must be more deeply and practically committed to deeds of compassion and social justice than traditional liberal churches and more deeply and practically committed to evangelism and conversion than traditional fundamentalist churches."[64] The cross addresses the problem of enmity with each other (Gen. 4) as well as the problem of enmity with God (Gen. 3). Change that is multi-layered and multi-dimensional encompassing all aspects of life will come only as we integrate both of these aspects of reconciliation and restoration through Christ.

Outline of the Book

In this book, my purpose will be to expand on the biblical and theo-logical basis for this conception of the JustMissional church. Part one lays a foundation for the church's missional identity in terms of the "already and not-yet" nature of the kingdom. Chris Wright and others have helped us see the kingdom as a central theme of Scripture. Others may prefer a "covenantal" approach, arguing that God's covenantal relationship with his people is the organizing center for understanding Scripture. But actually, the two approaches are not contradictory since God's covenant promises are kingdom promis-es.[65] The key question which has divided evangelicals is "what is the nature of the kingdom?" I attempt to steer a middle course between those who over-emphasize the dualism between the "secular" and "sacred" based upon a "two kingdom" model of mission and those who virtually collapse the two based upon a "one kingdom" trans-formational model of mission. On the one hand, an overemphasis on the distinction between the "ecclesial kingdom" and the "civil kingdom" often results in a privatistic retreat of the church from public life. On the other hand, some who use salvation language to refer to the transformation of all spheres of life through Christ's kingdom tend to flirt with a social gospel. One of my main argu-ments is that the church "prefigures" God's promise of future crea-tional restoration. Therefore, a concern for the "good news" of the gospel should heighten a commitment to *both* fulfill the evangelistic mandate and live out the kingdom principles of righteousness and justice.

In part two, I further develop this argument by showing that true worship of God and concern for his holiness cannot be separated from a concern for justice. Worship of God is closely connected to mission and the kingdom since all of redemptive history has as its goal the glory of God through Christ as the rightful ruler over the entire created universe (I Peter 4:11; Phil. 2:7-11). But the writings of the prophets in the Old Testament as well as the teachings of Jesus and his apostles make it abundantly clear that we cannot create a division between personal piety (devotion to God) and activism (justice). In other words, the inward life (what we often mean by "righteousness" or "piety") and the outward life (mercy and justice) are inseparable. There has been a tendency within evangelical circles to create a division between God's grace and love and his justice. However, these are not contrasting principles. As we will see, throughout Scripture God's grace and love are exhibited in a concern for justice on behalf of the needy and oppressed as well as in his work of redemption. God's grace flowing through us is manifested in the form of justice and mercy. Thus, to limit our obligation to evangelism is to limit the scope of God's work of reconciliation. Evangelism is the "ultimate" motive for works of justice and mercy; but it is not the "ulterior" motive.

All of this, of course, raises fundamental questions about the nature of the church's mission. Here, not only do we have to be clear about what is meant by the words "church" and "mission." We also must be clear on the meaning of the "gospel" to which the church is to bear witness. These are issues, of course, on which many articles and books have been written. Addressing them adequately will necessarily entail an examination of key "missional" texts in Scripture and the relationship between God's covenant with Israel and his "new covenant" with the church. This is the subject of part three where I further discuss the concept of the missional church and argue for the perspective of "integral mission," which seeks to re-unite or re-integrate those elements which have often been separated in the course of the church's history. It is my contention that there is continuity as well as development between the mission of Israel as the "people of God" in the Old Testament and the mission of the church (*ekklesia*) in the New. Moreover, careful analysis of central mission texts from Jesus to the apostle Paul reveals that our understanding of the gospel is incomplete apart from a concern for the poor and marginalized of society and a reconciliation of people to one another as well as to God through his son.

In the concluding chapter I attempt to draw some practical implications from the more theoretical discussion of the preceding chapters. In particular, I describe four practical out-workings of the JustMissional church. The first two characteristics begin with the internal life of the church. They are: (1) *vocational synergy*—or the combined effect of individuals with different vocational "callings" working together to accomplish the church's mission; and (2) *servant leadership*, or leadership which equips people in the body of Christ for ministry. The next two characteristics are more externally focused. They involve: (3) the creation of *missional networks* with other like-minded churches and organizations; and (4) *sustainable transformation*, or real long-term change that is Christ-centered and comes as we seek to address the spiritual, relational, physical, and emotional needs of people and communities holistically. To be sure there are other characteristics that could be noted. But these are qualities that are increasingly coming to define what have been called "Rising Influence" churches—or churches that mobilize their people to make an impact on their communities for Christ and his kingdom.

Notes

[1] Robert Fulford, *The Triumph of Narrative: Storytelling in the Age of Mass Culture* (New York, NY: Broadway Books, 1999). See also Leslie Leyland Fields, "The Gospel is More Than a Story: Rethinking Narrative and Testimony," *Christianity Today* (July/August 2012). See http://www.christianitytoday.com/ct/2012/july-august/the-gospel-is-more-than-a-story.html.

[2] Mae Elise Cannon, *Social Justice Handbook: Small Steps for a Better World* (Downers Grove, IL: IVP Books, 2009), p. 33.

[3] Ibid.

[4] John Stott, *Human Rights and Human Wrongs: Major Issues for a New Century* (Grand Rapids, MI: Baker, 1999), p. 20.

[5] See James J. Stamoolis, "A Brief history of Evangelical Involvement in Social Justice," in *Social Injustice: What Evangelicals Need to Know About the World*, ed. William J. Moulder and Michael T. Cooper (Lake Forest, IL: Timothy Center Press, 2011), p. 47.

[6] Ibid.

[7] Quoted in Stott, *Human Rights and Human Wrongs*, p. 21.

[8] Ibid., p. 20. See Donald W. Dayton, *Discovering an Evangelical Heritage* (NY: Harper and Row, 1976) and Timothy L Smith, *Revivalism and Social Reform in Mid-Nineteenth-Century America* (New York: Abingdon, 1957).

[9] John Wesley was the forerunner of the Clapham Sect led by William Wilberforce which was largely responsible for the abolition of the slave trade in England (1807) and ultimate emancipation (1833). Three days before his death in 1791, John Wesley wrote to Wilberforce to assure him that God had raised him up for his "glorious enterprise" and to encourage him not to be weary of well doing. See Stott, *Human Rights and Human Wrongs*, p. 19.

[10] Ibid., p. 20.

[11] Cannon, *Social Justice Handbook*, p. 52.

[12] Stott, *Human Rights and Human Wrongs*, p. 20.

[13] The following analysis is taken largely from George M. Marsden, *Fundamentalism and American Culture, New Edition* (New York, NY: Oxford University Press, 2006), pp. 86-93; 231-60.

[14] Postmillennialism argues that the messianic kingdom has been inaugurated by Christ's first advent and that prior to his second coming the messianic kingdom will grow until it has filled the whole earth. This growth is entirely supernatural and occurs through the preaching of the gospel and the outpouring of God's Spirit. The present millennial age will end with the second coming of Christ at which time the kingdom will be perfectly consummated. Premillennialism holds that the millennial kingdom does not arrive until *after* Christ's second coming. Most dispensational premillennialists argue that the messianic kingdom is inaugurated at the second advent, not the first, and that the world is getting progressively worse, not better. See Keith A. Mathison, *Postmillennialism: An Eschatology of Hope* (Phillipsburg, NJ: P&R Publishing, 1999).

[15] Marsden, *Fundamentalism and American Culture*, p. 86.

---

[16] Ibid.

[17] Ibid.

[18] Timothy Smith, *Revivalism and Social Reform*, p. 225.

[19] Marsden, *Fundamentalism and American Culture*, p. 88.

[20] In the nineteenth century evangelicalism included most major Protestant denominations and also newer revivalist groups including Methodist and Pentecostal holiness groups and premillennialists. By the end of the century American evangelicalism was beginning to polarize between theological liberals and conservatives. Fundamentalism might best be described as a militantly anti-modernist expression of evangelicalism. In the early twentieth century it found expression in the intellectual battle between evangelical leaders such as J. Gresham Machen who defended the "fundamentals" of true Christianity and philosophical materialism, evolutionism, and the higher criticism of Scripture. Ibid., pp. 4, 118-123, and 234.

[21] Ibid., p. 91.

[22] Smith, *Revivalism and Social Reform*, p. 58.

[23] Walter Rauschenbusch, *Christianity and the Social Crisis* (London: Macmillan, 1907), pp. 357, 391-400.

[24] Marsden, *Fundamentalism and American Culture*, p. 92.

[25] Ibid., pp. 232-33.

[26] Carl F. H. Henry, *The Uneasy Conscience of Modern Fundamentalism* (Grand Rapids, MI: Eerdmans, 1947), p. 45.

[27] Stott, *Human Rights and Human Wrongs*, p. 25.

[28] Marsden, *Fundamentalism and American Culture*, p. 254.

[29] Ibid.

[30] Ibid., p. 243.

[31] Ibid., p. 260.

[32] James Davison Hunter, *To Change the World: The Irony, Tragedy, and Possibility of Christianity in the Late Modern World* (New York: Oxford University Press, 2010).

[33] See the address by James Davison Hunter, "To Change the World," *Trinity Forum Briefing* (Vol. 3, No. 2, 2002). http://www.sallt.com/Websites/saltandlight /images/TO_CHANGE_THE_WORLD__HUNTER_.pdf

[34] Hunter, *To Change the World*, p. 95.

[35] Ibid.

[36] "To Change the World," p. 11.

[37] Ibid.

[38] Ibid., p. 228.

[39] In recent descriptions of the "missional church" the term "mission" is often used to refer to God's redemptive mission in the world *and* to the church's participation in God's mission. The term "missions" has the connotation of mission activity that is supported by the church and carried out by people from and in the church. In contemporary usage, however, "missions" is often thought of in terms of a "program" within the church which is separated from other aspects of church life (i.e., worship, community, and spiritual care) or even as the activity of "mission" organizations that frequently operate apart from "church" structures. What is often lost is the close interconnection between the "church" and "mission." Biblically, the "church's mission" is (or should be) an expression of and participation in

God's mission in the world. This does not exclude the importance of human organization. It is clear from the book of Acts that the early church made a concert-
ed effort to organize itself to carry out its mission task. But, as will be argued in
this book, this activity of the early church was never divorced from its corporate
calling as a "sent" people of God. As Charles Van Engen states, the church "lives
out its calling in the world through mission, finds its essential purpose in its participation in God's mission, and engages in a multitude of programs whose purpose is
mission. . . We cannot understand mission without viewing the nature of the
Church, and we cannot understand the Church without looking at its mission."
God's Missionary People: Rethinking the Purpose of the Local Church (Grand Rapids, MI:
Baker, 1991), p. 30. This serves as the basis for my use of the term "mission" in
this book.

[40] Christopher J.H. Wright, *The Mission of God: Unlocking the Bible's Grand Narrative*
(Downers Grove, IL: IVP Academic, 2006), p. 64.

[41] Ibid.

[42] Ibid., pp. 54-55.

[43] N.T. Wright, *The New Testament and the People of God* (Mpls, MN: Fortress, 1992),
pp. 39-40.

[44] Kevin J. Vanhoozer, *The Drama of Doctrine: A Canonical Linguistic Approach to Theology* (Nashville, TN: Westminster John Knox, 2005), pp. 17-18.

[45] Ibid., p. 22.

[46] Ibid., p. 25.

[47] Ibid., p. 44.

[48] Michael W. Goheen, "The Urgency of Reading the Bible as One Story," *Theology
Today* (Vol. 64, 2008), p. 472.

[49] Leslie Leyland Fields, "The Gospel is More Than a Story," p. 38.

[50] Ibid.

[51] The emergent/emerging church is a label that is used to define a subset of
churches that attempt to be more responsive to the post-modern mindset, which
places emphasis on experience, community and tolerance. They often express disil-
lusionment over the traditional institutional church, emphasize creative and experiential approaches to worship, are more flexible and ecumenical and less "judgmen-
tal" in their approach to theology, and adopt a more holistic approach to the role of
the church in society. Emergent leaders often express a desire for "a kinder, gen-
tler" version of evangelicalism that is devoid of the doctrinal dogmatism, moral
certainty, and an absolutist mindset that is unresponsive to the developments of
modern culture. See D.A. Carson, *Becoming Conversant with the Emerging Church: Understanding a Movement and its Implications* (Grand Rapids, MI: Zondervan, 2005).

[52] Fields, "The Gospel is More Than a Story," p. 38. In fairness to McLaren, it
should be noted that he professes to adhere to the classical doctrines of the Christian faith. In one of his books he states categorically, "I affirm, wholeheartedly and
humbly, the mystery of the Trinity and the incarnation, Jesus' role as savior and
Lord and head of the church, the affirmations of the ancient creeds." See *Finding
Our Way: The Return of the Ancient Practices* (Nashville, TN: Thomas Nelson, 2005), p.
33. McLaren rightly argues in this book that "we must rediscover our faith as a way
of life, not simply as a system of belief." (Ibid., p 3) However, as will be pointed

out in the next chapter, in other writings he redefines the meaning of "salvation" and downplays the importance of the traditional doctrine of the atonement.

[53] Trevin Wax, "The Gospel is More Than a Story: A Conversation with Leslie Leyland Fields," http:// thegospelcoalition.org/

[54] Vanhoozer, *The Drama of Doctrine*, p. 15.

[55] Ibid., p. 14.

[56] Fields, "The Gospel is More Than a Story," p. 38.

[57] "A Call to an Ancient Evangelical Future: The Full Text of an Appeal to Live the Biblical Narrative," *Christianity Today* (9/1/2006) See: http://www.christianitytoday.com/ct/2006/september/11.57.html?start=1

[58] Michael Goheen, *A Light to the Nations: The Missional Church and the Biblical Story* (Grand Rapids, MI: Baker Academic, 2011), p. 203.

[59] Ibid., p. 115.

[60] This diagram is an adaptation of a similar diagram by Ken Baker in "Kingdom Mission, p. 10.

[61] Ibid.

[62] Ibid., p. 4. More concretely, I am using the concept of the "missional church" to refer to a church body that: (1) is defined by missionary witness or is "on a mission" in its local community and beyond; (2) lives as an alternative community in the world as the "people of God" and an expression of God's future kingdom; and (3) views its own mission as rooted in God's redemptive mission in the world.

[63] For a development of this argument see Waldron Scott, *Bring Forth Justice: A Contemporary Perspective on Mission* (Grand Rapids, MI: Eerdmans, 1980), pp. xv-svi.

[64] Tim Keller, "The Missional Church,"
http://www.shenango.org/PDF/PMC/Tim%20Keller.pdf

[65] Vaughan Roberts, *God's Big Picture: Tracing the Storyline of the Bible* (Downers Grove, IL: InterVarsity, 2002), p. 21.

PART ONE

THE CENTRALITY OF THE KINGDOM
AND THE LORDSHIP OF CHRIST

Just before he ascended into heaven Jesus said to his disciples: "You shall be my witnesses" (Acts 1:8). These five parting words of Jesus are so familiar to us as Christians that we tend to miss their full significance. But there are some important things about them that should be noted. First, they define the *mission* that Christ gave to his disciples. They weren't just part of a "wish list." They were Jesus' marching orders. He further connects this mission with the coming of the Holy Spirit who later filled the group of believers at Pentecost. It was after this event that Jesus' followers are first called the "church" or *ekklesia* (Acts 5:11). So, secondly, these words define the fundamental activity and nature of the *church* operating under the power of the Holy Spirit. Third, the word "you" (plural) means that this mission is given to the entire church body or community of believers. In other words, it describes the *vocation* or calling of each individual believer who is part of the church or body of Christ. Fourth, the fact that these words are given by the *resurrected* Christ who ascended into heaven and is now enthroned on the right hand of God the Father (Col. 3:1) means that they are *doxological* in nature. That is, the mission that has been given to the church is intimately bound up with the worship of Christ and of God who rules over all of creation. Finally, and closely related to the fourth observation, this mission to be a witness is closely connected to Jesus' teaching concerning the kingdom (Acts 1:3) which he will return to fully establish in power and glory (Acts 1:11).

Although a kingdom of God has been a frequent source of debate among theologians and missiologists, it is hardly a major topic of conversation for the average churchgoer. However, I am convinced that the kingdom, properly understood, is the key to understanding not only the church's mission but the believer's role in fulfilling that mission. Indeed, there are a growing number of evangelicals who share the view that God's rule through Christ is a central unifying theme of Scripture. Noting that the Bible begins (Gen. 1-2) and ends (Rev. 19:22) with royal motifs, Kenneth Barker has suggested that the theological subject matter of all the biblical books may be delineated along kingdom-covenant lines.[1] Likewise, Arthur Glasser has stated that: "God's right to reign and rule over all of creation and over all the peoples of the world must be unequivocally understood. This brings together the message of Old and New Testament narratives because the Kingdom of God is one of the central, overarching themes of the Bible." In this sense, the whole Bible is the revelation of God's mission in human history.[2] The concept of the JustMissional church is rooted in the biblical picture of the church as the primary agent and participant in this story of God's redemptive mission in the world. My purpose in part one of this book will be to show how this theology of the church (i.e., "ecclesiology") as the embodiment of the kingdom is connected to the theology of God's saving purposes (i.e., "soteriology") and the theology of Jesus as Messiah and Lord (i.e., "Christology").

Notes

[1] Kenneth L. Barker, "The Scope and Center of Old and New Testament Theology and Hope," in *Dispensationalism, Israel and the Church: The Search for Definition*, ed. Craig A. Blaising and Darrell L. Bock (Grand Rapids, MI: Zondervan, 1992), p. 306.

[2] Arthur F. Glasser et. al., *Announcing the Kingdom: The Story of God's Mission in the Bible* (Grand Rapids, MI, Baker, 2003), pp. 17, 20

Chapter 1
The Kingdom as
Already and Not Yet

Much of the confusion in the minds of Christians about the kingdom stems from failure to define what we *mean* by the kingdom of God. Basically it means "God's sovereign rule," or "the dominion of God."[1] As I will show in the next chapter, however, God's reign also involves a realm and subjects. Many people think that the kingdom of God was only emphasized in the teachings of Jesus. However, it is also a major theme in the writings of Paul and the other New Testament authors. But before we delve further into what the Bible has to say about the kingdom it is necessary to give a brief historical background on evangelical views of the kingdom and what appears to be an emerging consensus among evangelical theologians.

Evangelicals and the Kingdom

From its earliest beginnings the evangelical movement has been beset by an internal squabble over kingdom questions. Is the kingdom future or present? Is it spiritual or material? What is the relationship of the kingdom of God to the church? Is it to be found in evangelizing the lost or in reclaiming the culture? By-and-large, this debate has centered on the differences between dispensational and covenantal interpretations of the church and kingdom.[2] Dispensationalists have seen God's promises to Israel as being fulfilled in a future millennial kingdom while the covenantalists have seen the church as *spiritually* replacing Israel.[3] More recently, however, there has been something of a "thawing" of the "cold war" between these two streams of evangelical theology as theologians have found points of agreement. According to Russell Moore, this "rapprochement" has come about as theologians in both camps have sought to find a "unifying center" for their respective theologies in the concept of the kingdom of God.[4]

The issue of the need for an evangelical consensus on the kingdom is really not so new. In the late 1940s, citing the lack of agreement among evangelicals on eschatology and the kingdom, the noted evangelical theologian Carl F.H. Henry called for a "deliberate restudy of the whole kingdom question" and attempts to find a "mediating position" between the "kingdom then" concept of fundamentalist dispensationalism and the "kingdom now" concept of the liberal Social Gospel. In efforts to avoid any tendency to identify the kingdom with any present social order, he argued, fundamentalists had erroneously relegated the kingdom to the age to come, thereby cutting off its relevance for addressing contemporary social concerns.[5] Henry was joined in this call for reformulation of kingdom theology by George Eldon Ladd, who (to the consternation of both dispensationalists and covenantalists) developed a new theological and exegetical synthesis based on the concept of Christ's reign as "already" and "not yet."[6] In many respects, Ladd was the forerunner of the theological consensus on the kingdom that appears to be emerging among many evangelicals.

It is important at the outset to clearly differentiate between "realized" and "inaugurated" eschatology. Proponents of realized eschatology deny or play down any future aspect of the kingdom. They argue that the kingdom of God has already arrived, that it is fully present through the person and work of Christ and can be fully experienced in the life of the Christian and the church. It must be said that there are some within the evangelical camp who, if they do not fully embrace this position at least verge on this understanding of the kingdom. In my view, this position is not biblically warranted. Inaugurated eschatology holds that the promises of the kingdom are *partially* realized in the present but await their complete fulfillment at the return of Christ. In the words of Blaising and Bock: "To call such eschatology inaugurated is only to say that the process of fulfillment has commenced; there is more—even much more—to come."[7] This tension between the "already" and "not yet" is found in the biblical description of salvation. Those who believe in Christ are saved now, but await a completion of that salvation in the future. In fact, as we will see, the apostle Paul often speaks of salvation in decidedly *eschatological* terms.

The Christocentric Focus of Inaugurated Eschatology

What should be emphasized, however, is that the *primary* focus of those who have arrived at the theological centrality of the kingdom is not the biblical history of salvation as such but the fact that this history is centered on the person of Christ. In other words, their primary concern is Christological. As Moore states:

> This is the key insight of inaugurated eschatology—namely, the fact that its central biblical referent is not a golden age within history or the timing of prophetic events, but instead is the One whom God has exalted as "both Lord and Christ— this Jesus whom you crucified" (Acts 2:36) . . . This Christocentric focus of inaugurated eschatology has necessitated that the rival theological systems within the evangelical coalition revise some of their more biblically problematic tenets, and jettison others.[8]

It is their understanding of the lordship of Christ, then, that has caused many evangelicals to recast their theology of end times (eschatology), salvation (soteriology) and the church (ecclesiology) in terms

45

of the kingdom of God. This Christologically-based understanding of theology in these three areas is depicted in the following diagram:

Figure 2. The Lordship of Christ and Theology

This chapter will focus on the first of these themes as it is found in Scripture. The next two themes will be discussed in the following chapters.

The New Testament Fulfillment of Old Testament Promises

Reading the biblical texts that speak of God's kingdom promises might be compared to watching a mystery movie or a detective drama.[9] In a detective show, the viewer is typically introduced to a crime scene and given clues that point to the perpetrator. Gradually, as the story unfolds, new evidence is introduced that clarifies earlier events. But only when the case is finally solved are all of the pieces brought together. At the end of the show there is often an "ah-ha" moment, as one sees connections that were not apparent or only partially understood earlier.

In the same way, the New Testament completes and expounds on concepts in the Old Testament. "As revelation proceeds, the texts themselves, New and Old Testament, are brought together in a way that links concepts together, so that both old and fresh associations are made (Matt. 13:52)."[10] This complementary emphasis does not mean that Old Testament promises are removed. It just means that new connections are made based on the progress of God's revelation. What was only partially grasped in the Old Testament as events unfolded is now more fully understood since we know how the story ends. Of course, since only God knows the *entire* story, as we interpret biblical texts we must be sensitive to the meaning of the divine author (based on the entire canonical promise in Scripture) as well as the meaning of the human author in his setting.[11]

It is not possible here to give a detailed description of this relationship between Old Testament "promise" and New Testament "fulfillment" in Christ. However, we can highlight some key passages. One of these is Isaiah 16:5, which gives a prophecy concerning the messiah who would be a descendant of David:

> *In love a throne will be established, in faithfulness a man will sit on it— one from the house of David—one who in judging seeks justice and speeds the cause of righteousness (NIV).*

Psalm 110, which is part of a group of Psalms known as regal (or royal) Psalms, describes this Davidic king as seated on the right hand of God (vs. 1)—an image denoting *active rule* beside God (cf. Ps. 16: 8-11; Ps. 132: 11).[12] Psalm 89 further describes him as the "first born" of God and the king above all kings (vs. 27) who will exercise authority over all of creation forever (vss. 21-29) and whose reign will be characterized by righteousness and justice (vs. 14). The Old Testament prophets frequently connect the rule of this Davidic king with the outpouring of God's Spirit. Isaiah, for example, describes the Spirit of God as resting on the Messiah who is characterized by wisdom and understanding (11:1-2). The prophets Ezekiel and Joel similarly present this Davidic ruler as mediating the cleansing work of the Holy Spirit among God's people (Ezek. 36:22-32; 37:24-28; Joel 2).

What is significant is how these Old Testament themes are adopted by the New Testament writers and applied to the person and work of Christ. First, numerous New Testament passages depict the risen Christ as the Davidic king who is enthroned at the right hand of God (Acts 2:33-36; 7:55-56; Rom. 8:34; Eph. 1:20-22; Col. 3:1; I Peter 3:22; Heb. 1:3, 13; 10:12; 12:2). Both Acts 2:34 and Hebrews 3:1 directly quote Psalm 110:1 to describe the inaugurated reign of Christ through his resurrection and ascension. In his speech in Acts 2 "Peter goes on to declare that this Lord (Jesus) sits by God's side until all enemies are a footstool for the Lord's feet, something that is yet to be fully realized. So inauguration is present, but consummation is not."[13] In Colossians, this description of Christ as "seated at the right hand of God" (3:1) is combined with references to "the kingdom of his son" (Col. 1:13) and the depiction of Christ as "first born of all creation" (Col. 1:15). We have seen that this is language the Psalmist uses to describe the supremacy of the Davidic king. It is used in this passage to describe Christ's preeminence over all creation (Col. 1:16-17). In Col. 1:18 Christ is further described as "the first born *from among the dead*," again indicating that the inauguration of Christ's reign as Davidic king took place at his resurrection.[14]

Secondly, the New Testament repeatedly emphasizes the role of God's Spirit in Jesus' ministry and resurrection as evidence of his Davidic kingship. The Gospels view the anointing of Jesus by the Holy Spirit at his baptism (Mark 1:9-12; cf. Ps. 45:6-7) and his miracles as evidence of the coming of the kingdom and a fulfillment of the Old Testament prophecy that the Spirit of God would come upon the Davidic king who would bring justice and hope to the nations (Matt. 12:15-21, 28; Isa. 42:1-4). Jesus describes his own ministry as a fulfillment of Isaiah's prophecy that the coming of God's Spirit would accompany the apocalyptic day of the Lord (Luke 4:18-21; Isa. 61:1). Undoubtedly recalling the Old Testament predictions that the Davidic king would give God's Spirit to his people, John the Baptist declares that Jesus would baptize people with the Holy Spirit (Matt. 3:11). This prediction was fulfilled with the outpouring of the Holy

Spirit at Pentecost, an event which Peter sees an eschatological act of the enthroned messianic King (Acts 2:33).[15]

Of particular significance is the way in which the apostle Paul characterizes the resurrection of Christ through God's Spirit *and* the believer's *participation* in Christ's resurrection through the Holy Spirit in terms of an "already/not yet" eschatology. In the book of Romans, Paul describes Christ's resurrection as the "first fruits" of the resurrection of the dead (15:20). This recalls the Israelite festival in the spring (Lev. 23:9-14) when the crops began to grow. The first shoots of wheat would be given to God as a token thank offering and were viewed by the worshiper as a pledge that a great harvest was to follow. Similarly, Paul sees the first resurrection as marking the beginning of Christ's reign which will culminate in the final resurrection of all the dead and his delivering of the kingdom to God (Rom. 15: 23-24). In Colossians, the believer's identification with Christ's death and resurrection is characterized as both a present reality and a future hope. As those who have been brought into his kingdom (Col. 1:13) through the Spirit they "have been raised with Christ" (Col. 3:1; cf. 1:22; 2:12). But they also look forward to Christ's future appearance when they "will appear with him in glory" (Col. 3:4).

In 2 Corinthians the apostle Paul speaks of the death and resurrection of Christ as the decisive event that signals the end of the old age and the beginning of the new (5:14-19).[16] His reference to a "new creation" in this passage echoes the words of the prophet Isaiah: "For I am about to create new heavens and a new earth. . ." (Isa. 65:17). Elsewhere, his description of himself and his readers as those "on whom the fulfillment of the ages has come" (1 Cor. 10:11) places the church at the critical juncture between the old age that is passing away (1 Cor. 7:31b) and the new age that has appeared in Christ. In this tension between the "already" and the "not yet" of redemption, the Spirit of God is a kind of "first installment" or "earnest money" that guarantees the final payoff (2 Cor. 1:22; 5:5). In this sense, the Holy Spirit working through the church is an eschatological sign that the power of God has already broken into the present time and a foretaste and assurance of God's future redemption.[17]

Implications for the Church

This picture in the New Testament of Christ's resurrection and ascension as the great "hinge of history" should revolutionize our thinking as Christians.

1. It should transform our understanding of worship.

In his book *How Does America Hear the Gospel?* William Dyrness points out that every religious conception is rooted in culture. Our experience of God, for example, is colored by the culture passed on to us by our parents and society. "Though we must find our meaning in God and his purposes, it will inevitably be expressed in the cultural forms we inherit."[18] Ideally, after conversion and as Christians mature in their understanding they will radically question certain parts of their culture and refine or affirm others through what Dyrness calls "prophetic discipleship." The larger setting still includes our peculiar cultural situation "but now this is seen in the light of the community of God's people to which we belong and the purposes of God laid out in Scripture."[19] There is a constant tension, then, between using cultural forms to communicate the gospel and allowing the Word of God to transform these forms as God's people move toward maturity.[20]

Americans (and westerners generally) have been deeply influenced by the philosophies of pragmatism and utilitarianism. The truth or value of something or an idea is tested on the basis of its "cash value," or the practical difference it makes in one's life. We want a gospel that "works," which is why our most famous evangelistic tool was written by a former business man and begins with the words "God loves you and has a wonderful plan for your life." It also explains the popularity of Rick Warren's *Purpose Driven Life*, Joel Osteen's *Become a Better You*, and a host of other Christian books that focus on how to become more personally fulfilled, overcome relational conflicts, or have a better marriage. Since westerners are socialized to place a priority on doing and making and to define reality in material and objective terms they are interested in how Christianity will be of use in their lives. But, as Dyrness has rightly warned, when even "Christian" methods—evangelistic tools, Christian life seminars, and so on—are made ends in themselves the gospel is trivialized. Ironically, the very success of Christianity in America may have blinded us to this fact.[21] A pre-occupation with means to the exclusion of our final purpose or goal in Christ and our allegiance to him as Lord of history introduces the danger of idolatry.

The cultural subversion of Christianity can be seen in the ways Jesus is "sold" in the modern age. The influence of the media and commercial advertising has become so pervasive that many Christians have uncritically adopted its methods to promote Christianity and Christ in the same way that companies promote cars or deodorants. Ernest Dichter, who is generally acknowledged as the inventor of image advertising, advised companies that the best technique for selling a product "is to paint for the customer a total picture of the kind of person he would like to be, and then make him believe your product is a necessary part of that picture."[22] To use a phrase made popular by tennis star Andre Agassi in a Canon commercial, "Image is everything." Some in the Christian media have viewed "image advertising" as the most effective communication technique for fulfilling the Great Commission. Bruce Cook, the former advertising agent for Coca-Cola, gave this rationale for the "I found it campaign," which he engineered in the late 1970s: "Back in Jerusalem when the church started, God performed a miracle there on the Day of Pentecost. They didn't have the benefit of buttons and media, so God had to do a little supernatural work there. But today, with our technology, we have available to us the opportunity to create the same kind of interest in a secular society."[23] The "product" that Cook and other Christian advertisers were supposedly promoting was

Christ. But in this media blitz, little emphasis was placed on the person of Christ himself as found in Scripture. This would have severely limited the ad campaign's marketing potential. Instead, like a commercial for Geritol, the ads showed pictures of youthful, healthy, and happy people who could testify to the therapeutic results in their lives. The point was to make the picture so appealing that the customer would want to see himself within the frame. In actuality, the product being sold was a lifestyle.[24] This confusion of advertising "to create an interest" with true witness can also be seen in campaigns that reduce Jesus' name to bright pink on a bumper sticker—which is even more egregious when one considers that in the Old Testament the Hebrews were never to pronounce the name for God (YHWH) because it was too sacred.

Today, image advertising has been taken to a new level by "branding," or creating an identity on the basis of brand names or labels. Again, what matters is not substance but style. With the proliferation of Christian merchandise—music, books, T-shirts, gifts, and jewelry—there seems to be an increased tendency in the church to substitute "Jesus-labels" for Jesus' lordship. In the words of Sky Jethani, "As total sales of religious products reaches $7 billion annually, it appears that God's people are constructing and expressing their identity through the consumption of Christ-branded products."[25] According to Pete Ward, the use of brands by Christians to construct an "identity" is what explains the wild success of WWJD bracelets. These products are endorsed as a legitimate way to "incarnate Christ" in our culture. Jethani has suggested, however, that their popularity has more to do with externally displayed products than with internally transformed values. "In a consumer culture 'incarnating Christ' no longer carries the expectation of Christians loving God and their neighbors, but rather the perpetual consumption of Christian merchandise . . ."[26] Another example of selling products that foster a "Christian identity" is the 1in3Trinity brand which "includes clothing for men and women as well as an energy drink, 'fused with the Fruit of the Spirit.'"[27]   Communicating Christianity as a "brand" in the same way that a company markets Calvin Klein clothing or an energy drink trivializes the gospel and is at odds with the biblical picture of Christ's *present* messianic rule.

2. *It corrects popular conceptions of heaven.*

The emphasis in Scripture on the present rule of Christ from heaven is also a corrective to our tendency to equate heaven simply with a future *place* where we will be with God forever.   The description that Christians are often so "heavenly minded that they are no earthly good" is an overstatement, but it contains a grain of truth.   In Scripture, the "not yet" of the kingdom is viewed in terms of a new creation.   This is reflected in the biblical hope of a rule of Christ as Messiah in a new heaven and a new earth (II Pet. 3:13; Rev. 21:1-4).   The emphasis of Scripture is not on a future heavenly existence but on a *new creation* through the power of Christ which is partially experienced in the present because of his presence there as risen Lord (Col. 1:5, 3:1-2; Eph. 1:3, 1:21; Phil. 3:20-21).[28]   Eternal life is therefore a life in which the divine blessings and characteristics of the age to come can be enjoyed and demonstrated, however imperfectly, here and now.[29]

This conclusion would seem to conflict with the Gospel of John, with its emphasis on the theme of "eternal life."   There is hardly a believer who is not familiar with the use of this term in John 3:16.   But the kingdom significance of "eternal life" is often missed in English translations.   For, it does not refer *primarily* to life that goes on forever with God.   The Greek word for "eternal" (*aionios*) is derived from the Greek word for "age" (*aion*).   Eternal life, then, is literally "the life of the age."[30]   According to Tasker, the word *aionios* is used seven times in John's gospel and in every instance it is associated with *life*. But the evangelist uses a different word when he speaks of something abiding "forever."   Therefore, "although the idea of duration is not absent from the word *aionios*, it is the different *quality* of life that it stresses. The Jews tended to think of time as a succession of ages, which would culminate in a final, blessed age, designated "the age to come."[31] When John speaks of "eternal life," then, he has in mind "life characteristic of that final age, which Christ inaugurated."[32] Although full enjoyment of this life lies in the future, believers in Christ have a foretaste of it in the present through his Spirit who abides in us.

This same overlap between the present age and the age to come is evident in I John 2:8, which states that "the darkness is passing and the true light is already shining." Light and darkness exist concurrently. "The age to come has arrived by virtue of the death and resurrection of Christ, but its arrival does not spell the immediate removal of evil and darkness."[33] While the Jews expected that all evil and darkness would be destroyed with the arrival of the new age, the apostle John states that the light shines without immediately or completely quenching darkness. The two, however, are not equivalent. John emphasizes the defeat of evil (it is passing away) and the triumph of light (it is shining).[34] He then draws out the ethical implications of this truth when he states: "We know that we have passed from death to life, because we love our brothers. Anyone who does not love remains in death." (I John 3:14) Interestingly, the verb that is used here (*metabiano*) is also used in John 5:24 to refer to "crossing over" from death to (eternal) life. Both passages therefore express the truth that because believers have passed into life and abide in life, the age to come is now a reality.[35]

Conclusion

By way of summary, then, we can say that the tension between the "now" and the "not yet" permeates the entire New Testament.[36] The New Testament is radically God-centered and focuses on the supremacy of God in Christ. But this emphasis on divine sovereignty and the Lordship of Christ is closely related to the history of salvation and the unfolding of God's promises in the Old Testament. God has begun to fulfill his saving promises, though he has yet to complete all that he promised. The word "salvation" is used to denote to both the present fulfillment of God's promises and the final fulfillment.[37] It is important that we keep in mind this connection between God's glory in Christ and salvation. "God works out his saving plan so that he would be magnified in Christ, so that his name would be honored . . . God's glory and humans' salvation are not in conflict. Rather, God is glorified in the salvation of his people."[38] In the next two chapters I will further explore the importance of these themes for understanding the gospel message and nature and purpose of the church.

Notes

[1] Steve Schaeffer, *Living in the Overlap: How Jesus' Kingdom Proclamation Can Transform Your World* (Enumclaw, WA: WinePress, 2010), p. 3.

[2] Russell Moore, *The Kingdom of Christ: The New Evangelical Perspective* (Wheaton, IL: Crossway, 2004), pp. 11

[3] Historically, dispensational theologians have emphasized the future physical fulfillment of the political, national, and territorial promises made to Israel. Covenant theologians have tended to see the kingdom as spiritual and already present. Dispensationalists have emphasized the dichotomy of Israel and the church. Although the salvation they receive—eternal life—is the same for both and both share basically the same spiritual purpose, there is an eternal distinction between Israel and the church. While Christ presently rules spiritually over the church he will establish a future physical millennial kingdom with a restored nation of Israel as its center. Most covenantal theologians, on the other hand, describe the church as "spiritually" replacing Israel. The covenantal land promises are posited as typological of the "spiritual" blessings of forgiveness of sins and eternal heavenly life. See Craig A. Blaising and Darrell L. Bock, *Progressive Dispensationalism*, p. 32; and Moore, *The Kingdom of Christ*, p. 119.

[4] Ibid., p. 22. Among dispensationalists, this recent move towards a "kingdom theology" is found in "progressive dispensationalism," which argues that there is a *holistic and unified* salvation that is progressively revealed in Scripture as the eschatological "Kingdom of God." Progressive dispensationalists agree with more traditional dispensationalists that there will be a literal fulfillment of the promises to Israel in a future millennial kingdom. However, unlike traditional dispensationalists

who view the church age as a "parenthesis" in God's plan of salvation, the progressive dispensationalists do not see the church as signaling a "secondary" redemption plan. Rather, the church as part of the *very same plan of redemption* in which the political-social and spiritual purposes of God complement one another. Similarly, while modified covenantalists continue to reject the idea of a future millennial kingdom they agree with progressive dispensationalists in emphasizing the unity and holistic nature of God's redemptive purposes to "restore and renew the human race and the cosmos" through the eventual triumph of the eschatological kingdom of God. Blaising and Bock, *Progressive Dispensationalism*, pp. 46-48 and Moore, The *Kingdom of Christ*, p. 24.

[5] Carl F.H. Henry, *The Uneasy Conscience of Modern Fundamentalism*, p. 51. Quoted in Moore, *The Kingdom of Christ*, pp. 22, 25-27.

[6] George Eldon Ladd, *The Presence of the Future: The Eschatology of Biblical Realism* (Grand Rapids, MI: Eerdmans, 1974). Quoted in Moore, *The Kingdom of Christ*, pp. 22, 32.

[7] Blaising and Bock, *Progressive Dispensationalism*, pp. 53, 97-98.

[8] Moore, *The Kingdom of Christ*, p. 56.

[9] Ibid., p. 98.

[10] Darrell L. Bock, "Hermeneutics of Progressive Dispensationalism," in *Three Central Issues in Dispensationalism: A Comparison of Traditional and Progressive Views*, ed. Herbert W. Bateman IV (Grand Rapids, MI: Kregel, 1999), p. 89.

[11] Ibid., pp. 88-90.

[12] See Darrell L. Bock, "The Reign of the Lord Christ," in *Dispensationalism, Israel and the Church*, p. 52.

[13] Ibid., p. 51.

[14] Blaising and Bock, *Progressive Dispensationalism*, p. 179.

[15] Moore, *The Kingdom of Christ*, p. 59.

[16] In this passage verse 17 should be translated "if anyone is in Christ *there is* a new creation" (NRSV). Paul is not merely talking about an individual subjective experience of renewal through conversion, but a renewal of the whole created order (cf. Rom. 8:18-25). See Richard B. Hays, *The Moral Vision of the New Testament: A Contemporary Introduction to New Testament Ethics* (San Francisco, CA: Harper Collins, 1996) p. 20.

[17] Ibid., p. 21.

[18] William A. Dyrness, *How Does America Hear the Gospel?* (Grand Rapids, MI: Eerdmans, 1989), p. 22.

[19] Ibid. p. 23.

[20] Ibid., p. 78. Kevin Vanhoozer argues that for the church to become an effective community of "cultural agents" (i.e., those who make a mark on culture rather than simply submitting to cultural programming) it must: (1) interpret culture in light of a biblical-theological framework; and (2) interpret Scripture by embodying gospel values and truths in concrete cultural forms. He proposes the following formula: Christian cultural agency = theological competence + cultural literacy + gospel performance. It is not enough to know doctrine. We must also be able to "read culture" by becoming culturally literate and critical thinkers. This involves neither a total condemnation nor a whole hearted affirmation of popular culture. "Nothing

is gained either by failing to recognize signs of common grace in culture or by reading the gospel into cultural texts where it is not present. Only when we truly understand what is happening around us can we engage our world intelligently and effectively (and evangelistically)." See "What is Everyday Theology? How and Why Christians Should Read Culture," in *Everyday Theology: How to Read Cultural Texts and Interpret Trends*, ed, Kevin J. Vanhoozer et. al.(Grand Rapids, MI: Baker Academic, 2007), p. 55.

[21] Dyrness, *How Does America Hear the Gospel?*, pp. 55-56.

[22] Quoted in Virginia Stem Owens, *The Total Image, or Selling Jesus in the Modern Age*, (Grand Rapids, MI: Eerdmans, 1980), p. 26.

[23] Ibid., pp. 27-28.

[24] Ibid., p. 28.

[25] Skye Jethani, *The Divine Commodity: Discovering Faith Beyond Consumer Christianity*, (Grand Rapids, MI: Zondervan, 2009), p. 54.

[26] Ibid., p. 54-55.

[27]Ibid.,

[28] Moore, *The Kingdom of Christ*, p. 62.

[29] Ibid., p. 18.

[30] Steve Schaefer, *Living in the Overlap*, p. 17

[31] R.V.B. Tasker, *The Gospel According to St. John* (Grand Rapids, MI: Eerdmans, 1977), p. 72.

[32] Ibid.

[33] Thomas R. Schreiner, *Magnifying God in Christ: A Summary of New Testament Theology* (Grand Rapids, MI: Baker Academic, 2010), p. 27.

[34] Ibid.

[35] Ibid.

[36] Ibid., p. 36.

[37] Ibid., pp. 16, 36.

[38] Ibid., p. 16.

Chapter 2
Salvation as Christ-centered and Holistic

Jim Wallis, the editor of *Sojourners* and the author of numerous books on the subject of the Bible and poverty, tells the story of how when he was a seminary student at Trinity Evangelical Divinity School he decided to go through the Bible and literally cut out with a pair of scissors all of the verses that had to do with the poor. Then, when he preached on poverty, he held up the tattered Bible and exclaimed "This is our American Bible, it is full of holes!" or words to that effect. In a recent book entitled *The Hole in Our Gospel*, Richard Sterns, the president of World Vision, USA, similarly argues that the typical Christian has a huge hole in his/her life that comes from ignoring the plight of the poor. "The idea behind [the book] is quite simple," he states. "It's basically the belief that being a Christian, or follower of Jesus Christ, requires much more than just having a *personal* and transforming relationship with God. It also entails *a* public and transforming relationship with the world."[1] This naturally raises the question, what is the gospel that is at the heart of the church's mission? Certainly, we would say that it is the "good news" of God redemption of the world. But what is that nature, scale, and scope of God's redemption?[2] My goal in this chapter will be to establish a basic theological framework for answering these questions, which I will address in further detail in later chapters.

Gospel Reductionism

In my view, there are two popular responses to these questions which involve a distortion or at least oversimplification of a true biblical understanding of the gospel. The first interprets the gospel as the salvation of individual souls and therefore sees the mission of the church as the rescue of individual souls from the world. [3] This view is found in popular methods of presenting the gospel, such as the Four Spiritual Laws and the Roman's Road. While personal salvation is indeed an important and necessary *part* of the gospel, to reduce it to these terms misses its full biblical content. What is often ignored or at least downplayed in many contemporary evangelical treatments of the gospel is that ethical living is intrinsic to the gospel itself. True, we are saved by grace through faith in Christ. But the apostle Paul frequently speaks of "obeying the gospel" to indicate that an ethical *living out* of the gospel cannot be separated from *believing* the gospel. The book of Romans begins and ends with the striking phrase "obedience of faith" (Rom. 1:5, 16:26)—a term that denotes "an obedience which consists in faith and an obedience that finds its source in faith." [4] As Chris Wright argues, the genitive expression "faith's obedience" means that the two verbs "to believe" and "obey" cannot be split apart. Obedience demonstrates the reality of faith.

> This understanding of the gospel as intrinsically ethical, a matter of obedience not just belief, is shared by Peter (Acts 5:32; I Peter 4;17), James (Jas. 2:14-26), John (I John 2;3; 3:21-24; 5:1-3), and the writer to the Hebrews (Heb. 5:9), and of course it goes back to Jesus himself (e.g., Matt. 7:21-27: 28:20; Luke 11:28; John 14:23-24). It would be worth pausing to read all these passages. And when you have finished reading them, is it still possible to say that the gospel is only a matter of saying a prayer of faith? [5]

Proponents of the "emergent church" often criticize treatments of the gospel as a "get-out-of-hell-free" and "go-to-heaven-when-you–die" card as resulting in a lack of social concern. The following words of Brian McLaren reflect the thinking of many in this movement:

> But now I wonder if this gospel about how to get your soul into Heaven after death is really only a ghost of the real gospel that Jesus talked about, which seems to have something to do with God's will being done on earth now, not just in Heaven later. . . Yes, I believe that the gospel has facts that deal with forgiveness of sins, but I feel unfaithful to Jesus to define the gospel by that one fact when I see our contemporary churches failing to address so many other essential gospel concerns—justice, compassion, sacrifice, purpose, transformation into Christlikeness, and ultimate hope.[6]

While we must strongly disagree with McLaren's opposition to the doctrine of heaven as having little to do with the gospel we can concur with him to the extent that an *over-emphasis* on heaven can lead to an escapist mentality which is unbiblical and reductionistic. As Russell Moore has stated, "Seeking first the Kingdom should not dampen Christian concern for social and political justice, but heighten it. After all, the priorities of the King—seen in his ultimate goal of the restoration of the creation—must become the priorities of the Kingdom colony, the church."[7]

The emergent church movement, however, tends towards another type of gospel reductionism. In their zeal to correct a dualistic and "other-worldly" interpretation of the gospel many in this movement over-emphasize the kingdom as a present reality. The *inaugurated* kingdom with its tension between the "already" and the "not yet" is often reduced to a *realized* "here and now" kingdom.[8] This over-realized view of the kingdom is evident in Rob Bell's statement that "The goal isn't escaping this world but making this world the kind of place God can come to."[9] For some within this movement the gospel is more about repenting of selfishness and following the moral example of Christ than it is about the doctrine of Christ's substitutionary sacrifice as an atonement for sins. According to McLaren, the gospel of the kingdom has little to do with Christ's atonement for the forgiveness of sins and everything to do with transforming the world towards peace and justice.[10] In the view of Steve Chalke, an emergent church leader from the UK, the doctrine of penal substitution is the moral equivalent of "cosmic child abuse."[11] While the cross is still important in this perspective, there is a tendency by some emergents to reduced it to a moral example of suffering under oppression. In the words of McLaren, "Jesus uses the cross to expose Roman violence and religious complicity with it" and display "God's willingness to accept rejection and mistreatment, and then respond with forgiveness, reconciliation, and resurrection."[12] This is not to say that there is not an ethical dimension to the cross. After all, the apostles Peter and Paul often use Jesus' suffering and sacrifice as an example for how Christians should live their lives and respond to mistreatment (I Peter 2:20-23; Rom. 5:3-8, 12:1, 9-21; Phil. 2:1-11). But to *reduce* it to these terms results in an impoverished view of Christ. A legitimate question to pose to these emergent leaders is, "How can there be a Kingdom, in the biblical sense, with a distorted Christology?" In other words, they seek to have a kingdom without a King.[13]

The Cosmic Scope of Redemption

To understand the relationship of the gospel (*euangelion*) to the kingdom we have to again look briefly at the Old Testament background. The cognate verb (*euangelizomai*), meaning "to announce, tell, deliver a (good or bad) message," is used in the Psalms (40:9-10; 96:2ff.) and Isaiah (41:27, 52:7) to herald Yahweh's victory over the world and his kingly rule.[14] The New Testament writers portray Jesus as both the announcer (or author) and subject of this message of salvation. In Mark 1:15, for example, Jesus is portrayed as the messenger who announces the arrival of salvation with the coming of God himself. His message of "good news" that the kingdom of God is near is the "message of peace" of Isaiah 52:7:[15]

> *How beautiful on the mountains are the feet of those who bring good news, who proclaim peace, who bring good tidings, who proclaim salvation, who say to Zion, "Your God reigns."*

The apostle Paul often assumes this concept of the gospel in his epistles. Notice how Paul defines the scope of the gospel in Colossians 1:15-23. First, because all things in the universe have been created by Christ (vs. 16) and he sustains all things (vs. 17) God has reconciled all things to himself through Christ "by making peace through his shed blood on the cross" (vs. 20). Next, Paul proclaims Christ's headship over the body (i.e., the church) as the "first born from among the dead" (vs. 18). This picture of Christ's relationship to the church expresses God's kingdom purposes to renew the *imago Dei* by conforming believers to the image of His Son, so that He would be the firstborn among many brethren (Rom. 8:29). After this survey of the cosmic significance of Christ's reign and his relationship to the church Paul talks about the personal reconciliation of the believer to God through Christ's atoning death (vss. 21-22). This, says Paul, is what constitutes the gospel that "has been proclaimed "to every creature under heaven" (vs. 23).[16]

The diagram below illustrates the relationship between these three dimensions of the gospel. On the one hand, the individual believer and the church experience the "in-breaking" of Christ's inaugurated kingdom by virtue of being united to him in his death and resurrection. At the same time, the personal regeneration of the individual and corporate renewal of the church by God's Spirit are a "foretaste" of future cosmic restoration of the natural order through the work of Christ. As Andrew Lincoln notes: "The resurrection and exaltation of Christ accomplish a new unity between heaven and earth, for Christ now has a heavenly body (I Cor. 15:42ff), a body of glory

(Phil. 3:21) and His humanity is now in heaven (Phil. 3:20F; Col. 3:1); Eph. 1:20ff, 6:9), and both serve as a pledge of the ultimate unity of the cosmos in Christ (Eph. 1:10).[17]

Figure 3. The Three Dimensions of Redemption

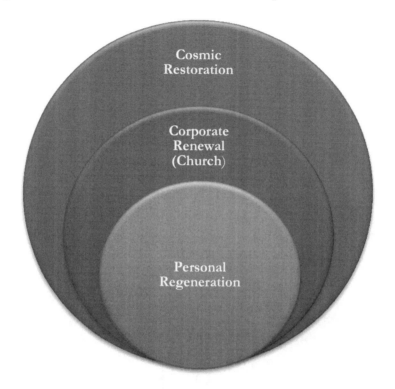

This picture of redemption, as Moore further points out, fits with the prophetic foreshadowing of new covenant redemption in the Old Testament as including spiritual, physical, bodily, social, relational, and political aspects (Ezek. 36:24-38; Jer. 31:31-36). These blessings are tied to the promised future consummation which is manifested in the resurrection from the dead and the outpouring of God's Spirit (Ezek. 37:12-14, 39:28-29). In his ministry "Jesus points to this holistic vision of Kingdom salvation by forgiving sins, casting out demons, and healing diseases by His authority as the Kingdom in person, the anointed King upon whom the Spirit rests (Matt. 12: 15-32,

15:29-31; Mark 1:21-39; Luke 4:18-10, 9:1-2, 11:20, 17:20; John 7:37-39)."[18]

God's Work in Creation and Redemption

The foregoing raises the question of whether there is a distinction between God's work in creation and his work in redemption. The view which has traditionally been held in the history of the church is that God's work in creating and sustaining the world is distinct from his work in redeeming it. "Everywhere, by general grace God works to sustain creation, preserve order, and create justice for all, including those who continue to reject Christ."[19] According to this "two kingdoms" model, the cultural mandate (also referred to as the "creation mandate") is rooted in God's command to exercise dominion over all the earth, subdue it, and develop its latent potential (Gen. 1:26-28; cf. Gen. 2:15) and has to do with God's providential rule over all of creation. God is not redeeming the cultural activities and institutions of this world, but is *preserving them* through the covenants he made with Adam and Eve and with Noah (Gen. 8:20-9:17) as representatives of all humanity. This work of *preserving* the world must not be confused with God's *redemptive* purpose, which is rooted in the covenant he made with Abraham and is fulfilled in the work of Christ. As redeemer, God already rules over those who are part of the "redemptive kingdom" which is manifest in the life and ministry of the church.[20] Christians presently live in these two kingdoms—as citizens of the "civil kingdom" (secular society) and members of the "ecclesial kingdom" (the church) where they operate as part of a new and separated community and recognize Christ's lordship over their lives.[21]

Many, if not all, advocates of the redemptive "transformation" of culture, on the other hand, reject the distinction between creation and redemption. The cultural mandate and the gospel mandate are essentially aspects of the one mission of God to restore and heal creation and bring it back into a covenantal relationship with him. To separate the two, they argue, restricts Christ's lordship over *all* of creation and creates an unwarranted dualism that compromises the holistic character of God's kingdom purposes in this world. In this "one kingdom" model, there is no division of life into a "secular" realm on the one hand and a "sacred" realm in which Christians do "kingdom" work on the other. Since Christ is renewing and redeeming all of creation his kingdom includes every aspect of life and everything the Christian does in his name is work of and for the kingdom.[22]

There are strengths as well as weaknesses in both of these models as they are often described. This is particularly true when it comes to understanding the church's mission and role in society. Advocates of the two kingdom perspective have argued that since the two realms—the "civil kingdom" and the "ecclesial kingdom"—have distinct areas of responsibility before God, neither should encroach upon the other. An overemphasis on this distinction has often resulted in the retreat of the institutional church from public life. David VanDrunnen argues, for example, that the institutions of the "common kingdom" (i.e., families, businesses, states) have the responsibility to care for the needy of this world. While Christians (or groups of Christians) have the responsibility on the basis of Scripture to show love and care for the neighbor (whether they are believers or not) and to cooperate with civic institutions in this endeavor the local church as an institution should focus on its own poor not the needy unbeliever. "The church's nature is spiritual and its authority is ministerial, thus it should not take up cultural tasks that Scripture has not entrusted to it." The concerns of the institutional church's outside its four walls are therefore spiritual not social or cultural.[23] In my opinion, this view of the church's social concern severely truncates its role in the public square and compromises its witness as salt and light in the world. The holistic and kingdom-oriented vision of redemption given in Colossians 1:20, 2 Corinthians 5:19 and other passages of Scripture prevents us from strictly bifurcating "spiritual" concerns from those of culture.[24]

But in reacting against this tendency for the institutional church to simply withdraw from the cultural and social spheres the temptation in some Christian circles has been for the pendulum to swing to the opposite extreme. As one reads the growing literature on the transformation of all spheres of life through the kingdom of God one gets the impression that everything—including protecting the environment, destroying the works of the devil and eradicating disease bearing microbes, advocating for mass transit, and working for world peace—falls under the scope of the church's mission. But, as Stephen Neill remarked years ago, "If everything is mission, then nothing is mission."[25] In other words, "mission" becomes so watered down and all-inclusive that it loses its meaning. Some who advocate mission as transformation argue that social action or justice is always "evangelistic" work "for no area of life is 'neutral,' supposedly immune from the effects of sin and the reach of redemption."[26] Furthermore, since sin is both personal and social, the language of salvation can be used to describe the "conversion" and healing of social structures as well as individuals.[27] Others talk about the "transformation" of entire cities, cultures, and nations.[28]

Ronald Sider correctly observes, however, that Scripture: (1) does not speak of conversion apart from explicit faith in Christ; (2) never talks about the presence of the kingdom apart from Christ's physical presence or where people consciously confess him as Savior and Lord; and (3) never uses salvation language to refer to environmental or socioeconomic improvement in the larger society beyond the church.[29] Therefore, it is theologically misleading to speak of the "transformation" or "conversion" of entire cultures, social structures and nations in the same way that we speak of the conversion of individuals.[30] Moreover, "unless we maintain some basic distinction between creation and redemption, Christianity merges with civilization. The basic New Testament distinction between the church and the world becomes difficult or impossible."[31] Somehow, then, we must find an elusive middle ground between the polar extremes of social and cultural withdrawal which is characteristic of many churches today and the form of cultural transformationism which is found in much contemporary thinking on mission.[32]

There is an interrelated nature to God's work in creation and redemption, but they are not one and the same. We should distinguish between a universal kingdom where God reigns providentially over the entire universe (Ps. 47:2, 8, 83:18, 103:19) and a redemptive kingdom where God reigns over his covenant people.[33] However, because God is a God of justice who rules the world in justice and because his justice is rooted in his love for all of creation, his work in sustaining creation and his work in redemption are interconnected. "When human sin produces devastation throughout the created order, God acts to both sustain that order and also to develop a plan of redemption that will, when completed at Christ's return, restore that created order to wholeness."[34] By the power of God's grace we can strive for human righteousness, though we must not confuse this human righteousness with the divine righteousness that belongs to the kingdom of God. Yet the human struggle for social justice can be a provisional reflection and foreshadowing of the perfect righteousness and justice of the kingdom.[35] Human action against misery and exploitation is therefore relevant to the divine work of redemption, although they are not the same.[36]

As Gary Breshears points out, a kingdom involves reign, a realm in which the reign is exercised, and subjects over who it is exercised. Currently, Christ reigns over the *church*, which should display the first fruits of kingdom righteousness and justice. "When the church speaks prophetically for righteousness in word and deed, she calls all people to a righteousness they have some knowledge of by virtue of their general-revelation-enlightened conscience (Rom. 2:14-16)."[37] But while Christ has won the decisive victory over the powers and authorities on the cross (Col. 2:15) their evil power is not totally broken and Christ will not exercise his kingly authority over the earth until his return. Therefore, when Paul says that all things have been reconciled to God (Col. 1:20) he does not mean that the cosmic redemption of all things has occurred. Rather, he is saying that there is no area of the cosmos that is not impacted by the cross and that God's decisive action that makes the redemption of the entire cosmos possible has taken place. In fact, in Colossians 1:15-20 Paul himself makes a distinction between creation and redemption when he talks about Christ as both the Creator and Sustainer of all things (vss. 15-17) and the Redeemer of all things (vss. 18-20). "The two activities are wonderfully and marvelously interrelated and complementary. But they are not identical."[38]

Implications for the Church

What are the implications of all of this for the church? There are at least three, which I will summarize here, and which we will develop further in later chapters.

1. Personal redemption is primary but holistic in nature.

A growing number of those who espouse a transformative model of gospel proclamation de-emphasize the traditional doctrine of substitutionary atonement. Gregory Boyd and others maintain that the "Christus Victor" theme which emphasizes Christ's defeat of the satanic powers is more in line with the kingdom motif in Scripture. One can appreciate their concern to avoid the overly privatistic and individualistic tendencies that have often been associated with the doctrine of penal substitutionary atonement. And one can agree that evangelicals have often (wrongly) downplayed the cosmic effects of Christ's work on the cross. But it will not suffice to replace one error for another. In fact, it is the very *priority* of personal regeneration through Christ's death and resurrection which makes cosmic redemption possible.[39] For it is through personal regeneration and the forgiveness of sins that individuals are brought into the kingdom (Col.

1:13, 2:13-14) and experience the holistic effects of redemption. It is only as individuals are first reconciled to God that they can experience true reconciliation with others as an expression of the new humanity (Eph. 2:15-16). And it is only through the work of the Spirit in regenerating the heart that there is a uniting of the individual to the pioneer of salvation (Heb. 2:10) who is the first born from among the dead and can claim the cosmos as his inheritance (Ps. 2:1-12; I Cor. 15:21-28). "The priority of personal regeneration is maintained precisely because salvation is seen, holistically, in terms of a bodily resurrection, the reversal of the Edenic curse, and the restoration of humanity as vicegerents of the created order."[40]

2. The church is central to God's kingdom purposes.

Some who adopt the mission as transformation perspective argue that the church is not necessarily the center of God's kingdom purposes. Fuller Seminary professors Ryan Bolger and Eddie Gibbs argue that Jesus was much more concerned with a kingdom than the church. The primary goal of mission should be to foster communities that embody the kingdom not start churches. The immediate goal is not whether the community becomes a church but whether the kingdom is expressed. To illustrate their point about "living in community" they refer to the conversation that a pastor had with a friend at a café. When the friend asked when the church service was the pastor responded "You just had it."[41] But the explicit teaching of Scripture is that the work of reconciliation is most present in and through the church which prefigures and embodies, however imperfectly, the final and ultimate reconciliation and healing of the world. The church is entrusted with the "ministry of reconciliation" that in Christ it might "*become* the righteousness of God" (II Cor. 5: 18-21). The unity of Jews and Gentiles in the body of Christ as the "new humanity" manifests God's plan to unify the entire cosmos and reconcile it to himself (Eph. 2:14-18; 3:10-11; Rom. 15:5-15). We would do well to remember that the proponents of the Social Gospel, including its pioneer Walter Rauschenbusch, advocated a non-churchly view of the kingdom. According to Rauschenbusch the early church regarded the church as a "temporary shelter" which unfortunately grew to be the "main thing." In his words, "The church is one social institution alongside of the family, the industrial organization of society, and the state. The Kingdom of God is in all these, and realizes itself through them all."[42]

3. The inauguration of the kingdom prevents both a privatistic withdrawal from society and overly optimistic triumphalism.

The church has often been beset by a negativistic withdrawal from society on the one hand and optimistic dominionism on the other. The one tendency is illustrated by the oft quoted analogy attributed to D.L. Moody that it does no good to polish the brass on a sinking ship. The other tendency can be seen in Rick Warren's recent global P.E.A.C.E plan. This plan to transform Africa, beginning with the nation of Rwanda, promotes transformation in the form of the "Christianization" of nations. Based on the Great Commission to make disciples of all nations and the Great Commandment to love God and our neighbors, it proposes to attack what Warren calls the five "global giants"—spiritual emptiness, egocentric leadership, extreme poverty, pandemic diseases, and illiteracy and poor education by **P**lanting churches, **E**quipping servant leaders, **A**ssisting the poor, **C**aring for the sick, and **E**ducating for the next generation.[43] Reworking the often used evangelical interpretation of America as a "chosen nation," Warren defends his view of Rwanda as the first "purpose driven" nation: "In the Old Testament, God took a small nation and blessed the world with it. . . Just as God used Israel to bring good news to the world, I believe God wants us to use Rwanda, this nation, in the 21st century."[44] This view both misunderstands the entirely unique role of Israel in salvation history and presents an overly idealistic view of social and political transformation.

The tension between the "already" and "not yet" of the kingdom means that while the church cannot simply withdraw from politics and social action it also must be mindful of the limits of such engagement. Through "prophetic evangelism" individual Christians and Christian communities can have a profound impact as salt and light in society. The gospel may be a powerful force for change in society, both in challenging false idolatries and abuse of power and changing the hearts of individuals. The influence that Christians like Luther, Wilberforce, Wesley, and Whitfield had in changing the social and political structures of their day speaks to the power and influence of the future kingdom in invading society at large. But both history and Scripture also speak to the implacable resistance of sin to large-scale societal transformation. The "not yet" of the kingdom means that the church will continually struggle against the evil principalities and powers until the return of Christ. Changes will always be partial, imperfect, and temporary—as is evidenced by the fact that those very societies, nations, and even churches that were once most impacted by the Reformation and Great Awakenings are now heavily secularized. The following words sum up this continual tension in the present age:

> Although the decisive victory over the forces of evil has been won, the conflict still rages (Ephesians 6:11,12). Christ is risen; the Spirit has been poured out upon the church; the powers of the coming age are at work in the world, but the end is not yet. Hosts of darkness resist God's sovereignty; rampant evils oppose His will. To repent and believe is to side with God's purpose in this conflict—assured of ultimate victory, while contending God's righteousness in every sphere of life (I Corinthians 15:54-57; Acts 26:16-18).[45]

Conclusion

In this chapter I have argued against versions of the gospel which reduce it to either the salvation of individual souls or "kingdom ethics." The gospel is both faith and obedience. It is also both personal and cosmic in its scope. This is evident from Ephesians where Paul connects human redemption with the bringing of "all things in heaven and on earth" under the headship of Christ (Eph. 1:10). Paul also connects soteriology with a theology of the kingdom. By virtue of being united with the resurrected Christ the believer is transferred into the eschatological kingdom of God. At the same time, an ethic of the kingdom is not possible apart from Christ's redemption of the believer through the cross. A proper understanding of the gospel of the kingdom should also prevent us from either creating too great a separation between God's work in creation and his work in redemption or of simply collapsing these two aspects of God's activity in the world. God's ongoing work of sustaining creation and his plan of salvation are marvelously interrelated. But they are not the same. Christ's victory over sin through the cross signifies an in-breaking of the "age to come" into our present history. But this victory is not complete and Christ's lordship over all of creation is yet to be fully realized. This tension between the "now" and the "not yet" prevents Christians from both an isolationist withdrawal from the world and an overly optimistic triumphalism. Presently, Christ's rule is (or should be) most fully manifested in and through the church, which Paul describes as "the new humanity" (Eph. 2:15) and connects with the "new creation" (II Cor. 5:17). These basic motifs of "cross," "new creation," and "redeemed community" (or church)[46] in Paul's theology will be explored in greater detail in the next chapter and in chapter 12.

Notes

1 Richard Stearns, *The Hole in Our Gospel: What Does God Expect from Us?* (Nashville, TN: Thomas Nelson, 2009), p. 2.
2 Christopher J. H. Wright, *The Mission of God's People: A Biblical Theology of the Church's Mission* (Grand Rapids, MI: Zondervan, 2010), p. 31.

[3] Moore, *The Kingdom of Christ*, p. 121.

[4] See Andreas Kostenberger and Peter T. Obrien, *Salvation to the Ends of the Earth: A Biblical Theology of Mission* (Downers Grove, IL: InterVarsity, 2001), p. 182, n. 48. Kostenberger and Obrien point out that "the apostle has in view the believer's total response to the gospel, not simply his or her initial conversion. . . This notion of a total response accords well with the parallel expression of 15:18, "the obedience of the Gentiles' (NRSV), which focuses not simply on the nations coming to faith or their acceptance of the gospel, but on their initial response *and* constancy in Christian conduct as well."

[5] Wright, the *Mission of God's People*, pp. 195-6.

[6] Quoted in Todd L. Miles, "A Kingdom without a King? Evaluating the Kingdom Ethic(s) of the Emerging Church," http://www.sbts.edu/resources/files/2010/02/sbjt_121_miles.pdf (Paper delivered at the annual meeting of the Evangelical Theological Society, November 2007), p. 91.

[7]"Moving Forward with a Kingdom Consensus." Interview with Russell Moore (http://www.angelfire.com /tn/steveweaver/Russell_Moore_Interview.pdf)

[8]Todd Miles, "A Kingdom without a King?" p. 97.   Another emergent church leader states: "We have totally reprogrammed ourselves to recognize the good news as a means to an end—that the kingdom of God is here. We try to live into that reality and hope. We don't dismiss the cross; it is still a central part. But the good news is not that he died but that the kingdom has come." Brian McLaren similarly states that the gospel is about "social transformation arising from the presence and permeation of the reign of Christ." (Ibid., p. 91) Elsewhere, in criticizing what he calls the "skyhook Second Coming" view of dispensational pretribulationists, he writes that they have "marginalized Jesus with all his talk of the kingdom of God coming on earth, being among us now, the presence and permeation of the reign of Christ." See *Generous Orthodoxy* (Grand Rapids, MI: Zondervan, 2004), pp. 237-8. In a book co-authored with McLaren, Tony Campolo is similarly critical of dispensational premillenialism. He writes: "This is a theology that—with its implicit threat of being left behind, of time running out—is used by Dispensational preachers to great evangelistic effect. It has been a very effective goad to evangelism. . . To the contrary, the history of the world is infused with the presence of God, who is guiding the world toward becoming the kind of world God willed for it to be when it was created. Human history is going somewhere wonderful." Quoted in Larry Pettegrew, "Evangelicalism, Paradigms, and the Emerging Church," *The Master's Seminary Journal* (Fall 2006), p. 169.

[9]Quoted in Miles, "A Kingdom without a King?," p. 97.

[10] David VanDrunen, *Living in God's Two Kingdoms: A Biblical Vision for Christianity and Culture* (Wheaton, IL: Crossway, 2010), p. 24. McLaren contrasts the "conventional view" that Jesus saves sinful human beings from the righteous wrath of God with the "emerging view" that through his suffering, death, and resurrection Jesus inserted into history "a seed of grace, truth and hope" that "will, against all opposition and odds, prevail over the evil and injustice of humanity and lead to the world's ongoing transformation into the world God dreams of." See Brian McLaren, *Everything Must Change: Jesus, Global Crises, and a Revolution of Hope* (Nashville: Thomas Nelson, 2007), pp. 79-80.

[11] Steve Chalke and Alan Mann, *The Lost Message of Jesus* (Grand Rapids, MI: Zondervan, 2004). See also "The Redemption of the Cross" in *The Atonement Debate: Papers From the London Symposium on the Theology of the Atonement*, ed. D Tidball, D Hilborn and J Thacker (Grand Rapids, MI: Zondervan, 2008), pp. 249-266. In fairness to Steve Chalke it should be pointed out that he rejects only one version of the doctrine of substitutionary atonement. See: Tom Wright, "The Cross and the Caricatures: A Response to Robert Jenson, Jeffrey John, and a New Volume Entitled Pierced for Our Transgressions." www.virtueonline. org/portal/ modules/news/article. php?storyid=5895#.U6g_z6gQAmJ

[12] McLaren, *Everything Must Change*, pp. 158-60. Dave Tomlinson likewise argues that people are saved through the cross of Christ, but not in the sense that Christ died in the sinner's place. The doctrine of substitutionary atonement must be rejected because it "makes God seem fickle, vengeful, and morally underhanded." Rather, Christ's death on the cross demonstrated "God's love, which always forgives, rather than through a once-for-all event of forgiveness. What is changed, then, is not God's attitude toward us, but our attitude toward him." See Pettegrew, "Evangelicalism, Paradigms and the Emerging Church," p. 173.

[13] Miles, "A Kingdom without a King?," pp. 91, 99.

[14] Colin Brown, ed., *The New International Dictionary of New Testament Theology, Vol. 2* (Grand Rapids, MI: Zondervan, 1979), pp. 108-9.

[15] Kostenberger and Obrien, *Salvation to the Ends of the Earth*, p. 273.

[16] Lit. "in all creation under the heaven." The gospel "is God's trumpet call to the whole creation . . ." Robert M. Carson, *Tyndale New Testament Commentaries: The Epistles of Paul to the Colossians and Philemon* (Grand Rapids, MI: Eerdmans, 1972), p. 49. The Greek work *ktisis* denotes the sum total of what God has created (Cf. Rom. 1:20). But, according to Zodhiates, here it probably refers specifically to mankind as God's creation. See Spiros Zodhiates, *The Hebrew-Greek Key Study Bible* (Chattanooga, TN: AMG Publishers, 1986), p. 1705.

[17] Quoted in Moore, *The Kingdom of Christ*, p. 110.

[18] Ibid., pp. 110-11.

[19] Ronald J. Sider, *Good New and Good Works: A Theology for the Whole Gospel* (Grand Rapids, MI: Baker Books, 1993), p. 202.

[20] Van Drunen, *Living in God's Two Kingdoms*, p. 15.

[21] This idea of "two kingdoms" is expressed in many of Luther's writings. Luther distinguished between the kingdom of God (or of Christ) which is made up of all who believe in and profess the name of Christ and the kingdom of the world, or the organized society of men. The kingdom of God is realized in the church while the kingdom of world is realized in the state. Instrumentally, these are two means by which God governs the world. Luther's view of the state is closely connected with his concept of "natural orders" or stations of life (family, vocation, state, economics, and the empirical church) which he viewed as part of God's design to continue his creation and preserve it from disorder caused by sin. On the other hand, God accomplishes his work of redemption through the gospel which is proclaimed by the church. See Otto W. Heick, *A History of Christian Thought, Vol. I* (Philadelphia, PA: Fortress, 1965), p. 339.

22 VanDrunen, *Living in God's Two Kingdoms*, pp. 18-19. We have seen that this view is embraced by proponents of the emergent church. It is also found among some neo-Calvinists. In *Creation Regained: Biblical Basics for a Reformational Worldview* (Grand Rapids, MI: Eerdmans, 1985) Albert Wolters argues that the "redemption in Jesus Christ means the *restoration* of an original good creation. . . In other words, redemption is *re-creation*." Therefore, although fallen, everything that God created—whether social, relational, cultural or personal—is part of God's good creation is meant to be redeemed and brought under Christ's lordship. The church is called to take part in this on-going and unfolding creational work of God. The same perspective can be seen in mission movements, such as the Disciple Nations Alliance. In *Life Work: A Biblical Theology For What You Do Every Day* (Seattle, WA: YWAM, 2009) Darrow Miller argues that because Christ has won the decisive battle through the cross "God is at work in the world, redeeming his creation, building his kingdom . . ." Therefore, "in the midst of brokenness, redeemed man is to work to redeem culture and transform nations." (p. 109). As David Hegemen summarizes this perspective: "Thus God seeks to create a community of redeemed men and women who are quipped for every good work. We are redeemed so that we may work! The human race is brought back to a state of righteousness so that we might return to our Edenic calling to develop ("work") the earth into a glorious garden-city and finally take possession of our long-awaited inheritance." See *Plowing in Hope: Toward a Biblical Theology of Culture* (Moscow, Idaho: Canon, 1999), p. 71.

23 VanDrunen, Living in Two Kingdoms, pp 158-69.

24 Moore, *The Kingdom of Christ*, p. 121.

25 Stephen Neill, *Creative Tension* (London: Edinburgh Press, 1959), p. 81.

26 See Paul Marshall, *Thine is the Kingdom: A Biblical Perspective on the Nature of Government and Politics Today* (Grand Rapids, MI: Eerdmans, 1984), p. 37.

27 Ibid, See also Richard Mouw, *Political Evangelism* (Grand Rapids, MI: Eerdmans, 1973), p. 13; and Orlando Costas, *From the Periphery: Missiology in Context* (Maryknoll, NY: Orbis, 1982). This broader understanding of salvation as including the emergence of justice and wholeness (*shalom*) in society is reflected in the argument that the Mission of God (*missio Dei*) and God's kingdom must be identified with the movement of his Spirit in the world. Craig Van Gelder and Dwight Zscheile argue that the world (not just the church) is the field of God's ongoing activity and presence through the Spirit. The church must therefore discern and participate in what God is doing in the world. "Human salvation involves sharing in the community of Christ, which finds its [mission] through taking part in Christ's ministry in the world." See *The Missional Church in Perspective: Mapping Trends and Shaping the Conversation*, (Grand Rapids, MI: Baker Academic, 2011), pp. 112-13. Ray Anderson likewise argues that both the world and the church are reconciled to God through Christ. "Through the incarnation of God in Christ the world has been reconciled to God (2 Corinthians 5:19 . . . The church does not possess Christ for itself but finds Christ in the world." See *An Emergent Theology for Emerging Churches* (Downers Grove, IL: InterVarsity, 2006), p. 192. After a careful survey of the words used for "salvation" in the Old and New Testaments, Ronald Sider and James Parker III conclude that "the overwhelming volume of biblical usage points toward the narrower usage of salvation language." This does not mean that salvation is only per-

sonal or individual. Certainly, salvation is both vertical and horizontal, personal and social. "But it is all within the context of conscious confession of Christ." See: "How Broad is Salvation in Scripture?," In *Word and Deed: Evangelism and Social Responsibility*, ed. Bruce J. Nicholls (Grand Rapids, MI: Eerdmans, 1985), p. 105.

[28] See Bob Roberts, *Glocalization: How Followers of Jesus Engage a Flat World* (Grand Rapids, MI: Zondervan, 2007), pp. 40-44; Luis Bush, "A Call to Transformation," (http://www.ausprayernet.org). Use of the word "transformation" may be legitimate when talking about limited social change produced by the gospel. However, the word is often used in conjunction with the concept of "discipling nations" which presupposes spiritual conversion. See, for example, Darrow L. Miller, *Discipling Nations: The Power of Truth to Transform Cultures* (Seattle, WA: YWAM, 1998). At the same time, it is important to see that there are differences in emphasis among those who call for a "transformation" of social structures. Those who represent what I would call the "missional transformation" perspective tend to see the fall as resulting in patterns of domination and oppression by social, political, and economic systems. In this view, social transformation takes place through: (1) evangelism; (2) the church as a "counter-system," characterized by loving and sharing relationships among believers who seek to live out the principles of the kingdom; and (3) social and political action in defense of the social and economic rights of the poor and oppressed. See, for example, James F. Engel and William A. Dyrness, *Changing the Mind of Missions: Where Have We Gone Wrong?* (Downers Grove, IL: InterVarsity, 2000) and Robert Linthicum, *Transforming Power: Biblical Strategies for Making a Difference in Your Community*, (Downers Grove, IL: InterVarsity, 2003). The "Christianization of culture" perspective argues, on the other hand, that social transformation comes from *within* social institutions as are individuals changed by the gospel become a moral and spiritual force in their respective spheres of influence and false worldviews are replaced by the Christian worldview. In this way, other cultural spheres besides the church in which Christians operate (or what is often referred to as the "marketplace") are legitimate vehicles for the extension of Christ's reign throughout the earth. This perspective especially sees capitalism combined with Christian principles of stewardship as the best means for combating poverty and other social ills.   Examples of this perspective include Darrow Miller, *Discipling Nations*; and Ed Silvoso, *Anointed for Business; How Christians Can Use Their Influence in the Marketplace to Change the World* (Vetura, CA: Regal, 2002).

[29] Sider, *Good News and Good Works*, pp. 158-65; 196ff.

[30] Ibid., p. 159f. This is not to dispute that fact, as Sider points out, that there are cases in more communal and less individualistic societies where an entire village turns to Christ or that evangelism should address the whole person in community not isolated individuals. "But if repentance and conversion are genuine in 'community evangelism,' each person makes a *personal* decision and enters into a *personal* (as well as corporate) relationship with the living God. At the core of biblical faith is the radical truth that God calls each person to respond to Christ's invitation. In evangelism, we address only persons, not social structures, because only persons can become disciples of Christ." (Ibid., p. 160)

[31] Ibid., p. 207.

[32] See Mark A. Snoeberger, "History, Ecclesiology, and Mission, or Are We Missing Some Options Here?" (http://www.dbts.edu/pdf/macp/2010/Snoeberger, %20 History%20Ecclesiology%20and%20Mission.pdf). I agree with the assessment with the need for a "middle ground" expressed in this article, although I disagree with the author's own position of its composition.

[33] Gerry Breshears, "The Body of Christ: Prophet, Priest, or King?" *Journal of the Evangelical Theological Society* 37/1 (March 1994), pp. 7.

[34] Sider, *Good News and Good Works*, p. 204.

[35] See Donald G. Bloesch, *Freedom for Obedience: Evangelical Ethics for Contemporary Times* (San Francisco, CA: Harper and Row, 1987), p. 233.

[36] Stephen Charles Mott, *Biblical Ethics and Social Change* (New York: Oxford University Press, 1982), p. 102-3.

[37] Breashears, "The Body of Christ: Prophet, Priest, or King?," pp. 7, 10.

[38] Sider, *Good News and Good Works*, p. 207.

[39] Moore, *The Kingdom of Christ*, pp. 110, 114-15.

[40] Ibid., p. 111.

[41] See Russell D. Moore and Robert E. Sagers, "The Kingdom of God and the Church: A Baptist Reassessment," (http://www.sbts.edu/resources/files/2010/02/sbjt_121_moore_sagers.pdf) pp. 72-72.

[42] Walter Rauschenbusch, *A Theology for the Social Gospel*, (New York: Macmillan, 1917; reprinted by Nashville, TN: Abingdon, 1981), pp. 145, 222,

[43] Timothy C. Morgan, "Purpose Driven in Rwanda: Rick Warren's Sweeping Plan to Defeat Poverty," *Christianity Today* (October 2005).

[44] Gary F. VanderPol, *The Least of These: American Evangelical Parachurch Mission to the Poor, 1947-2005*, Th.D. Dissertation, Boston University School of Theology, 2010, p. 273.

[45] From the "Evangelism Manifesto" of the Christian Reformed Church and Reformed Churches in America. Quoted in Steve Schaeffer, *Living in the Gap*, pp. 152-3.

[46] See Hays, *The Moral Vision of the New Testament*, pp. 19-36, 196-99.

Chapter 3
The Church as the
Sign of the Kingdom

Some churches are going to great lengths to attract people to their Easter services. One church in south Las Vegas invited people to "join us as we celebrate Easter. . . with power packed worship experiences and tons of fun for the kiddies." It featured an "Easter Carnival" with live music, bounce houses, face painters, and a variety of food vendors. During the Saturday evening and Easter Sunday worship services the church raffled away TVs, iPods, and other items. To enter the raffle those who attend were required to "purchase" a raffle ticket with ten cans of food.[1] Another church in the Bay Area attracted 23,500 people to its Easter service by offering millions of dollars in prizes, including 16 free cars, televisions, and furniture. Besides the larger prizes, the church gave away 15,000 prize packs with coupons for free goods and services such as a chiropractic exam, Hooks baseball tickets, a week's membership to Gold's Gym, and a night's stay for dogs at the Pooch Pad. In response to the criticism that the church was promoting consumerism and bribing people to come to church, the pastor defended the prize give-away as a way to "get them in here and get them saved . . ." The prizes, he argued, are a metaphor for getting into heaven. "The true ultimate give-away was

Jesus dying on the cross."[2]   While we might view the actions of these churches as extreme and outside the "mainstream," they are simply a logical extension of the attractional model of church growth which dominates Christian thinking today.

It is now conventional wisdom among leaders in many evangelical churches that we must learn from the marketing strategies of modern corporations and businesses.   Lyle Schaller, who is one of the most popular church consultants, argues in his book *The Very Large Church* that consumerism is now just a "fact of life."   He then goes on to coach pastors how to appeal to spiritual consumers, but says nothing about how the church ought to transcend cultural values.[3]   The same mentality is reflected in the "homogeneous church growth principle" which has had a major influence in our churches and justifies market segmentation on the basis of the sociological observation that people gravitate to people who are like them.   Consequently, as the adage goes, Sunday morning is the most segregated time of the week.   But as Michael Horton states: "When we allow something other than the gospel to determine the identity of the church, our mission becomes an extension of the powers of the present age rather than the in-breaking of the age to come."[4]

Needed—Churches that Reflect, Not Just Churches that Attract

Research indicates that there has been a dramatic increase in the number of megachurches[5] in the U.S. from just 10 in 1970 to 1,200 in 2005.   Today over half of the church goers attend the largest 10 percent of churches in the U.S.   What often goes unnoticed is the fact that, on average, 50 smaller churches close their doors every week.[6] Over the last four decades there has also been a steady decline in the percentage of Americans who attend church on a regular basis. "Seeker friendly" megachurches typically focus on being "culturally relevant."   The "megaministry principle" is that church size and growth ought to match the potential offered by wide stretches of suburban sprawl.   And in order to capture this potential the architecture of most megachurches closely resembles that of a theatre and the suburban shopping mall.[7]

Pemkumar Williams points out that the architectural design of the typical megachurch embodies two fundamental values: control and choice. The mall banishes outside threats of disruption and distraction. It incorporates a variety of elements like interior landscaping, controlled lighting, and temperature to create a positive atmosphere. Megachurches reflect this desire for control. This is not bad in itself. But "when this involves advertising, programming, management, and leadership of a large number of people responsible for a variety of activities all geared towards creating the best possible impression on the visitor, there is a tendency to control the process so as to guarantee the product."[8] The role of the Spirit tends to get "squeezed out" in the process. The mall-like spaces of megachurches also enable them to offer a wide variety of programs and activities that cater to the modern suburbanite. The constant refrain of church consultants is that churches must continually incorporate new features and add new services if they want to effectively compete for today's religious consumers. "Along with multimedia auditoriums, today's thriving churches also include coffee shops, bookstores, food courts, auto repair shops, day care centers, weight rooms, and themed children's facilities complete with Nintendos and talking animals . . . These megachurches are self-contained cities where the faithful can worship, eat, shop, work and play."[9]

The megachurch concept challenges us to create an inviting and accepting atmosphere that is open to outsiders and creates bridges between the "human city" and the "holy city." But "by too closely copying the human city (or the suburb) it might be that the mall like church is less along Scriptures trajectory for theological community than it hopes to be."[10] Referring to the growing concentrations of Christians in large congregations of over two thousand members, Tom Sine expresses the concern that such churches "tend to become very accomodationist to the values of dominant consumer culture in order to ensure high numerical growth and don't invite members into a more serious, whole-life faith."[11] I believe he is right. If our churches are to be truly faithful to Scripture, they need to focus less on *attracting* people through a multitude of programs, promotional gimmicks, and perfectly orchestrated worship services and focus more on *reflecting* the righteousness of Christ's future kingdom.

Years ago Carl Henry wrote in his book *A Plea for Evangelical Demonstration*: "Proclamation of the gospel-truth is doomed unless pulsating life renders the spoken word potent even before it is preached . . . Only the gospel truth *demonstrated* can fully expose the counterfeit character of what often passes for truth in thought and word, but is devoid of Biblical love and justice, holiness and joy."[12] (Emphasis mine) The early Christians knew, Henry argued, that it was their spiritual vision of the cosmos under Christ and their proclamation of God's justice and of Jesus' justification which gave them perspective and power. He maintained that loss of this perspective and power in the modern church would render it impotent.[13] His prophetic warnings are as true for the church today as when he wrote them.

Before proceeding further it is important to have a working definition of the "church." Kevin Giles points out that there is often little agreement on a definition of what constitutes "the church." After discussing various understandings of the church he suggests that it is best described as a "Christian community," or a gathering of people who are united to Christ and to each other by Christ's ministry, death, and resurrection. Although a Christian community without any institutional form is impossibility, the church is not just a sociological phenomenon. It is God's creation in Christ. Christians are united in a common fellowship (the horizontal dimension) because they are united in Christ (the vertical dimension).[14] In the New Testament the church is sometimes viewed as the world-wide community of Christians, sometimes as a community of Christians in one location, and sometimes as those who met together in a particular home location. This three-fold usage calls into question the usual meaning of the expression "the local church." Protestants often think of "the church" as referring primarily to a group of Christians who actually gather together—the third designation above. But the fact that Paul, Luke and other NT writers speak of Christians in one area as the church (*ekklesia*)[15] suggests that we should think of all Christians in one geographical area, not just those in a specific congregation, as "the local church."[16]

The New Testament conception of the church challenges the radically individualistic orientation of western culture. The worldview of Scripture presupposes that the individual is always part of a larger social collectivity which is primary. To become a follower of Jesus by necessity means becoming part of a larger spiritual family. "To suggest that the Bible is ultimately about individual salvation, or that the church is but a local assembly of individuals who are bound together only by their personal associations, or that each individual congregation is in no profound way linked with other congregations, introduces ideas alien to biblical thinking. Those who suggest such things reflect their own cultural values, not the values of the biblical writers."[17] This corporate and communal concept of the church is profoundly important for understanding its connection to the kingdom of God.

The Church as the Initial Manifestation of the Kingdom

In ecclesiastical (e.g., Catholic) models of the kingdom the church is viewed as the custodian and embodiment of God's reign. This conception of the kingdom is reflected in the words of the well-known hymn of Timothy Dwight:

> I love thy kingdom, Lord, the house of thin abode,
> the church our blest Redeemer saved with his own precious blood.[18]

I would be wrong, however, to *equate* the church with God's kingdom. Rather, it is (or ought to be) a manifestation, however imperfect, of the future kingdom. Others have described the church as a "beachhead of the new creation" and "sign of the new age,"[19] a "workshop of kingdom righteousness"[20] and a "Kingdom colony."[21] All of these descriptive phrases are meant to convey the biblical picture of the church as a community of believers which, although it still struggles with sin in the present age, has begun to participate in the powers and blessings of the age to come through the indwelling of the Holy Spirit. As Carl Henry puts it: "When Christianity discusses the new society, it speaks not of some intangible future reality whose specific features it cannot yet identify, but of the regenerate church called to live by the standards of the coming King, and which in some respects already approximates the kingdom of God in present history."[22]

The apostle Paul frequently uses kingdom or kingdom-like language to describe the church and enjoin Christ-like behavior. In 1 Thessalonians, believers are corporately called to live lives worthy of God "who calls you into His kingdom and glory." (1 Thess. 2:12). In I Corinthians they are commanded to abstain from immorality and idolatry as those "upon whom the ends of the ages have come" (1 Cor. 10:11). In Colossians, Paul similarly has in mind the *corporate church* not just individuals when he describes Christ's redemptive work as the transferring of believers "from the domain of darkness" into the "kingdom of the Son" (Col. 1:13). In Ephesians, he describes the cosmic reign of Christ as finding its initial expression and fulfillment within the church "which is his body, the fullness of him who fills everything in every way." (Eph. 1:22). These and many other passages in the New Testament speak of the church as the primary arena in and through which the holiness, righteousness, and justice of the kingdom are to be manifested in the present age.[23]

The New Testament uses numerous images, metaphors, and pictures that connect the church with prophetic promises of a restored Israel and a future kingdom. One of the most significant of these is the picture of the church as the temple of the Holy Spirit. While this image is usually thought of in individualist terms, only once in the New Testament is it applied to individual Christians. In every other case it is applied to the Christian community or church as a corporate and communal entity.[24]   While we will refer to this temple imagery a number of times in this book, here we will look at its significance for understanding the church as a *sign* of God's future kingdom.

In the Old Testament the temple is associated with the presence of the Spirit and God's holiness. Gregory Beale shows, further, that in the prophets the earthly temple is seen as a reflection of the heavenly or cosmic temple of God.[25]   In Isaiah 6:2-4, for example, the temple is associated with a picture of God's glory which fills the entire earth: "Holy, holy, holy is the Lord Almighty, the whole earth is full of his glory."   In the last chapter of Revelation these themes are brought together in dramatic fashion. In Revelation 21:3, John pictures the new heavens and new earth in terms of an end-times temple which literally encompasses the entire earth and where God fills the entire earth with his presence: "And I heard a loud voice from the throne saying, 'Look! God's dwelling place (i.e., tabernacle) is now among the people, and he will dwell with them. They will be his people, and God himself will be with them and be their God.'"

The eschatological significance of the image of *church* as the "temple" of the Holy Spirit can be seen in a number of New Testament passages. In 2 Corinthians 6:16 Paul explicitly connects the church with the end-times temple when he states: "For we are the temple of the living God. As God has said 'I will live with them and walk among them, and I will be their God, and they will be my people." Paul is here quoting from Ezekiel 37:26-27, which is a prediction of the coming temple. So, he is saying that Christians are the initial fulfillment of the actual prophecy of the end-time temple.[26]   In 1 Corinthians 3:16 Paul further describes the church as "God's temple" in which his Spirit resides.

In the New Testament this image of the church as the temple of the Holy Spirit has four-fold significance, as the figure below indicates:

Figure 4. The Church as the Temple of the Holy Spirit

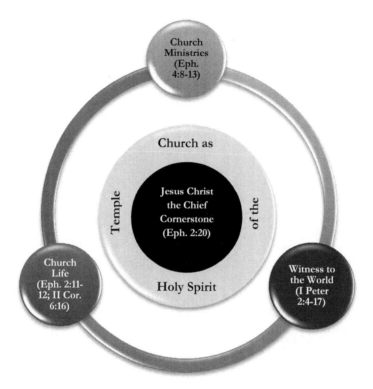

First, and most importantly, it connects the church to Jesus Christ, the chief cornerstone. "In him," says Paul, "the whole building is joined together and rises to become a holy temple." (Eph. 2:20).[27] In the same chapter, this temple imagery is further linked to Paul's description of the life of the church as a "new humanity," where both Jews and Gentiles are reconciled to each other and to God through the cross (Eph. 2:14-18). Next, Paul invokes temple imagery when he describes the church as being "built up" through the ministries of the apostles, prophets, evangelists, pastors, and teachers, the purpose of which is to "to equip God's people for works of service" (Eph. 4:11-12, cf. 2:22-24; I Cor. 3:10-14). He further indicates that these divine giftings are directly related to the inaugurated reign of Christ (4:8-13). Finally, in I Peter the image of the church as "living stones that are being built into a spiritual house" (2:4) is connected to its mission to be a witness in word and deed to the Gentile nations (vs. 12), government authorities (vss. 13-17) and economic authorities (vss. 18-24).

Implications for the Church

Again, there are several practical implications of this picture of the church as the inaugurated form of the kingdom. I will focus on three areas of church life and ministry in particular: (1) identification with Christ in the ordinances of the church; (2) the internal social ministry of the church; and (3) the external ministry of the church to the world.

1. The church's observances of the ordinances of baptism and the Lord's Supper should convey their eschatological significance.

Because of a tendency to view both baptism and the Lord's Supper in individualistic terms, Christians in the western world often miss the importance of both of these ordinances as pointing to the future kingdom. In Romans 6:1-11 Paul describes baptism in terms of an inaugurated "already/not yet" eschatology: "If we have been united with him like this in his death, we will certainly also be united with him in his resurrection . . . Now if we died with Christ, we believe we will also live with him" (vss. 5, 8). For Paul, then, baptism is a sign, not just of our union with Christ in the present, but also our future resurrection with him in the *eschaton*.[28] Similarly, Jesus teaches his followers to view the Lord's Supper as both a remembrance of his sacrificial death and a symbol of the future messianic meal in the Kingdom of God (Luke 22:16-17, 20). "The Lord's Supper is the meal in which the baptized and believing church enjoys already the taste of what the final kingdom will bring in its fullness."[29] Paul conveys this experience of living between the beginning of the end and

the consummation of the end when he states that through the ongoing practice of the Lord's Supper we "proclaim the Lord's death until
he comes" (I Cor. 11:26).[30]

*2.   The church must seek to reflect the kingdom righteousness in its internal so-
cial life before it addresses the need for righteousness in social and political structures.*

A local church with which I am familiar has as its slogan the words:
"A different way of doing church." But, as Reggie McNeal reminds
us, the key to an authentic and dynamic Christianity that has an effective witness to the world is not to become better at *doing* church but
to learn to *be* the church. Churches in North America often reflect
the malaise of the culture around them because they have lost their
identity.[31] In recent years, the tendency among evangelicals has been
to seek change through politics. But churches cannot legitimately
protest the lack of "family values" in Washington D.C. if they have
not addressed the sins of divorce, pornography, and spousal abuse in
their own ranks. Calls to defend the rights of the unborn will increasingly fall on deaf ears if there is not a similar concern for the
rights of children born into extreme poverty.   Christian protests
against "big government" and "out-of-control" spending on social
services lack credibility if there are not also efforts to develop "parallel structures" to help the needy, particularly fellow-believers in our
local churches who have lost their jobs because of economic problems that that still impact many of our communities. "The church is
the test community for social and political righteousness. If we don't
or can't pursue it here, we really have nothing to say there. If we seek
it among ourselves, even though we fall short, we have something to
say, and our imperfections help to keep us humble."[32] Churches
which exhibit righteousness and justice internally are a witness to the
rest of the world of the righteousness and justice which will characterize Christ's future kingdom on earth.   This is particularly important in the area of race relations. A church which is deeply divided by culture and race in effect denies the very reality of the kingdom

itself—one which will be made up of people from "every tribe and language and people and nation" who have been purchased by Christ's blood, and will serve God and reign on earth (Rev. 5:9-10).

3. Social concern must be part of the church's witness to the coming kingdom.

One of the most vexing issues in our churches has been whether ministries of mercy and social justice ought to be coupled with evangelism as an essential part of the missional outreach of the church to unbelievers. Michael Horton argues that, while individual believers have the responsibility to show mercy to their neighbors (Christian and non-Christian) as part of their general duty as Christians "none of the principle passages usually adduced actually supports the emphasis on social action (i.e., service ministries to the civil community) as an element of the Great Commission."[33] There is, he argues, a tendency to confuse the Great Commandment with the Great Commission. In his view, they are on different planes. The Great Commandment is rooted in law and calls every person—believer and unbeliever alike—to neighborly love while the Great Commission is rooted in God's act of redemption and calls believers to proclaim the gospel to everyone. To confuse to two is to confuse the gospel with the law. It also involves a failure to distinguish between the church as an *organization* entrusted with the means of grace and the church as an *organism* consisting of believers who are salt and light in the various spheres of society and in their communities. It is this distinction between the church as a place and the church as a people that has become confused in contemporary talk about the church transforming society.[34] Horton is concerned that loving our neighbor will become a pretense for evangelism and that the gospel will be turned into the social gospel. Moreover, "the church cannot say or do everything that needs to be said and done by Christians working alongside non-Christians in society."[35] These are legitimate concerns as we have already noted in our discussion of some interpretations of mission as the "transformation" of society and nations. But this is not a sufficient basis for avoiding biblically balanced and well-reasoned approaches to integrating word and deed in the ministry of the church.

I will address the issue of evangelism and social concern in greater detail in later chapters. Here, several points can be made in response to Horton's argument. First, many of the New Testament passages enjoining "good works" are not limited to Christians as individuals. Rather, they are addressed to Christians corporately as the church. Jesus' command to be "salt and light" so that people "may see your good deeds and praise your Father in heaven" (Matt. 5:16) is directed to the community of believers as a new covenant people of God which he describes as a "city on a hill" (vs. 14). The imagery used by Jesus parallels God's command to the nation of Israel to be a "light to the nations" by reflecting his righteousness and justice (Isa. 42:6; 51:4). Paul's instruction in Galatians 6:10 to "do good to all people, especially those who belong to the household of believers" comes at the end of a series of exhortations to godly living which are addressed to the entire church as a corporate body. The word "therefore" connects this verse to the previous verses which speak of the dual outcomes of the ways of the flesh as reaping destruction and the way of the Spirit as reaping a harvest, thereby indicating that persistence in "doing good" is a matter of eternal kingdom significance. The connection between the ethical behavior of believers and the witness of the church to God's plan of redemption is most evident in I Peter 2:9-12, where Peter draws out the missional implications of the corporate behavior of Christians as a "chosen people" and "holy nation:" "Keep your conduct among the Gentiles honorable, so that when they speak against you as evildoers, they many see your good deeds and glorify God on the day of visitation." (I Pet. 2:12, ESV) Almost certainly, these words of Peter are based on a recollection of Jesus' teaching in Matthew 5:16. And, as we have seen, this entire passage is heavily eschatological in nature. All of these passages, then, connect social responsibility with witness by the church to God's wider mission.[36]

Second, I agree with Tim Keller's observation that "Evangelism is the most basic and radical ministry possible to a human being. . . . But just as good works are inseparable from faith in the life of the believer, so caring for the poor is inseparable from the work of evangelism and the ministry of the Word."[37] Keller rightly argues that, although our long range objective should always be the salvation of those to whom we minister "we should not give aid only because a person is open to the gospel, nor should we withdraw it if he or she does not become spiritually receptive."[38] Otherwise, social concern becomes simply a carrot for conversion. At the same time, it should always be clear that the motivation for our aid is our Christian faith, and every effort should be made to find non-artificial and non-exploitative ways to connect ministries of the Word and gatherings for teaching and fellowship with ministries of social concern.[39]

Finally, when churches neglect social ministry they are often replaced by either para-church organizations or secular non-profits. The result is that the local congregation forfeits this aspect of witness in the community to the righteousness of the kingdom and many individual giftings in the church body that could be mobilized for the advancement of Christ's kingdom are simply not utilized. While Michael Horton and others who share his views may argue that individual Christians still have the responsibility to join with their non-believing neighbors in addressing issues of common concern, practically speaking the exact opposite usually occurs. When a local congregation uses all of its resources on ministries that are internally oriented, the typical church goer shifts his or her volunteer labor from the community to serving in the church. The result is that *both* the church body and its members "withdraw" and become useless in the betterment of the community. While it is true that the church as an institution cannot carry out corporately all of the activity that it equips its members to do, there are many ways in which it can work through "missional networks" to mobilize the people of its congregation for service in their communities and still be the church.[40] The graphic below illustrates this relationship:

Figure 5. The Church, Kingdom, Providence, and Missional Networks

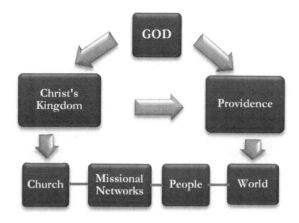

The church as a witness to Christ's kingdom and missional networks made up of congregations, agencies, non-profits, and individuals can work together for common causes and on the basis of a common grace that is rooted in God's providential care for the world.   I will discuss the importance of missional networks in greater detail in the last chapter.

Conclusion

The New Testament presents a "kingdom ecclesiology" that is rooted in a unifying story. As Richard Hays summarizes this "story:"

> The God of Israel, the creator of the world, has acted (astoundingly) to rescue a lost and broken world through the death and resurrection of Jesus; the full scope of that rescue is not yet apparent, but God has created a community of witnesses to this good news, the church. While awaiting the grand conclusion of the story, the church, empowered by the Holy Spirit, is called to reenact the loving obedience of Jesus Christ and thus to serve as a sign of God's redemptive purposes for the world.[41]

The New Testament writers use a number of metaphors to convey this nature of the church as an eschatological community. The church is variously described as the people or elect of God (Gal. 6:16; I Pet. 1:1; 2:10); a new humanity (Eph. 2:15) and new creation (Gal. 6:15; cf. II Cor. 5:17); the one body of Christ (I Cor. 12:13); and the temple of the Holy Spirit and God's temple (I Cor. 3:16-17). This means, on the one hand, that we cannot conceive of redemption and atonement through Christ in purely individualistic terms. God redeems a community, not just individuals (Eph. 1:4; 5:25-27; Col. 1:13). The believer's new freedom *in Christ* "is not merely an independence *from* certain things, but also an independence *for* others."[42] Through God's Spirit individuals are transferred out of a broken relationship with both God and others and enabled "to live a kind of life that will extend and deepen that new community itself."[43] This social dimension to the gospel is treated in greater detail in chapter 12.

A kingdom ecclesiology means, further, that the message of salvation cannot be divorced from a witness to the righteousness and justice of the kingdom, both in the church's corporate life and its relationship to the world. The church is not just the "evangelistic machinery." As part of the "good news" we call the gospel, it has been placed on this earth to both proclaim the gospel of the kingdom and exemplify it.[44] As Moore reminds us, a "recognition of the Kingdom orientation of the church . . . serves to make sense of the specific way in which the church is the arena in which the holistic and relational aspects of the Kingdom manifest themselves."[45] This brings us to the meaning and significance of justice in Scripture.

Notes

[1] See http://www.thechurchlv.com/easter-2012
[2] See http://www.caller.com/news/2010/apr/04/churchs-giveaway-attracts-thousands/

[3] Jethani, *The Divine Commodity*, pp. 19-20.

[4] Michael Horton, *The Gospel Commission: Recovering God's Strategy for Making Disciples* (Grand Rapids, MI: Baker Books, 2011), p. 131.

[5] Megachurches are typically defined as churches with a weekly attendance of at least 2,000 people.

[6] Jethani, *The Divine Commodity*, p. 89.

[7] See Premkuman D. Williams, "Between City and Steeple: Looking at Megachurch Architecture," in *Everyday Theology*, ed. Vanhoozer, pp. 115f.

[8] Jethani, *The Divine Commodity*, p. 122.

[9] Ibid., p. 89.

[10] Williams, "Between City and Steeple," p. 130.

[11] Tom Sine, *The New Conspirators: Creating the Future One Mustard Seed at a Time* (Downers Grove, IL: IVP Books, 2008), pp. 205-206.

[12] Carl F.H. Henry, *A Plea for Evangelical Demonstration* (Grand Rapids, MI: Baker, 1971), p. 83.

[13] Ibid., p. 69.

[14] Kevin Giles, *What on Earth in the Church? An Exploration in New Testament Theology* (Downers Grove, IL: InterVarsity, 1995), pp. 8-18.

[15] In a later chapter I will discuss in greater detail the meaning of the word *ekklesia* in relation to the concept of the "people of God" which has its roots in the Old Testament.

[16] Giles, *What on Earth is the Church?* pp. 185-86.

[17] Ibid., pp. 20-21.

[18] See Howard A. Snyder, *Models of the Kingdom: Gospel, Culture and Mission in Biblical and Historical Perspective* (Eugene, OR: Wipf and Stock Publishers, 1991), pp. 68-69.

[19] Michael Goheen, *A Light to the Nations: the Missional Church and the Biblical Story* (Grand Rapids, MI: Baker Academic, 2011), p. 165

[20] Blaising and Bock, *Progressive Dispensationalism*, p. 289.

[21] Moore and Sagers, "The Kingdom of God and the Church," p. 76.

[22] Carl F. H. Henry, *God, Revelation, and Authority, Vol. IV: The God Who Speaks and Shows* (Wheaton,. IL: Crossway, 1999), p. 522.

[23] Moore, *The Kingdom of Christ*, pp. 146f.

[24] Goheen, *A Light to the Nations*, p. 179.

[25] G.K. Beale, *The Temple and the Church's Mission: A Biblical Theology of the Dwelling Place of God* (Downers Grove, IL: InterVarsity, 2004), pp. 45ff. .

[26] Ibid., p. 253-54.

[27] I Peter 2 also describes Christ as the "cornerstone" (vs. 6) and "capstone" (vs. 7) of the temple. This language is eschatological in nature and is used in the Psalms and Isaiah to describe the coming Davidic king (See Isa 28:16; Ps 118:22).

[28] Moore and Sagers, "The Kingdom of God and the Church," p. 77

[29] Geoffrey Wainwright, *Eucharist and Eschatology* (New York: Oxford University Press, 1981), p. 134.

[30] Steve Schaeffer, *Living in the Gap*, p. 37.

[31] Reggie McNeal, *The Present Future: Six Tough Questions for the Church* (San Francisco, CA: Jossey-Bass, 2003), p. 17-18.

[32] Blaising and Bock, *Progressive Dispensationalism*, p. 290.

[33] Horton, *The Gospel Commission*, p. 224.

[34] Ibid., pp. 226-43.

[35] Ibid. pp. 227and 236

[36] See Wright, *The Mission of God*, pp. 387f.

[37] Tim Keller, "The Gospel and the Poor," *Themelios* 33-3 (December 2008), p. 17. Available at: http://s3.amazonaws. com/tgc-documents/journal-issues/33.3/ Themelios_33.3.pdf

[38] Ibid., p. 18.

[39] Ibid.

[40] See Missional Network, "Community Transformation Partnerships: An Opportunity for Churches to Join in the Long-Term Transformation of the Communities," http://www.missionalnetworkweb.com/Files/ Community%20 Transformation.pdf

[41] Hays, *The Moral Vision of the New Testament*, p. 193.

[42] Robert Banks, *Paul's Idea of Community, rev. ed.* (Peabody, MA: Hendrickson, 1994), p. 19.

[43] Ibid., p. 20.

[44] Harvie M. Conn, *Evangelism: Doing Justice and Preaching Grace* (Grand Rapids, MI: Academie Books, 1982), pp. 18-19.

[45] Moore, *The Kingdom of Christ*, p. 154.

PART TWO

KINGDOM WITNESS, JUSTICE, AND WORSHIP

Mission is not the ultimate purpose of the church. God's glory is. All things are being worked out according to his purpose and plan, which is the demonstration of his glory (Eph. 1:11). God's mission is the manifestation of his magnificence. His glory is therefore the fuel and goal of missions. Mission is God's chosen means to his glory.

Jonathan Edwards referred to four dimensions of "God's passion for his glory."[1] First, God is glorious whether he does anything to demonstrate it or not. God could have remained the only being in existence and not created a single thing, and his glory and power would exist nonetheless. God's glory does not depend on our existence. But, secondly, God is glorified in his creation (Psalm 96). Edwards spoke of this as a "disposition in the fullness of divinity to flow out and diffuse itself:"

> Therefore . . . we may suppose that a disposition in God, as an original property of his nature, to an emanation of his infi-

nite fullness, was what excited him to create the world; and so, that the emanation itself was aimed at by him as the last end of creation.[2]

God is therefore glorified when his creation (especially human-kind which is created in his image) fulfills the purpose for which it was created. Third, God is glorified when we come to him in worship, praising his name and his works of salvation. The apostle Paul makes this clear when he states that we were chosen in Christ before the creation of the world "to the praise of his glorious grace" (Eph. 1: 4-6). Finally, God is glorified when we proclaim his glory to the nations. In Romans the apostle Paul indicates that the ultimate goal of his own mission of calling the nations to the obedience of faith is that they might "glorify God for his mercy" (Rom. 1:5, 15:8, 16: 26-27). To demonstrate that this purpose of his mission is a fulfillment of God's promise to Abraham that he would be a blessing to all nations, Paul quotes a series of verses from the Old Testament (Rom. 15:9-12):

> [A]s it is written: 'Therefore I will praise you among the Gentiles; I will sing hymns to your name.' And again it says, 'Rejoice, O Gentiles with his people.' And again, 'Praise the Lord, all you Gentiles, and sing praises to him, all you peoples.' And again, Isaiah says, 'The Root of Jesse will spring up, one who will arise to rule over the nations, the nations will hope in him.'[3]

The book of Revelation ends with a glorious vision of people from all nations praising God and walking in the light of his glory in a new heaven and new earth (Rev. 19:1-8, 21:1-5, 22-24). But it goes even further in stating that all of creation, not just all peoples, will be united in praise to God through Christ:

> Then I heard every creature in heaven and on earth and under the earth and on the sea, and all that is in them, singing: "To him who sits on the throne and to the Lamb be praise and honor and glory and power, forever and ever!" (Rev. 5:13)

God's mission and the mission of his church are inseparably linked. Therefore, the church's mission in the present age begins and ends with God's glory.

Closely related to the subject of worship and God's glory is the issue of idolatry. An idol might be defined as "whatever your heart clings to or relies on for *ultimate security*" and "whatever claims the ultimate loyalty that belongs to God alone."[4] It is, as the 16th century reformer John Calvin described the second commandment, anything that acts as a substitute for true worship of God.[5] If God's glory is the ultimate purpose and goal of the church's mission then idolatry is its polar opposite. Chris Wright puts it well: "Since God's mission is to restore creation to its original purpose of bringing all glory to God himself and thereby enable all of creation to enjoy the fullness of blessing that he desires for it, God battles against all forms of idolatry and calls us to join him in that conflict."[6] A biblically informed missional approach to idolatry therefore demands that we understand the variety of ways human beings make gods for themselves and the whole breadth of the Bible's exposure of its deleterious effects, especially on humans as the crown of God's creation.[7]

Chapter four looks at how various temptations to idolatry in our society threaten true worship in the church. The next two chapters examine the relationship between justice and God's holiness in the Old and New Testaments. The final chapter in this section draws some practical implications for Christians and the church.

Notes

[1] John Piper, *God's Passion for His Glory: Living the Vision of Jonathan Edwards* (Wheaton, IL: Crossway, 1998, 2006).
[2] Ibid., p. 155.
[3] II Sam. 22:50; Ps. 18:49; Duet. 32:43; Isa. 11:10.

[4] G.K. Beale, *We Become What We Worship: A Biblical Theology of Idolatry* (Downers Grove, IL: InterVarsity, 2008), p. 17.

[5]Ibid., p. 19.

[6] Wright, *The Mission of God,* p. 188.

[7] Ibid. Also, Beale, *We Become What We Worship*, p. 18.

Chapter 4
The Noise of
Solemn Assemblies

In his book *Crumbling Foundations* (1984) Donald Bloesch observes that "idol worship" is a particular challenge to the Western church, for we live in a period of unprecedented technological advance and the erosion of the metaphysical foundations of Western culture. The dominant religion is the religion of the Enlightenment, which worships humanity and has disdain for any serious concern for the glory of God.[1]   In this context, Bloesch sees two great dangers for the church.   One is a succumbing of the church to the norms of the technological society—utility, productivity, and efficiency—which glorify personal achievement, experience, and success.   This often results in an individualistic piety that ignores the crying needs of humanity and social justice.[2]   The opposite danger is for Christians to identify with social movements of reform on both the right and left of the political spectrum to such an extent that the spiritual dimensions of their mission are sacrificed.   These sociopolitical ideologies "make social restructuring an ultimate concern and thereby become secular salvations."[3]   As I will seek to show in this chapter, these tendencies continue to be the two main temptations facing the church in America which should have as its ultimate goal the glory of God.

The Church and Consumerism

Unless you belong to a church which espouses a gospel of "health and wealth," you have undoubtedly heard a sermon or two on the dangers of materialism. This is certainly an issue, particularly as Christian holidays become more and more consumer driven. During the Christmas season the check-out line becomes more a symbol of the meaning of Christmas for the vast majority of Americans than the manger or the cross. The check-out line reflects our vision of the "good life," characterized by sex, beauty, health, information/knowledge, convenience, wealth, and celebrity. While each of the elements (with the exception of celebrity and convenience) may have a place, the checkout line puts our loves out of order and indicates the subtle impact that culture can have on our priorities. The "good life" envisioned by the gospel relativizes what the checkout line sets forth as essential.[4] However, being "in but not of" the checkout line pertains not simply to our lifestyles as Christians. There are a growing number of observers of worship in our evangelical churches who argue that the threat of consumerism is not just the temptation to make material goods (and related values) the center of life. A deeper and more subtle threat to the church is that the *worldview* of consumerism has become the dominant framework through which Christians in America understand everything, including the gospel, church, and even our worship of God himself.[5]

It will help to get some historical perspective. In the 1950s America was emerging from the turbulent years of the Second World War. Technology and industrialization impacted every aspect of American culture. Concurrently, there was a revolutionary transformation of the American economy into what Kenneth Galbraith aptly described as the "affluent society," leading to the expansion of the middle class and the pervasive influence of the middle class values and outlook of consumption, individualism, pragmatism, affluence, and success. In this cultural context, Peter Berger, a theologically astute sociologist, observed a curious paradox. On the one hand, religion was accorded considerable prestige, with a vast majority of the American population attending church services and a large number of people showing an interest in religious matters. Unlike today, there was no fear that America was becoming a "Godless" country. At the same time, Berger observed, American society was highly secularized and religion had less and less influence in broad segments of American life.[6] What accounted for this paradox? Berger argued that the religious establishment in America enjoyed popularity because it had accommodated itself to and even buttressed the secular values of the "way of the middle" and the middle class "way of life." In an affluent culture that catered to self-indulgence and personal cravings, churches had become institutions of "religious consumption." By and large, the religious establishment fostered a religion of complacency and sanctified the political and social status-quo. It was with the middle class that this "fusion" between religion and culture was the strongest.[7]

True Christian religion will always be in tension with the world and have a prophetic dimension. But, in Berger's view, institutionalized religion in America guarded against this by "inoculating" church goers with "small doses of Christianoid concepts and terminology" which effectively "immunized" them from any real encounter with the Christian message.[8] Theological construction, he argued, provided the criteria by which churches could judge themselves. Without it, religion would become mere expediency at the institutional level and experience at the personal level.[9] But American culture militated against any real intellectual effort. Consequently, in churches the emphasis tended to be placed on emotional pragmatism and on religion as a means to "psychological well-being" rather than any real honest confrontation with the Christian message. Berger concluded: "The way is opened for the attitude of the religious consumer, who shops around the denominational supermarket for just the right combination of spiritual kicks and thrills to meet his particular psychological needs."[10]

Fast forward to today. Gone is the optimism and cultural euphoria of the 1950s. We are faced with political gridlock, economic crisis, and terrorist threats at every turn. A shrinking middle-class is under pressure as never before. Evangelicals bemoan the loss of "Christian" values and a growing indifference to the faith of our founding fathers. The steady decline in recent years in the percentage of our population that attends church on a regular basis adds to the perception that Christianity is being pushed more and more to the peripheries of American life. But if Berger's analysis of religion in America has any validity, it appears that the more things change the more they stay the same. Following the events of September 11, 2001 the officials of the U.S. government urged Americans to go shopping. This was also the response of government officials to the oil crisis in the Gulf Coast and is an important part of our government's "answer" to economic crises in general. While the purpose of this "advice" has been to stimulate an imperiled economy, the message it sends to the rest of the world is that the "American way of life," which is under attack by terrorists and other destructive forces, is clearly identified with the values of consumerism. In a free market society "the Market" comes to take on the attributes of a "god."

If the solution to our economic woes is to encourage Americans to consume the same apparently holds true for an embattled church. So church-growth experts recommend that the way for church leaders to win back alienated customers is to market the church through elaborately staged "contemporary worship events" featuring films, dramas, visual effects, and upbeat music.[11] One pastor defends this experience-based approach to worship this way:

> It is our desire not merely to have a church service, but to create an experience through song, video, messages, and any other tools the Holy Spirit might place in front of us . . . I be-

lieve a boring church is a sin! So, we are going to always do all we can to make sure that when a person attends our church on Sunday that it is one of the best hours of their week. I believe people should look forward more to church than *24, Lost,* or *American Idol.*[12]

While evangelicals protest loudly against immoral content in the media they often fail to critically examine their own parallel forms of "Christian entertainment" which "make bold attempts to compete with mainstream offerings." Thus, they generate publicity for the very media they are criticizing.[13] Most pastors would not, of course, claim to be competing with Hollywood or network TV. Their motivation for embracing entertainment is to impact lives. As Tim Stevens and Tom Morgan state in their book *Simply Strategic Growth: Attracting a Crowd to Your Church:* "We are about entertainment to the extent that it allows us to captivate the minds and hearts of those who do not yet know Jesus."[14] To that end, they recommend staging a worship experience that includes music that is upbeat and celebratory. To infuse the proper level of energy into the worship service they recommend "pumping up the volume" because "louder music creates more energy." In addition, polished performers on the stage should "practice looking happy" and leaders should make sure that they are "strategically using humor."[15] In this scenario, worship "succeeds to the extent that it can arouse interest and provide entertainment."[16]

Use of entertainment in worship is, of course, not new. Staged performances and use of music to create a proper "mood" for spiritual transformation were part of the revivals of Charles Finney, Dwight L. Moody, and Billy Graham. Entertainment, if used properly, is not incompatible with worship and it is correct to want worship to be relevant. But, as Quentin Schultz reminds us, worship should reach beyond merely pragmatic biases (what works now!) to engage principles of underlying past worship as evident in Scripture and church history.[17] True worship is never simply a pleasurable experience that minimizes the tension between the church and the world. It does not distract us from our sin before a holy God. Nor does it "sentimentalize and neutralize the Christian images of the naked horror of Calvary and the blazing glory of Easter morning."[18] It is not based on manufacturing feelings in the believer or on meticulously controlling movements on a stage. "Genuine praise challenges our secularity and idolatries and narcissism by concentrating not on our feelings of happiness, but on qualities in God."[19] Intensity of worship is not gauged by the loudness of music on a decibel chart but by the depth of sincerity in the human heart. We want to help people to experience God. But "there are times when God remains hidden or when the appropriate response to the sense of divine presence is the awe-filled silence of the humbled heart."[20]

In a culture that is driven by the biases of consumerism and technology it is also easy to lose sight of the social dimensions of worship. Jesus' concern for the marginalized in society—the poor, weak, broken, and dispossessed—does not fit well with the tendency in the current evangelical establishment to promote images of clean cut, upper-middle class, and photogenic media celebrities.[21] Given current technologies, the emphasis on personal choice and convenience (which is the hallmark of consumerism) tends towards cultural and ethnic homogeneity and can even result in the loss of a felt need for corporate worship altogether. People attending one church in California that has pioneered video venues can choose from *eighteen* different worship options each weekend based on worship style, time slot, or location. When given this amount of choice, most people will pick a worship community that fits with their particular style, perspective, life-stage, and ethnicity.[22] Another mega-church not only has video venues but also an iPhone application which allows users on-the-go to watch both past and live services on the phone's 3 ½ inch monitor. This new technology offers what consumer consultants call a "point of entry" for new potential members and is intended as a supplement rather than substitute for communal worship. But it does also make it easier for highly mobile tech-savvy young adults to ignore the warning of Hebrews to "forsake not the assembling of yourselves together" (Hebrews 10:25). To accommodate the hectic pace of Christians one drive-in church in Florida mimics fast food restaurants like McDonalds and Burger King by giving communion bread and juice in sealed plastic containers as people drive in and then listen to the service from their cars.[23] Even more extreme are the so-called "virtual churches" that use online networks like Facebook. In his book *SimChurch*, for example, Douglas Estes argues that virtual churches are real churches and can offer real community. He even entertains the possibility that the sacraments of Baptism and the Lord's Supper can be participated in by meditating on an image of the sacrament on the computer screen. Here, there is even less understanding of the church as Christ's embodied community in the world.[24]

Darrell Guder is right when he argues that when there is a separation of the gospel message of salvation from the gospel message of the kingdom of God and a separation between the saviorhood of Jesus Christ and his lordship the gospel itself tends to be reduced to a form of Christianity that is consumer-based and market-driven. The gospel is primarily directed to meeting individual needs and local churches are run as "businesses," where giving, membership numbers, growth, and attendance are evidence of a healthy religious bottom line.[25] As the church becomes more socially acceptable and respectable the claims of Christ as Lord of life and history are never heard, "because such claims burst the boundaries of the safely reduced gospel which ensure that Christianity will never be as radical in our social setting as in fact it must be."[26] Whenever the church, for whatever reason, ceases to function as an incarnational witness of God's people in community to the kingdom the danger is great that the gospel will be reduced to the minimum of an individualized and privatized faith.

The Church and Sociopolitical Ideologies

The other danger, already alluded to, is that the church will become captive to ideologies of either the left or the right. As Donald Bloesch states: "Christians on both the theological left and right have been tempted to align themselves uncritically with social protest movements and have suffered a crisis of identity as a result . . . Ideological alignments accelerate rather than counter the secularization of the church."[27] Michael Horton even more forcefully warns: "Christians on the left and the right have a delusional obsession with politics that verges on idolatry."[28] Forgetting that Christ's kingdom transcends and stands in judgment over every social and political ideology, the current tendency among many evangelicals is to think that the future of America hangs on the next election. Talk-show pundits are often elevated to the status of political icons and Christians are divided based on whether they watch Fox News or CNBC. This is not to say that public policy issues are unimportant or that Christians do not have the responsibility to vote their consciences. But general principles derived from Scripture are not always easily applied to the specifics of public legislation and God's word does not always offer specific policy prescriptions.[29] The rhetoric on both the evangelical left and right in politics today tends to be simplistic in interpreting Scripture and applying it to public policy.[30] Furthermore, once *any* system or ideology is elevated to the status of being divinely inspired (and therefore beyond divine criticism) we are guilty of turning an economic or political idea into a religion.[31]

Perhaps more disturbing is the confusion of the American flag with the symbols of the Christian faith—as if the "American way of life" has any relationship to God's kingdom and national patriotism has any connection with our allegiance to Christ as King of kings and Lord of lords. Francis Schaeffer was particularly struck by the presence of the American flag in the front of the church and the mixed signals that it sends:

> In the United States many churches display the American
> flag. The Christian flag is usually put on one side and the
> American flag on the other . . . So, if by having the American
> flag in your church you are indicating to your young people
> that there are two equal loyalties or two intertwined loyalties,
> you had better find some way out of it. . . . It must be taught
> that patriotic loyalty must not be identified with Christianity .
> . . Equating any other loyalty whether it is political, national,
> or ethnic with our loyalty to God is sin, and we better get our
> priorities right now.[32]

When we recite the Pledge of Allegiance in a church context we signify that we have a divided loyalty to the nation and to God's kingdom and when we sing the National Anthem or "God Bless America" in a worship service we place God in service of national goals and
aspirations in a way that is tantamount to national idolatry.   In addition, as Schaeffer also warned, we risk rejection of the gospel message because of the church's alignment with a politics of patriotism
and nationalism.[33]

As I have argued in the previous chapters, the gospel of God's grace
and redemption is universal as well as personal in scope. His work of
redemption encompasses all of creation. Through the cross, God has
"disarmed the powers and authorities" (Col. 2:15) and is "reconciling
the world to himself" (II Cor. 5:18).   This is the basis for what
Guder calls "prophetic evangelism."   To evangelize prophetically
means proclaiming God's rule—which both spells the ultimate end
of orders of rebellion and restores creation to its original wholeness.[34]
The church is necessarily involved in this ongoing struggle against
demonic powers (Eph. 6:12) until Christ's return when every "dominion, authority and power" will be destroyed (I Cor. 15: 24-25).
Prophetic evangelism addresses the distortion of creation that occurs
when humans ignore God and his commands and erect their own
idolatrous substitutes (Rom. 1:18-32). Donald Bloesch puts it well
when he states:

The Gospel has politically revolutionary implications because it descralizes the holy places of culture religion; it demythologizes the myths which society has created for itself and by which it is enabled to survive; and it calls into radical question the current absolutes that enthrall the political and academic establishments and that have their source in man's idolatrous imagination. In short, the Gospel is a direct threat to the pantheon of the gods, whether these go under the names of science, sex, the national heritage, the racial consciousness, the proletarian utopia or any other. The Gospel poses an unmistakable challenge to every kind of political totalitarianism which demands from its subjects unconditional allegiance, even if it should use the cloak of Christianity to broaden its appeal.[35]

Thus, while the church must avoid aligning itself with any particular political party or platform, this does not mean that it should also avoid addressing social as well as personal evils in society based upon the imperatives of God's universal law. Evangelicals often avoid any discussion of "social sin" or injustice and prefer to concentrate on sin at the personal level. Paul's injunction in Romans 13:1 to "submit to governing authorities" is also frequently cited as a justification for political quietism and the acquiescence of Christians to unjust governments. However, in stating that there is no authority except that which is established by God, Paul places definite limits on political authority. Moreover, in adding that government is "the servant of God for *good*," he assumes that the acts of government ought to be judged according to the highest standards of God's moral law.[36] Paul himself asserted his rights as a Roman citizen and proclaimed God's righteousness and future judgment before the Roman political authorities (Acts 24:10-24).

Conclusion

Almost 50 years ago Harry Blamires, a British theologian, made a plea for a reformation in evangelical thinking. "The Christian mind," he wrote, "has succumbed to a secular drift to a degree unmatched in Christian history . . . Except for a very narrow field of thinking, chiefly touching questions of strictly personal conduct we Christians in the modern world accept, for purposes of mental activity, a frame of reference constructed by the secular mind and a set of criteria reflecting secular evaluations."[37] More recently, other evangelical thinkers have renewed Blamire's critique of evangelical "anti-intellectualism."[38] Os Guinness cogently argues that one of the reasons for the ineffectiveness of evangelicals in public life is the lack of a public philosophy that defends the common good. Without a common vision for the common good, "evangelicals are open to the charge that we are tribespeople rather than citizens" and "that our real concern is not justice but 'just us.'"[39] Guinness identifies a number of reasons for this "scandal" of the evangelical mind—some which have been touched in this chapter. One is a narrow pietism which replaces theological depth with an emphasis on the relational, therapeutic, charismatic, and the managerial (i.e., church growth).[40] A second factor is a pragmatist mindset which fosters a "piety of prosperity" and a utilitarian view of religion as a means to health, wealth, popularity, and peace of mind.[41] A third reason is the consumerist lifestyle of "creating and devouring" which reduces the church to "simply another customer center that offers designer religion and catalogue spirituality to the hoppers and shoppers of the modern world."[42] Finally, many evangelicals have replaced Christian discernment with tabloid and talk-show truth which, in the political arena, resorts to "truth-as-power play."[43]

Guinness' warnings to contemporary evangelicals are a reaffirmation of Carl Henry's view that a Christian doctrine of society "cannot be depicted in full force apart from an emphasis on both the holy demand of God for personal righteousness and universal social justice and God's gracious provision for a new man and a new society on the basis of redemptive grace."[44] The next two chapters explore in greater detail this relationship between God's holiness and his concern for righteousness and justice in every area of human relationships.

Notes

[1] Donald G. Bloesch, *Crumbling Foundations: Death and Rebirth in an Age of Upheaval* (Grand Rapids, MI: Zondervan, 1984), p. 20-21.
[2] Ibid., pp. 30-31, 66.
[3] Ibid., pp. 31, 39.
[4] See Jeremy D. Lawson et. al., "The Gospel According to Safeway: The Checkout Line and the Good Life," in *Everyday Theology*, ed.Vanhoozer, pp. 63-79.
[5] Jethani, *The Divine Commodity*, p. 12. See also A. Daniel Frankforter, *Stones into Bread: A Critique of Contemporary Worship* (Louisville, KY: Westminster John Knox, 2001).
[6] Peter Berger, *The Noise of Solemn Assemblies: Christian Commitment and the Religious Establishment in America* (Garden City, New York: Doubleday, 1961), pp. 30-9.
[7] Ibid., p. 46
[8] Ibid., p. 116.
[9] Ibid., p. 124
[10] Ibid., p. 126.
[11] Frankforter, *Stones into Bread*, p. 140.
[12] Jethani, *The Divine Commodity*, p. 74.
[13] See Quentin J. Schultze and Robert Woods Jr. eds., *Understanding Evangelical Media: The Changing Face of Christian Communication* (Downers Grover, IL: InterVarsity Press, 2008), p. 283.
[14] Tim Stevens and Tony Morgan, *Simply Strategic Growth: Attracting a Crowd to Your Church* (Loveland, CO: Group, 2005), p. 24. Quoted in Jethani, *The Divine Commodity*, p. 75.
[15] Ibid.
[16] Frankforter, *Stones into Bread*, op. cit., p. 141.
[17] Quentin J. Schultze, *High-Tech Worship? Using Presentational Technologies Wisely* (Grand Rapids, MI: Baker Books, 2004), pp. 17-19.
[18] Berger, *Noise of Solemn Assemblies*, p. 118.
[19] Frankforter, *Stones into Bread*, p. 135,
[20] Ibid.,
[21] Schultze and Woods, eds., *Understanding the Evangelical Media*, p. 288.
[22] Jethani, *The Divine Commodity*, p. 127.

23 Charles Anderson, "The Business of Busyness; Or, What Should We Make of Martha?" in *Everyday Theology*, ed, Vanhhoozer, p. 156.

24 Douglas Estes, *SimChurch: Being the Church in the Virtual World* (Grand Rapids, MI: Zondervan, 2009).

25 Darrell L. Guder, *The Continuing Conversion of the Church* (Grand Rapids, MI: Eerdmans, 2000), pp. 188-98.

26 Ibid., p. 190.

27 Bloesch, *Crumbling Foundations*, pp. 31, 39.

28 Horton, *The Gospel Commission*, p. 238.

29 See Carl F. H. Henry, "Linking the Bible to Public Policy," in *Biblical Principles and Public Policy: The Practice*, ed. Richard C. Chewning Colorado Springs, CO: NavPress, 1991), pp. 27-8.

30 Horton, *The Gospel Commission*, pp. 211, 229,

31 Michael S. Horton, *Beyond Culture Wars: Is America a Mission Field or Battlefield?* (Chicago, IL: Moody Press, 1994), p. 56.

32 Ibid., p. 34

33 Ibid.

34 Darrell L. Guder, *Be My Witnesses: The Church's Mission, Message and Messengers* (Grand Rapids, MI: Eerdmans, 1985), p. 175.

35 Donald G. Bloesch, *Essentials of Evangelical Theology, Vol. 2: Life, Ministry and Hope* (New York: Harper and Row, 1978), p. 170.

36 Mott, *Biblical Ethics and Social Change*, p. 150. Gordon Spykman similarly argues on the basis of Romans 2:14-15 that "God's first word for creation remains basic; it is neither abrogated nor withdrawn . . . By it God maintains his abiding claims on all persons and all societies, including the institutions of state, church, home, school and other associations in society. His word, first published in creation, then republished in Scripture, seeks to heal our life relationships in society and the state." Man's response to God's norms has been distorted by sin. Nonetheless, "the order of society points responsively to an ultimate order beyond itself as the source and criterion of its meanings." See "The Principled Pluralism Position," in *God and Politics: Four Views on the Reformation of Civil Government*, ed. Gary Scott Smith (Phillipsburg, NJ: Presbyterian and Reformed, 1989), p. 83.

37 Harry Blamires, *The Christian Mind: How Should A Christian Think?* (London: SPCK, 1963), pp. 3, 7.

38 See Mark A. Noll, *The Scandal of the Evangelical Mind* (Grand Rapids, MI: Eerdmans, 1994); and Os Guinness, *Fit Bodies, Fat Minds: Why Evangelicals Don't Think and What to Do About It* (Grand Rapids, MI: Baker Books, 1994).

39 Ibid., p. 17. Carl Henry also argues that the remnants of God's moral claim of the basis of the *Imago Dei* "supply an inner contact point between Christians and the secular community for bringing into relationship the good in the Christian revelational understanding and the general or public conception of the good." See *The Christian Mindset in a Secular Society: Promoting Evangelical Renewal and National Righteousness* (Portland, OR: Multnomah, 1984), p. 121.

40 Ibid., p. 38

41 Ibid., p. 57

42 Ibid., pp. 109-10

[43] Ibid.., pp. 112-14. Cal Thomas and Ed Dobson similarly talk about the error made by many on the religious right of focusing on the objective without regard for the methods. The result is damage to both the church and the state. They write: "The damage to the church is caused by those who appear to the 'unchurched' to be interested in ushering in the kingdom by force. The damage to the state is that at the precise moment when government needs the moral principles the church can offer, too many in both the liberal and conservative wings of the church have deserted their primary territory and gone lusting after the temporal power associated with the kingdom of this world. The church then becomes an appendage of the state rather than its moral conscience. It is transformed from a force not of this world into one that deserves to be treated as just one more competitor for earthly power. It is seen as just another lobbying group to which politicians can toss an occasional bone to ensure loyalty." Cal Thomas and Ed Dobson, *Blinded by Might: Why the Christian Right Can't Save America* (Grand Rapids, MI: Zondervan, 1999), pp. 182-83. They also acknowledge the error of the Christian right of focusing on issues of the family, abortion and homosexuality to the exclusion of issues of poverty, racial equality, and the environment. See also Joel Hunter, *A New Kind of Conservative* (Ventura, CA: Regal, 2008).

[44] Henry, *A Plea for Evangelical Demonstration*, p. 120.

Chapter 5
Justice and Covenant
in the Old Testament

In a much discussed article entitled "What Makes Mission Christian" Christopher Little offers a two-pronged critique of holistic approaches to mission which emphasize the inseparability of evangelism and social ministry. Theologically, he maintains, it results in a "horizontalization" of mission. And on a practical level it invariably draws resources away from evangelism. Noting that holistic mission draws heavily upon the concept of the kingdom of God, he argues that evangelicals need to replace the kingdom of God with the glory of God as the defining biblical motif in mission. God's glory was the ultimate goal of the Pauline mission. And, "if the chief end of mission is the glory of God, the means of mission must reflect this priority."[1]

Little is right to emphasize God's glory as the ultimate purpose and goal of mission. We can agree that the greatest motivation for giving glory to God is his merciful provision of salvation through Christ (Rom. 15:8-9; Eph. 1:3-8). Little is further correct in pointing to the excesses among some adherents to transformational mission, with their emphasis on an "over-realized eschatology." But there are two major shortcomings in Little's argument. First, he simplistically equates this particular approach to mission with holism in general, which is a broad concept incorporating a variety of mission models. Secondly, and more importantly, his assumption that the motif of the kingdom of God is something other than and opposed to the mission of God's glory is simply untenable biblically.[2] As we have seen in previous chapters, the inauguration of the kingdom is a major theme in Paul's theology of salvation and the church. Russell Moore points out that, "the New Testament does not present the glory of God as abstracted from the mission of Jesus, but instead presents it as finding its expression in His incarnation, atonement, and exaltation. The entire sweep of redemptive history therefore finds its goal in the glory of God *in Christ*." And the doxological and soteriological goals both "find their purpose and fulfillment in Jesus' inheritance of the kingdom."[3]

Little's argument nonetheless resonates with many evangelicals who are uncomfortable with the notion of social justice, particularly in the context of missions. It is important for us to be clear, then, about what the Old and New Testaments say about justice, as an attribute of God and expression of his holiness and as a response of God's people. The focus of this chapter is on the Old Testament. The next chapter looks at justice in the New Testament.

Understanding Righteousness, Justice, and Mercy

God's universal command to be a people of justice and mercy is spelled out in Micah 6:8: "What does the Lord require of you but to act justly and to love mercy and walk humbly with your God." This "Micah Mandate" is "one of those great biblical definitions of true religion" which ""utterly transcends dispositions or dispensations."[4] The same triad of virtues is described by Jesus in Matthew 23:23 as summing up the "weightier matters of the law" thereby securing them as central paradigms of mature faith and a balanced Christian life.[5] The words, "what does the Lord require of you?" signify that we should intently seek after justice, mercy, and humility before God.

By combining these three virtues, Micah is indicating that the vertical dimension of our relationship to God and the horizontal dimension of human relationships are interrelated. We tend to equate worship with prayer and songs of praise to God. While these elements are indeed important, Micah says that true worship of God is also connected to mercy and justice. All of our efforts for justice are empty unless they are accompanied by humility before God and utter dependence on him. By the same token, if we are to be in a right relationship with God there must be a burning desire for justice and mercy in our personal lives and in the life of the church.

But what is the meaning of justice and mercy? Since the common understanding of these terms is often different from their meaning as intended by the authors of the Bible it is important to have a clear understanding of their use in Scripture.

Justice in the Old Testament

The following table summarizes the key Hebrew words that are associated with our term "justice."

Figure 6. Words for Righteousness, Justice, and Mercy in the Old Testament

	Original Word	English Translation
Hebrew	*sedeq/ sedeqa*	righteousness, justice
	mishpat	justice, judgment
	hesed	mercy, love

The two words righteousness and justice are often found together in the Old Testament and are frequently interchangeable:

> *The Lord loves righteousness and justice*
> *The earth is full of his unfailing love (Psalms 33:5)*

Let justice roll down like water,
and righteousness like an ever-flowing stream (Amos 5:24)

When righteousness and justice are paired together they form a single comprehensive idea known as a *hendiadys* (e.g. Gen. 18:19; Ps. 33:5, 103:6-7). The nearest English equivalent is "social justice."[6]

The root meaning of righteousness (*sedeq* and *sedeqa*) is "straight"—or a standard against which other things are measured. *Sedeq* refers to the abstract principle of righteousness while *sedeqa* refers to the concrete acts (to "act righteously") in relationships. *Sedeqa* is often the object of the verb "to do" (*asah*) and means to "do justice." While most people today tend to give the term "righteousness" a religious meaning (i.e., prayer, Bible study) or view it in terms of private morality (i.e., sexual chastity), in the Old Testament it is a highly relational concept and has the meaning of treating all relationships in family and society with fairness, generosity, and equity.[7]

The Hebrew word for justice (*mishpat*) comes from a root which in its widest sense means "to put things right," or intervene (whether within or outside a court of law) in a situation that is wrong, oppressive, or out of control and "fix" it.[8] Legally, it has the meaning of acquitting or punishing every person on the merits of the case, regardless of race or social status. But it also has the broader meaning of giving people their legal rights. *Mishpat* is then giving people what they are due, whether punishment, protection or care.[9] As it is commonly used in the Old Testament, justice is a call for action—something you do—not simply a principle of evaluation. In the words of Chris Wright, "Justice as an appeal for a response means taking upon oneself the cause of those who are weak in their own defense."[10]

The third term (*hesed*) is the Hebrew word for mercy, or God's unconditional grace and compassion. In Micah 6:8, *mishpat* places the emphasis on action while *hesed* emphasizes the motive behind the action.[11] Frequently, it is paired with *sedeqa* (righteousness) to describe

God's action (Ps. 36:10) or to describe the requirements of human ethical response (Hos. 10:12). The element of mercy or benevolence is often so closely tied to righteousness, that in later Hebrew it became the usual term for almsgiving to the poor (Dan. 4:24; cf. Matt. 6:1).

Conclusions about the Nature of Justice in the Old Testament

Based upon this brief survey of words in the Old Testament, we can draw the following conclusions about the nature of justice. First, it involves care for the most vulnerable members of society. This is why in the Old Testament *mishpat* is often described as taking up the cause of the widows, orphans, immigrants, and the poor. God's concern for the protection of the economically vulnerable, particularly those who are most likely to be victims of gross injustice, is apparent throughout Scripture. Over and over again, God's people are called to care for widows, orphans, immigrants, and the poor:

> *This is what the Lord Almighty says: Administer true justice, show mercy and compassion to one another. Do not oppress the widow or the fatherless, the immigrant or the poor. (Zechariah 7:10-11; cf. Deut. 27:19; Jer. 22:3; James 1:27)*

In Old Testament times, these four categories of people were often destitute and close to starvation. This "quartet of the vulnerable" stands for those who have no social power and are therefore most susceptible to abuse. Today it could be expanded to include the unborn, homeless, refugees, many single parents, and elderly people.[12] It also includes those caught in the terrible and inhumane practices associated with human trafficking—i.e., child slaves in India who work sixteen hours a day to harvest tea that is drunk by middle-class consumers and sew carpets that adorn their sitting rooms; bonded laborers in South Asia, Latin America and Africa who accrue or inherit debts that can never be repaid; slaves who harvest coffee in

Kenya and Ethiopia, and agricultural products in the U.S; and those caught in the world-wide sex trade.

Second, justice consists of right relationships—with God and others in family and society.   This theme is particularly prominent in the book of Job. At one point, for example, Job states in his defense:

> *If I have denied justice to my menservants and maidservants when they had a grievance against me, what will I do when God confronts me? What will I answer when called to account? . . . If I have denied the desires of the poor or let the eyes of the widow grow weary, if I have kept my bread to myself, not sharing it with the fatherless . . . If I have seen anyone perishing for lack of clothing, or a needy man without a garment, and his heart did not bless me for warming him with the fleece from my sheep, if I have raised my hand against the fatherless, knowing that I had influence in court, then let my arm fall from the shoulder, let it be broken off at the joint. For I dreaded destruction from God, and for fear of his splendor I could not do such things. (Job 31:13-23)*

This aspect of justice is closely connected with the Hebrew concept of *shalom*—or wholeness, completeness, and harmony for both the individual and the community.   It is the restoration of the spiritual, physical, economic, and social well-being which God originally intended before the Fall.[13]

Third, justice means to act with generosity. While we tend to equate generosity with charity, or acts of kindness that are optional for the believer, this is foreign to Scripture. Both the Old and New Testaments characterize generosity as one of the marks of living "justly" and lack of generosity as being "unjust."   In condemning Israel for its injustices, Ezekiel identifies over-consumption and indifference towards the poor as one of the "sins of Sodom" (Ezekial 16:49). In a later verse, he equates not committing robbery with actively giving food and clothing to the poor (Ezek. 18:16; cf. Matt. 25:31-46). The implication is that lack of generosity is tantamount to robbery.[14]

It is not possible in this chapter to give a detailed exposition of all of the major passages in the Old Testament that talk about justice. My purpose is limited to showing that these three aspects of justice—protection and care for the most vulnerable members of society, right relationships characterized by fairness and equity and generosity to the poor and needy—are viewed in the Old Testament as essential to true worship of God and full obedience to his commands by those who are in a covenantal relationship with him.

It All Begins With God

The constant message throughout Scripture is that justice begins with God. Therefore, if we want to be like God, and know him, we must be persons of justice. Two themes in the Old Testament are of particular importance: (1) the relationship between God's justice and his holiness; and (2) God's covenantal relationship with Israel, in which the Israelites were to imitate God's righteousness and justice.

Justice as an Expression of God's Holiness

As we have seen, in the Old Testament the words for justice and righteousness are almost inter-changeable, both indicating conformity to God's standards of holiness and moral excellence.[15] God's justice and his holiness go together like two blades on a pair of scissors. God's justice comes from his holiness; and his holiness demands justice.

This close relationship between justice, righteousness, and holiness is seen especially in the great "holiness code" of Leviticus 19. In this passage, the Israelites are commanded: "Be holy because I, the Lord your God, am holy." (19:1). Holiness is then defined as: (1) loyalty to God alone (19:3-4); (2) generosity to the poor (19:9-10); (3) personal honesty and integrity (19:11-13; 16); (4) practical compassion for the disabled and respect for the elderly; (19:14; 32); 5) judicial impartiality in treatment of rich and poor (19:15); (6) love for one's neighbor (19: 18, 34); (7) fair treatment and payment of employees (19:24); (8) sexual integrity (19: 20-22, 29); (9) equality before the law for immigrants and ethnic minorities (19:33); and (10) honesty in business practices (19:35). Thus, while we tend to make a distinction between moral purity and personal piety on the one hand and justice on the other, in this passage personal and social holiness are inseparable. Both are an expression of the character of God. As Walter Kaiser states: "In this great chapter on moral holiness (Lev. 19) the emphasis falls on social justice. . . . In Leviticus if you want to be holy, don't pass out a tract; love your neighbor, show hospitality to the stranger and be a person of justice."[16]

The relationship between God's justice and his holiness is also evident in the book of Isaiah. In chapter six, Isaiah describes his encounter with God. The angels sing:

> *Holy, holy, holy is the Lord God Almighty;*
> *the whole earth is full of his glory*

At the sound of their voices, the prophet cries out:

> *Woe is me, for I am a man of unclean lips, and I live among a people of unclean lips, and mine eyes have seen the King, the Lord Almighty (Isaiah 6:3-5)*

When Isaiah has a vision of God's holiness he becomes acutely aware of his sin and the sinfulness of the society around him. What is the nature of this sin? It is evident from chapter one that it involved a failure to live according to God's commands regarding justice. In 1:2-20, known as the "Great Assiz," God calls on all of heaven and earth to hear his case against his people (1:2). His people do not know him (1:3), and they have abandoned him, despised him, and turned away from him (1:4). Therefore God is justified in bringing judgment against his people (1:5-9). Israel was a very religious nation, giving sacrifices unto the Lord (1:11) and celebrating the festivals and the Sabbath (1:13-14). But they hated justice (1:12) and were a violent people (1:15b). Instead of more religious ceremony, God calls on his people to repent of their sins, stop doing evil, and start seeking justice for the widow and the orphan:

Your hands are full of blood;
wash and make yourselves clean.
Take your evil deeds out of my sight!
Stop doing wrong, learn to do right!
Seek justice, encourage the oppressed
Defend the cause of the fatherless;
plead the case of the widow
Come now, let us reason together, says the Lord
Though your sins are as scarlet,
they shall be white as snow
Though they are red like crimson,
they shall be like wool (Isa. 1:16-18)

The chapter concludes with God's intention to purge the nation of evil and injustice and restore justice and righteousness (1:24-27) and a declaration of his judgment not only on Jerusalem but on all corrupt civilizations (1:28-31).

This chapter in Isaiah and many other passages in the Old Testament express four basic truths about God and justice.[17] First, he loves justice and conversely hates injustice. Oppression of the weak and poor is an affront to his very nature while kindness to the needy honors him (e.g., Isa. 61:8; Prov. 14:31, 19:7). Second, God has compassion on all who experience injustice (e.g., Isa. 49:13; Ps. 9:9, 12; 12:5). Third, defending the cause of the weak, the stranger, and the oppressed is central to his very nature as creator of the universe (e.g., Ps. 146:1-2, 5-9). Finally, because God abhors injustice, he acts in his

righteousness and holiness to judge and condemn those who perpe-
trate injustice and allow it to flourish (e.g., Ps. 34:15f; Amos 1:3-2:3).
As John Stott states:

> It is clear from these Old Testament passages that God hates
> injustice and oppression everywhere. Indeed, wherever right-
> eousness is to be found in our fallen world it is due to the
> working of his grace . . . Here, then, is the living God of the
> Bible. His concerns are all embracing—not only the "sacred"
> but the "secular," not only the religious but nature, not only
> his covenant people but all people, not only justification but
> social justice in every community, not only his gospel but his
> law. So we must not attempt to narrow his interests. Moreo-
> ver, ours should be as broad as his.[18]

Justice and God's Covenantal Relationship with Israel

In the Old Testament, the foundation for all ethical conduct is God's
grace as manifested in his covenant with Israel. The purpose of this
covenant, which was first made with Abraham, is expressed in Genesis 18:19: "I have chosen him (Abraham) *so that* he may teach his
children and his household after him . . . *to do righteousness and justice.*"
While the long term goal of the covenant was for Israel to be a blessing to the nations, its immediate objective was the creation of a
community of righteousness and justice.[19] The basic *motivation* for
justice and righteousness is God's own character and his gracious actions on behalf of the Israelites.

In this context, there are two "signs of the covenant" that are closely
linked to righteousness and justice: circumcision and the Sabbath.
Following their release from bondage in Egypt, Moses repeatedly
speaks of God's redemption of his people as the basis for "doing justice." And he specifically connects this covenantal relationship to
circumcision:

Circumcise your hearts, therefore, and do not be stiff-necked any longer. For the Lord your God is God of gods and Lord of lords, the great God, mighty and awesome, who shows no partiality and accepts no bribes. He defends the cause of the fatherless and the widow, and loves the alien, giving him food and clothing. And you are to love those who are aliens, for you yourselves were aliens in Egypt. (Deut. 10: 16-19)

Do not deprive the alien or the fatherless of justice, or take the cloak of the widow as pledge. Remember that you were slaves in Egypt and the Lord your God redeemed you from there. That is why I command you to do this. (Deut. 24: 17-18)

Moses' command to "circumcise your hearts" (Deut. 10:16) is significant, for the act of circumcision is a fundamental sign of the covenant and a metaphor for covenantal obedience.[20] "Heart circumcision" is an unbroken relationship with God and passionate commitment to his ways. In Deuteronomy 15, imitation of God's deep compassion for the poor, weak, and oppressed is characterized in terms of an unstinting generosity towards the poor and needy that would result in the elimination of poverty (Deut. 15:4).

The prophet Jeremiah likewise describes those who neglect justice for the poor and downtrodden as being "circumcised in the flesh" but "uncircumcised in the heart" (Jer. 9:25-26). He goes on to describe true knowledge of God in terms of doing justice by defending the rights of the poor and needy:

He (i.e., Joseph) did what was right and just.
so all went well with him.
He defended the cause of the poor and needy
and so all went well.
Is that not what it means to know me?
declares the Lord (Jer. 22:15b-16)

This passage is only one of numerous passages in the Old Testament that link true knowledge of God with justice. To know God is to engage with him in acts of justice and compassion. Failure to imitate these characteristics of God is tantamount to failure to really know him or his gracious acts of redemption on our behalf.[21] In the words of Timothy Keller:

> The logic is clear. If a person has grasped the meaning of God's grace in his heart, he will do justice. If he does not live justly, then he may say with his lips that he is grateful for God's grace, but in his heart he is far from him. If he doesn't care about the poor, it reveals that at best he doesn't understand the grace he has experienced, and at worst he has not yet really encountered the saving mercy of God. Grace should make you just.[22]

The Old Testament law also clearly stipulates that Sabbath-keeping is not simply an external ritual. It must be accompanied by righteousness and justice. In Exodus 20:8 Moses calls upon the Israelites to "remember the Sabbath day, to keep it holy." This command has a three-fold significance. First, the word "remember" points back to God's resting on the seventh day (Gen. 2:2). Second, the instructions "to keep it holy" require acknowledgement of this day as sacred because of God's deeds and declaration. And third, the command bridges one's obligation to God (the first three commands) and his duties to others (the last six commands).[23]

The sacredness of the Sabbath as a "sign" of Israel's covenantal faithfulness to God therefore has clear social and economic dimensions, and a strong ethical rationale. As Chris Wright points out, the "rhythm of the sabbath" stipulates that all should work and all (including slaves) should rest. It is therefore a form of "employee protection."[24] The regulations regarding the sabbatical year likewise stipulate that every seventh year the land should lie fallow so that the poor might get food from it (Exod. 23:10-11) and there should be a release of pledges taken for debt (Deut. 15:2). These laws are based on the concept of divine ownership of land and are described as "a sabbath to the Lord" (Lev. 25:4). But their intended practical purpose is humanitarian—to help the impoverished and the debtor. Serving God and caring for other people are inseparably bound together.[25]

In the prophetic books of the Old Testament willful disregard for the poor is frequently linked to violation of the Sabbath (Amos 8:5-6; Isa. 58:3-14; Jer. 17:19-27). The OT prophets are particularly critical of those who were scrupulous in their religious observance while subverting justice or ignoring the plight of the needy and oppressed. Over and over again, they pronounce God's judgment on the religious leaders and people of Israel and Judah who engage in a multitude of sacrifices and burnt offerings but neglect justice for the poor. The prophet Amos declares:

> *Even though you bring me burnt offers and grain offerings,*
> *I will not accept them.*
> *Though you bring choice fellowship offerings,*
> *I will have no regard for them.*
> *Away with the noise of your songs!*
> *I will not listen to the music of your harps.*
> *But let justice roll on like a river,*
> *righteousness like a never-failing stream!*
> *(Amos 5:22-24; cf. Isa. 1:13-15; 58:6-7)*

In this and other passages, the prophets address sins of both omission and commission. The people they describe are more concerned with their own conspicuous consumption and pleasure than with protecting the rights of the poor (Amos 3:15; 6:4; 8:5; Isa. 5:8-13); and more interested in the details of sacrifice than taking care of the widows and orphans (Isa. 1:13-17). Particularly to blame are the civil and religious leaders who twist the law and subvert justice. (Isa. 3:14-15, 5: 23-25). In Isaiah they are described by God as a "people [who] come near me with their mouth and honor me with their lips, but their hearts are far from me" (Isa. 29:13).

Conclusion

The Israelites had a misplaced confidence that because they were God's chosen people he would hear their prayers and accept their sacrifices despite their violence, duplicity, greed, self-indulgence, and indifference towards the poor. They were oblivious to God's anger towards them. So, the prophet Isaiah uses the strongest language possible to arouse them out of their spiritual and moral stupor. He calls them a harlot (Isa. 1:21). As John White points out, a harlot or prostitute is on the lowest rung of sexual sins.[26] It is a term used by the prophets to denote God's feelings towards a treacherous spouse. To God the sins of Israel amounted to treachery, ingratitude, and violation of a holy relationship. Therefore, he says to the Israelites:

> *When you spread out your hands in prayer, I will hide my eyes from you;*
> *even if you offer many prayers, I will not listen (Isa. 1:15)*

To the extent that we as Christians exhibit the same attitude and conduct as the ancient Israelites the message of the prophets is the same for us as it was for them. If our lives fail to reflect God's heart for justice and mercy our songs of praise are only noise in his ears, our offerings and religious observances are meaningless, and our most eloquent prayers are an affront to him.

Notes

[1] Christopher R. Little, "What Makes Mission Christian?," *International Journal of Frontier Mission* (Summer 2008), pp. 67-70. This article is an expanded version of an article that appeared in *Evangelical Missions Quarterly* (January 2006).

[2] See Steve Hawthorne's response to Little in "Responses to Little's 'What Makes Mission Christian?," *International Journal of Frontier Missiology* (Summer 2008), pp. 77-8.

[3] Moore, *The Kingdom of Christ*, p. 103

[4] George Grant, *The Micah Mandate: Balancing the Christian Life* (Nashville, TN: Cumberland House, 1999), pp. 12-13.

[5] Ibid.

[6] Christopher J. H. Wright, *Old Testament Ethics for the People of God* (Downers Grove, IL: InterVarsity, 2004), pp. 255, 257.

[7] Timothy Keller, *Generous Justice: How God's Grace Makes Us Just*, (New York: Dutton, 2010), p. 10.

[8] Wright, *Old Testament Ethics for the People of God*, p. 256.

[9] Keller, *Generous Justice*, p. 4

[10] Wright, *Old Testament Ethics for the People of God*, p. 257.

[11] Keller, *Generous Justice*, p. 3

[12] Ibid. p. 4.

[13] Cannon, *Social Justice Handbook*, p. 24-5.

[14] Keller, *Generous Justice*, p. 17

[15] Gary Haugen, *Good News about Injustice: A Witness of Courage in a Hurting World* (Downers Grove, IL: InterVarsity, 1999), p. 71.

[16] Walter C. Kaiser, "Leviticus," in *New Interpreter's Bible: Genesis to Leviticus* (Nashville, TN: Abingdon, 1994), p. 1136.

[17] Haugen, *Good News about Injustice*, pp. 69-70.

[18] Stott, *Human Rights and Human Wrongs*, pp. 33-4.

[19] Wright, *Old Testament Ethics for the People of God*, p. 266.

[20] Ibid., p. 341.

[21] Ash Barker, *Make Poverty Personal: Taking the Poor as Seriously as the Bible Does* (Grand Rapids, MI: Baker Books, 2009), p. 88.

[22] Keller, *Just Generosity*, pp. 93-4.

[23] See Bob Deffinbauth, "The Meaning of the Sabbath (Exodus 20:8-11)," http://bible.org/seriespage/ meaning-sabbath-exodus-208-11.

[24] Wright, *Old Testament Ethics for the People of God*, op. cit., p. 296.

[25] Ibid., pp. 296-97.

[26] John White, *The Golden Cow: Materialism in the Twentieth-Century Church* (Downers Grove, IL: InterVarsity, 1979), pp. 22.

Chapter 6
Justice and Worship
in the New Testament

Evangelicals are often reticent to get involved in issues of justice for a number of reasons. Three common objections, in particular, call for a brief response. First, it is often assumed that the concern for social justice is largely limited to the Old Testament. However, it is also a constant theme in the New Testament. As we will see, a concern for justice is evident in the gospels and Jesus' ministry (Matt 21:32, 23:12; Mark 12:40; Luke 11:38-42); the book of Acts (2:44-5, 4:32-35); the Pauline epistles (II Cor. 8:13-15, 9:9); the book of James (1:27, 2:15-16, 5:46) and I John (3:16-20).

Second, it is often argued that involvement in issues of justice detracts the church from the central priority of evangelism. This assumes that the two are inevitably in conflict—the more one concentrates on justice the less attention he will give to evangelism, and vice versa. But it is better to see them as complementary and integrally related to each other. To paraphrase the oft quoted words of John Stott, evangelism without a concern for justice treats the individual as a bodiless soul; while an exclusive concern for justice without evangelism treats him as a soulless body:

Our neighbor is neither a bodyless soul that we should love only his soul, nor a soulless body that we should care for its welfare alone, nor even a body-soul isolated from society. God created man, who is my neighbor, a body-soul-in-community. Therefore, if we love our neighbor as God made him, we must inevitably be concerned for his total welfare, the good of his soul, his body and his community.[1]

Finally, those on the conservative end of the political spectrum often maintain that a concern for social justice reflects a "liberal" political and social agenda. Years ago, the Grand Rapids Report (1982) addressed the issue of the "political" and "social" nature of justice by drawing the following distinction between "social service" and "social action:"[2]

Figure 7. Social Service and Social Action

Social Service	Social Action
• Relieving human need • Philanthropic activity • Seeking to minister to individuals and families • Mercy	• Removing the causes of human need • Political and economic activity • Seeking to transform the structures of society • Justice

The Report goes on to describe sociopolitical action in this way:

It looks beyond persons to structures, beyond rehabilitation to the reform of the prison system, beyond improving factory conditions to securing a more participatory role for the workers, beyond caring for the poor to improving—and when necessary transforming—the economic system (whatever it may be) and the political system (again, whatever it may be), until it facilitates their liberation from poverty and oppression.[3]

Here, we can agree that caution must be exercised to avoid "politicizing" the gospel, as I have discussed in previous chapters. We must recognize the limits of social action. This will be further address in the next chapter. But this does not mean that we should restrict our efforts to acts of mercy, as evangelicals have a tendency to do. Jesus directly confronted acts of oppression and injustice which were rooted in the social, political, and religious systems of his day, though he did not have a "political" agenda. Referring to the need for evangelicals to recover the biblical concern for abuses of human rights Carl Henry stated:

> If the church preaches only divine forgiveness and does not affirm justice, she implies that God treats immorality and sin lightly. If the church proclaims only justice, we shall all die in unforgiven sin without the Spirit's empowerment for righteousness. We should be equally troubled that we lag in championing justice and in fulfilling our evangelistic mandate. We should realize that the Great Commission is dwarfed and even maligned if one implies that God is blindly tolerant of social and structural evil, that he forgives sinners independently of a concern for justice . . . The local church should identify the most grievous injustices—local, regional, and national—and strive to rectify them, in concert with all who seek to right the wrong.[4]

The purpose of this chapter is to look at justice in the New Testament, though again my focus will be on those passages which connect justice to worship and a concern for God's holiness. As with the Old Testament, it is important to begin with a basic definition of the various Greek words in the New Testament that are connected with justice.

Righteousness, Justice, and Mercy in the New Testament

In the New Testament, the *dikaios* word group which speaks of justice is found over two hundred times.[5] English translations often obscure the connection of this term with the Old Testament concepts of justice and righteousness. The Greek translation of the Hebrew Bible/Old Testament, or Septuagint, uses the word *dikaiosune* for *sedeq* (righteousness, justice) over 90 percent of the time. One can legitimately infer from this that in the New Testament, as in the Old, righteousness and justice are interconnected. But modern translations of the New Testament typically translate the word *dikaiosune* as "righteousness" rather than "justice."[6] This has contributed to the erroneous tendency within evangelical circles to equate righteousness with personal piety and morality and detach it from the public sphere.

According to Nicholas Wolterstorff, "in linguistic circles of the New Testament writers, *dikaiosune* did not refer definitively either to the character trait of righteousness . . . or to the social condition of justice, but was ambiguous between the two."[7] A proper translation should be based upon the context. Actually, there are many instances in the New Testament where "justice" would probably be a better translation than "righteousness." Wolterstorff argues that almost all English translations may have missed the central place that justice had in the teachings of Jesus.[8] Consider, for example, the difference in meaning if the word "justice" is substituted for "righteousness" in these words of Jesus from the Sermon on the Mount:

Blessed are those who hunger and thirst after righteousness/justice (dikaiosune) for they shall be filled. (Matt. 5:6)

Blessed are those who are persecuted because of righteousness/justice (dikaiosune), for theirs is the kingdom of heaven. (Matt. 5:10)

The word *krisis/krisin* is found 47 times in the New Testament and is translated "judgment" or "justice." It has the primary meaning of rendering a judgment or decision according to justice or injustice, right or wrong.[9] This is the word that Jesus used when he criticized the Pharisees for tithing the mint, dill, and cumin and neglecting justice, mercy, and faith, or love of God (Matt. 23:23; Luke 11:42; cf. Mic. 6:8).

The three main words for mercy or compassion in the New Testament are *eleos/elleo* (65); *oiktirmos* (5); and *splanchna* (11). As we have indicated, mercy (*eleos*) is closely associated with righteousness and alms as opposed to mere ritual purity (Matt. 6:1; Luke 11:41) and the giving of one's possessions to the poor (Luke 12:33). In the parable of the Good Samaritan, mercy (*splanchna*) is characterized in terms of a deep heart-felt compassion at the sight of human need and an attitude of complete willingness to use all means, time, strength, and life for saving our neighbor at the crucial moment.[10]

Jesus and the Religious Establishment

As will be shown in chapter ten, Jesus' viewed his entire ministry as a partial fulfillment of the Old Testament prophecy that the "servant of the Lord" would "bring justice to the nations" (Isa. 42:1). Here, however, the focus will be on just one aspect of his ministry—his relationship to the religious establishment of his day.

Jesus' Confrontations with the Pharisees

Jesus' concern for righteousness and justice is particularly evident in his confrontations with the Pharisees and other leaders of the religious establishment. The Pharisees were religious legalists. Their name literally meant "the separatists" because they were pre-occupied with remaining untainted from the world. They made a sharp division between the "spiritual" and "material" and regarded the spiritual realm to be superior to the material. That's why they fastidiously observed the details of religious piety and ceremonial purity.[11] While both Jesus and the Pharisees saw themselves as "fulfilling" the law, they had diametrically opposed views of what was entailed in obedience to the law. Jesus' interactions with and concern for the marginalized—the sick (especially leprosy sufferers), "sinners," tax-collectors, prostitutes—and his healings on the Sabbath went against the dominant theology and ethics of the religious leaders of his day.[12]

In a way that was reminiscent of the Old Testament prophets, Jesus had scathing remarks against the Pharisees and other religious leaders for their violation of Old Testament principles of justice and mercy. On one occasion he describes them as teachers of the law "who devour widows houses and for show make lengthy prayers" (Mark 12: 38-40). On another occasion he describes the Pharisees as "clean on the outside of the cup and dish," but inside are "full of greed and wickedness." They go to great lengths to tithe everything they have but neglect justice and the love of God (Luke 12:39-42; cf. Matt. 23:23). As Keller points out, the term "neglecting justice" in this context probably means lack of care or concern for the poor: "Behind their excessive religious observances are lives that are insensitive to the vulnerable classes. In Jesus' view, this revealed that they did not know God or his grace at all."[13]

What prompted these harsh words by Jesus? In Israel the ruling elite consisted of three groups—the Herodians, the scribes and Pharisees, and the Jerusalem clerical aristocracy. These three communities of non-Roman power were supported primarily by an oppressive system of taxation. The wealth of the priestly hierarchy came largely from the temple tax required of all Jews and from the sale of sacrificial animals and the profits of money changers in the temple. This group was well known for its sumptuous feasts and banquets, which consumed much of their income.[14] About 80 percent of the population consisted of peasants or farmers who worked the land owned by the elite. From the harvested crops "the typical farmer had to give 50 percent to the owner of the land. Twenty-five percent went for land taxes to be paid to the Herodian kings and the Roman government, and 10 percent went for taxes to the Jewish clerical aristocracy for the running of the temple and the religious apparatus of Israel. In other words, 85 percent of the typical farmers' annual income went to pay for taxes and other liabilities."[15]

According to Jewish law, the poor were required to pay the temple tax. But they were also to be given tax relief aid. For example, the poor tax required that every third and sixth year the tithe of one's produce must be stored up and distributed to those in need, including widows, orphans, Levites, and strangers. But this was often neglected.[16] Other forms of assistance to those in need included distributions to the poor at high feast days and weekly and daily care for the poor through the local synagogue. But the poor often did not receive the compassion or help called for in Old Testament law. Walter Pilgrim notes: "They were despised by the religious teachers and excluded from the most sacred precincts. They were far too burdened with laws and taxes and with systematic fleecing of their goods and property."[17]

The Pharisees and other religious leaders were particularly adept at finding ways to circumvent the requirements of Old Testament law regarding justice and mercy.[18] For example, they had a way of avoiding the law concerning debts through a practice called *prosbol*.[19] Following poor harvests the peasants would have to borrow money at exorbitant rates from the rich in order to survive. When they were unable to repay their debts they would fall into debt slavery and frequently lose their possessions and land. While these transactions were considered "legal," the prophet Amos described them as a way of "buying the poor with silver" (Amos 8: 6). To prevent this from happening, the Torah specified that people had to be released from their debts every seven years. While this law was considered binding, the religious leaders of Jesus time found a way of getting around it by turning the title to a loan over to a court during the seventh year and then returning it afterward. As a result, the rich got richer while the poor often spiraled deeper and deeper into debt until they were reduced to becoming prostitutes or beggars on the streets.[20] Another favorite practice involved declaring goods as *corban*—an offering to God—so they could be set aside for God and not used for any other purpose, including supporting parents in times of need (Mark 7: 9-13). Because of this practice, Jesus quotes Isaiah 29:13 in describing the Pharisees and teachers of the law as hypocrites who set aside the commands of God in order to follow their own traditions (Mark 7:6-13).

Jesus' Cleansing of the Temple

For the Jews, of course, the Jerusalem Temple was the center of public worship and service to God. It was the established sanctuary where God would manifest himself to his covenant people and where they could experience his majesty, glory, and holiness. The temple itself was a small building where only priests could enter, with one half consisting of the Holy of Holies and the other room containing an altar at which priests offered incense and prayer. Outside the temple there were three successive courts: the Court of Priests, the court of Israel (which only Jews could enter), and the court of the Gentiles. The whole temple area was a crowded and noisy area—accommodating not only visitors but also hundreds of priests and their assistants to take care of the details of sacrifice, stalls with sacrificial animals, and money changers who converted outside coinage to the required coins needed to purchase animals. As we have seen, this entire religious system which was supported by the temple tax and the rents collected by the priests from those who needed space to do their work was a source of considerable wealth and power.[21]

Jesus' protest against the commercial activity in the temple is recorded by all four gospels (Matt. 21:12-13; Mark 11:15-17; Luke 19:45-46; John 2:13-17). In the first three gospels his action of overturning the tables of the money changers is accompanied by verbal reference to two prophetic texts in the Old Testament—Isaiah 56:7 and Jeremiah 7:11. The first of these ("My house shall be called a house of prayer for all the nations") evokes the eschatological vision of Isaiah 55-66 in which God will restore and redeem Jerusalem and bring all nations there for true worship. Jesus' radical act was therefore a parable of judgment against the temple, not only because of its misuse as a place for economic enterprise, but also because it represented Israel's rejection of God's commandments and ultimately of Jesus himself.[22] The second phrase ("You have made it a den of robbers") is an allusion to Jeremiah's Temple Sermon (Jer. 7:1-15) which is a vehement call for repentance and condemns Israel for oppression, stealing, murder, adultery, false swearing, and idolatry while continuing the charade of temple worship.[23] There is evidence from various Jewish writings that the money changers were robbing people and that excessive prices were being charged by those who were selling animals used in temple sacrifice.[24] These practices were in sharp contrast to Jesus' teachings concerning justice and mercy and his practice of healing on the Sabbath (cf. Matt. 12:6-8). It is significant that directly after this episode, those who were forbidden to enter the temple because of their deformities were accepted by Jesus—the "blind and the lame came to him in the temple, and he healed them" (Matt. 21:14).

It is important to see that the temple cleansing is framed by Jesus' cursing of the fig tree (Mark 11:14) and its withering (Mark 11:20) which signified that the temple with its sacrificial system would become barren and empty and be replaced by Jesus himself (Matt. 26:59-61; Mark 14:57-58). Jesus' self-identification with the temple is also underscored in Matthew 12:6. In addition to foreshadowing Jesus' future sacrifice, these passages also signify that God's glorious presence is manifested uniquely in Jesus in a greater way than it was ever manifested in a physical temple structure.[25] In Matthew 12:6-8 Jesus' description of himself as superior to the temple occurs in the context of offering eschatological Sabbath rest to people (Matt. 11:28-30). Jesus therefore describes himself as the "Lord of the Sabbath." But this Christological argument is coupled with an appeal to Hosea's words "I desire mercy not sacrifice" (Hos. 6:6). We have seen that in the Old Testament prophets observance of the Sabbath was closely connected with the practice of righteousness, justice, and mercy. Jesus' practice of healing and doing good on the Sabbath is an outworking of his claim that he came to fulfill the law and bears witness to what he calls "the weightier matters of the law: justice, mercy, and faithfulness" (Matt. 23:23).[26] Jesus' healings on the Sabbath also signify the inauguration of the kingdom and the beginning of the new creation. His words and actions concerning the range of practices associated with the temple system of his day are therefore a forceful demonstration against idolatry and injustice and a sign that he is about to bring in a new order in accordance with Isaiah's vision of a future kingdom characterized by justice and true worship of God.[27]

In Mark's gospel the cleansing of the temple is part of a whole series of Jesus' final teachings in the temple area, which begin in 11:12 with the cursing of the fig tree and conclude in 13:1-2 with Jesus' prediction of the destruction of the temple. In this section, Mark brings Jesus' teachings to a close in a triple series marked by the word *scribe* (12:28, 35, 38).[28] The first of these teachings centers on Jesus' verbal exchange with one of the teachers of the law. In this exchange, the scribe asks Jesus: "What is the greatest commandment?" There are two important things to notice about Jesus' response.[29] First, he connects the double command to love God and love one's neighbor with the ancient *shema* of faith in One God (Deut. 6:4), thereby indicating that "affirmation of the one God who is 'Lord' is inseparably part of the 'chief commandment.'"[30] Belief in one God is necessarily connected to obedience to the moral law. Second, Jesus' response "there is no other command greater than these" (Mark 12:30b) indicates that the two commands (love of God and love for one's neighbor) *together* comprise the "chief command" about which the scribe is inquiring. Together they encapsulate the essence of the law. Victor Furnish summarizes the significance of this "double commandment" in this way:

Loving the neighbor is no less an act of obedience than loving God and is part of the total response to the sovereign claim of God under which man stands. One's response to God—setting aside self-will, renouncing one's own claims— is to be paradigmatic for one's relation to his neighbor. [31]

In Mark's version of this encounter the scribe not only repeats Jesus' words but emphasizes that this Great Commandment is "more important than all of the burnt offerings and sacrifices" (Mark 12:33). Jesus responds that the scribe has spoken "wisely" and is not far from the kingdom of God (Mark 12:34). Following this exchange, Jesus pronounces God's judgment on the teachers of the law for their injustice and false religiosity (Mk 12:38-40). Throughout this entire section, then, Jesus demonstrates that justice and mercy are inseparably connected to worship and love of God.

Community Ethic or Social Ethic?

A number of commentators argue that the New Testament passages which talk about justice and mercy are directed primarily, if not exclusively, to relationships within the Christian community. Some see little in the New Testament (or even the Old Testament) that points to the Christian responsibility to the larger society.[32] In response to this argument, two observations can be made.

1. Various passages in the New Testament focus on "neighborly love" in the context of the church.

First John appears to have a more restricted understanding of justice in view when it states: "If anyone has material possessions and sees his brother in need but has no pity on him, how can the love of God be in him?" (I John 3:17) Here, the use of the word "brother" is a designation for other believers. Likewise, James is addressing the issue of favoritism in the church when he talks about unequal treatment of rich and the poor as a violation of the command to love one's neighbor (Jas. 2:8-9). And when he enjoins mercy towards widows and orphans (1:27) and other brothers or sisters who are destitute and in desperate need of food and clothing (2:14-27) as an expression of true religion and true faith he has in mind relationships within the body of Christ. Finally, recent interpretations of Matthew 25:40 ("whatever you did for one of the least of these brothers of mine") view it as a reference to feeding and clothing other Christians in need, particularly itinerant Christian teachers dependent on hospitality from their family of faith.[33] This interpretation seems to be supported by Matthew's use of the expression "these little ones" to refer to disciples in need of help, again in a missionary context (Matt. 10:42). In my view, the parable of the Sheep and Goats in Matthew 25:31-46 underscores the need for basic humanitarian concern towards those within the church, particularly who have suffered loss as a result of their personal witness to faith in Christ. Such "intentional humanitarianism" is both an expression of our oneness in Christ and a global witness to the transforming effect of the new life in Christ.[34]

These observations are basically in keeping with the argument developed in previous chapters that since Christ presently rules over the church, it should display the first-fruits of kingdom righteousness and justice. This is why some of the harshest judgments in the New Testament are directed towards those who are guilty of fraud and favoritism in the church. This can be seen in the harsh criticism that James employs against those in the church who glory in their own status and position and are indifferent to the plight of the poor, even in the context of worship (1:9-11; 2:2-4, 5-12, 15-16; 4:13-17). James' strongest words are reserved for wealthy landowners who, in their opulence and greed for money, defraud workers of their wages. To these people he says, "You have fattened yourselves in the day of slaughter" (5:5b).[35]

The same righteous indignation is leveled by the apostle Paul at wealthy Christians in the Corinthian church who neglect the needs of the poor in their practice of the Lord's Supper (I Cor. 11:17-34). As in all other cities, the early Christians celebrated the Lord's Supper in homes, typically after a communal meal. These shared meals—or "agape meals"—were a regular part of church practice, and provided a setting for the community's response to the needs of the poor while also reinforcing a distinct Christian identity.[36] As Paul's words indicate, eating together, ritualized in the sharing of the Lord's Supper, re-enacts the central meaning of the gospel. When believers remember the broken body and shed blood of Christ in sharing the bread and cup they also symbolize their unity as believers in Christ and celebrate the reconciliation and love available to us through His sacrifice.[37] Paul is shocked to find out that the wealthy Christians are eating sumptuous meals together in the absence of the poorer Christians. Consequently, the poorer Christians are left with little or nothing to eat:

> *When you come together, it is not the Lord's Supper you eat. For as you eat, each of you goes ahead without waiting for anyone else. One remains hungry, another gets drunk. (I Cor. 11:20)*

Instead of symbolizing the unity and love of God's people, the Lord's Supper was being practiced in such a way that it reflected the conflicts, divisions, and selfishness of the world. In a manner that is reminiscent of the prophets' condemnation of the meaningless religious practices of the Israelites and Jesus' rebuke of the Pharisees, Paul states that the wealthy Christians have shown contempt for the church of God and humiliated the poor (I Cor. 11:21). By not recognizing the "body of the Lord" when they take the Lord's Supper, they in effect deny the reality of God's grace in their own lives and in the life of the church, and eat and drink God's judgment on themselves (I Cor. 11:29).

2. Other passages indicate that "neighborly love" cannot be limited to relationships within the church.

The New Testament, however, gives no basis for limiting acts of love to the Christian community. In Paul's theology the believer who receives God's grace through faith in Christ is released from sin by the power of God's Spirit and becomes a slave to righteousness (Rom. 6:11-18). In Galatians 5:13, Paul states that this freedom in Christ should result in service to one's neighbor in love. He calls this "faith expressing itself through love" (Gal. 5:6). Following Jesus' teaching, Paul views love for one's neighbor as summing up the meaning of the entire law (Gal. 5: 14; Rom. 13: 9; cf. Lev. 19:6). Paul universalizes neighborly love when he says that the Christian's responsibility is to do good "to all people" (Gal. 6:9-10). The phrase "doing good" in this passage means concrete acts of kindness, not merely having good relations. And while Paul enjoins that special attention should be given to needs within the body of Christ ("especially those who belong to the family of believers"), he assumes that Christians have a general social responsibility to people outside the church.[38]

The same universal application of love can be seen in II Corinthians 9:6-13, where Paul urges the Corinthian church to take part in the relief effort for the poor in Jerusalem following the famine that struck Palestine in 46 AD (Acts 11:29). Citing God's grace as the motivation for love and invoking the Psalmist's praise of the just and righteous man who "scatters abroad his gifts to the poor" (II Cor. 9:9; cf. Ps 112:9), he states that men will praise God for their obedience to the gospel and their generosity "in sharing with *them and with everyone else*" (emphasis mine). The reference to "all" or "everyone else" coupled with "them" indicates that Paul is encouraging liberality to all people not just poor believers in the church.[39]

Elsewhere, Paul also specifically interprets the love command as applying to the Christian's relationships with outsiders as well as to his relations with other Christians (I Thess. 3:12; II Thess. 2:17, 3:13). Citing Proverbs 25:21 and perhaps recalling Jesus' words, Paul urges believers to show neighborly love in both word and action even towards their enemies (Rom. 12:19-21; 13:9-10; cf. Luke 6:35-36). The context of Paul's command to show mercy towards one's enemies is particularly significant, since it comes at the end of a list of examples of what it means to give our bodies in sacrificial service to God as a "*spiritual act of worship*" (Rom. 12:1, emphasis mine).

Of course, the clearest and most forceful example in the New Testament of universal love (including love for one's enemy) is Jesus' parable of the Good Samaritan. Here, Jesus definitively breaks away from traditional restrictions on what it means to love one's neighbor. In this story, he describes the plight of a Jewish man who falls into the hands of robbers, is beaten, stripped of his clothes, and left "half dead" on the side of a highway winding through the mountainous region between Jerusalem and Jericho (Luke 10: 30). With obvious reference to the religious leaders of his day, Jesus describes the apathy and indifference of a priest and Levite—two devout clergymen—who see the man lying on the side of the road but pass by on the other side. These men conform to the external requirements of the religious law. But their godly identities are outward facades that mask the absence of divine love and mercy, even towards a fellow Jew. The further ironic twist in the story is that the person who shows compassion is a Samaritan—a label synonymous with ungodliness and heresy to the Jewish audiences of his time.[40] The intended contrast could not be greater. Two Jews with top religious credentials refuse to lift a finger to help another Jew, who is a brother in the faith. But a Samaritan—a man despised by the Jews—goes out of his way to show mercy to a man who, for all intents and purposes, is his enemy.

The message of Jesus' parable of the Good Samaritan is clear. Upholding basic human rights must transcend barriers of religious and ethnic identity. In commenting on the parable, John Wesley insisted that love of neighbor means "universal benevolence," "embracing neighbors and strangers, friends and enemies . . . the good and gentle, but also . . . the evil and unthankful . . . every soul that God has made."[41] Reflecting on the social distance that often insulates those who could help from those in need Wesley stated:

> One great reason why the rich in general have so little sympathy for the poor is because they so seldom visit them. Hence it is that [according to the common observation] one part of the world does not know what the other suffers. Many of them do not know, because they do not care to know: they keep out of the way of knowing it—and then plead their voluntary ignorance as an excuse for their hardness of heart.[42]

The parable of the Good Samaritan is part of the biblical tradition which enjoins God's people to show sacrificial hospitality to the stranger—to act fairly toward strangers (Exod. 22:21) and not oppress them (Exod. 23:9), provide food for them (Lev. 19:10), and love them as their own (Lev. 19:34).

Christine Pohl reminds us that loving the neighbor across cultural and geographic boundaries can lead to overlooking the needs of people right on our doorstep. "There is no explicit discussion about excluding them, they are simply overlooked. Historically, this often happened to the poor and infirm. Today we face this danger as many churches ignore the urban poor or never notice the elderly or disabled people in their own communities."[43] The New Testament instructs us to give generously out of our abundance (I Tim. 6:18-19) and frequently warns of the seductive and destructive power of riches, which can blind us to the needs of the poor right in front of us. The Rich Fool is excluded from the kingdom of heaven because he places a covetous pursuit of material goods above love of God and love of the poor (Luke 12: 13-21, 32-34). The rich man in Luke 16 is condemned, not for his wealth per se, but for ignoring the plight of poor Lazarus at his gate.[44] John Schneider puts it well:

The strong obligation-generating power is in the immediate moral proximity of someone in dire need. What makes the behavior of the rich people in these parables so very hideous and damnable is not that they had wealth, or even that they enjoyed it. It is that they do so, like the rich in Amos, in spiritual obliviousness to grievous human suffering that was as near to them, in the moral sense, as it could be. It was not merely that they neglected "the poor," but that they neglected a human being in need directly in front of them.[45]

Whatever the meaning of "the least of these" in Matthew 25, then, these three parables—the Good Samaritan, the Rich Fool, and the Rich Man and Lazarus—all clearly indicate Jesus' intention to broaden its meaning to include anyone in need of human care.[46]

Conclusion

It is significant that, as in the Old Testament, some of the strongest affirmations in the New Testament of God's concern for justice and mercy are given in the context of worship. When Jesus drove the money changers out of the temple he was opposing a religious system in which true love and worship of God had been corrupted by love of money and abuses of power and privilege. Many of his conflicts with the Pharisees occurred over the meaning of the Sabbath. His own practice of reaching out to the marginalized and healing the sick on the Sabbath stood in sharp contrast to the abuses of justice by the religious leaders of his day. By linking his identity as "Lord of the Sabbath" with the words of Hosea, "I desire mercy not sacrifice," (Matt. 12: 6-8; cf. Hos. 6:6) he reaffirmed the Old Testament teaching that true worship of God cannot be separated from a commitment to mercy and justice. This connection between true worship and justice and mercy is also evident in Paul's rebuke of wealthy Christians in Corinth for selfishly neglecting the poor in their practice of the Lord's Supper (I Cor. 11:17-34) and in James' sharp criticism of favoritism and indifference to the needs of the poor and needy when believers came together for worship (Ja. 2:1-14).

Within Christian (particularly evangelical) circles, "piety" is often associated with the individual's worship of God. The life of love for God is variously called piety, spiritual growth, sanctification, Christian maturity, and Christlikeness. Largely because of the pietistic tradition, devotion to God has been defined by evangelicals largely in inwardly spiritual and experiential terms. But I have argued in this chapter that in the teachings of both Jesus and his apostles there is also a social dimension to love for God. The early believers in Jerusalem who were filled with the Holy Spirit at Pentecost responded by selling their possessions and giving to anyone who was in need (Acts 2:42-45). The deep experience of salvation and worship of God led directly to generosity for the poor.[47] I think Harvie Conn is correct when he states: "To be interested in things spiritual is to be interested in all of life, now touched by the healing hand of the Holy Spirit . . . God's interests cannot be programmed for action into sacred or 'spiritual' categories. . ."[48] True spirituality integrates the spiritual and the physical. The New Testament simply gives no basis for separating the love of God from love for others, or the spiritual from the social. In fact, love for God and love for neighbor are so deeply intertwined that Jesus can refer to both as "one" command. The consistent teaching of the New Testament is that believers with this world's goods who fail to respond in a tangible way to needy brothers and sisters in Christ do not in fact know God despite their prayers and pious professions (Matt. 25:31-46; Jas. 2:14-26; I John 4:7-8). The Good Samaritan and other passages in the New Testament make it clear that a similar concern for the needy must be extended to non-believers.

In a community near where Kathi and I live, there is a ministry to children called Side Walk Sunday School. The founder of this ministry, Louie Reyes, tells of how when he was a young man, he was deeply disturbed when he saw a little boy walking along-side of the road with no shoes and barely any clothes. What was even more disturbing to him was that neighbors on their way to church drove by the boy, apparently oblivious to his plight. This experience motivated Louie and his wife to start a ministry to children in local communities ravaged by crime, drugs, poverty, and illiteracy. After weeks of visiting neighborhoods and inviting children, the ministry began to grow and children began attending the church which he had started. The children were increasingly open to the gospel. But the influx of children from poor communities was bothersome to a number of the adults, many of whom subsequently left the church. In effect, bringing children in from the ghetto ran the "church out of the church." But Louie and his wife did not abandon their vision to minister to poor children. Now, after years of sacrifice, the Side Walk Sunday School is a vibrant ministry serving children in over 11 cities and at-risk communities.[49] Kathi and I have visited this church. It is not without its weaknesses. But the story of this ministry is a stirring example of what it means to "love your neighbor as yourself."

We evangelicals pride ourselves in dotting our i's and crossing our t's theologically. But orthodoxy is not just about having the right beliefs. It is also about having the right practice and behavior. Jesus was comfortable eating with the social outcastes of his day. He ministered to the poor and broken-hearted. Yet in both our church structures and our lifestyles have we, his modern followers, isolated ourselves in middle class, religious ghettos?[50] If so, perhaps it is time to rethink our priorities.

Notes

1 John R.W. Stott, *Christian Mission in the Modern World* (Downers Grove, IL: Inter-Varsity, 1975), pp. 29-30.
2 Stott, *Human Rights and Human Wrongs*, p. 27.
3 Ibid.,

[4] Carl F. H. Henry, "A Summons to Justice," *Christianity Today*, 36 (July 20, 1992), p. 40.

[5] Cannon, *Social Justice Handbook*, p. 20.

[6] Robert L. Foster, "Understanding Justice in the New Testament. See www.sbl-site.org/assets/pdfs/TBv2i5_ Fosterjustice.pdf

[7] Nicholas Wolterstorff, *Justice: Rights and Wrongs* (Princeton, NJ: Princeton University Press, 2010), p. 112.

[8] Ibid., pp. 110-13.

[9] *The NAS New Testament Greek Lexicon* (http://www.biblestudytools.com/ lexicons/greek/nas/)

[10] Colin Brown, ed., *Dictionary of New Testament Theology, Vol. 2* (Grand Rapids, MI: Zondervan, 1971), pp. 599-600.

[11] Grant, *The Micah Mandate*, pp. 71-3.

[12] Christopher J. H. Wright, *Knowing Jesus Through the Old Testament* (Downers Grove, IL: InterVarsity, 1992), pp. 237-38.

[13] Keller, *Generous Justice*, pp. 51; 200.

[14] Walter E. Pilgrim, *Good News for the Poor: Wealth and Poverty in Luke-Acts* (Mpls, MN: Augsburg, 1981), p. 42.

[15] Linthicum, *Transforming Power*, p. 63.

[16] See Pilgrim, *Good News for the Poor,* p. 45.

[17] Ibid., p. 46.

[18] Joseph A. Grassi, *Informing the Future: Social Justice in the New Testament* (New York: Paulist, 2003), p. 109.

[19] Ibid.

[20] Linthicum, *Transforming Power*, p. 63.

[21] Grassi, *Informing the Future*, pp. 121-22.

[22] Beale, *The Temple and the Church's Mission*, p. 179.

[23] See Hayes, *The Moral Vision of the New Testament:*, p. 334.

[24] For example, Leviticus 12:6-8 stipulated that after an Israelite woman gave birth she was to bring an animal sacrifice to the temple, preferably a sheep. But if she were poor and could not afford the price of a sheep she could take two doves or two pigeons for the sacrifice, one for a burnt offering and one for a sin offering. According to the Jewish Mishnah, because of their greed those who were selling birds increased their prices so much that the poorer women of the community could not afford them. Both the Talmud and the historian Josephus describe the greed and injustices that were committed by many of the high priests of the first century who walked the temple courts. (http:www.biblehistory.net/Jesus_ Cleansing_Temple.pdf)

[25] Beale, *The Temple and the Church's Mission,* p. 178,

[26] Hayes, *The Moral Vision of the New Testament*, p. 100.

[27] Ibid., p. 335.

[28] Grassi, *Informing the Future*, p. 125.

[29] See Victor Furnish, *The Love Command in the New Testament* (Nashville, TN: Abingdon, 1972), pp. 25-30.

[30] Ibid., p. 26.

[31] Ibid., p. 63.

[32] Mott, *Biblical Ethics and Social Change*, p. 35.

[33] See Kevin DeYoung and Greg Gilbert, *What is the Mission of the Church? Making Sense of Social Justice, Shalom and the Great Commission* (Wheaton, IL: Crossway, 2011), pp. 162-63.

[34] Commentators have disagreed over the meaning of the phrase "the least of these my brethren" in Matthew 25:40. The majority hold that it refers to the oppressed and suffering humanity. See, for example, R.V.G. Tasker, *The Gospel According to St. Matthew: An Introduction and Commentary. Tyndale New Testament Commentaries* (Grand Rapids, MI: Eerdmans, 1962), p. 238. However, this interpretation does not square with Matthew's use of an almost identical phrase ("these little ones") in 10:42 to refer to the disciples of Jesus who are in mission activity. Furthermore, in every case where Matthew uses the word "brethren" it refers to either natural-born kin or to disciples of Christ. In Matthew 12:46-50 Jesus insists that the term means his disciples (cf. 5:47, 23:8, 28:10). See W.D. Davies, *The Setting of the Sermon on the Mount* (London, Cambridge University Press, 1966), p. 96. A third problem with this interpretation is that if often leads to the conclusion that since Jesus identifies *himself* with the "least of these of his brethren" (Matt. 25:34-36) he is "hidden" or present in the hungry, thirsty, the strangers, the naked, the sick, and the imprisoned of the world, not just the believing community. See Jurgen Moltmann, *The Church in the Power of the Spirit* (New York: Harper and Row, 1977), p. 126, See also Martin R. Tripole, "A Church for the Poor and the World: At Issue With Moltmann's Ecclesiology" *Theological Studies*. (http://www.ts.mu.edu/readers/ content/ pdf/42/ 42.4/42.4.6.pdf) The theological and missiological implications of this conclusion are too complex to discuss at this point. But some are right in pointing out that improper exegesis at this point has been used to justify almost any missional paradigm. See, for example, Christopher Little, "Christian Mission Today: Are We on A Slippery Slope? My Response," *International Journal of Frontier Missiology* 25:2 (Summer 2008), p. 88. In light of these problems with the traditional view, D.A. Carson and others argue that the phrase "the least of these my brethren" refers to the disciples that Jesus sends out on missionary activity (cf. Matt. 10:40-42). See *Matthew, Mark and Luke: Expositor's Bible Commentary* (Grand Rapids, MI: Zondervan, 1984), p. 520. People from all nations are judged, then, not according to their works but on the basis of how they treat Christ's emissaries who are sent out by him and how they respond to the gospel message. (Little, "Christian Mission Today," p. 88). This interpretation is consistent with the fact that Jesus' parable of the sheep and goats in Matt. 25 is part of the Olivet Discourse which describes that the "gospel of the kingdom" as being preached in all the world for a witness to all nations (Matt. 24:14). However, this second view tends to be too narrow in its conception of "mission." Besides verbal proclamation of the gospel, the church is also a witness in its *inner community life* to the new life in Christ. Jesus often spoke of the persecution that would accompany the church's world-wide witness. It is likely, therefore, that the phrase "to least of these my brethren" has reference to the needy *within the church* itself, particularly those who experience loss for the sake of Christ. Thus, while Jesus may have in mind the unbeliever's response to the gospel of the kingdom, this parable speaks specifically to humanitarian concern *within the body of Christ* and its evangelistic implications: "By this shall all men know that you

are my disciples if you have love one for another" (John 14:35). In other words, it addresses the essential need for "intentional humanitarianism" towards those who have suffered loss because of their witness to Christ. For, "whatever you did for one of the least of these brothers of mine, you did it for me" (Matt. 25:40). See John L. Amstutz, "Humanitarianism With A Point: A Second Look at the Parable of the Sheep and the Goats Missiologically," *International Journal of Frontier Mission* 9:4 (October 1992).

[35] While some argue that these wealthy landowners must be unbelievers, the context of the entire book would suggest that James has in mind some within the Christian community. See David P. Nystrom, *James: The NIV Application Commentary* (Grand Rapids, MI: Zondervan, 1997), p. 267-68.

[36] Christine Pohl, *Making Room: Recovering Hospitality as a Christian Tradition* (Grand Rapids, MI: Eerdmans, 1999), p. 42.

[37] Ibid., p. 30

[38] Mott, *Biblical Ethics and Social Change*, p. 36.

[39] Ibid., p. 36.

[40] Jethani, *The Divine Commodity*, p. 65.

[41] Pohl, *Making Room*, p. 76.

[42] Ibid.

[43] Ibid., p. 79.

[44] DeYoung and Gilbert, *What Is the Mission of the Church?* p. 167.

[45] Quoted in Ibid., p. 167.

[46] See Pohl, *Making Room*, p. 23.

[47] See Keller, *Generous Justice*, p. 4.

[48] Harvie M. Conn, *Evangelism,* p. 64.

[49] http://www.sidewalksundayschoolkids.com/beta_history.html

[50] John White, *The Golden Cow*, p. 83.

Chapter 7
We Become
What We Worship

In his enlightening and thought-provoking book *We Become What We Worship*, Gregory Beale argues that "God has made all people to reflect, to be imaging beings."[1] Adam and Eve were created in God's image for the purpose of reflecting his character and glory and filling the earth with it (Gen. 1:26-28). But instead of obeying God's commands and trusting in him, they chose to follow the words of the serpent. This disobedience also ultimately entailed self-worship in that "Adam decided that he knew what was better for him than God did, that he wanted to advance himself at all costs, and that he trusted in himself, a created man, instead of in the Creator."[2] The effort of Adam and Eve to become "like God" by autonomously setting up their own ethical law was blasphemous and resulted in their expulsion from the garden. When the Israelites followed after other gods they also "resembled what they revered, which was an expression of retribution for their idolatry and led to their spiritual ruin. What Isaiah and the faithful remnant of the Old Testament and the believers of the early church epoch revered, they resembled for their restoration and blessing. The same is true for us today."[3]

Beale reminds us that, while the Israelites were guilty of worshipping wooden, stone, and metal images in a way that is not characteristic of the church today, the biblical warnings about idolatry are still very relevant to us in the twenty-first century since even by New Testament times idolatry took such non-literal forms as trusting in dead tradition or in money.[4] It behooves us, therefore, to conclude our survey of worship and justice in the Bible with a discussion of some implications for Christians living in what is still one of the most prosperous nations on earth.

Giving Generously

Skye Jethani writes in his book *The Divine Commodity* of an experience he had traveling through Cambodia. Driving through the outskirts of Phnom Penh he saw countless factories lining the streets. "What are these?" he asked David, his missionary host. "Garment factories," he replied. "Clothing is one of the largest industries in Cambodia. Labor is so cheap that most of the brands you buy were probably made here at one time or another: Wal-Mart, Banana Republic, Gap—you name it."[5] The missionary went on to explain that many of the factories are built and then later abandoned by American companies as they move to other countries in search of cheaper labor. When the factories shut down, the girls who were lured from the countryside to work in them are suddenly out of work. To survive, many of them become prostitutes. Skye and his missionary friend then drove to a village about an hour outside of the city. As they arrived, David explained that every adult in the village had HIV/AIDS. "The men will travel to the city to sell their crops. They also visit the brothels, contract the virus, and then bring it home and infect their wives. They're not educated and they don't understand how HIV is transmitted."[6] David and his missionary co-workers have dedicated themselves to educating these villagers about AIDS, caring for them as they succumb to the disease, and then building orphanages to care for the children when their parents die.[7]

A number of years ago, Michael Jordan was strongly criticized in the press for his association with Nike because the shoes that Nike was selling for upwards of $100 a pair were being made by people (many of them children) who worked for pennies an hour under deplorable conditions. We might legitimately fault Jordan for profiting from his association with a corporation that engaged in slave labor. But, few of us in the evangelical community stop to think about how the lifestyles we so enjoy are connected to systems of structural as well as personal sin. In the words of Jethani:

> We can casually browse the racks at the Gap without any thought to the workers who manufactured the clothing. We are oblivious to the factory conditions, the worker's poverty, families, or health. Instead, as we peruse the store we are conditioned to think only about our desires. "Will those pants make me look fat?" "Is that purse in style?" "Can that shirt work with my jacket?" We are deluded into believing the items we purchase had no story before they appeared at the store. They exist simply to meet our desire.[8]

Some might object to these words as creating "false guilt." Kevin DeYoung and Greg Gilbert argue that "*Justice, as a biblical category, is not synonymous with anything and everything we feel would be good for the world.*"[9] While some Christians view the gap between the rich and the poor or advocating for a living wage as "justice" issues, the concept of justice in the Bible, they argue, is a more "prosaic" category that has to do with not showing partiality, not stealing, not swindling, and not taking advantage of the weak. They continue: "We dare say that most Christians in America are not guilty of these sorts of injustices, nor should they be made to feel that they are."[10]

To a point, I would agree. First, before engaging in a sweeping critique of free market capitalism, we should acknowledge that there are multiple sources of poverty. So, while we might decry some of the evils of "corporate capitalism," we must also speak out against the evils of extreme government corruption, brutal dictatorships, militarism, mismanagement, tribalism, and even genocide which are widespread in the majority world.   All of these injustices are grievous sources of poverty and point to the brokenness of a world infected by sin.[11] Second, one of the great dangers in addressing issues of grievous injustice is that calls for social "restructuring" will result in a politicization of the gospel.   It bears repeating that we must be careful not to identify the gospel with any particular political, economic, or social agenda.   Finally, we are all caught in the web of a fallen world.   In this context, Luther spoke of the natural orders as instituted by God to preserve a semblance of order, yet at the same time necessarily and thoroughly corrupted by sin.[12] For this reason, none of us can fully escape the dilemma of being complicit in systemic social injustices.

These qualifications, however, do not entirely get us off the hook. We should bear in mind that God condemns sins of *omission* as well as sins of *commission* (Obad. 1:10-11; Ezek. 16:48-50; Prov. 24:11-12; Luke 16:19-21).   The Old Testament prophets announced God's judgment on those Israelites who were guilty of an idolatrous attachment to *cultural values* of opulence and avarice that undergirded and justified systems of greed and injustice (Amos 4:1-2; 6:4-7).[13] Speaking of the dangers of an over-attachment to material things among Christians in America, Timothy Keller writes:

> Your money flows most effortlessly toward your hearts greatest love. In fact, the mark of an idol is that you spend too much money on it, and you must try to exercise control constantly. Saint Paul has written, if God and his grace is the thing in the world you love most, you will give your money away to ministry, charity and the poor in astonishing amounts (II Cor. 8:7-9). Most of us, however, tend to overspend on clothing, or on our children, or on status symbols such as homes and cars. Our patterns of spending reveal our idols.[14]

Keller goes on to say that our most painful emotions also reveal our idols. A person who is driven to frantic activity and overwork should ask himself, "Do I feel that I *must* have this thing to be fulfilled or feel significant?" When we ask questions like that and we "pull your emotions up by the roots," as it were, we will often find our idols clinging to them.[15]

These observations apply not just to lay people in the church. David Nystrom recalls a conversation that he had with a denominational administrator during a gathering of church leaders in the Detroit area. As they enjoyed a meal in the cafeteria of a lovely church, the administrator cast his gaze around the room and said in a low tone: "Sometimes I worry about the money we spend on ourselves. How many starving children could be fed for a year with the money spent on making this facility beautiful, as opposed to merely functional?"[16] In our consumptive market-driven culture the temptation is great for church leaders in America—particularly leaders of our megachurches—to undertake projects of church expansion or "renovation" in an effort to idolatrously extend an image of themselves or their church buildings. This is reflected in recent statistics on spending patterns of American churches compiled by Empty Tomb, a mission research and advocacy organization. In 1920 the percentage of giving to missions from the total offering was 10.09 percent, or just a little more than a dime per dollar. In 2003 conservative and evangelical denominations gave just 2.6 percent (or less than 3 cents a dollar) and more liberal mainline denomination gave a mere .9 percent (one cent) on overseas work. Much of this difference in spending patterns between the contemporary church today and churches in the 1920s is due to the increasing amounts of money that are spent on the abundance of internal programs and on salaries for staff to run the sprawling church campuses which have become the norm today. According to the authors of this report "the numbers demonstrate an increased emphasis on internal operations over the broader mission of the church."[17] Another recent survey of churches across America similarly found that nearly 95 percent of the typical church's ministries are limited to members alone.[18]

Also sobering is the fact that giving among North American church-goers was higher during the Great Depression (3.3 percent of per capita income in 1933) than it was after a half-century of unprecedented prosperity (2.5 percent of per capita income in 2004).[19] Other research on patterns of giving by American evangelicals compared to other segments of the population shows mixed results. According to research in giving conducted by George Barna in 2008, although conservative "born-again" Christians are twice as generous as their more liberal counterparts only 9 percent of Americans who describe themselves as "born-again" tithed in 2007.[20] A similar survey conducted by Barna in 2012 found that more than three quarters (79 percent) of evangelicals gave to a cause they believed in over the previous year while only 28 percent of those who identified themselves as having a faith other than Christian did the same. Evangelicals are also among the faith groups that donate the most. However evangelicals are the least likely (28 percent) to give to a non-profit organization outside their church. About 12 percent of those who identified themselves as "born again" (evangelical and non-evangelical) gave 10 percent or more of their income to a church or non-profit in 2012. This is about par with the average giving over the past decade.[21] According to research conducted by the Empty Tomb, evangelicals as a whole give about four percent (and all "Christians" only 2.43 percent) of their income to the church.[22] The conclusion that can be drawn from these statistics is that American evangelicals are more generous than other groups, religious and non-religious.[23] However, we are not as generous as we ought to be, based on biblical teaching. As one church minister puts it, "God doesn't grade on a curve."[24] Noting the correlation between the rise in personal income and a relative decrease in giving to Christian causes generally (especially Christian charity and missions) Sylvia Ronsval, the executive vice-president of Empty Tomb, states: "What we are seeing is a wholesale accommodation to culture . . . The way we are spending our money is like a thermometer of our spiritual condition—and there is not a lot of encouragement."[25]

These statistics also have a bearing on the question of how many resources should be spent on issues of social concern and justice compared to evangelism. Social and humanitarian ministries, it is argued, invariably consume the lion's share of time, money, and personnel resources so that little is left for evangelism and church development.[26] How this issue is framed has a bearing on the conclusions that are drawn. To begin with, we should not look at this in terms of a zero-sum game. In his recent book, *Boundless Faith*, Robert Wuthnow observes that in the American church, evangelism is coming to be defined as showing Christian love through humanitarian work,[27] and "service is redefined as evangelism."[28] This can lead to what Jim Pleuddemann calls "halfistic mission."[29] Rightly understood, however, a concern for justice is not in conflict with a concern for evangelism. As I have argued, from a biblical standpoint the two are necessarily interconnected. Since the poor make up the greatest percentage of the unreached in the unevangelized areas of the world, both word and deed are critical in reaching the lost for Christ and God's greater glory.

Furthermore, while there is a need to overcome the dichotomy and resulting imbalance of resources which often still exists between humanitarian and evangelistic ministries, this should be viewed in the context of the equally unbiblical imbalance which exists between the amount of resources that Christians spend on themselves and the resources that are spent for ministries to their unbelieving neighbors around the world. Eighty percent of the world's evangelical wealth is in North America. If all evangelical church members in North America gave just 10 percent of their incomes, there would be more than enough to fund the fulfillment of the Great Commission.[30]

Defending the Rights of the Oppressed

I am not suggesting, of course, that the issues of poverty can be addressed simply by a more generous sharing of resources. First, money which is not given wisely can lead to unhealthy dependency. We will discuss this issue in a later chapter. But, further, money alone does not address the root causes of poverty and injustice. It is at this point that Christians historically have divided into two political camps—capitalism and Marxist socialism. Both ideologies are touted by Christians as the most "biblical" response to human misery. Evangelicals in America are often uneasy with the concept of "social justice" because of its association with state sponsored redistributions of wealth to address conditions of poverty and inequality. Christians in Europe, on the other hand, are more inclined to accept statist interventions to alleviate what they view as the excesses of capitalist greed and acquisitiveness. But as Michael Horton rightly argues, *ultimately* "it does not matter what brand of politics one accepts, as both Marxism and capitalism are cut from the same cloth of Enlightenment modernity."[31] Neither the capitalistic nor the socialistic ideology seeks the spiritual good of society. Both believe that humans are basically good and that social problems can be addressed by structural change which "unleashes" human potentialities. Above all, "both are idolatrous: Capitalism replaces God and his prominence with the 'Invisible Hand of the Market,' whereas Marxism makes an idol out of the state. One looks to the state as the liberator, the other to the market, but both are essentially materialistic and hostile to spiritual realities."[32]

This is not to say that capitalism is not preferable to socialism as an economic system. In practical terms, it is easy to argue (in my estimation) that capitalism is superior. Proponents of free market capitalism point out, for example, that the global marketplace has reduced poverty around the world. Kevin DeYoung and Greg Gilbert argue that "the biggest consumers of goods and resources are also the most productive creators of jobs and wealth."[33] That may be the case, although the bigger picture is more of a mixed bag. Like any economic system, capitalism has its "winners" and its "losers." There can be Christian inputs into capitalism as we will discuss in the last chapter. But it is still a man-made system that is infected by sin. More to the point is that the very success of capitalism has had a deleterious effect on the church itself. David Wells discusses in detail how the modern church's worship of self rather than God has resulted in a "psychologizing" of Scripture, as preachers attempt to be practical in addressing the "felt needs" of people in their congregations. In today's market-driven church, he argues, Christianity is largely reduced to meeting the religious consumer's desire for idolatrous self-fulfillment.[34]

According to Wells, a further consequence of the privatizing and psychologizing of Christianity is that sin is often viewed as a personality flaw rather than a moral failing. This, he argues, is nothing less than a transformation of the Christian faith. We can agree. However, one of the defining characteristics of evangelicalism over the past century has been a pervasive individualistic orientation. This has resulted in a tendency for evangelicals to view sin almost exclusively in personal terms. Most evangelicals, as I have previously noted, are reticent to address social as well as personal evils in society.[35] To the extent that evangelicals are involved in social concern we also prefer to concentrate on acts of social service, such as giving out clothes to the needy or serving a meal to the homeless at Thanksgiving. Instead of directly confronting conditions or structures that cause poverty or oppression, we prefer to believe that social reform will take place "one heart at a time" through personal evangelism. [36] Yet the Old Testament prophets, Jesus, James, and even Paul, all directly confronted the perpetrators of injustice in their day. According to Robert Linthicum, of the 116 incidents recorded in the gospels in which Jesus was confrontational, 66 were confrontations of representatives of the religious, political or economic systems of either Israel or Rome.[37]

It is true, of course, that there can be no lasting change in society without a change in the hearts of individuals. Conversion characterized by a new relationship with God and a new direction in relationships is central to social change. But is it socially naïve to assume that limiting our efforts to personal evangelism and social service is sufficient in addressing many cases of injustice around us.[38] This is poignantly illustrated by the following story as told by Robert Linthicum. While serving as a student ministry intern, he worked among black teenagers in a government housing project in a U.S. city. A fourteen-year-old girl named Eva began attending one of his Bible studies. One day she came to him in deep distress. "Bob," she said, "I am under terrible pressure and I don't know what to do. There is a very large gang in this project that recruits girls to be prostitutes for wealthy white men in the suburbs. They are trying to force me . . ."[39] He urged her to resist their demands and keep attending the Bible study. Then he went home for summer vacation. He recounts:

> Three months later I returned and Eva was nowhere to be found. The other youth told me she had stopped coming about a month after I had left. I went to Eva's apartment. As soon as she saw me she burst into tears. 'They got to me, Bob,' she said. 'How could you give in like that' I unsympathetically responded. 'Why didn't you resist?' She told me a story of terror. 'First they told me they would beat my father. . . and they beat him bad. I had no alternative. So I gave in.' 'But, Eva' I said, 'why didn't you get some protection? Why didn't you go to the police?' Eva responded, 'Who do you think *they* are?'

Linthicum relates how up until that moment he had viewed sin in strictly individual terms. Then he began to realize that much of the city's legal and political system was itself set up to benefit the rich at the expense of the poor.[40]

As the above story illustrates, there are a number of different aspects to injustice, like sex trafficking of minors, each of which requires a different type of intervention. At the lowest level there are the conditions of poverty which expose children to gang violence, drug and alcohol abuse, and prostitution. According to the Children's Defense Fund, children living in families with incomes of less than fifteen thousand dollars are twenty-two times more likely to be abused or neglected than children living in families with incomes of thirty thousand dollars or more.[41] Then there are the perpetrators of abuse (i.e., the gangs, pimps, and wealthy customers). Finally, there are those in positions of authority who abuse their power. Gary Haugen, director of the International Justice Mission, points out that often operating in collaboration with those who exercise coercion there are "hidden forces," or those esteemed people of power and authority who abuse that power and lie about it.[42]

The Bible speaks of four types of intervention to address the needs of victims: (1) victim rescue; (2) perpetrator accountability; (3) structural prevention; and (4) victim assistance (see chart below).[43]

Figure 8. Four Types of Justice Intervention

Type of Intervention	Scripture	Text
Victim rescue	Psalm 82:3-4	"Defend the cause of the weak and fatherless, maintain the rights of the poor and oppressed. Rescue the weak and the needy; deliver them from the hand of the wicked."
Perpetrator accountability	Psalm 10:2,15	"Break the arm of the wicked and evil man; call him to account for his wickedness that would not be found out."
Structural prevention	Psalm 10:18	"[Defend] that fatherless and the oppressed, in order that man, who is of the earth, may terrify no more."
Victim assistance	Psalm 146:7-9	"He upholds the cause of the oppressed and gives food to the hungry. . . lifts up those who are bowed down . . . watches over the alien and sustains the fatherless and the widow."

Victim rescue is intervention on behalf of those presently suffering abuse—the prisoner who is illegally detained or tortured, the girl being held in prostitution, or the child in bonded servitude. *Perpetrator accountability* is intervention after the abuse has taken place to bring the perpetrator to account for their actions and seek just compensation for the victim. *Structural prevention* consists of efforts to ensure that the victim and other vulnerable people are not abused again and prevent abuse from happening in the first place. In addition to addressing the human sin condition through evangelism and discipleship, it involves addressing the conditions of poverty that expose the weak and vulnerable to abuse. It means not only giving people food, but defending their right to food and the basic necessities of life and empowering them to become self-sufficient through efforts like job training and micro-business development. It may also include efforts to bring about changes in local or government agencies. *Victim assistance* involves physical, emotional, and spiritual support for victims *after* they have been rescued from abuse—i.e., shelter or transitional housing, counseling, spiritual care, job training, etc.

The people of God therefore pursue mercy and justice when they go beyond simply meeting personal needs and act to alter or alleviate abysmal social conditions which accentuate human poverty and misery and make people more vulnerable to acts of cruelty and oppression. Church leaders also fulfill this mandate when they make general pronouncements about God's concern for justice and his judgment on those guilty of oppression and brutality and when they cooperate with other agencies and organizations (Christian and non-Christian) to hold perpetrators of injustice accountable. Local churches obey this injunction when they bring God's moral law to bear on more grievous injustices in their teaching and provide avenues for church members to use their spiritual gifts to help victims of abuse.

Engaging Justice Politically

One of the thorniest issues, of course, is how the church as an organ-izational entity ought to respond when confronted with structures of injustice and oppression. In my view, a "Christ-against-culture" posi-tion must be held in tension with the "Christ-transforming-culture" position.[44]   On the one hand, the church is a political and social force when it acts as a "counter-community." When Christ describes the Christian community as "the light of the world" (Matt. 5:14) he gives a startling picture of the social impact that the church should have as an alternative social reality. The image of *light* in Scripture is that of a positive, aggressive force that combats darkness. In the book of Isaiah it is associated with the forces of justice that oppose the rod of oppression (Isa. 9:2, 4-5, 7).[45] But Christians can also seek creative social reform through politics, while at the same time recog-nizing the limits of politics and avoiding the excessive use of power in reform.[46] Failure to keep both perspectives in view often results in an idolatrous attachment to ideologies on both the left and the right.

The experience of the church with apartheid in South Africa is in-structive in this regard. According to John de Gruchy and Steve de Gruchy (as well as other leading theologians who challenged the ra-cially-based system of segregation) the Reformed churches in South Africa were not segregated until the mid-nineteenth century revivals led by holiness preacher Andrew Murray and pietist missionaries. It was under the influence of such evangelicals, they argue, that the Dutch Reformed Church concluded at its Synod of 1857 that it was permissible to hold separate services for blacks and whites. This de-cision was rationalized on the basis of the missionary strategy for "church growth" prevalent at the time that the gospel should be communicated to each nation and group in ways appropriate to their culture. This was akin to the widely influential "homogeneous unit principle" popularized by Donald McGavran that people gravitate to people who are like them.   While mixed congregations in South Af-rica continued to exist, what was meant to be an exception in 1857 became the rule. The missionary strategy therefore had enormous ramifications for the church. While it facilitated the growth of indigenous congregations it "divided the church along racial lines in a way that was recognized even then as theologically unsound."[47]

In his powerful treatise, *The Uneasy Conscience of Modern Fundamentalism* (1947), Carl Henry comments that he posed the following question to a group of evangelical pastors about their preaching:

> How many of you, during the past six months, have preached a sermon devoted in large part to a condemnation of such social evils as aggressive warfare, racial hatred and intolerance, the liquor traffic, exploitation of labor or management, or the like—a sermon containing not merely an incidental or illustrative reference, but directed mainly against such evils and proposing the *framework* in which you think solution is possible?[48]

Not one of the pastors, Henry recounts, could say that he had preached such a sermon.[49] The church's separation from culture allows it to pronounce God's judgment on evil and demonstrate a better way of life. But a church that mimics the values of the surrounding culture loses its prophetic voice. It is simply silent.

Henry thought that Christians as citizens ought to be politically engaged for the betterment of society and that evangelical leaders and pastors had to do a better job of "enunciating theological and moral principles that have a bearing on public life" and in proposing "frameworks" for solutions to specific problems of social injustice. But he argued that the church as an institution has neither the authority nor the competence in most cases to offer specific policy prescriptions. In expressing basic agreement with Henry, Richard Mouw suggests the further need for "intermediate organizations" between the institutional church and Christian citizens which can focus on specific areas of cultural and political involvement and present well-reasoned and Scripture-based proposals on specific issues.[50]

But while politics can be an avenue for limited reform it is folly to assume that entire cultures can be transformed through political means. One gets the impression from some proponents of "transformational politics" that the kingdom of God will be ushered in through our efforts of social and political reform. Robert Linthicum argues, for example, that Jesus' allusion to the Old Testament Year of Jubilee in his description of his ministry in Luke 4:18-19 is a prescription for a social and political liberation that will "bring in" God's kingdom. Jesus, of course, cared deeply about the poor. But neither he nor the early church espoused such a program for social reform. As we have previously argued, there will always be an unresolved tension between the present and future dimensions of God's reign. The jubilee concept may suggest general principles of justice and compassion for a comprehensive and redemptive response to human need, particularly within the body of Christ.[51] But it cannot be applied literally—nor does it mean that there will be a society in which "none will be rich, none will be poor and all of us will live at shalom with each other."[52] Such applications of Scripture verge on Marxist idealism. Moreover, they obscure the central importance of personal regeneration for true social reformation and put the focus on our own political efforts. God alone will bring about the final restoration of his creation, though Scripture indicates that through our prayers, godly living, and kingdom witness we can speed the day of its coming (Acts 3:19-21; II Peter 3:11-12).

Conclusion

Christians must continually guard against allowing their theology to be shaped and molded by prevailing cultural norms and practices—or what Sherwood Lingenfelter calls "social games."[53] Evangelicals are particularly sensitive to this when it comes to the tendencies of liberals to reshape theology in political categories of social justice. But have we equally allowed the values of our affluent materialistic society to shape our attitudes and actions towards the poor, disadvantaged, and socially vulnerable of the world?

This brings me back to Beale's argument that humans were created by God to be imaging beings—if we do not reflect God and his character, we will reflect something else in creation. "We either commit ourselves to God, identify with his name and become like his character, or we commit ourselves to some object of the creation and become like that thing."[54] This idea of becoming what we worship is implicit in the Old Testament description of idolatry as exchanging the glory of God for the image of an idol (cf. Ps. 106:19-21). Beale points out that what is exchanged is not only the *object* of worship (God for another god) but also the glorious *character* of the true God potentially reflected among his people for identification with the *character* of a false idol.[55] Thus when the Israelites worshiped Baal, performing sexual rituals as a fertility rite, they became as detestable as their god (Hos. 9:10).[56] And when they ran after worthless idols made of wood they lost their capacity to reflect God's character of justice and mercy (Jer. 2:11, 34; 7:5-11; Micah 5:12-6:8). They became spiritually and morally insensitive and void, just like the idols they worshipped (Ezek. 12:2).[57]

Beale's study of idolatry merits careful reflection by Christians who live in a culture that glorifies wealth, comfort, and self-indulgence. We have seen that in both the Old and New Testaments God's people are commanded to imitate his concern for the poor, marginalized, and oppressed. But to the extent that the church becomes conformed to the values of this world, it risks the same spiritual and moral consequences of idolatry as the Israelites. Chasing after the idol of material goods can turn us into consumers of the latest fashion who give no thought to the oppression of men, women, and children in sweatshops and other forms of slave labor. The idol of sexual excess can make us blind to sexual violence, the degrading of women's bodies as mere objects for sexual gratification, and the commercial sexual exploitation of women and children. Pursuing the idols of fame and fortune turns us into worshippers of success who have little regard for the poor, the outcaste, and the homeless who don't "deserve" our attention. The idols of racial pride and eth-

nic identity prevent us from acknowledging the evils of racial prejudice and cultural intolerance. The danger of these forms of worldliness is that they often make sin seem normal and righteousness to be
strange.[58]   We are so comfortable with the values of an affluent, materialistic, and self-indulgent society that we become anesthetized to
their harmful effects.   In these areas, as in every other area of the
Christian life, God tells us to keep ourselves from idols (I John. 5:21).

Notes

[1] Beale, *We Become What We Worship*, p. 284.

[2] Ibid., p. 134,

[3] Ibid., p. 284.

[4] Ibid.

[5] Jethani, *The Divine Commodity*, p. 39.

[6] Ibid.

[7] Ibid., pp. 39-40.

[8] Ibid., p. 40

[9] DeYoung and Gilbert, *What Is the Mission of the Church?*, p. 176.

[10] Ibid.

[11] This point was made in recent remarks by Dr. Craig Ott, professor of missions at
Trinity Evangelical Divinity School, Deerfield, IL.

[12] See George W. Forell, *Faith Active in Love: An Investigation of the Principles Underlying
Luther's Social Ethics* (Mpls, MN: Augsburg Publishing House, 1954), pp. 142ff.

[13] Commenting on Amos' condemnation of the "cows of Bashan" in Amos 4:1-2,
Ron Sider notes: "The women involved may have had little direct contact with the
impoverished peasants. They may never have realized clearly that their gorgeous
clothes and spirited parties were possible partly because of the sweat and tears of
toiling peasants. In fact, they may even have been kind on occasion to individual
peasants. . . But God called these privileged women 'cows' because they profited
from social evil. Before God they were personally and individually guilty." See *Rich
Christians in an Age of Hunger* (Dallas, TX: Word, 1990), pp. 106-7.   Evangelicals
seem to be guilty of inconsistency when they picket abortion clinics which profit
from the evil of late-term abortions or refuse to purchase products from companies
that endorse gay marriage but turn a blind eye when it comes to corporations that
subject workers to inhumane conditions.

[14] Timothy Keller, *Counterfeit Gods: The Empty Promises of Money, Sex and Power and the
Only Hope That Matters* (New York: Dutton, 2009), p. 168.

[15] Ibid., p. 170.

[16] Nystrom, *James*, p. 276.

[17] Of every dollar given to a Protestant church in America the amount that goes to overseas missions is two cents. By contrast, of very dollar taken in by Antioch Presbyterian Church in Chonju, Korea 70 cents goes to missions. See Edward Veith, "Who Gives Just Two Cents for Missions? We do, to our Shame," *World Magazine* (October 22, 2005). Available at: http://www.worldmag.com/ articles/11176

[18] Thom S. Rainer, "Seven Sins of Dying Churches," *Outreach Magazine*, 5 no. 1 (January-February 2006), p. 16.

[19] "Key Statistics on Generous Giving," http://library.generousgiving.org/page. asp? sec=4&page=311

[20] See "New Study Shows Trends in Tithing and Donating," *The Barna Group* (April 14, 2008). Available at: http://www.barna.org/barna-update/article/18-congregations/41-new-study-shows-trends-in-tithing-and-donating

[21] See "Barna poll: Tithing stable in 2012; evangelicals content with their personal financial status." http:// churchexecutive.com/archives/barna-poll-tithing-stable-in-2012-evangelicals-content-with-their-personal-financial-status

[22] Ruth Moon, "Are American Evangelicals Stingy?" *Christianity Today* (February 2011) See: http://www. christianitytoday.com/ct/2011/February/areevangelicals-stingy.html

[23] One exception is the Mormons, who are the most generous of all religious groups in America.

[24] Moon, "Are American Evangelicals Stingy?"

[25] Russell G. Shubin, "Where Your Treasure Is. . . A Fresh Look at our Life and Our Resources in Light of the Kingdom" *Mission Frontiers*, (September 2001), p. 12. See: http://www.missionfrontiers.org/pdfs/23-3-Whereyourt reasureis.pdf

[26] Little, "What Makes Mission Christian?" pp. 67.

[27] Robert Wuthnow, *Boundless Faith: The Global Outreach of American Churches* (Berkeley, CA: University of California Press, 2010), p. 135.

[28] Ibid., p. 142.

[29] Jim Pleuddemann, "Is Social Justice the Same as Evangelism?" http://missionary impossible.blogspot.com /2010/ 11/is-social-justice-same-as-evangelism.html

[30] "Key Statistics on Generous Giving."

[31] Horton, *Beyond Culture Wars*, p. 56.

[32] Ibid.

[33] DeYound and Gilbert, *What Is the Mission of the Church?*, pp. 87-88.

[34] Beale, *We Become What We Worship*, p. 294. See David Wells, *Losing Our Virtue* (Grand Rapids, MI: Eerdmans, 1998). See also Paul C. Vitz, *Psychology as Religion: the Cult of Self-Worship* (Grand Rapids, MI: Eerdmans, 1977), pp. 66-82.

[35] See Dennis P. Hollinger, *Individualism and Social Ethics: An Evangelical Syncretism* (Lantham, MA: University Press of America, 1983).

[36] Keller, *Just Generosity*, p. 127.

[37] Linthicum, *Transforming Power*, p. 171.

[38] Keller, *Generous Justice*, p. 127.

[39] See Robert C. Linthicum, *City of God, City of Satan: A Biblical Theology for the Urban Church* (Grand Rapids, MI: Zondervan, 1991), pp. 45-7. This story is recounted by Keller in *Generous Justice*, p. 128,

[40] Ibid.,

[41] David Anderson, "Unleashing the Family: Safe Families for Vulnerable Children," in *A Heart for the Community: New Models for Urban and Suburban Ministry*, ed. John Fuder and Noel Castllanos (Chicago, IL: Moody Press, 2009), p. 422.

[42] Haugen, *Good News about Injustice*, pp. 129-30.

[43] Ibid., pp. 155-7.

[44] These concepts of "Christ Against Culture" and "Christ Transforming Culture" are taken from H. Richard Neibuhr's classic, *Christ and Culture* (NY: Harper and Row, 1956). In his typology, the "Christ Against Culture" view emphasizes Christ's lordship as the sole authority over the Christian as opposed to other authorities. If we are to follow Christ we must reject any loyalty to culture. This is expressed in John's statement: "Do not love the world or anything in the world. If anyone loves the world, the love of the Father is not in him." (I John 2:15). This view often emphasizes separation from the world. The "Christ Transforming Culture" perspective is more optimistic about the ability of Christians to change culture. While still affirming the universality of sin, it holds that cultures can be converted to reflect the values of God's kingdom. One example of this view is Calvin, who emphasized the positive, third use of the law, to bring about social reform.

[45] See Mott, *Biblical Ethics and Social Change*, p. 137.

[46] Ibid., p. 197.

[47] John de Gruchy and Steve de Gruchy, *The Church Struggle in South Africa: Twenty-Fifth Anniversary Edition* (Minneapolis, MN: Fortress, 2005), pp. 8-9.

[48] Henry, *The Uneasy Conscience of Modern Fundamentalism*, p. 4.

[49] Ibid.

[50] See Richard Mouw, "Carl Henry Was Right," *Christianity Today*, January 2010, http://www.christianity today. com/ct/2010/january/25.30.html?start.

[51] See Wright, *The Mission of God's People*, pp. 111-12. We will discuss this further in chapter nine.

[52] Referring to Luke 4:18-19, Robert Linthicum states: "So what Jesus was doing by reading Isaiah 61:1-2 in the synagogue and proclaiming, 'Today, this Scripture has been fulfilled in your hearing'? In essence he was proclaiming this message: 'You wealthy and powerful, as well as the people—you are to keep the entire jubilee and not just one regulation of it. I have come to bring about the setting free of this great people, so that none of us will be rich, none will be poor and all of us will live at shalom with each other.' Jesus had come proclaiming a reversal of his entire society, so that wealth, power and religious control would no longer be lodged in the hands of a few while all the rest were thrust into ever deeper poverty. That is what Jesus meant by the kingdom of God." Later he states that the "essential mission of the church is to work for the transformation of the world into God's kingdom . . . We are to be about winning people to Christ, confronting political systems, transforming economic systems and converting religious (or value-creating) systems." *Transforming Power*, pp. 60-61, 116-17.

[53] Sherwood Lingenfelter, *Transforming Culture: A Challenge for Christian Mission* (Grand Rapids, MI: Baker Books, 1008), p. 30.

[54] Beale, *We Become What We Worship*, pp. 304-5.

[55] Ibid., p. 87.

[56] Ibid., p. 105.
[57] Ibid., p. 122.
[58] Ibid, p. 300.

PART THREE

KINGDOM WITNESS AND THE MISSION OF THE CHURCH

Go to the local Wal-Mart store and you will be hard pressed to find anything made in America. The "global village" offers unparalleled opportunities for travel, communication, and interaction with persons from diverse cultures and religious backgrounds. It also forces mission agencies, missionaries, and local churches to respond to *both* the beneficiaries and marginalized losers in the global marketplace. Deeply entrenched problems such as civil strife, ethnic genocide, poverty and malnutrition, mass migrations of refugees, disease (especially A.I.D.S), and human trafficking plague the poorest nations of the world to which many missionaries are called. These global realities make it imperative that we clearly define the mission of the church. But, as we have already seen (and as anyone who is at all familiar with contemporary missions knows) this is a highly contentious issue.

The Meaning of Mission

Answering the question "what is the church's mission?" is not as easy as it would seem. For it presupposes a number of other issues. To begin with, our assumptions about the nature of the church shape our view of missions just as our view of mission influences our conception of the church. So, it is essential that we have a biblically informed understanding of the church. Furthermore, it important that we are clear on what we mean by the word "mission." It is often noted in mission literature that the noun "mission" does not even appear in the Bible. Charles Van Engen notes that from a biblical perspective, what is emphasized regularly is the concept of being sent, with an emphasis on the authority and purpose of the sender. In the New Testament the words *apostello* (apostle) and *pempo* (send) are used almost interchange-ably.[1] According to the *Theological Dictionary of the New Testament*, the word *apostellein* becomes a theological term meaning "to send forth to service in the kingdom of God with full authority (grounded in God)."[2] William Larkin Jr. argues that in the Bible "'mission' is the divine activity of sending intermediaries whether supernatural or human to speak or do God's will so that God's purposes for judgment or redemption are furthered."[3] Based upon this definition, mission comprises six elements: (1) a sender, along with the sender's purpose and authority in sending; (2) the act of sending, or a commission and authorization that leads to movement; (3) the agents, or "those who are sent;" (4) the particular task of those on mission; (5) the intended result or goal of the mission; and (6) mission's comprehensive framework of God's salvation history.[4]

Key Questions

Given this overall definition, there are a number of questions which bear on the subject of the church's mission:

- What is the biblical-theological meaning of the word *ekklesia* (church)? What is the significance of this term for understanding the church's mission? How appropriate is it to speak of the "missional" church? Can we speak of the church, not just individual "specialized" missionaries, as "sent" on a mission?

- What is the gospel? Is the gospel more correctly summarized in terms of forgiveness of sins and regeneration through the cross of Christ, or should it be more broadly understood in terms of the coming of the kingdom through the ministry and person of Christ that creates a redeemed community? How is the gospel related to the whole salvation history "story-line" of the Bible? How is the gospel shared? Is it shared only by words or also by deeds?

- How should we interpret some of the key "mission" texts in the Bible (i.e., the Great Commission)? What is the relationship between the Great Commission and the Great Commandment in understanding the "mission" of the church? Is there an ethical and social component to the church's mission?

- Is it is proper to speak of "mission" in the Old Testament? If so, in what sense? And, how is the mission in the Old Testament in the context of God's covenant relationship with Israel related to mission in the New Testament and God's "new covenant" with the church?

- How is Paul's mission related to the mission of Jesus? Is there continuity or discontinuity between the mission of Paul and the mission of Jesus?

This, of course, is a daunting list of questions, some of which have already been partially discussed in previous chapters. What we will attempt to do in the following chapters is construct an overall biblical-theological framework which pulls together some key missional concepts and addresses these key issues in greater detail.

Notes

1 Charles Van Engen, "'Mission' Defined and Described," in, *MissionsShift:: Global Mission Issues in the Third Millenium*, ed., David J. Hesselgrave and Ed Stetzer, (Nashville, TN: B&H Publishing Group, 2010), pp. 1-11.
2 Ibid, p. 11.
3 William J. Larkin Jr., "Mission," in *Evangelical Dictionary of Biblical Theology*, ed., Walter A. Elwell (Grand Rapids, M: Baker, 1996), p. 534.
4 William J. Larkin Jr., "Introduction," in *Mission in the New Testament*, ed. Larkin J. Larkin Jr. and Joel F. Williams (Maryknoll, NY: Orbis, 1998), pp. 3-4.

Chapter 8
The Mission
of God's People

I remember in the late 1960's and early 1970's watching a popular TV show called "Mission Impossible." The series followed the exploits of the IMF (Impossible Mission Force), a small team of secret agents involved in covert operations around the world against dictators, evil organizations, and crime lords. Most episodes began with the leader of the IMF, Jim Phelps, receiving directions via a hidden tape recorder and an envelope with pictures and instructions explaining the mission. The tape recorded message usually went something like this: "Good morning/afternoon Mr. Phelps . . . Your mission, Jim, should you decide to accept it is . . . As always, should you or any of your agents be caught or killed, the Secretary will disavow any knowledge of your actions. This tape will self-destruct in ten seconds. Good luck, Jim." Smoke would then billow from the tape recorder.[1] The mission, of course, would always be accepted and accomplished, often in dramatic fashion and against incredible odds.

The early believers were similarly given a mission (Matt. 28:19-20)—which, humanly speaking, must have seemed at times to the small band of disciples to be "Mission Impossible." Think of the obstacles they faced. The fledgling church of the first century experienced ridicule, slander, loss of employment, beatings, and even death at the hands of individuals, hostile crowds, and religious and political authorities who were determined to wipe out the Christian faith.[2] Yet, this small group of Jesus followers grew to be the most significant movement the world has ever known. Why is this? I think in large measure it had to do with how the early church understood and lived out under the power of the Holy Spirit its identity as the people of God, an identity that is closely connected with the New Testament term *ekklesia*.

What's in a Name? Recovering the New Testament Concept of Ekklesia

In the New Testament, the name most frequently used to designate the Church is *ekklesia*. Jesus said he would build his *ekklesia* (Matt. 16:18). This was the word the early followers of Jesus used to describe themselves following Pentecost (Acts 5:11, 8:1). The term arises out of a combination of two Greek words: the verb *kaleo* ("to call") and the presupposition *ek* ("out of"). So it literally means "the called out ones" or a *group of persons who are called out for a purpose*. But who are these people? Who calls them? And for what purpose are they called?

To understand the theological significance of *ekklesia* we must briefly look at its Old Testament roots. Early Jewish scholars who translated the Hebrew Scriptures into Greek (the Septuagint) used the term *ekklesia* for the Hebrew word *qahal* ("assembly").[3] In the Old Testament, the "assembly" of Israel is described as a people of God's own possession or "the people of God."[4] When the people of Israel are first gathered by God to be established as his covenant people, they

are described as "the whole assembly" (Deut. 5:22) and this significant day is referred to as "the day of assembly" (Deut. 9:10, 10:4,
18:16). In each of these instances, the Septuagint uses *ekklesia* to
designate "assembly." As a covenant nation, Israel was to reflect
God's glory and be a witness to his truth and grace among the nations. "The Old Testament *ekklesia* is a people constituted and gathered by God, and called to participate in his salvific work."[5]

Clearly, then, the use of the term *ekklesia* by Jesus and the early
church is steeped with Old Testament meaning and imagery. The
connection between the Old and New Testaments is brought out
forcefully by the apostle Peter: "Once you were not a people, but
now you are the people of God; once you had not received mercy,
but now you have received mercy" (I Peter 2:10). Peter describes the
characteristics of the church as a "people of God" in terms of holiness and moral purity (2:9, 11), verbal witness to God's saving grace
and mercy (2:9-10), and good works (2:12, 15). It is further significant that Peter is addressing *Gentile* believers scattered throughout
Asia Minor, not Jews!

In the next four chapters we will explore in greater detail this theme
of the fulfillment of Old Testament promises and expectations in the
New Testament, especially as it pertains to the church's mission. My
main concern at this point is simply to show that this conception of
ekklesia as the "called out" people of God ties the contemporary
Christian community to God's covenant promise with Israel. Just as
Israel had a mission of being God's vehicle for blessing the nations
(Gen. 12:3) so the church is called to participate in and be a witness
to God's plan for the redemption of all of creation.[6]

Sadly, much of this rich biblical meaning behind the word "church"
has been lost. Actually, the word "church" as it is often used in our
Western culture is a poor substitute for the original Greek word
ekklesia. Over the centuries Christian thinking has placed increased
emphasis on the intellectual, institutional, and organizational aspects

of church life. The meaning of "church" as it is used in the English language today reflects this historical development. Thus, Webster defines our English word "church" as:[7]

- a building for public and especially Christian worship
- the clergy or officialdom of a religious body
- a body or organization of religious believers; as a) the whole body of Christians; b) Denomination (eg. The Presbyterian church); c) Congregation
- a public divine worship (eg. go to church every Sunday)
- the clerical profession (e.g. considered the church a possible career)

When I conduct workshops in churches one of the exercises I might do is to ask participants to give me images that they associate with the word "church." These images are then drawn on a white board. Often, the images that come to people's minds are physical images (i.e., pulpit, pews, sanctuary, and so on), which portray the church as a "place" where Christians gather, although on deeper reflection virtually all will agree that the church is not a building! The question then is: how we can recapture the New Testament understanding of the church?

The Missional Church

In recent years the idea of the *missional church* has captured the imagination of many Christians. However, the sundry uses of the term "missional" has created a great deal of confusion. Some have used it in connection with marketing the church to make it more attractive to the postmodern individual and stimulate church growth. Others who advocate the emergent church have equated it with the kingdom of God. But, as we have observed, there are those in this movement which describe the kingdom in such a way that the centrality of the cross and of Christ himself are obscured and in some cases even re-placed by the ethical "teachings" of Jesus. Both of these trends re-flect a concept of the church and mission that, in many ways, contradicts the views of those who were the first to introduce the concept of the missional church.[8]

The Meaning of Missional

One of the first books to address this topic is *Missional Church: A Vision for the Sending of the Church in North America* (1998). In this seminal work, the authors use the term "missional" to emphasize the essential nature and vocation of the church as God's called and sent people.[9] These authors see the church in North America as beset by three critical weaknesses: (1) an individualistic notion of mission that diminishes the importance of the ecclesial community; (2) an accommodation of the gospel and church life to the powers of Western culture that undercuts the nature of the church as an alternative community; and (3) a privatization of faith occasioned by the collapse of Christendom.[10] According to Darrel Guder, one of the authors of this study, an unfortunate result of Christendom (in which the church was established by the state) is that the corporate character of the people of God has been almost exclusively defined in institutional categories. "The biblical emphasis on God's calling, forming, and sending of a people has been diluted and distorted by church institutions." But the correct response to this form of reductionism, he argues, is not to resort to (Western) individualism, which focuses exclusively on *personal* salvation and calling. In Scripture, "[t]he personal encounter with Christ is always and immediately linked with incorporation into his body, the Church. The purpose of personal calling is the formation of the witnessing community . . . . The apostolic strategy was not only to 'save souls' but to form witnessing communities whose members' testimony to God's salvation formed the center of their gospel proclamation."[11]

Historically, two theological concepts have been foundational to this understanding of the missional church. The first is a focus on the already/not yet reign (kingdom) of God, which I have discussed in previous chapters. This focus on the kingdom of God does not (as we will see) mean doing away with a "Great Commission theology," which has been the emphasis of the Protestant missionary enterprise for over two centuries. But it does reframe the necessity of obeying the Great Commission within the larger context of the reign of God.[12] The second foundational concept is *missio Dei*—or the mission of God.[13] Basically, this means that mission has its source in God the Father who sent his Son to reconcile all things to himself. From Genesis to Revelation, God's mission manifests itself in the unfolding history of mighty redemptive acts that culminate in the renewal of all creation through the person and work of Jesus Christ. [14] Inherent in the concept of the *missio dei* is the recognition that God is a sending God, and the church is sent.[15] The church's mission is therefore a necessary part of the story of God's redemptive purpose. The church is an instrument of God's mission. Further, if the church's mission is part of God's mission in the world then this mission defines the church and is the responsibility of the whole church, involving all of God's people.

The *missio Dei*, however, is another one of those theological concepts that has been the source of much confusion and debate. From the beginning, a fundamental issue has been whether the *missio Dei* should have a "redemption" focus or a "creation" focus:

> Should the *missio Dei* be understood primarily in relationship to God's work of redemption and thereby see the church as the primary way in which God works in the word—a *specialized* way of understanding God's work in the world? Or should the *missio Dei* be understood as the broader agency of God in relation to all creation and God's continuing care of that creation—a *generalized* way of understanding God's work in the world? [16]

Clearly, these two approaches have led to divergent understandings of the missional church. In the first more traditional understanding of mission, the primary focus is on the ecclesial community (the church) which has its origin in the salvific work of Christ and continues his mission in the world through the power of his Spirit. As a sign and foretaste of the kingdom the church witnesses to the reign of God and his redemptive purposes in the world. Although the work of God's Spirit is not limited to the church, it is both the primary agent God's saving work and its locus. From this perspective, "missional" refers to the specific task of local churches to advance the kingdom of God through its members both locally and around the world. The second mission paradigm shifts the focus away from the church to the salvific and providential work of God's Spirit in secular history to accomplish his purposes for humankind and all of creation. In moderate versions of this missional approach the church seeks to discern what God is already doing in the world and then "participates" in God's continuing redemptive mission. More liberal and ecumenical versions of this perspective, however, diminish the centrality of Christ in Scripture, reject the universal claims of the gospel, and virtually eliminate the distinction between the church and the world. The goal of mission is *shalom* or the humanization of society; and the church is simply one of many other social institutions that work together to transform oppressive political, social and economic structures. Unfortunately, there are evangelically-oriented emergents who seem to uncritically embrace this perspective.

Missions or Missional?

It should be apparent to the reader that the focus of this book is more in line with the first of these views on the missional church. Rightly understood, mission is church-centered, and the church is mission-centered.[17] In saying that mission is "church-centered" I do not of course mean to suggest that mission is simply the extension of a local church or denomination. We must affirm that God is providentially at work in all of creation, not just in the church, and that there is a general revelation that is discerned through common grace. But mission is church-centered in the sense that the church is central to God's mission in the world. As Rudolf Schnakenburg states,

"Christ's reign over the world is realized in a special manner in the Church and becomes there a concrete reality of grace."[18] As the primary agent of God's action in history, the church (i.e. the body of Christ) has been granted the same power which raised Christ from the dead and put everything under his feet (Eph. 1:19-23). It is this power, present through the Holy Spirit, which animated and energized the first century church and is available to the church today. The church is "mission-centered" because Christ is head of the church and God is reconciling the world to himself through Christ (II Cor. 5:19; Col. 1:20) "Thus, the *mission* of the Church is to be Christ's witness in the world, being, doing, and saying that witness as a continuation of his ministry, incarnating the gospel for the sake of the world, for which he died."[19] It is this outward call that should define the purpose and function of the inward life of the church.[20]

A church that has a "missional mindset" is different from being a church that is simply "missions minded." Consider for a moment how missions is structured in most churches, even those with a strong missions emphasis. Typically, there is a missions committee that is made up of about 6-8 people. Initially, they may be involved in crafting the church's "mission statement." But most of their time is spent making decisions on how money in the missions budget ought to be allocated. The missions committee is one of a number of other committees in the church and "missions" is simply one program among many other programs or departments in the church's organizational chart. The problem with this approach to mission is that it creates a separation in the church between its members and its mission that inhibits the church from developing a true mission dynamic. There is generally little synergy between the missions committee and the other ministries of the church, and a limited sense of ownership of the church's mission by most members of the congregation beyond contributing financially to the support of missionaries that are sent out from the church. In fact, competition for funds can produce tension rather than cooperation between the missions committee and other ministries of the church.[21] Bob Roberts puts it well:

"We have segmented and compartmentalized the different dimensions of the church and thereby failed to understand its function in terms of the whole."[22]

The Internal and External Focus of the Missional Church

The concept of the missional church therefore has significant practical implications for church life, structure, and leadership. Some discussions of the missional church create a false dichotomy between an external and internal focus. An examination of *ekklesia* in the New Testament reveals that both elements are important. As Michael Gohen states:

> The church is a community gathered for certain activities whereby their new life in Christ is nourished. The church is not any less the church when it is then scattered throughout the week. Both are important and it seems difficult to hold these together. A diminishment of the institutional nature of the church will mean a loss of the very way God has established that his people nourish and strengthen their kingdom life. A diminishment of the scattered nature of the church will lead to introverted church-centrism.[23]

This dynamic relationship between the inward/outward movements of the missional church is depicted in the wheel diagram below.[24] The hub of the wheel represents the Christians gathered for worship, instruction, fellowship, and mutual edification. The outer rim represents the Christians scattered and deployed in various "missional outposts" in the community and beyond. The missional outposts consist of different ways in which believers interact with non-believers (through work, friendships, partnerships for addressing community issues, etc.) with the ultimate purpose of kingdom witness. But they are also closely connected with each other since outreach is never simply an individual effort. The spokes represent missional practice and leadership within the local church.

Figure 9. The "Inward"/"Outward" Movement of the Mission-al Church

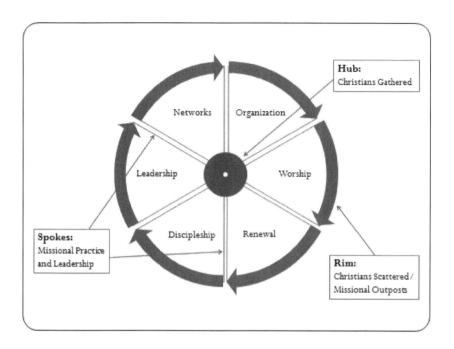

This model of the church is different from the "maintenance" model of many churches, where the focus is on maintaining the organizational structure, which is typically pyramidal with descending levels of power and responsibility. Since real growth and impact occurs at the rim where lay Christians rub shoulders with non-Christians, the wheel's energy and focus is always directed outward, as if the wheel were in motion creating centrifugal force.[25] But the direction and energy comes from the hub as the leadership equips lay people to witness and serve through the enabling power of the Holy Spirit. The inward/outward dynamic of the missional church is discernible in six key areas: (1) discipleship; (2) leadership; (3) networks; (4) organizational structure; (5) worship; and (6) renewal. Some of these areas of the missional church will be discussed more fully in later chapters. For now, they can be briefly summarized as follows:

Discipleship: The three elements of right knowledge, obedience, and action are related to each other in discipleship. Much of the discipleship in the contemporary church is based on the premise that if people have right knowledge this will automatically produce right behavior. So, many pastors and church leaders stress the importance of small group Bible studies and focus on solid biblical instruction and teaching from the pulpit. This is indeed important. But the biblical concept of the "mind" incorporates the entire person including his will and emotions, not just the mental faculties (Matt 22:37; Rom. 12:1-2). Gaining knowledge through biblical instruction is essential to transformation. In this sense, right thinking forms the basis for new ways of acting. But knowledge is best assimilated and understood in the context of life application. This means that right thinking does not take place without right action. Right action leads to right thinking just as much as right thinking leads to right action.[26] Knowledge and obedience are linked together when there is *both* reflection and action based on the Word of God. This means, further, that discipleship or "spiritual formation" is never simply an in-house affair. True discipleship does not take place unless there is engagement with the world. At the heart of multiplying healthy churches is the multiplication of responsible, committed, and reproductive disciples.

Leadership: As I have indicated, in most churches (especially large churches) leadership tends to be top-down and bureaucratic. In the missional model, by contrast, leadership is less hierarchical, more network-focused, and service oriented. Usually, the laity simply has a supportive role while the pastor/staff do most of the ministry. But this is the reverse of what Ephesians 4:11-12 says: "And he gave some as apostles, and some as prophets, and some as evangelists, and some as pastors and teachers, *for the equipping of the saints for the work of service*, to the building up of the body of Christ . . ." Biblically, then, the role of the pastor/staff is to equip laity and the role of the laity is to do ministry. Bill Easum rightly states that the key is for the church to develop a culture of equipping where the entire congregation is mobilized for ministry rather than the normal twenty percent.[27] The primary way lay ministry is effective is through team-based ministry rather than committees. Most churches are dominated by committees that easily become ingrown and bureaucratic and even political. Healthy teams, on the other hand, have a clear calling and are missionally focused. Churches with an effective lay ministry generally have cell groups or small groups that are designed to multiply themselves by raising up new leaders in the context of doing ministry.

Networks: The concept of the missional church gives credence to what some have described as a "synergistic" approach to mission.[28] Instead of simply helping to support and fund missionary "professionals" to impact the world, local churches operating out of this mission model are more likely to adopt a *multi-pronged strategy.* As "cells of the kingdom" they mobilize and empower members of the congregation to utilize the *diversity of gifts* for the accomplishment of the missionary mandate locally as well as globally. This "grass roots" approach to mission emphasizes partnerships through networks of congregations and other connectional structures that facilitate missional collaboration. Rather than trying to do everything on its own, a local church will focus on several things it does well and partner with other churches, volunteer organizations, and mission agencies both at home and abroad to realize common objectives.[29]

Organizational Structure: From a missional standpoint, what a church *is* determines what it does; and it organizes what it does. So, organization flows from the church's missionary nature and purpose. This is the reverse of the pattern of many churches in which organization and structure shape and define what they do.[30] Furthermore, as Van Engen states, "In missionary churches the effectiveness of leaders is not measured by what they do or do not accomplish, but by how the people of God are equipped."[31] This may require a careful rethinking and re-envisioning how a church is structured and organized.[32] Church leaders must align the vision that they have for their congregation with what Jesus called his followers to be and do. At the same time, vision alone is not enough. There must also be an effective organization that unleashes people with purpose to *achieve* the vision.[33] Therefore, using the wheel model, a missional congregation is composed of a system of networked, complementary, and integrated missionary "outposts" dedicated to and united by a single vision. Finally, it is important that the church's missional actions in the world are *culturally appropriate* and *contextually relevant*. This requires flexibility and a willingness to adapt to change as leaders discover with the congregation as a whole what structures and processes are most effective in a particular context.

Worship: This dimension of the church's life is usually viewed as taking place corporately. But in Romans 12:1, Paul encourages his readers to "offer your bodies as living sacrifices, holy and pleasing to God—this is your spiritual act of worship." He then describes this act of worship in terms of nonconformity to the world, spiritual renewal of the mind, humility, and mutual edification through the use of spiritual gifts, and love for one another and those outside the body of Christ, even those who might be considered to be its enemies. Worship therefore is not just a public gathering of people who experience God and offer praises to him. It should also be evident in our private walk with God and in public practice as we seek to live lives of sacrificial witness to him. The gathering of believers in worship and mutual edification is then complemented by a sending movement into the world as we seek to demonstrate who we are in and with Christ.[34]

Renewal: In one of the most helpful books I have read on this subject, Robert Lewis and Wayne Cordeiro point out that culture is the most important social reality of a local church. "Leaders today need to build a culture, because a church is an organism more than it is an organization." Furthermore, churches must be value-driven, not program driven. For "ultimately our church culture resides not in buildings, programs, or printed proclamations but in people who say 'this is what God wants us to become.'"[35] What implications does this have for church renewal? The diagram below illustrates the three foundational elements of a church's culture: (1) God' kingdom agenda; (2) a church's identity—who we are; and (3) our unique setting.

Figure 10. Elements of a Church's Culture and Kingdom Witness

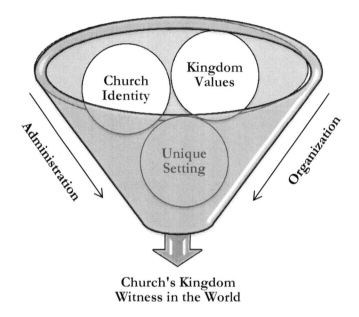

Church's Kingdom
Witness in the World

God's kingdom values set the agenda for the church—including what we do, what we think and who we are. This is "kingdom culture building."[36] Yet, every local church is unique and it lives out kingdom values in its own unique way and in its own unique setting. A local church must therefore continually identify and re-valuate the core values of its culture in light of kingdom values. And it must shape the nature of its kingdom witness in the world according to the unique giftings of the congregation and the needs represented in its particular social setting under the guidance of the Holy Spirit. This is a continual process that must involve the entire congregation and requires an openness to change that makes adaption and renewal part of the culture of the church.[37]

The Church and Integral Mission

The practice of the missional church, as I have described it brings us to the concept of "integral mission." In this approach, the mission of God is bigger than simply the salvation of souls. Although this aspect of the gospel is immensely important, exclusive focus on this as the task of the church fails to understand the full scope of God's mission in the world. As Rene Padilla, one of the key proponents of integral mission, states "The salvation that the gospel proclaims is not limited to man's reconciliation with God . . . It has to do with the recovery of the whole man according to God's original purpose for creation."[38] This involves a significant paradigm shift in the traditional approach to the church's mission.

Two Dichotomies

There has been a tendency in the history of the church, particularly in the West, to create two dichotomies. The first of these, as we have already discussed, is a dichotomy between the life and mission of the church. The second dichotomy involves a separation of the proclamation of the gospel in word from a "living out" of the gospel in deed. In this traditional approach, the "mission" of the church is to save souls and plant churches, mainly in foreign countries, through evangelism. The agents of mission are principally cross-cultural missionaries, who are supported by the local church. With this mission model, which is still operative in most evangelical churches today, it is possible for a local church to have a strong mission emphasis but have no significant influence or impact on its surrounding neighborhood. Moreover, since "mission" is largely limited to evangelistic outreach and "love of neighbor" is viewed primarily as the responsibility of individual believers, the corporate vocation of the church as God's covenant people is separated from the life of the individual Christian and ethics is separated from ecclesiology.

Integral mission seeks to overcome these dichotomies. The dictionary definition of "integral" is "entire, complete, or whole." It is "that which is necessary to the completeness of the whole" or "the parts that together constitute a whole." *Integral mission* therefore is mission that is made up of parts which constitute a single undivided whole. It is concerned with re-uniting or integrating those elements that have historically been separated. In this approach to mission, the church communicates the gospel through everything it is, says, and does. Its purpose is to incarnate and model the values of the kingdom of God and be a witness in word and deed to the gospel of Jesus Christ for the transformation of life in all its dimensions, both at the individual level and on the social or community level.[39]

As one reads the book of Acts, for example, it becomes apparent that what the church does and says in the world is necessarily connected to what it is as a community of believers. As the true remnant of the people of God spoken of in the Old Testament, the church is not just a neutral bearer of a message. It is a witness to that message by its very nature and existence. This means that Luke (and the New Testament as a whole) sees the social nature as well as the message of the church as a vital and integral part of the mission of God in the world.[40]

As Rene Padilla points out, there is nothing in this view of mission which precludes the role of "specialized" ministries such as those exercised by the apostles, prophets, evangelists, pastors and teachers referred to in Eph. 4:11. But what is important is that these gifts of leadership are part of a community of gifts that complement each other and contribute equally to the accomplishment of God's mission by the church as a witness to Jesus Christ.[41] Evangelism and the planting of churches by those commissioned to do so is still a critical part of the church's mission. But the churches that are planted should be integrated into the life of the communities in which they are planted. Moreover, Christian mission must be "glocal"—both global and local. One of the anomalies in missions today is that churches will spend thousands of dollars to send short-term missions teams to do "ministry" among the disadvantaged in cities that are located hundreds and even thousands of miles away, but have only limited (if any) involvement with disadvantaged populations of the communities or cities where they are located.

This view of integral mission also requires that we rethink what we mean by evangelism. Usually, priority is placed on evangelism over against social concern because the spiritual is more important than the material. Emphasis is therefore placed upon the "salvation of souls." However, biblically, the spiritual refers to the presence of God with his creation in which he renews and blesses it. Evangelism therefore involves witnessing in word and deed to the personal healing in every area of life that comes as individuals are reconciled to God through Jesus Christ. From this perspective, the spiritual has priority because there is nothing more important than a personal relationship with God. But this does not exclude a concern for the physical or material since "spirituality" simply means "seeking to live our lives in response to and cooperation with, the radically passionate and compassionate Spirit of God."[42] As the Micah Network puts it, "In integral mission our proclamation has social consequences as we call people to love and repentance in all areas of life. And our social involvement has evangelistic consequences as we bear witness to the transforming grace of Jesus Christ."[43]

Integral Mission and Church Structures

There is the story of an oriental master who allowed one of his disciples to live in a small shack by a river. Every morning the disciple washed his shorts—one of his few possessions—and hung them on a tree. One day the rats tore them to shreds. So the disciple had to go begging in the village to buy new ones. But the rats tore these up as well. So the disciple decided to get a cat to get rid of the rats. But this introduced a new problem. In addition to meeting his own needs, the disciple also had to beg for milk to feed the cat. In time, the disciple acquired a cow so he would have permanent source of milk for his cat. But he then realized that he needed fodder for the cow. With the increasing demands of the animals the disciple found that he had less and less time to devote to his spiritual life. So he purchased some land around the shack and arranged for two peasants to cultivate it. But the peasants needed supervision. So the disciple decided to get married and gave this task to his wife. Over time, through the ingenuity of his wife and a number of other arrangements, the disciple became the richest man in the neighborhood. One day, much later, the master came by and was astonished to find the disciple living in a stately mansion instead of an old shack. Seeing the disciple coming out from his new house, the master pointed to the mansion and exclaimed "What is this?" The disciple replied, as if it were the most natural thing in the world, "Though you might find it hard to believe, master, it was the only way I could preserve the shorts!" In commenting upon this story, Hugo Santos remarks, "The bizarre picture it presents can teach us something about a phenomenon that is common to organizations: the purpose for which they are created is always at risk of being pushed into second place, leaving as the primary objective the survival of the organization itself."[44]

Some years ago, I served as a short-term missionary teacher at a very small Bible college that was located in a small town about 200 miles north of Anchorage, Alaska. In addition to the college, there was also a medical clinic and a Christian radio station. While a few of the missionaries lived among the residents in the town, it was more economical for most of the missionaries to live in homes that were clustered together on land next to the radio station and college. As the number of missionaries grew so did the number of houses on the missionary compound. To further save money, the mission then decided to create a missionary food co-op. So it purchased a large truck to haul food from Anchorage, where it was purchased in bulk. Instead of going to the food market located in the town, the missionaries usually bought the cheaper food at their own store. Understandably, there was growing resentment on the part of a number of the local residents that the missionaries were not helping to support the businesses in their community. Again, I am sure there were valid practical reasons for the decisions that were made by this particular mission. But the cumulative effect of these efforts at "good steward-ship" was that the missionaries became more and more detached and isolated from the very people they were sent to serve.

The same phenomenon can be observed, I believe, with many of our local churches. In most of the major cities in the U.S. there are numerous large church structures that are boarded up or have been demolished—the result of "white flight" to the suburbs from inner city neighborhoods. One church with which I am very familiar was at one time located in the heart of the city. But it has since moved to a large campus that is more like an island separated from the rest of the community. The building where people of the church used to meet has been torn down and replaced by a bank. Similar stories have been repeated over and over again in cities large and small across the U.S. It is true, of course, that the line between "city" and "suburb" is often blurred. There is a wide variation in the racial and ethnic make-up of suburbs. But the overall pattern is clear. Whites have migrated to predominantly white communities, and churches follow. [45] This is particularly true of white middle-class evangelicals. Tim Keller notes that when it comes to the inner city, "Protestant (evangelical) Christians are the least urban religious group and thus have the least impact culturally."[46]

The reasons for this "suburbanization of the church" are varied and complex, though I would suspect that a primary rationale has been a concern for self-preservation.[47] It can, of course, be argued that the suburbs also need the gospel. But has the numerical growth of churches in the suburbs had a tangible impact even on the communities we inhabit? While some cases it probably has, I would suggest that generally speaking it has not. More often than we would like to admit, a concern for safety, security, and personal comfort and a pre-occupation with the maintenance of organizational systems and structures take precedence over the stated aims and concerns of the church.

Robert Putman observes that, whereas evangelicals are more generous philanthropically and are more involved in activities within their own religious community, they are less likely than mainline Protestants to be involved in the broader community and to participate in programs for social improvement. While there are some notable exceptions such as Charles Colson's Prison Fellowship Ministries, most evangelical volunteering "supports the religious life of the congregation itself—teaching Sunday School, singing in the choir, ushering at worship services—but does not extend to the broader community as much as volunteering by members of other faiths."[48] A recent study by Ellison Research (Phoenix, AZ) corroborates this assessment by Putman. In 2006, a random sample of 504 Protestant pastors were asked what their first spending priority would be if they were recipients of an unexpected financial windfall. The top priority among all Protestant pastors (31%) was to build, expand, or update their church's buildings and facilities. This was followed by increasing community evangelism activities (16%), paying off debt (12%), adding staff (10%) and giving to foreign missions (7%). There were significant differences between the clergy of evangelical and those of mainline denominations. Evangelical pastors were much more likely than mainline pastors to put a high priority on new or better facilities (38% to 22%), while mainline pastors put a higher priority on social programs than did evangelicals (13% to 2%). Among Southern Baptist clergy, 43 percent said having better/newer facilities was a priority while one 1 percent would use the financial windfall for social programs.[49]

Integral Mission and Community Relief and Development

There are many local churches that are reticent to get involved in their communities out of a fear that they will be overwhelmed by people with needs and inundated with the requests for help from the poor. This may be particularly true of churches that are located in the inner city. But I have also observed this attitude among churches that are located in more affluent suburbs. This is especially an issue with attempts to move from relief to development. Relief does for others; development enables others to do for themselves. On the one hand, relief (or betterment) is generally ineffective in addressing the real deep-rooted needs of a community and can often end up doing more harm than good if it does not lead to development. As Robert Lupton states:

> Betterment is easier and it feels better. How heartwarming it feels to volunteer as a server for the Thanksgiving feast for the homeless! . . . But as anyone will attest who has spent any extended time in such 'mercy' activities, there is an ugly side that inevitably reveals itself. Greed, manipulation, a sense of entitlement, resentment—somehow these darker instincts are never far below the surface among the recipients of one-way charity. And even in the best of scenarios, when relationships between givers and receivers appear to be genuinely thankful and gracious, the tendency toward unhealthy dependency is ever-present.[50]

On the other hand, development is difficult and time consuming. Moreover, there are those who believe that evangelism and development programs just don't mix. "It is virtually impossible to offer development services alongside programmed evangelism," it is argued, "without communicating to the community that you are prepared to buy their allegiance to the Christian faith, and that your services are provided on the condition they eventually pay homage to your religious agenda." Members of the community will "play the game" so long as there is the expectation of continued economic benefit.[51] In response to these pressures, many evangelical agencies simply divide their ministry into separate church planting and development departments. Often, development activities are undertaken by separate parachurch organizations which have limited, if any, connection to the local church. But, again, this creates a very disjointed gospel. As will be argued in subsequent chapters, the Great Commission to "make disciples" cannot be separated from the Great Commandment. Nor, in my estimation, can true development take place apart from evangelism and discipleship through the local church.

Circle-Urban Ministries, which is located in the Austin community of Chicago, is an excellent example. Its former executive director, Glen Kehrein, describes his experience in 1968 of standing on the roof of Moody Bible Institute and watching the smoke billowing from the riots that followed the death of Dr. Martin Luther King Jr. These riots fueled racial panic and a mass exodus of whites from the Austin community. Soon businesses, institutions, and churches (including 27 evangelical churches) followed. Called to live out his faith in a new way and to impact a declining community with God's love, Kehrein formed CUM as an outreach arm of Circle Church in 1974. The ministry took a major step in 1983 when it joined in a faith-and-works partnership with a newly planted Rock of our Salvation Evangelical Free Church. In describing the amazing story of this ministry, Kehrein writes: "My experiences have wrought in me a strong conviction that true Christian community development can be done only from a church base."[52] This relationship between community development and the faith community can take different forms. But, in the final analysis, real spiritual growth and nurture can only be provided in the local church.[53]

One of the problems in community development is that it can easily become simply a program, when in fact true development is a process that at its core is relational and is led by God's Spirit. Without an emphasis on forming personal relationships, conflict, and tension between community development efforts and programed evangelism is inevitable. The mission that I am currently a part of has as its goal the integration of ministries of social concern with relational evangelism, discipleship and church planting. In our crisis response ministry, for example, emphasis on the work of rebuilding homes following a disaster is a vehicle into building relationships. As meaningful relationships are formed and as people begin to share their personal stories there can be a mutual exploration of ways to find genuine, loving, just, long-term, and sustainable solutions to the needs of individuals and to specific needs within the community. In this process, opportunities arise to share the gospel and the "way of Christ" in a manner that is non-confrontational, non-judgmental and non-controlling. Here, exhibiting the love of Christ is the key as people are dignified as God's image bearers and they begin to feel something of God's love for themselves and for others. Individuals are invited into Bible studies where they can discover for themselves what it means to be a follower of Christ. These "discovery Bible studies" are linked to an existing church plant—or, as they grow and multiply, they can lead to a new church plant.

There is, of course, no guarantee of success in every instance. In even the most ideal circumstances community development and renewal is challenging and requires long-term commitment. And there will always be people who try to take advantage of our efforts to help them. When Jesus healed the ten lepers, only one ever expressed any gratitude or gave any indication of a heart-change that resulted in faith (Luke 17:11-19). Still, Jesus continued to combine acts of justice and compassion with an announcement of the good news of the kingdom.

Conclusion

To have a proper understanding of the church's mission we must first of all recover a biblical understanding of the church itself. Contemporary Christians "must relearn the language of Scripture with respect to the church."[54] Under the influence of modern culture we have largely replaced a biblical view of *ekklesia* with an institutionalized model of the church. Most American (and Western) Christians have learned to read their New Testaments through the modern lens of institutionalism. We need to rethink our entire concept of the church and learn to see it afresh through the lens of NT authors. This will require a "paradigm shift" regarding what it means to be part of the body of Christ.[55]

In this chapter I have suggested that the concepts of the "missional church" and "integral mission" are helpful in this regard. The concept of the missional church roots the essence and identity of the church in its call to participate in the ongoing drama of God's redemption and serve as a witness to his future kingdom. Integral mission seeks the transformation of all dimensions of life as the gospel message is proclaimed and the values of God's kingdom are lived out in the life of the faith community through the power of the Holy Spirit. The purpose of the chapters that follow is to show how this understanding of the church and its mission is rooted in the Old Testament concept of the "people of God" and is a central theme of the New Testament, from Jesus' mission to Paul's Gentile mission.

Notes

[1] Danny Biederman and Robert Wallace, *The Incredible World of Spy-fi: Wild and Crazy Spy Gadgets, Props, and Artifacts from TV and the Movies* (San Fransisco, CA: Chronicle Books, 2004), p. 82.

[2] There are numerous references in the New Testament to the persecution of the early Christians (Matt. 10:28, 23: 34-36; Luke 6:22, 12:4; Acts 7:1-8:1; 12:1-5; 14:5, 19; 16:19-40; 19:28-29; 22:4; I Peter 2:12, 20-21; 4:12; 5:8-9; II Tim. 4:5-6. II Thess. 2:14-15; Rev. 2:2-3. 9-13). This persecution was not limited to Jerusalem or to Jews hostile to Christianity. I Peter indicates a general persecution of Christians (1 Peter 1:6; 4:12, 16) in Asia Minor north of the Taurus (1 Peter 1:1; note especially Bithynia) and elsewhere (1 Peter 5:9). The book of Acts portrays the political authorities as initially sympathetic towards Christians (Acts 13:8, 18:17). This changed, however, with the Emperor Nero's attempt to make Christians the scapegoat for the great fire in Rome on 19 July 64 AD. The "fiery trial" spoken of in I Peter 4:12 may be a reference to the subsequent persecution of Christians. Peter and Paul may have been among the 977 Christian martyrs. Thereafter, the ruling class of the empire regarded Christianity as an "evil religion" with no legal standing which had to be eliminated. (See W.H.C. Frend, *The Rise of Christianity* [Philadelphia, PA: Fortresss, 1984], pp. 109-10.) The persecution of the church increased in the 2nd century and culminated with the most severe persecutions under Diocletian and Galerius at the end of the 3rd and beginning of the 4th centuries.

[3] Stanley J. Grenz, *Theology for the Community of God* (Grand Rapids, MI: Eerdmans, 2000), p. 464.

[4] Ibid., p. 465.

[5] Gohen, *A Light to the Nations*, p. 161.

6 Wright, *The Mission of God*, pp. 65-87.

7 http://www.merriam-webster.com/dictionary/church

8 Todd Billings, "What Makes a Church Missional?" *Christianity Today* (March 5 2008). See the article at: http://www.christianitytoday.com/ct/2008/march/16.56.html

9 Van Engen, "Mission Defined and Described," p. 24.

10 See Michael W. Goheen, "Historical Perspectives on the Missional Church Movement: Probing Lesslie Newbigin's Formative Influence," *Trinity Journal for Theology and Ministry.* http://www.missionworldview. com/wp-content/uploads/2011/06/Historical-Perspectives-on-Missional-Church.pdf

11 Darrell L. Guder, "Defining and Describing 'Mission'" in *MissionShift*, ed. Hesselgrave and Stetzer, pp. 54-5.

12 Craig Van Gelder and Dwight J. Zscheile, *The Missional Church in Perspective*, pp. 28-9.

13 David Bosch defines *missio dei* in terms of "the mission of God," or "God's mission." See *Transforming Mission: Paradigm Shifts in Theology of Mission* (Maryknoll, NY: Orbis, 1991), pp. 389-90.

14 Gohen, "Historical Perspectives on the Missional Church Movement," p. 68.

15 See Ed Stetzer, *Planting Missional Churches: Planting a Church That's Biblically Sound and Reaching People in Culture* (Nashville, TN: B&H Academic, 2006), pp. 20, 28. As we have noted, in both the Old and New Testaments, "mission" is regularly associated with the concept of being sent.

16 Gelder and Zscheile, *The Missional Church in Perspective*, p. 30.

17 See Joel Holm, *Church Centered Mission: Transforming the Church to Change the World* (Joel Holm Ministry Resources, 2004).

18 Rudolf Schnackenburg, *God's Rule and Kingdom*, J. Murray, trans. (New York: Herder and Herder, 1963), p. 313. Quoted in Van Engen, *God's Missionary People*, p. 110.

19 Guder, *Be My Witnesses*, p. 109.

20 Ibid., pp. 108-9.

21 Holm, *Church Centered Mission*, pp. 28-9.

22 Bob Roberts Jr., *Transformation: How Glocal Churches Transform Lives and the World* (Grand Rapids, MI: Zondervan, 2006), p. 26.

23 Gohen, "Historical Perspectives on the Missional Church Movement," p. 82.

24 This model is adapted from the "Spoke-and-Wheel Management Model" in Bishop Claude E. Payne and Hamilton Beazley, *Reclaiming the Great Commission: A Practical Model for Transforming Denominations and Congregations* (San Francisco, CA: Jossey-Bass, 2000), p. 76.

25 Ibid., pp. 74-7.

26 See Alan Hirsch, *The Forgotten Ways: Reactivating the Missional Church* (Grand Rapids, MI: Brazos Press, 2006), pp. 122-24.

27 See Bill Easum, "Role of Lay Leadership." http://churchconsultations.com/community/com-resources/articles/articles-by-bill-easum/role-of-lay-\leadership/

28 See Bruce Camp, "Major Paradigm Shifts in World Evangelization," *International Journal of Frontier Missions* (July/August, 1994), pp. 135-36.

29 Van Gelder and Zscheile, *The Missional Church in Perspective*, p. 160.

[30] Ibid., p. 158.

[31] Van Engen, *God's Missionary People*, p. 176.

[32] Ibid., pp. 163-176.

[33] Robert Lewis, *The Church of Irresistible Influence: Bridge-Building Stories to Help Reach Your Community* (Grand Rapids, MI: Zondervan, 2001), pp. 75-6.

[34] Gelder and Zscheile, *The Missional Church in Perspective*, pp. 152-53.

[35] Robert Lewis and Wayne Cordeiro, *Culture Shift: Transforming Your Church from the Inside Out* (San Francisco, CA: Jossey-Bass, 2005), pp. 1, 19, & 187.

[36] Ibid., pp. 20-4.

[37] Ibid., pp. 113-26; 169-79.

[38] C. Renee Padilla, *Mission Between the Times* (Grand Rapids, MI: Eerdmans, 1985), p. xx.

[39] See C. Rene Padilla, "What is Integral Mission?" http://lareddelcamino.net/en/images/Articles/ what%20is% 20integral%20mission%20cr%20padilla.pdf

[40] Christopher J. H. Wright, *Walking in the Ways of the Lord: The Ethical Authority of the Old Testament* (Downers Grove, IL: InterVarsity, 1995), p. 171.

[41] C. Rene Padilla, "Introduction: an Ecclesiology for Integral Mission," in *The Local Church, Agent of Transformation*, ed., Tetsunao Yamamori and C. Rene Padilla (Buenos Aires: Kairos, 2004), pp. 46-7.

[42] Dave Andrews, "Integral Mission, Relief and Development," p. 8. See: http://www.daveandrews.com.au/articles/Integral%20Mission%20in%20Relief%20and%20Development.pdf

[43] "Micah Network Declaration on Integral Mission." See: http://www.micah network.org/integral-mission

[44] Hugo N. Santos, "Church Structures: The Perspective of Institutional Psychology," in *The Local Church, Agent of Transformation*, ed., Yamamori and Padlla, pp. 206-7.

[45] William Julius Wilson has document this white flight in his book, *The Truly Disadvantaged: The Inner City, the Underclass and Public Policy* (Chicago: University of Chicago Press, 1987). Examining the population migrations within the thirty-three most populous metropolitan areas, Wilson found that while the black populations of the central cities were growing substantially, white and middle class residents migrated to the suburbs. Between 1950 and 1980, the populations in the central cities lost more than 9 million whites and added more than 5 million blacks, many of them from the rural south (pp. 100-01). In his study of the history of two Dutch Reformed congregations in Chicago, Robert Swierenga writes: "Mobility has always been a hallmark of church life in Chicago, the nation's second city. Congregations grew, flourished, and declined as their upwardly mobile members moved to newer subdivisions or more distant suburbs, where spacious new homes with gardens on tree-lined streets beckoned. Finally, the mother churches followed their members and sold the beloved edifice to other ethnic groups. Eventually, urban renewal projects, new land uses, or simple decay dictated that the buildings fall to the wrecker's ball. The first Dutch Reformed churches, erected in the 1850s and 1860s, suffered this fate. The earliest buildings still used for worship date from the 1890s, and all now house African American congregations." (See: "A Tale of Two Congregations: Acculturation and its long-term impact on Chicago's West-Side Reformed Church-

es," http://www.calvin.edu/henry/ISSRC/I mages/swierenga.pdf) The suburbanization of the white middle-class church and its consequences for the inner city have been addressed in a number of books, including Gibson Winter, *The Suburban Captivity of the Churches* (New York: Macmillan, 1962); Harvie Conn, *The Urban Face of Mission* (Phillipsburg, PA: P&R Publishing, 2002); and Harvie Conn and Manuel Ortiz, *Urban Ministry: The Kingdom, the City and the People of God* (Downers Grove, IL: IVP Academic, 2010).

[46]Tim Keller, "A Biblical Theology of the City," http://theresurgence. com/files/pdf/tim_keller_2002_a_ biblical_ theology_of_the_city.pdf, p. 6.

[47] Patrick Donohue states that, while caution must be exercised in ascribing motives for the white flight to the safety of the suburbs, "one wonders if the idols of self-protection, comfort, and ethno-centricity have motivated such migration." ("The Suburban Churches Role in Urban Mission," MA Thesis, Reformed Theological Seminary. http://www.rts. edu/Site/Virtual/Resources/Student_Theses/ Donohue%20-%20Urban%20Missions%20.pdf, p. 7.)

[48] Robert D. Putman, *Bowling Alone: The Collapse and Revival of American Community* (New York, NY: Touchstone, 2000), pp. 77-8.

[49] See Ron Sellers, "New Improved Facilities Top Churches' Wish List for Unexpected Money," *Facts & Trends*, May/June 2006, 6-9. http://www.lifeway. com/lwc/files/lwcF_corp_factsandtrends_06MayJune.pdf See also: http://www. grey matterresearch.com/index_files/Spending_Priorities.htm

[50] Robert D. Lupton, *Compassion, Justice and the Christian Life: Rethinking Ministry to the Poor* (Ventura, CA: Regal, 2007), p. 50.

[51] Dave Andrews, "Integral Mission, Relief and Development," p. 9.

[52] Glen Kehrein, "The Local Church and Christian Community Development," in *Restoring At-Risk Communities: Doing It Together and Doing It Right*, ed., John M. Perkins (Grand Rapids, MI: Baker, 1995), p. 163.

[53] Ibid., p. 171,

[54] Frank Viola, *Rethinking the Wineskin: The Practice of the New Testament Church* (Present Testimony Ministry, 2001), p. 185.

[55] Ibid., pp. 185-87.

Chapter 9
Israel as a
Light to the Nations

A number of scholars are reticent to find any emphasis on "mission" in the Old Testament. According to Eckhard Schnabel, for example, the universalistic dimension of Israel's faith provides the salvation-historical foundation for early Christian mission and illuminates its structure. But it "cannot be identified with mission in the sense of an active endeavor of Israelite or Jewish messengers who seek to win non-Israelites or non-Jews to faith in YHWH and for integration into Israel."[1]   Others, however, see a focus in the Old Testament involving a mission of the people of God that is directed towards others who are not a part of the community of faith. It may be present in rudimentary form, since God's universal plan for the salvation of the world is not always plainly perceived by God's people as it progressively unfolds in the course of human history. But it is there nonetheless.[2] The purpose of this chapter is to show that the development of Israel's missionary mandate is highlighted in five passages (or groups of passages) which describe: (1) God's covenant with Abraham (Gen. 12:1-3, 18:19); (2) Israel's role as a priestly kingdom and holy nation (Exod. 19:3-6); (3) The Law and Israel's witness among the nations (Deut. 4:32-40); (4) Israel as a "royal priesthood" (II Sam

7:11-17; cf. Ps 2:7-9, 67:1-7, 72:11-17, 96:2-9); and (5) Israel as a light to the nations (Isa. 42:6-7, 43:10-12, 49:6).

God's Covenant with Abraham

The universal dimensions of God's mission are explicitly described for the first time in God's covenant with Abraham. In this Great Commission of the Old Testament God says to Abraham: *"Leave your country, your people and your father's household and go to the land I will show you. "* (Gen. 12:1) This imperative to "go" is followed by a series of blessings:

I will make you into a great nation
and I will bless you;
I will make your name great,
and you will be a blessing.
I will bless those who bless you,
and whoever curses you I will curse;
all peoples on earth will be blessed through you.
(12: 2-3)

Walter Kaiser argues that this text provides "the formative theology" for "a divine program to glorify himself by bringing salvation to all on planet earth."[3] While some deny that this text contains anything like a missionary mandate, it should be noted that following this command to go, Abraham built alters and called on the name of the Lord in many of the places where he traveled and lived (Gen. 12:7,8; 13:4, 18; 22:9-12). In this way, he witnessed about his faith in YHWH.[4] Moreover, on two other occasions God repeats his promise that all of the nations will be blessed through Abraham (Gen. 18:18, 22:18). Kaiser stresses that the three-fold promise of blessing in Genesis 12:2 ("I will make you into a great nation;" "I will bless you;" "I will make your name great") is immediately followed by two purpose clauses: *"in order that* you may be a blessing . . *so that* all the peoples on the earth will be blessed through you" (emphasis mine). Abraham and his nation were to be blessed *so that* they might be a channel of blessing to others.[5] Basically, then, the meaning of this passage is that if Abraham does what he is commanded and if God follows through on his promises, the result will be universal blessing.[6]

But what is the nature of this blessing and who will be blessed? The usual interpretation of this passage, of course, is that it refers to God's plan to bless the world through Abraham's progeny out of which would come the promised messiah. And, indeed, this is the meaning that the apostle Paul gives this passage when he describes it as the "gospel in advance" (Gal. 3:8). In addition, Jesus' command in the Great Commission to make disciples "of all nations" (Matt. 28:19) reaffirms God's promise in Gen. 22:18.[7] In the next chapters we will further expand on these allusions to the Old Testament in the New. Ultimately, then, the recipients of blessing are those who place their faith in Christ. However, the text suggests that there is an additional and more proximate focus in God's commission to Abraham. Chris Wright argues that God's command to "go . . . and be a blessing" has an ethical and missional dimension of helping the nations experience "all the good gifts that God longs for people to enjoy in this world."[8] Blessing, in other words, is restorative as well as redemptive. Also, it has both a vertical and horizontal dimension. On the one hand, those who seek to live life in relationship to God are blessed by him (the vertical). On the other hand, there is a relational element as those who are blessed by God reach out to bless those around them (the horizontal).[9] Kevin DeYoung and Greg Gilbert strongly disagree. They maintain that this passage contains neither an imperative to "be a blessing" nor a moral agenda. "The call of Abram is not about a community blessing program." Clearly, they continue, this "is a glorious mission text announcing God's plans to bless the whole world. But the blessing is not something we bestow on others as we work for human flourishing."[10]

My own view is closer to Wright's. The parallels between God's commission to Abraham and his commission to Adam are too obvious to ignore. Numerous commentators have noticed that Adam's commission to "be fruitful and multiply and fill the earth" (Gen. 1:28) is passed on to Abraham and his descendants, who are to multiply "as the stars of the heavens." (Gen. 22:17, 26:3, 26:4, 28:3, 35:11-12). Beale argues on the basis of Genesis 1:26-28 that "the presence of God . . . was to be extended throughout the whole earth by his image bearers, as they themselves represented and reflected his glorious presence and attributes." This goal of spreading the glorious presence of God "would occur especially by Adam's progeny born in his image and thus reflecting God's image and the light of his presence as they continued to obey the mandate given to their parents . . ."[11] Adam, however, failed to obey God. So, God raised up other Adam-like figures to whom his commission is passed on.[12] From this perspective, we can agree with Wright that Abraham and his descendants were also to be a blessing in the sense that they would be an *example*, or witness—religiously, morally, and ethically—to all the peoples of the earth. Abraham was chosen to be a teacher of righteousness and justice, a role that was to be passed on to his descendants. In this sense, he was a model of God's mission in the world.[13]

This is brought out most forcefully in Genesis 18:19 where Abraham is contrasted with the wickedness of Sodom and Gomorrah. These twin cities are the prototype of a fallen and sinful world that stands under God's judgment. But, contrary to popular perceptions, the sin of Sodom was not limited to sexual immorality. As Ezekiel clearly states, its people were "arrogant, overfed and unconcerned; they did not help the poor and the needy." (Ezekiel 18:49). The suffering of some people in or near Sodom was so great that they cried out in pain against its oppression and cruelty (Gen. 18:20-21).[14] In this context, God describes his covenant with Abraham:

> *For I have chosen him, so that he will direct his children and his household after him to keep the way of the Lord by doing what is right and just,* **so that** *the Lord will bring about for Abraham what he has promised for him"* (Gen. 18:19, emphasis mine).

In this passage, the fulfillment of God's promise to Abraham of blessing the nations is conditional upon doing what is right and just, or following "the way of the Lord." As we have seen, the Hebrew word for "just" means, in the broadest sense, to intervene in a situation that is wrong, oppressive, or out of control, and fix it. In the midst of a world characterized by evil and suffering, God wanted a nation distinguished by his own ethical and religious priorities—in this way it would fulfill his promise of being a blessing to the nations.[15] The logic and syntax of Genesis 18:19 combine election, ethics, and mission. "The ethical quality of life of the people of God is the vital link between their calling and their mission. There is no mission without ethics."[16]

Israel's Role as a Priestly Kingdom and Holy Nation

The next passage of importance for our discussion is Exodus 19:3-6, which describes the inauguration of the Sinaitic covenant and describes the chosen people of Israel as a priestly kingdom and a holy nation. Again, there are differences of opinion on the missionary significance of this text. Referring to the description of Israel as "a kingdom of priests," (v. 6) Kaiser states "It is here that Israel's missionary role became explicit, if any doubt had remained."[17] Wright similarly argues that, "this conception of national priesthood has an essentially missional dimension" and gives Israel "the priestly function of being the agent of blessing."[18] Schnabel, however, maintains that the focus of Exodus 19 is on the relationship between the chosen people and YHWH and that the reference to Israel as a "priestly kingdom" simply means that the people of Israel have a unique access to him as only priests can be close to YHWH.[19]

This passage, however, must be read within the context of the book of Exodus as a whole. God's promise to Abraham is reaffirmed to Moses (Exod. 3:6-8, 6:2-8) who leads the Israelites out of captivity in Egypt. The purpose of the ten plagues in Egypt and the crossing of the Red Sea was not just to demonstrate the impotence of the Egyptian gods (Exod. 12:12) but also to help "the Egyptians to know" that the God of Israel was the Lord (Exod. 7:5, 17, 8:22, 14:4,18).[20] It is also in Exodus that the clan becomes the covenant people of God. Expression such as "Yahweh's people," "your people," or "my people" occur for the first time (Exod. 3:7, 15:16; Num. 11:29).[21] Exodus 19:4-6 is therefore a key programmatic statement of God that serves as a "hinge" between the Exodus narrative (Exod. 1-18) and the giving of the law and covenant (Exod. 20-24).[22]

The overall structure of this passage is also important in determining its meaning. There are two parts to this text—God's redemptive action (19:4) and Israel's response (19:5-6):

Figure 11. Structure of Exodus 19:4-6

God's Redemptive Action (19:4)	Israel's Response (19:5-6)

• You have seen what I have done
• How I carried you on eagle's wings. . .
• *Now therefore. . .*
	• *If* you will obey me fully
	• You will be
	  o a treasured possession
	  o a priestly kingdom
	  o a holy nation

The description of Israel as being transported on eagle's wings followed by the words "now therefore" supplies the *motive and rationale* for what follows. Because of God's gracious act of deliverance of the Israelites from Egypt, they were to obey him fully and fulfill their covenantal obligations. Israel is then given three specific ministries, all of which are conditional on covenantal obedience: (1) to be God's *treasured possession*; (2) to serve as a *kingdom of priests*; and (3) to be a *holy nation*.[23] Closer examination of each of these descriptive phrases indicates the "missionary" nature of Israel's role as a nation.[24] First, the Hebrew word that is translated "special possession" refers to valuables of any kind (i.e., jewels) or moveable goods that were not attached to the land. The implication is that Israel was to be like a treasure that God could move around and disperse as he pleased. Second, the accompanying phrase "out of all nations" (v. 5) indicates both God's universal scope and interest in all nations as well as the uniqueness of Israel relative to all other nations. "The effect of this double affirmation is that Israel is going to live on a very open stage. There will be nothing cloistered or closeted about Israel's existence or history."[25]

Third, the function of the Levitical priest was to serve as a mediator between God and the Israelites. In the same way, Israel as a "priestly nation" was to adopt a mediatorial role in the midst of the nations. DeYoung and Gilbert object to the view that Israel was to mediate God's blessing to the nations as a kind of "incarnational presence," since the primary function of the priests in administering sacrifices was to placate God's anger.[26] However, the priests also had the function of teaching the law (Lev. 10:11; Deut. 33:10; Jer. 18:18; Mal. 2:6-7; Hos. 4:1-9) and blessing the people in the name of YHWH (Num. 6:22-27). The phrase "kingdom of priests" points to Israel's missionary role *as a whole community*. So, this passage indicates that the *whole nation* was to function as a mediator of God's will, moral and ethical demands, and saving purpose to the surrounding nations.[27]

Finally, the description of Israel as a "holy nation" further highlights Israel's ethical distinctiveness and call to service. As in the Abrahamic covenant, this aspect of Israel's calling has both a vertical and horizontal dimension. Vertically, it signified that Israel was ethically distinctive and given wholly to God as a nation. This idea of being "set apart" is emphasized in Leviticus 20:26: "You are to be holy to me because I, the Lord, am holy, and I have set you apart from the nations to be my own." We have seen that "being holy as God is holy" (Lev. 19:2) involved more than correctness in religious ritual. It also meant living with integrity, righteousness, and justice in every area of life. But, as a holy nation, Israel was "set apart" for a purpose and for God's use—to serve other nations. Putting it all together, then, "Israel's *identity* (to be a priestly kingdom) declares a *mission*, and Israel's *mission* demands an ethic (to be a holy nation)."[28]

The Law and Israel's Witness among the Nations

One of the reasons given for the view that Israel does not have a missionary call or vision is that such a task is not specified or elaborated in the Mosaic Law.[29] In this vein, Schnabel writes:

> If Ex 19:6 formulates a missionary task for Israel among non-Israelites, this task, formulated in the context of the inauguration of the Sinaitic covenant, would be a fundamental obligation, and we would be justified to expect that this task is specified and elaborated in the Sinaitic law. However, the Sinaitic law contains neither individual stipulations for a "missionary" activity of Israel, which would be indispensible in the context of the Holiness Code, nor stipulations that regulate the entry of pagans into God's people.[30]

The assumption, here, is that "missionary activity" consists of the type of evangelism that Christians usually have in mind—that is, going outside one's boarders and preaching. In other words, was Israel's witnessing active or passive? Did they go to foreign countries and speak about their God and his love for the nations? It is true that there are only a few examples of this type of active witness in the Old Testament.[31] But their importance cannot be discounted. The most dramatic instance of missionary activity in this sense is the story of Jonah. The emphasis of this entire book is on the universality of God's salvation and his love for all, even for the enemies of his people (Jonah 3:1-10, 4:6-11).[32] Daniel has been described as another "foreign missionary." Through his witness and that of his three friends, Nebuchadnezzar, the king of Babylon, was converted to faith in the Most High God (Dan. 4). Daniel also witnessed to the last Babylonian king, Belshazzar (Dan. 5), to Darius the Mede and high Medo-Persian officials (Dan. 6) and possibly also to Cyrus (Dan.

1:21, 6:28, 10:1).[33] One of the most celebrated stories of Gentile conversion in the Old Testament is the healing of Namaan, the commander of the army of Syria (II Kings 5:1-19). He is introduced to the God of Israel through the initiative and witness of a young Israelite girl who was in captivity in Syria. Following his healing through the prophet Elisha he refers to God as "Yahweh" (the name reserved only for those who had a personal relationship with him) and speaks of making a "burnt offering" to him. Elisha's response ("go in peace") indicates that Namaan's new-found faith, however imperfect, was genuine (vss. 15-19).

These and other "missionary" narratives in the Old Testament make it clear that God's mission in the Old Testament was not limited to Israel or exclusively Jewish.[34] However, the emphasis of the Old Testament—and Mosaic Law in particular—is that the people of God were to be an "object lesson" or a living example to other people and nations of God's grace. It is important to keep in mind that the pentateuchal law functioned as an expression of God's grace and provided a framework by which the people responded to God's acts of redemption. The Ten Commandments were placed in the tabernacle as a "testimony" or "witness" to God's saving acts—not only their deliverance from Egypt (Exod. 20:2) but also of his presence with and providential care of them in the wilderness. Israel, in turn, was to bear witness to God's saving presence and be a "testimony" of his truth to the nations, both verbally and by obeying his Law.[35] This link between obedience and witness to God's presence and the wisdom and righteousness of his Law is evident in these words of Moses to the Israelites:

> *See I have taught you decrees and laws as the Lord my God commanded me, so that you may follow them in the land you are entering to take possession of it. Observe them carefully, for this will show your wisdom and understanding to the nations, who will hear about these decrees and say, "Surely this great nation is a wise and understanding people." What other nation is so great as to have their gods near them the way the Lord our God is near us whenever*

we pray to him? And what other nation is so great as to have such righteous decrees and laws as this body of laws I am setting before you today? (Deut. 4:5-8)

The same linkage between obedience to the law and missional witness is expressed in Deut. 28:10 where the Israelites are told:

The Lord will establish you as his holy people . . . if you keep the commands of the Lord your God and walk in his ways. Then all the peoples of the earth will see that you are called by the name of the Lord, and they will fear you.

The Monarchy and Israel as a "Royal Priesthood"

During the monarchial period the three institutions of prophet, temple (including the priesthood), and king were given by God to help the nation of Israel fulfill its calling as a priestly kingdom in its relationship to surrounding nations.[36] In II Samuel 7:11-17 God promises David that an eternal kingdom would come from his offspring or "seed." This is part of God's universal plan to bring salvation to all nations through Israel. Two missionary Psalms (67 and 96) eloquently express this universal mission.[37] Both Psalms focus on God's promise to bless all nations through Abraham. Psalm 67 takes the Aaronic benediction of Num. 6:24-26 (which invokes God's blessing on the nation of Israel) and applies it to all the peoples and nations on the earth. There are two other noteworthy features of this Psalm. First, instead of using the name Lord or YHWH (which denotes a covenantal and personal relationship to God) it uses the name *elohim*, which expresses God's relationship to all peoples, nations, and creation. Furthermore, this Psalm makes it clear that the purpose for enlarging this blessing is "that your (i.e., God's) ways might be known on the earth, that your (i.e., God's) salvation among all nations" (vs 2). Psalm 96, which is the only Psalm to use the verb "proclaim" or "declare," similarly calls believers to "proclaim [God's] salvation day after day, his glory among the nations, his marvelous deeds among all peoples . . ." (vss 2-3). George Peters notes that there are over 175 references in the Psalms of a universalistic nature relating to the nations.[38]

The kings of Israel were to help fulfill Israel's missional identity and role in two ways.[39] First, they were to defeat idolatrous nations, foster righteousness and justice, and promote temple life. In accordance with God's covenant with David, the kings were expected to lead the nation of Israel in bearing "testimony" to the Law and all that it represented.[40] Secondly, the kings were to be a symbol of the future universal and gracious rule of God over Israel and all nations. This is made explicit in Isaiah 55:4-6, where God says that he had made David "a witness to the peoples." In the same vein, Psalm 72 indicates that the Abrahamic blessing will be extended to all nations through the rule of a king in the line of David: "All the nations will be blessed through him and they will call him blessed" (v 17).

Likewise, the temple was a symbol of Israel's task to expand God's presence to all the nations.[41] The geographic location of Israel—being at the crossroads of Middle East international routes between Egypt and Assyria or Babylon—was significant in this regard. The prophets envision the temple in Jerusalem as a "mega-world center" of worship of the one true God (Isa. 2:2-4).[42] In his prayer of dedication for the temple, King Solomon echoes this theme when he asks God, not only to hear the prayers of the Israelites but also that he would respond to the prayers of foreigners who are drawn to the temple "so that all of the peoples of the earth may know your name and fear you . . . and may know that this house I have built bears your name" (I Kings 8:27-30, 41-43). Solomon indicates this larger missional purpose for building the temple in a letter to Hiram, the King of Tyre (II Chr. 2:3-6) who then replies with words of praise to the Lord for his righteous acts on behalf of Israel: "Because the Lord loves his people, he has made you their king . . . Praise be to the Lord, the God of Israel, who made heaven and earth!" (II Chr. 2:11-12).

The Prophets and Israel as a Light to the Nations

Israel, of course, failed miserably in its mission. The people as a whole did not live up to the standards of the Mosaic covenant and successive kings of both Israel and Judah failed to uphold the ideals of the Law. In this context, God inaugurates a new covenant through his prophets. It is the prophetic vision of this new covenant that serves as a bridge between the status of the Law in the Old Testament and its significance in the New. Isaiah and the other prophets make it clear that this "new covenant" would consist of a new relationship with God (Jer. 31:33, 32:38-40; Ezek. 37:23,27; Isa. 54:5-10), a new experience of forgiveness (Ezek. 36:25, 37:23) and a new obedience to the Law (Jer. 31:33). In Jeremiah the new covenant is described in terms of a "new heart:"

> *I will give them a heart to know that I am the Lord; and they shall be*
> *my people and I will be their God, for they shall turn to me with their*
> *whole heart (Jer. 24:7)*

In this new covenantal relationship God will write the law on people's hearts (Jer. 31:33) rather than on stone tablets. Ezekiel further describes this "heart transplant" in terms of transformation through God's spirit:

> *A new heart I will give you and a new spirit I will put within you; and I*
> *will remove from your body the heart of stone and give you a heart of*
> *flesh. I will put my spirit within you, and make you follow my statutes*
> *and be careful to observe my ordinances (Ezek. 36:26-27).*

Chapters 40-55 of Isaiah are especially important in bringing out the scope of the new covenant. Isaiah 42:1-4 describes it in terms of the coming of the "Servant of God" who will fulfill the role and mission of Israel and "bring justice to the nations:"

> *Here is my servant who I uphold,*
> *my chosen one in whom I delight;*

> *I will put my spirit upon him*
> *and he will bring justice to the nations . . .*
> *In faithfulness he will bring forth justice;*
> *he will not falter or be discouraged*
> *until he establishes justice on earth*

In Isaiah 42:6 this servant of YHWH is described as a "covenant for the people." This phrase is to be understood through its parallelism with the next phrase "light for the nations," which is repeated in Isaiah 49:6 and explicated in terms of YHWH's salvation "going to the ends of the earth."[43] Here, Isaiah looks forward to a *restored* and *reconstituted* Israel that would be the agent of God's universal saving purpose:

> *It is too small a thing for you to be my servant*
> *to restore the tribes of Jacob*
> *and to bring back those of Israel I have kept.*
> *I will also make you a light for the Gentiles,*
> *that you may bring my salvation to*
> *the ends of the earth*

The call of the "true Israel" to be a "witness" is made explicit in Isaiah 44:8 where the Israelites are told "Do not tremble, do not be afraid. Did I not proclaim this and foretell it long ago? You are to be my witnesses." And again in Isaiah 43:10-12 the prophet states:

> *You are my witnesses, declares the Lord*
> *and my servant who I have chosen,*
> *so that you may know and believe me*
> *and understand that I am he.*
> *Before me no god was formed*
> *nor will there be one after me.*
> *I, even I, am the Lord,*
> *and apart from me there is no savior.*
> *I have revealed and saved and proclaimed—*

I, am not some foreign god among you.
"You are my witnesses," declares the Lord, "that I am God."

In these passages the designation of Israel as a "witness" becomes a link between its election as a particular people and its mission to declare God's saving purpose, which is universal in scope.[44]   Chris Wright states: "This eschatological and universalizing development of the covenant trajectory through the Old Testament story is what leads directly to the missionally charged language of fulfillment in the New."[45]

Conclusion

Richard Backham suggests that this development of Israel's mission is best understood in terms of a movement of the biblical narrative from the particular to the universal.[46] This movement from the one to the many can be described in terms of three interrelated "thematic trajectories." There is the singling out of Abraham, followed by Israel and then David.   Abraham is chosen precisely that he might be a blessing to the nations—a promise that is repeated four times in Genesis (18:18, 22:18, 26:4, 28:14). The Abrahamic call to "go . . . and be a blessing" has double focus, in that it both foreshadows the ultimate blessing to all nations through God's redeemer (salvation) and involves a conditional command to faithfully reflect God's religious and ethical priorities *among* the nations.   In the second thematic trajectory God reveals himself to the nations through the nation of Israel.   In both the Sinaitic (Exod. 19:4-6) and Deuteronomic (Deut. 4:5-8, 28:10) covenants God's acts of deliverance on behalf of his people are at the same time a universal self-revelation of his sovereign will and purpose.   By living as a society in conformity with the demands of the Law, Israel is to function as a servant nation representing God and his character before all the nations of the world.[47] The third trajectory moves from God's enthronement of David to the coming of God's universal rule over all of creation.[48] The Old Testament is highly ambivalent about earthly kings.   Israel's kings are often portrayed as corrupt, tyrannical and oppressive and objects of censor by Israel's prophets.   At the same time, the Davidic king is the earthly representative of God's rule of justice. Both the Psalms and the prophets express the hope of a truly ideal ruler from the seed of David who will bring salvation to the nations and fully embody God's rule of righteousness and justice.

The chart below summarizes this development of Israel's mission in terms of the four elements of "commission," "agent(s)," "task," and "result/goal:"

Figure 12. Summary of Mission in the Old Testament

	Abrahamic Covenant (Gen. 12:1-3; 18:9)	Covenant with Israel (Ex. 19: 4-6)	Law and Israel's Witness (Deut. 4:5-8; 28:10)	Israel as Royal Priesthood (Monarchy)	Israel as Light to the Nations (Prophets)
Commission	"Go... and be a blessing."	"You have seen... therefore, if... you will be..."	"Observe [the law]... so that they will know..."	The Davidic covenant & promise of God's universal rule	"New covenant" with restored & reconstituted Israel
Agent(s)	Abraham & his descendants	Israel as a "people of God."	Israel as a society (social, economic, legal, political and religious)	Institutions of prophet, temple (priest) and king	Righteous remnant, the eschatological people of God
Task	Ethical and missional	Priestly kingdom and holy nation	Ethical example and witness to God's law	Proclaim God's salvation, glory and marvelous deeds (Ps. 96:2-3)	Witness and light to the nations
Result/ Goal	Universal blessing	Israel as God's people on behalf of all nations	"All the peoples of the earth will see..."	Future universal and everlasting kingdom	New creation & God's glory

We can conclude, then, that a recurrent theme in the Old Testament is that the universality of God's purposes embraces the particularity of his chosen means. The redemptive dimension of Israel's election centers on the fact that Israel was chosen for the sake of other nations.[49] We have seen that the Old Testament contains stories of active witness. But Israel's primary mission among the nations was to *be* something, not to go somewhere.[50] This is the ethical dimension of Israel's visibility among the nations. As Chris Wright states: "The question of Israel's ethical obedience or ethical failure was not merely a matter between themselves and Yahweh, but was of major significance in relation to Yahweh's agenda for the nations (cf. Jer. 4:1-2)."[51]

All of this raises the question of the relationship between Israel's mission and the mission of the church. On the one hand, there is continuity between the two. As the Messiah spoken of in the Old Testament, Jesus both embodies the election of Israel and fulfills the prophetic expectations that the Servant of God would bring the blessings of salvation, justice and glory to the ends of the earth. Jesus gives a mission to the church which is rooted in his own identity and Spirit. Wright points out that the continuity between Israel and the church as the new "people of God" is evident in the fact that Jesus' words to his disciples "You are my witnesses" (Acts 1:8) is almost certainly intended by Luke to be an echo of the same words spoken by Yahweh to Israel in Isaiah 43:10-12.[52] As previously mentioned, there is also the obvious parallel between God's promise to Abraham that through his offspring "all nations on earth" will be blessed (Gen. 18:18, 22:19) and Jesus' command to make disciples "of all nations" (Matt. 28:19). God's command to the Israelites to walk in his ways therefore has paradigmatic significance for followers of Christ who have inherited the same role in relation to the nations and are also described as a royal priesthood and a holy nation (I Peter 2:9). "In the Old as well as the New Testament, the ethical demand on those who claim to be God's people is determined by the mission with which they have been entrusted."[53]

But there are also some important differences between Israel's mission and that of the church. Israel's missionary significance lay primarily (though not exclusively) in *centripetal* categories—with the nations coming *towards* Israel as an attractional force. Israel's role of being a witness to the nations is not understood in the New Testament sense of bringing the message of Yahweh to the nations but "in the sense of being a people of God whose life shall inquire after Yahweh" (cf. Isa. 43: 10-11).[54] This is why the temple, Jerusalem, and Zion are given central roles in universalistic passages in the Old Testament. In Isaiah, for example, the eschatological picture is one of all nations streaming to the temple in Zion and kings bringing the "wealth of the nations" to Jerusalem (Isa. 2:2, 60:11). The concept of outward *centrifugal* movement or expansion is not entirely absent, as we see in the book of Jonah. But even Jonah has a difficult time comprehending that God's love and mercy extends to nations beyond the borders of Israel—especially those that are its sworn enemies (Jonah 3:10-4:11).

By the time of Jesus, the more exclusivistic strands of Judaism had hardened into ardent nationalism. Although some non-establishment Jews engaged in missional outreach to foreigners,[55] the religious establishment practiced an exclusionary version of Judaism that centered on oral traditions and distinctive markers of Jewish identity. After years of subjugation under Roman rule, the Israelites looked forward to the coming of a messiah who would "trample" the Gentiles, and "dash them to pieces like pottery with a rod of iron," not one who would bring salvation to the gentile nations. Forgetting the message of the prophets that Israel's salvation is to take place in the last days *for the sake of* the nations, they looked "instead to an apocalyptic future of salvation and blessing for gathered Israel alone—and vengeance and wrath for the Gentiles."[56] It is in this historical context that we must understand both Jesus' mission and his Great Commission to the church.

Notes

1 Eckhard J. Schnabel, *Early Christian Mission, Vol. I: Jesus and the Twelve* (Downers Grove, IL: InterVarsity, 2004), p. 60.
2 See Jiri Moskala, "The Mission of God's People in the Old Testament," *Journal of the Adventist Theological Society* 19/1-2 (2008), pp. 41-3.
3 Walter C. Kaiser Jr., *Mission in the Old Testament: Israel as a Light to the Nations* (Grand Rapids, MI: Baker, 2000), p. 13.
4 Moskala, "The Mission of God's People in the Old Testament," p. 46. Beale argues that these shrines of worship or informal sanctuaries constructed by Abraham and the other patriarchs in Genesis "pointed to Israel's later tabernacle and temple from which Israel was to branch out over all the earth . . . This pilgrim-like activity 'was like planting a flag and claiming the land' for God and Israel's future temple, where God would take up his permanent residence in the capital of that land." *The Temple and the Church's Mission*, pp. 97-9.
5 Kaiser, *Mission in the Old Testament*, p.18. See also Walter C. Kaiser Jr., "Israel's Missionary Call," in *Perspectives on the World Christian Movement: A Reader*, ed., Ralph D. Winter and Steven C. Hawthorne (Pasadena, CA: William Carey Library, 2000), p. 12.
6 Wright, *The Mission of God*, p. 201. Wright points out that, grammatically, there are two imperative verbs in this passage: "go" (v. 1) and "be a blessing" (vs. 2b). "However, it is a feature of Hebrew. . . that when two imperatives occur together the second imperative may sometimes express either the expected result or the intended purpose of carrying out the first imperative. . . Either way, the message of the combined halves of the text clearly is that if Abraham does what he is told, and if God does what he says he will do, the result will be blessing all round."
7 Beale, *The Temple and the Church's Mission*, p. 175.
8 Wright, *The Mission of God*, p. 221.
9 Ibid., pp. 208-15. See also Wright, *The Mission of God's People*, pp. 67-68.
10 DeYoung and Gilbert, *What is the Mission of the Church?*, 31-3.
11 Beale, *The Temple and the Church's Mission*, op. cit., pp. 83-4.
12 Ibid., p. 93.
13 Wright, *The Mission of God*, p. 358.
14 Ibid. p. 359.
15 Ibid., p 366.
16 See Chris Wright, "The Old Testament and Christian Mission," *Evangel* (Summer 1996), p. 40.
17 Kaiser, "Israel's Missionary Call," p. 13.
18 Wright, *The Mission of God*, p. 331.
19 Schnabel, *Early Christian Mission*, Vol., 1, p. 71. Kevin DeYoung and Greg Gilbert employ Schnabel's arguments to support their view that this passage has no missional significance. See *What is the Mission of the Church?*," pp. 34-6.
20 Moskala, "The Mission of God's People in the Old Testament," pp. 47-8.
21 See John Goldingay, *Theological Diversity and the Authority of the Old Testament* (Grand Rapids, MI: Eerdmans, 1987), p. 64.

---

[22] Wright, *The Mission of God*, p. 330.

[23] See Kaiser, *Mission in the Old Testament*, cit., pp. 22-3,

[24] These points are taken largely from Kaiser, *Mission in the Old Testament*, pp. 22-3 and "God's Missionary Call," pp. 13-14; Wright, *The Mission of God*, pp. 329-33; 369-75; and Wright, *Walking in the Ways of the Lord*, p. 135.

[25] Wright, *The Mission of God*, p. 371.

[26] DeYoung and Gilbert, *What is the Mission of the Church?*, p. 35.

[27] There are two New Testament passages which further support this interpretation of Israel's priestly role. In a passage to which we have already alluded, Peter makes obvious reference to this Old Testament text when he describes the church as "royal priesthood" and "holy nation," *so that* "you may declare the praises of him who called you out of darkness into his wonderful light." (I Peter 2:9). Peter's use of this Old Testament text to engage his readers in ethical conduct and missionary witness indicates that he saw the Israel's role in the same light and regarded the church's mission as in continuity with the mission given to Israel. The apostle Paul also describes his missionary activity in *priestly and mediatorial* terms when he states that it is his "priestly duty" to bring the gospel to the Gentiles so that they might become an offering acceptable to God (Rom. 15:16).

[28] Wright, *The Mission of God*, p. 375.

[29] See DeYoung and Gilbert, *What is the Mission of the Church?*, p. 35

[30] Schnabel, *Early Christian Missions, Vol. 1*, pp. 71-2.

[31] Moskala, "The Mission of God's People in the Old Testament," p. 48.

[32] See Kaiser, *Mission in the Old Testament*, op. cit., pp. 69-71.

[33] See Moskala, "The Mission of God's People in the Old Testament," p. 50.

[34] Kaiser, *Mission in the Old Testament*, p. 49.

[35] See Moskala, "The Mission of God's People in the Old Testament," p. 55; and Beale, *The Temple and the Church's Mission*, p. 119.

[36] See Gohen, *A Light to the Nations*, pp. 54-60.

[37] Moskala, "The Mission of God's People in the Old Testament," p. 51-2.

[38] George W. Peters, *A Biblical Theology of Missions* (Chicago, IL: Moody Press, 1972), p. 116.

[39] Gohen, *A Light To the Nations*, p. 56

[40] Beale points out that II Chr. 23:11 says that when Joash was crowned king, they placed the "testimony" in his hands, signifying that he was to uphold the Law and all it stood for; cf. also II Chr. 34:28-33. See The *Temple and the Church's Mission*, p. 120.

[41] Beale, "Eden, the Temple and the Church's Mission," *Journal of the Evangelical Theological Society*, 48/1 (March 2005), p. 19.

[42] Moskala, "The Mission of God's People in the Old Testament," pp. 50-1.

[43] Wright, *The Mission of God*, p. 352.

[44] For as discussion of Isaiah 40-55 as depicting the restoration of the people of God see David W. Pao, *Acts and the Isaianic New Exodus* (Grand Rapids, MI: Baker Academic, 2000), pp. 45-59; 111-46.

[45] Wright, *The Mission of God*, p. 352

[46] See Richard Bauckham, *Bible and Mission: Christian Witness in a Postmodern World* (Grand Rapids, MI: Baker Academic, 2003); and "Revealing God's Character to the Nations," (http://theology.drvinson.net /ot/insights/revealing-god).

[47] See Michael Grisanti, "Israel's Mission to the Nations in Isaiah 40-55: An Update," *The Master's Seminary Journal* 9/1 (Spring 1998), p. 40.

[48] Baukham, "Israel: Revealing God's Character to the Nations."

[49] See Christopher J. H. Wright, "Truth with a Mission: Reading All Scripture Missiologically," *Southern Baptist Journal of Theology* 15/2 (2011), pp. 9-12.

[50] Ibid., p. 12.

[51] Ibid., p. 13.

[52] Ibid., p. 9-12.

[53] Ibid., p. 13.

[54] Grisanit, "Israel's Mission to the Nations in Isaiah 40-55," p. 62.

[55] See Glasser, *Announcing the Kingdom*, pp. 174-76.

[56] Goheen, *A Light to the Nations*, pp. 71-2.

Chapter 10
Jesus' Mission and
the Great Commission

I. Howard Marshall has argued that the theology of the New Testament springs out of the missionary movement of the early church. Theology, in turn, shapes the continuing mission of the church.[1] Moreover, the New Testament writers saw themselves as heirs of the religion expressed in the Old Testament and in continuity with the people who worshipped the God of Abraham, Isaac, and Jacob.[2] The identity of the early Christian movement and its mission was not shaped in a theological vacuum. Pre-eminently, it was a product of its interaction with and experience of salvation through the risen Christ. But, in a very real sense, the early believers also interpreted their identity and experience with God through the Holy Spirit as a mirror reflection of Old Testament prophecies regarding the restoration of Israel. On the one hand, they saw their experience as a direct though partial fulfillment of God's promises to the faithful remnant of Israel. At the same time, they interpreted Old Testament prophecies in light of that experience.

My purpose in the next three chapters, then, will be to examine how Jesus' mission and the mission of the early church are both rooted in and expand on the Old Testament themes of promise and fulfillment. Since space does not permit a detailed exposition of mission in the New Testament, my purpose, again, will be to focus on some key "programmatic" texts. This chapter will focus on Jesus' understanding of his mission and how he defined the mission of his disciples as recorded in the gospels. We will look at two familiar missional statements by Jesus: (1) his announcement of his earthly ministry in Luke 4:16-21; and (2) his giving of the Great Commission to his disciples as described in Matthew's gospel (Matt. 28:16-20; cf. Mark 13:10; Luke 24:44-49).

Some Preliminary Considerations

At the outset, I should explain why I have chosen to focus on these two texts. First, over the past two hundred years or so, the Protestant missionary enterprise has appealed to Matthew's version of the Great Commission to support global missions outreach. This passage in Matthew is therefore a key mission text. Unfortunately, because it is generally lifted out of its Matthean context, it is also often been misunderstood. Jesus' announcement of his ministry as recorded in Luke (4:16-21) is obviously important in its own right for understanding his earthly mission. But Luke's account is also significant because of its connection to the book of Acts as the first of a two-part volume. As Bosch points out in his magisterial survey of mission in the New Testament, Luke intentionally structured his two volumes in the way he did to demonstrate the essential unity between Jesus' mission and the mission of the early church.[3] This is obviously important to our survey.

Before delving into the meaning of these two passages, however, it is important to set them within the context of the message of the gospels as a whole. In his ground-breaking work *How God Became King: The Forgotten Story of the Gospels*, N.T. Wright argues that the usual "orthodox" interpretation of the gospels is characterized by the "missing middle." That is, in many classic Christian circles, including those that go broadly under the name "evangelical," the focus is on the birth, death, and resurrection of Christ with relatively little attention given (except for some select passages) to the middle part between these two book-ends.[4] Partly in reaction to this trend, others with a more liberal bent have privileged the middle part of the gospels—the stories of Jesus' care for the poor, the sick, the weak—and screened out the "odd supernatural stuff" at either end.[5] Both of these reductionist approaches to the gospels have resulted in a distorted understanding of what they are all about. Most importantly, there has occurred a split between the "cross" and the "kingdom." Those who emphasize the cross focus on the ancient creeds as well as the "gospel" of forgiveness of sins through Jesus' death and "sola fide" (faith alone) in Christ as the basis for "going to heaven." On the other hand, those who emphasize the "kingdom" often espouse a "social gospel" which focuses on Jesus' ethical teaching and holds him up as an example of how one ought to live. "We have lived for many years now with 'kingdom Christians' and 'cross Christians' in opposite corners of the room, anxious that those on the other side are missing the point, the one group with its social-gospel agenda and the other with its saving-souls-for-heaven agenda."[6] But the reality, Wright argues, is that both kingdom and cross are part of one another and are part of a larger whole (which includes the incarnation and resurrection). The writers of all four gospels bring kingdom and cross together into a unity that is greater than the sum of its parts.[7]

So, how do the gospels bring kingdom and cross together? To employ the title of Wright's book, they are the story of *how God became king on earth as in heaven. In other words, the story of the gospels is how Jesus who embodied the living God of Israel inaugurated the kingdom of God through his ministry and especially through the cross and resurrection.*[8] This is why, in Matthew's Gospel, the resurrected Christ triumphantly declares: "All authority in heaven *and on earth* has been given to me" (Matt. 28:18). The early Christian writers believed that the new creation has begun, though it will be completed and fully implemented in the future. "Jesus is ruling over that new creation and making it happen through the witness of his church."[9]

Wright invites us to see that there are four dimensions (which he compares to four speakers) to this unity of cross and kingdom. The first dimension is that *the story of Jesus is the completion of the story of Israel.*[10] In Jesus' time, the Old Testament hope in the restoration of Israel found expression in the ministry of John the Baptist. The angel, who announces John's conception, describes this ministry in terms of turning people's heart to the "wisdom of righteousness" (Luke 1:16). In the book of Matthew, John's prophetic ministry of calling people to repentance "for the kingdom of God is near" is described as a fulfillment of Isaiah's words:

> *The voice of one calling in the desert:*
> *"Prepare the way of the Lord."*
> *(Matt. 3:3; Isa. 40:3; cf. Mal. 3:1; Mark 1:2)*

Jesus uses this same Isaianic terminology in describing John's ministry as one of showing people "the way of righteousness" (Matt. 21:32; cf. Isa. 40:14). In accepting John's baptism and endorsing his message, Jesus makes it clear that he "saw his own mission in terms of the fulfillment of the great expectations of the restoration of Israel. If John was the one who had been sent to prepare Israel for its eschatological restoration by God himself, then Jesus was the one who had been sent to accomplish it."[11]

It is no accident that the words of Jesus as he hung on the cross ("My God, my God, why have you forsaken me") that are recorded by Matthew (27:46) and Mark (15:34) are the opening words of Psalm 22. This Psalm moves from intense suffering of the suffering servant to a celebration of God's victory and kingdom:

> *All the ends of the earth will remember*
> *and turn to the Lord,*
> *and all the families of the nations*

will bow down before him,
for dominion belongs to the Lord
and he rules over the nations
(Ps. 22:27-28)

"Here the whole sequence is laid out. The sufferer goes all the way down to death, and somehow he is rescued, not only for his own sake, but also so that YHWH'S 'kingdom,' that is, his sovereignty over the nations, might become reality."[12]

Jesus sees this eschatological fulfillment of Israel's hopes as present as well as future. In Matthew's account, following his temptation by Satan in the wilderness, Jesus begins his public ministry with the words "repent, for the kingdom of heaven is near" (Matt. 4:17). In Luke's description of Jesus' "inaugural address," after making reference to Isaiah's prophecy of salvation through the Messiah (Isa. 61:1-2), Jesus announces: "Today this scripture is fulfilled in your hearing" (Luke 4:17). At the same time, Jesus instructs his disciples to pray for the coming of God's kingdom in the future (Matt. 6:9; Luke 11:2) and he gives a parable about a future kingdom feast or banquet to which people in the streets and alleys are invited (Matt. 22:2-14; Luke 14:16-24). The question, of course, is in what sense Jesus affirms the presence of the kingdom, yet also views it as coming in the future.

Michael Goheen rightly observes that there are two aspects to Jesus' teachings concerning the kingdom: (1) It is the *dynamic power* of God that opposes evil in all of its forms (pain, sickness, death, demon-possession, and personal sin); and (2) it is the arrival of *eschatological salvation* or redemption into which people can enter by repentance and faith.[13] Jesus' miracles and exorcisms point to God's kingdom as "already" present. On one occasion, Jesus declares: "If I drive out demons by the finger of God (e.g., the "Spirit of God" in Matt. 12:28) then the Kingdom of God has come to you" (Luke 11:20). In Exodus the "finger of God" is associated with the miracles that were performed by the power of God and which eventually resulted in the release of Israelites from bondage in Egypt (Exod. 8:19). In both gospels, Jesus' announcement of God's reign and his miracles are closely linked. When the twelve disciples are sent on their initial mission (which is a prototype of the church's mission), Jesus instructs them to announce the coming of God's kingdom and to heal the sick (Luke 9:2; Matt. 10:7-8). These two characteristics are combined in Jesus' own ministry (Matt. 9:35). "The reign of God is present in the physical world, not just in the hearts of those who receive him. It is present in the relief of suffering of a physical body."[14] Jesus' miracles also signify the rescue of people from the power of sin and Jesus' authority to forgive sin (Matt. 9:4-6; Luke 4:22-25). Ultimately, then, they point to the supreme miracle of Jesus' death and resurrection, which paves the way for the final exodus, or eschatological redemption.[15]

The second dimension is that *the story of Jesus is the story of Israel's God.*[16] In other words, Jesus is the one through whom Israel's God will accomplish his redemptive purposes for Israel and the whole world. The prophet Ezekiel emphasizes the theme of Israel's redemption in the "shepherd" passage, which speaks of the Lord YHWH searching for his scattered sheep and rescuing them (34:11-12, 23-24, 31). The same prophet describes the divine glory leaving Jerusalem and then returning to a rebuilt temple. Both of these themes are taken up in the gospels—the first in descriptions of Jesus as the "good shepherd" who lays down his life for the sheep (Luke 10:11, 14-16) and the second in John's statement that "the word became flesh" and "tabernacled, made his dwelling among us, and we beheld his glory" (John 1:14). This theme of redemption, of course, is not limited to Israel. As N.T. Wright states, "God is the creator and redeemer of the world and Jesus' launch of the kingdom—God's worldwide sovereignty on earth as in heaven—is the central aim of his mission, the thing for which he lived and died, and rose again."[17] Looking at Matthew and Luke, we can see that there is a difference in emphasis. Matthew focuses on Jesus as teacher, while Luke stresses the blessings of salvation and the positive quality of what Jesus offers. But in both Matthew and Luke (as in the other two gospels) there is a concern with salvation in the broad sense.[18] This is why for Luke, as well as for Matthew, the central thrust of Jesus' message is repentance and forgiveness of sins, which is to be preached to "all nations" (Luke 24:46-49). Jesus' mission cannot be understood apart from the events of Easter through which there is fulfillment of the Old Testament expectation of universal salvation.[19]

The third dimension is *the launching of God's renewed people*.[20] In other words, "Jesus announces his kingdom and summons his followers to share in the work of announcing and inaugurating it."[21] As I have argued previously, this renewed "people of God" is grounded in and in continuity with the people of Israel. Israel is to be fulfilled, not replaced. At the same time, the new community of Jesus' followers is a signpost of the future church.[22] Here, the gospels give prominence to Jesus' ethical teaching and call to discipleship. Jesus calls his followers to a new way of living that is not only possible through God's Spirit but mandatory. Yet, the gospels do not present the kingdom as an ideal social order that is possible through human striving. The ethic of the kingdom is based on the decisive renewing act of God.[23] For example, Jesus' instructions to forgive "seventy-times-seven" (Matt. 18:22), is probably a veiled reference to the year of jubilee according to which debts were to be forgiven every "seven times seven" years. In other words, Jesus is proclaiming a "jubilee of jubilees" and signifying that the new age is here, the age of forgiveness and that his people are to embody it. The cross, which inaugurates the new age, is therefore not *just* about "how to have your sins forgiven." It also furnishes an agenda in which the forgiven people demonstrate to the world a new way of life based on the act of God which ends the reign of sin and death.

This brings us to the fourth dimension in the gospels, *the clash of the kingdoms*. This is evident from Jesus' temptation in the wilderness during which Satan promises Jesus authority over all of the kingdoms of the world if he will only worship him (Luke 4:5-7). In this context, N. T. Wright speaks of the confrontation between God's kingdom and Caesar's kingdom and of the victory of the former over the latter.[24] It is at this point that Wright probably over-reaches in describing the political dimensions of God's kingdom. He seems to come close to a "realized eschatology" when he states: "The establishment of God's kingdom means the dethroning of the world's kingdoms, not in order to replace them with another one of basically the same sort . . . but in order to replace it with one whose power is the power of the servant and whose strength is the strength of love."[25] Nonetheless, he is correct in the sense that Jesus' announcement of God's kingdom represents a "great reversal" of political and social power and "the coming kingdom already made its power felt in Jesus' judgment against the pride of power."[26] Jesus' announcement and inauguration of the kingdom cannot be reduced to a political program. But neither is it politically or socially irrelevant. For it signifies God's cosmic sovereignty and his eventual victory of over all the powers, human and superhuman.

It is from the vantage point of these four dimensions of the relationship between "kingdom" and "cross" in the gospels that we need to approach the two missional statements of Jesus in Matthew and Luke. This is not to say that there are not some important differences between the two gospels. As the chart below indicates, these two gospels reflect significantly different concerns:

Figure 13. Different Emphases of Mathew and Luke

	Disciple (*mathetes*)	Poor (*ptochos*)
Matthew	73	5
Luke	36	10

The concept of "discipleship" is a dominant theme in Matthew, and central to his understanding of the church and mission. The term "disciple" (*mathetes*) is twice as frequent in Matthew as it is in Luke.

More significantly, there are differences in nuances of meaning given to the word. While Luke (as well as Mark) sees the expression "disciples" as applying only to the Twelve, Matthew gives it a much broader meaning and regards the first disciples as prototypes for the church. Hence, Matthew is often referred to as the "gospel for the church."[27] Luke's interest, on the other hand, is in the poor and other marginalized groups of society. This is reflected in the fact that the word poor (*ptochos*) occurs ten times in his gospel compared to five times in Matthew. In addition, other related terms indicating want and need are much more frequent in Luke as are references to the rich. In fact, Luke has been called an "evangelist of the rich" because he "wants the rich and respected to be reconciled to the message and way of life of Jesus and the disciples, he wants to motivate them to a conversion that is in keeping with the social message of Jesus."[28] These differences notwithstanding, Matthew and Luke each in their own way give a picture of Jesus' mission and commission which integrate the four dimensions or themes outlined above. Since, chronologically, Jesus' announcement of his earthly ministry preceded his giving of the Great Commission to his disciples we will look first at the passage in Luke.

Jesus' Announcement of His Earthly Ministry (Luke 4:16-21)

Following his baptism by John (Luke 3:21-22) and his temptation in the wilderness (4:1-13), Jesus is reported by Luke to have come to Nazareth. There on the Sabbath he entered the synagogue and was handed the scroll of the prophet Isaiah, from which he read these words:

The Spirit of the Lord is on me,
because he has anointed me
to preach good news to the poor.
He has sent me to proclaim
freedom for the prisoners
and recovery of sight for the blind,

to release the oppressed,
to proclaim the year of the Lord's favor.
(Luke 4:16-19)

Then Jesus rolled up the scroll and exclaimed: *Today this scripture is fulfilled in your hearing* (vs 21). Luke clearly sees this inaugural sermon as a key to understanding Jesus' ministry. At issue is how to interpret and understand Jesus' reference to preaching good news to the poor (vs. 18) and the subsequent verses.

This question, of course, has been the source of considerable debate. There are two extremes of interpretation. At one extreme there are those who interpret these verses literally as referring to socio-political liberation.[29] Evangelicals who espouse mission as transformation would not go to the extreme of liberation theology, but they do maintain that these verses announce a program for social and political reform. Graham Cray argues that the anointing of God's Spirit on Jesus signifies the inauguration of an era characterized by the forgiveness of sins, physical healing, deliverance from demonic possession, the restoration of liberty, the end of oppression and the initiation of major social and economic reform. God's favor is available to all who respond. But the focus of Jesus' ministry is on the poor. "Preaching is Good News to the poor only if it announces God's active intervention on their behalf to restore justice."[30]

At the opposite extreme are those who tend to spiritualize these verses. According to this interpretation, the poor are the "humble poor" who acknowledge their total dependence upon God. Such poor are often also economically poor, since the materially destitute are generally more apt than the rich to be responsive to God. But the emphasis is on spiritual poverty. In this vein, Kevin DeYoung and Greg Gilbert argue: "Therefore, Jesus' mission laid out in Luke 4 is not a mission of structural change and social transformation, but a mission to announce the good news of his saving power and merciful reign to all those brokenhearted—this is, poor—enough to believe."[31]

Then, there are others who take mediating positions of one form or another. John Yoder, for instance, argues that that the fulfillment Jesus promised was an historical reality, but it was not a social event. Rather, it involved "a visible socio-political, economic restructuring of relations among the people of God, achieved by his intervention in the person of Jesus as the one Anointed and endued with the Spirit."[32]

The great danger in interpreting a text such as this one is that the reader's own social circumstances will influence his/her response to it. As Michael Prior aptly states, "Does one embark on the examination of a text in the hope of having one's own predispositions confirmed, or is one prepared to place oneself under the power of the word of the text if it should invite a radical change of values and lifestyle? To be sensitive to one's own pre-understanding may turn out to be more fundamental to understanding a text than any inquiry into its putative meaning."[33] It is critical, then, that we allow the text to challenge, reshape, correct, and enlarge *our* understanding rather than impose our particular presuppositions on it.[34]

To understand these verses it is necessary to examine: (1) the relationship of Luke 4:16-21 to the gospel as a whole and Luke's primary purpose for writing Luke-Acts; (2) the Old Testament background, particularly of the passages in Isaiah from which this text is taken; and (3) the meaning of "poor" (*ptochos*) and other key terms in this passage, especially in the context of Luke's gospel.

The Purpose of Luke-Acts

Scholars are in general agreement that Luke 4:16-30 is a programmatic text which gives the basic summary outline of Luke's writings as a whole (see chart below). As Walter Pilgrim states: "Jesus is here introducing us to his two volumes and providing us with glasses, as it were, by which we are to read all that follows."[35] This passage introduces in summary fashion a number of themes that Luke develops and which undergird his understanding of the Christian mission: the fulfillment of scriptural promises of salvation in Jesus; good news to the poor; repentance and forgiveness of sins; and salvation for "all nations"—all of which have meaning only in the context of Jesus' death and resurrection as the Messiah.[36]

Figure 14. Luke 4:16-30 as a Programmatic Text

Luke 4:16-30	Theme in Luke-Acts
"Today this Scripture is fulfilled in your hearing." (4:21)	Announcement and fulfillment of God's salvation through Jesus' ministry
". . . he has anointed me to preach good news to the poor. . ." (4:16-19)	Statement of the content of Jesus' ministry based on Isaiah
Two stories of Elijah's and Elisha's ministries to non-Jews (4:24-27)	Movement of the gospel from the Jews to the Gentiles
Jesus' rejection by the people of Nazareth (4:28-30)	Foreshadowing of Jesus' final suffering and rejection

There can be little doubt that salvation and the related themes of repentance and forgiveness are central to Luke's two-part volume. This is evident, first, from his choice of words. The words *soteria* and *soterion* ("salvation") occur six times each in Luke and Acts, while they are not used at all in Matthew and Mark and only once in John. Moreover, in both his gospel and in Acts, Luke gives prominence to the words *metanoeo* ("repent") and *metanoia* ("repentance"), which are also linked closely to *hamartoloi* ("sinners") and *aphesis* ("forgiveness")[37]

Luke's concern with salvation is also apparent from how he structures his work. In his study of Luke, Hans Conzelmann shows that Luke develops the theme of salvation history in terms of three epochs or time periods: (1) the epoch of Israel, up to and including John the Baptist; (2) the epoch of Jesus' ministry; and (3) the epoch of the church, beginning at Pentecost.[38] At both the end of his gospel (24:47-48) and the beginning of Acts (1:8; cf. 2:38-39) Luke's emphasis is that the gospel of repentance and forgiveness should be communicated by Jesus' witnesses to all nations, beginning in Jerusalem. Here, Luke employs a specific geographic structure to show the connection between Jesus' ministry and the church's role and identity. In Luke, Jesus' ministry unfolds progressively *toward Jerusalem*: beginning with his ministry in Galilee (4:14-9:50); then proceeding with the journey from Galilee to Jerusalem (9:51-19:40); then culminating in the final events in Jerusalem (19:41-24:53). In Acts, the church's mission proceeds in three phases that move progressively *from Jerusalem* (1:8), beginning with the events in Jerusalem itself (1-7); followed by Samaria and the coastal plains (8-9); and finally to all parts of the Roman Empire, culminating in Paul's arrival at Rome (10-28).[39] In employing this structure, Luke's emphasis is on the *universal thrust* of Jesus' mission and that of the church, as a fulfillment of Old Testament prophecy (i.e., Luke 19:45-6, 24:40-47; Acts 10:1-48, 13:46-7).

One of the distinctive features in Luke's theology of salvation is the amount of attention that he gives to Jesus' concern for the poor, sinners, and other marginalized groups in society. Jesus befriends and shows compassion to three groups of people that were usually rejected by the Jews of his day: (1) those with physical defects (blind, lame, lepers); (2) those who exploited the Israelites for personal gain (tax collectors); and (3) political and social enemies (Samaritans and Romans). Michael Goheen quotes Donald Senior and Carroll Studhlmueller on the significance of these associations:

> These provocative associations of Jesus are not incidental to his ministry. The extension of compassion, loyalty, and friendship across well-defined boundaries of exclusion was a parable in action, a way of vividly communicating Jesus' understanding of God and of the quality of his rule. The setting Luke gives for the mercy parables of chapter 15 makes this point: Jesus defends his friendship and table fellowship with

the "tax collectors and sinners" (15:1-2) by telling three parables of God's own scandalous mercy. Both Jesus' association and his parables are challenging statements about the nature of God who is coming to rule a transformed Israel.[40]

Jesus therefore challenges the nationalistic particularism and exclusivism of Jewish groups and radically redefines the traditional Jewish conception of election and participation in God's reign.[41] This brings us to the passages in Isaiah that Jesus quotes in his inaugural sermon.

Old Testament Background and Jesus' Use of Isaiah

There are three significant things to note about Jesus' use of Isaiah in Luke 4:16-21—all of which have perplexed interpreters of this passage. First, most of the quotation comes from Isaiah 61:1-2. But Jesus not only quotes from Isaiah 61. He also inserts a phrase ("to let the oppressed go free") from Isaiah 58:6 *between* Isaiah 61:1 and 61:2. What is the significance of this insertion? Secondly, the words "to proclaim the year of the Lord's favor" (4:19; cf. Isa. 61:2a) are an obvious reference to the Old Testament *Year of Jubilee* which stipulated that every 50 years debts were to be cancelled, slaves set free, and land that had been sold to pay off debts was to be returned to the original family. In what sense does Jesus use this concept in this passage? Third, Jesus does not read the rest of Isaiah 61:2 ("and the day of vengeance of our God"). Why does he omit these words?

To answer these questions, let's first look more closely at these passages in Isaiah. Isaiah 61 reflects the period of the return of Jewish exiles to a devastated Jerusalem after a half-century of captivity in Babylon. In these verses the prophet expresses the hope of messianic redemption and restoration, both spiritually and physically, for God's people. By this time the language of jubilee no longer had a strictly economic meaning, but was used metaphorically or symbolically to express a future eschatological vision of salvation. However, it could still function as an ethical demand for justice in the present.[42] Isaiah 58 is a prophetic denunciation of social injustice. The context of this passage is reflected in Nehemiah 5, which describes how poor Jews were forced to pay taxes levied by the Persian king. To pay these taxes they had to mortgage their vineyards and homes and even sell their children into slavery to rich fellow-Jews who took advantage of their plight.[43] As we observed in chapter five, Isaiah 58 is one of many passages in the Old Testament that indict the wealthy for hypocritically engaging in religious activities in the very process of oppressing the poor (vss. 3-5). To be recipients of God's blessing they must free the oppressed, share their food with the hungry, provide the poor with shelter, and clothe the naked (vss. 6f). The people of Jesus' day were undoubtedly familiar with these passages. And it is likely that when Jesus spoke these words he had in mind the people of his own day who suffered from the oppressive burdens of debt and taxation.

Given this Old Testament background, some argue that Jesus' mission involved a literal fulfillment of the Year of Jubilee in terms of socio-political restructuring. However, this view is problematic for several reasons. First, there is very little evidence, if any, that the jubilee legislation was implemented or practiced at any time in Israel's history.[44] Second, the descriptions of Jesus' ministry in the gospels do not indicate that it involved socio-political upheaval or a program of social reform.[45] In fact, thirdly, any interpretation of this passage as a manifesto for political liberation or a popular uprising involving a literal fulfillment of the jubilee runs counter to the universalistic thrust of Luke-Acts. This, in my opinion, is why Jesus omits the reference in Isaiah 61:2 to God's vengeance, since these words would have undoubtedly been interpreted by Jesus' listeners as a call for political and social liberation from Roman rule and oppression. This further explains why the congregation in the synagogue reacts so violently to Jesus' description of God's mercy on the Gentile widow Sidon and on Naaman, the Syrian. Whereas, the Jewish expectation was that salvation would be limited to them as God's elect, "Jesus not only omits any reference to judgment on Israel's enemies but also reminds his listeners of God's compassion on those enemies (4:25-27), a fact that fills all in the synagogue with wrath (v 28)."[46]

The core of Jesus' message, then, is that the "good news" of Isaiah 61 is for *all* who are oppressed. Luke's use of the word *aphesis* ("liberation") is important here. He uses the word five times in the Gospel (1:77, 3:3, 4:18 twice, and 24:47) and five times in Acts (2:38; 5:31, 10:43, 13:38, 26:18). In every case, with the exception of Jesus' quotation from Isaiah 61, the meaning is liberation or freedom from the bondage of sin. Forgiveness of sins is therefore a major element in Luke's understanding of "liberation."[47]

However, this does not mean that Luke 4 does not have definite ethical or social implications. First, the sins that people are freed from include *social* sins, not just personal sins (Luke 3:7-14; cf. Isa. 1:18). Furthermore, both the Old Testament background and Jesus' concern for the poor and social outcastes as portrayed in Luke's Gospel prevent us from simply spiritualizing this section of Scripture, as many evangelicals are wont to do. In the Old Testament, the jubilee was closely connected with the Exodus.[48] We have seen how, in the Old Testament covenant, Israel's liberation from Egypt is given as the motivating force for obedience of God's people to the Law. As a redeemed people the Israelites must reflect the character of their redeemer in the way they behave towards others. Leviticus 25, which gives the stipulations of the jubilee, echoes this language of redemption. God's great redeeming act of caring generosity and justice stands as the model and motivation for the behavior enjoined in the jubilee legislation.[49] In Luke as well, forgiveness of sins is no "cheap grace"—it entails a response of obedience to Jesus which means giving up possessions and responding to the needs of the poor.[50] It is very likely, then, that *both* Leviticus 25, with its emphasis on redemptive and restorative justice (modeled after the exodus), and Isaiah 61, with its emphasis on the jubilee as an eschatological symbol of the new Age, are operative in Jesus' use of jubilee imagery in Luke 4. To see further how and why this is the case, we now turn to an examination of the meaning of *ptochos* ("poor") and related terms (i.e., blind, sick, etc.) in this passage and Luke's gospel as a whole.

The Meaning of Ptochos ("Poor") and Related Terms

Before looking at the meaning of *ptochos* it is important to address briefly the theme of "eschatogical reversal" in Luke's gospel. That this is a major theme is evident from the number of occasions in Luke's account of Jesus' ministry where God's reign is characterized in terms of a reversal in status—between the proud and powerful and those who are humble and weak (1:46-53); those who seek God's kingdom and those who don't (6:20-26; cf. 22:28-30); Jew and Gentile (13:28-30); the rich and poor (16:19-31). Walter Pilgrim suggests that these texts, which express a "great reversal," are part of the oldest traditions in the gospels.[51] This was a message of hope for those who believed and obeyed. But it was not for the future only for it expressed an ethic of redemptive living that should be the operative principle for those who were committed to seeking God's kingdom (Luke 6:21-23; cf. Matt. 5:3-10). Jesus was not an idealistic optimist announcing the coming of a perfect social order through human action, political or otherwise. But the "already" aspect of the kingdom meant that the action of God is already making itself felt and calls for decisive action. Moreover, Jesus' announcement that God's kingdom is at hand calls into question the values of the present order.[52] Chris Wright gives this modern day parable to contrast the ethic of God's kingdom with the ethic of modern day society:

> Once upon a time there were certain banks who, though their own great folly, found themselves in danger of collapse under mountains of toxic debt that they could not repay or even understand. So they went to their governments, who had mercy on them and took their debts away with their thousands of billions of dollars taken from their tax-payers. Then these same banks came across many individuals whose taxes had rescued them, who owed them small debts of a few thou-

sand dollars or pounds, but they showed them no mercy at all and took away their homes because they couldn't pay up. Which goes to show that redemption in our fallen world seems to work very nicely for the rich and powerful but is hard to come by if you're poor. Jesus' idea of redemption in the kingdom of God operates differently.[53]

This brings us to the argument that the "poor" to which Jesus was specifically referring were the "pious poor," or those who in their afflictions humbly depended upon God's mercy. We can certainly agree on the importance of this concept in Luke. It is emphasized in Mary's Magnificat (Mark 1:50) and presupposed in the other depictions of eschatological reversal. However, Luke also connects Jesus' mission of announcing "good news" to the poor with concrete deeds of compassion towards people in need, the sick, the demon possessed, and blind. This is clear from the obvious parallels between the recipients of good news in the quotation from Luke 4 and the objects of mercy referred to in other passages in Luke, as summarized in the chart below.

Figure 15. The "Poor" as Recipients of Good News in Luke

	4: 16-18	7: 18-23	14:13	14:21
Recipients of "good news"/ mercy	The poor, broken-hearted, captives, blind; op-pressed	The demon-possessed, blind, lame, sick, lepers, dead, deaf & poor	The poor, crippled, lame & blind	The poor, crippled, lame, & blind

In Luke 7:18-23, Jesus is responding to John the Baptist's query as to whether he is the expected Messiah. Using the exact same words from Isaiah 61:1 as are used in Luke 4 ("good news is preached to the poor"), Jesus gives a list of those who are objects of his ministry and healings. Both the deeds and words of Jesus are "signs" of the presence of the kingdom in Jesus. Similarly, when Jesus dines in the home of prominent Pharisee (14:1) he states that invitations to feasts should be given, not to the friends, relatives or rich neighbors but to the poor, the crippled, the lame, and the blind (14:13). These are the very same people who are invited to the Great Banquet (Luke 14:21). In each of these instances a literal understanding of recipients is clearly intended.[54]

Richard Mouw reminds us that following Christ means following the example of Christ's redemptive work by reaching out to the spiritually broken, the poor, the sick, and the oppressed. "In this sense, the Christian way is rooted in very different values and commitments, and comforts from the motivations found among those whose loyalties are to the present age. And so the path of Christian discipleship and the life of the people of God constitute a radical alternative to contemporary styles of living."[55]

Luke's social and ethical concerns are also evident in the contrasts that he makes between the rich and the poor. Luke often characterizes the rich as those who are greedy and bent on making money (12:13-21), indifferent to the needs of the poor (16:19-31), and choked by preoccupation with riches and pleasures of the world (8:14). The selfishness of the rich ruler (18:22-25) is contrasted with the total selflessness of the poor widow who gave everything she had (21:1-4). Putting all of these stories together leaves little doubt that when Luke speaks of the *ptochos* he means those who are lacking in the essentials for subsistence.[56] However, it is not the rich per se that are condemned or the poor blessed, but the rich in the context of rejection of God and the poor in the context of trust in God and a positive response to the gospel of the kingdom (6:20-26).[57] Luke's emphasis is that all are in need of repentance and forgiveness of sins. Enslavement to sin and the values of this world can take various forms. The "poor" are ultimately, then, all of those who are in need of release from those things which oppress their souls, minds, and lives (19:10).

At the same time, we must not downplay Luke's concern for just relationships among those who would seek to live by the values of God's kingdom. In Luke's gospel one's use of money is illustrative—it is a sign or symbol—of his/her response to Jesus and the kingdom he inaugurates. But generosity and alms are not merely illustrative, for they express the reality of God's reign to which they point.[58] William Larkin points out that Luke introduces the concept of "economic repentance" (Luke 3:3-14). For the rich this means that they must repent of all behaviors that are incompatible with the kingdom. They must make restitution if their riches have been acquired wrongfully (19:8); make involvement with the poor and social outcastes part of their lifestyle (14:13-14); and use their financial resources for the benefit of the poor (18:22). "In these ways the poor will find themselves empowered and their conditions alleviated, as they participate, with the rich, as valued and cared-for members in the kingdom. This economic repentance is just as revolutionary in its way as any call for a program for economic justice, which redistributes wealth through governmental or military coercion."[59]

The Great Commission: Mission as Discipleship (Matt. 28:18-20)

The commission of the risen Christ to his disciples as recorded in Matthew is one of most familiar and oft quoted passages in the New Testament:

> *All authority in heaven and on earth has been given to me. Therefore go and make disciples of all nations, baptizing them in the name of the Father and of the Son and of the Holy Spirit, and teaching them to obey everything I have commanded you. And surely I am with you always, to the very end of the age. (Matt. 28:18-20)*

Unfortunately, this very familiarity can become an obstacle to truly understanding these words of Christ. As with Luke 4, the Great Commission in Matthew cannot be properly understood without considering both the Old Testament background and its relation to the Gospel as a whole. Therefore it is important that we first grasp the larger context of this passage. We will then look at the nature of discipleship in Matthew and examine the meaning of key concepts ("nations;" "baptizing;" and "teaching") that are associated with making disciples.

The Great Commission in Relation to the Old Testament and Matthew's Purpose

Concerning the Old Testament background, it is clear, as we have already pointed out, that the reference to "all nations" in Matthew 28:20 is an echo of God's promise to Abraham in Genesis 22:18 (cf. 12:2-3). Jesus' words as recorded by Matthew indicate, therefore, that God's promise to Abraham, which embraced all nations, was now being realized.[60] A second observation, as Chris Wright points out, is that the Great Commission follows the covenant structure in the book of Deuteronomy.[61] This is depicted in the following table:

Figure 16. The Covenant Structure of the Great Commission

Covenant Structure in Deuteronomy	Great Commission (Matt. 28:18-20)
Self-introduction of God ("I am YHWH")	"All authority. . . has been given to me. . ."
Imperative demands of covenant relationship	"Therefore, go and make disciples. . ."
Promise of blessing	"And surely I am with you always. . ."

Wright concludes: "The Great Commission is nothing less than a universalized covenant proclamation. " Even the language of the Great Commission, with its emphasis on divine authority and obedience, is almost pure Deuteronomy.[62]

These connections with the Old Testament take on further significance in light of the fact that the Great Commission, as the final pericope, pulls together many themes in the Gospel and summarizes its essential message. Two early pericopes, in particular, reveal Matthew's concern to show that Jesus is the true Israel. Jesus' temptation by Satan in the wilderness for forty days (Matt 4:1-11) echoes Israel's forty years in the wilderness. Jesus' responses to Satan are taken directly from Moses' words to the Israelites (Matt 4:4, cf. Deut. 8:3; Matt 4:7, cf. Deut. 6:16; Matt. 4:10, cf. Deut 6:16). But where Israel failed in the face of temptations Jesus succeeded.[63] Jesus' temptation is followed by his choosing of the twelve disciples (Matt. 4:18-22), which commentators generally agree represent the twelve tribes of Israel. The Twelve therefore signify the restoration of true Israel through Jesus who performs various types of healings—miracles which were prophesied to be part of Israel's end-time restoration to God (Matt. 11:4-6, 23-25; cf. Isa. 32:3-4, 35:5-6, and 42:7, 16).[64]

As I have argued repeatedly, Jesus' miracles point to the final restoration of creation and signify the "in-breaking" of God's new order. Matthew views Jesus' miracles of healing as a fulfillment of Isaiah's prediction that the servant of the Lord would establish justice (Matt. 12:15-21; cf. Isa. 42:1-4). Malachi had similarly prophesied that the "son of justice" would "rise with healing in his wings" (Mal. 4:2). Mott rightly states: "The nature of Jesus' healing ministry as serving physical and social needs has too often been overlooked when miracles have been interpreted primarily as authenticating the gospel, rather than bringing deliverance."[65] On a number of occasions, Matthew (as well as the other gospels) presents Jesus' motivation for healing as one of simple compassion (Matt 14:14, cf. Mark 6:34; Matt. 15:32, cf. Mark 8:2; Matt. 9:36 (cf. 9:35 and 10:1); 20:34; Mark 5:19; Luke 7:13). On other occasions, he performs a miracle in response to a plea for compassion (Matt. 9:27, 15:22, 17:5, cf. Mark 9:22; Matt. 20:30-31, cf. Mark 10:47-48 and Luke17:13, 18:38-39). Matthew summarizes the *activity* of Jesus' mission as going about *teaching* in the synagogues, *preaching* the good news of the kingdom, and *healing* every disease and sickness among the people (Matt. 4:23). Jesus instructs his disciples to repeat this same ministry of preaching, proclaiming and healing (Matt. 10:7-8, 27).

We should make a final point concerning the book of Matthew before turning to an analysis of the Great Commission. Following the choosing of the twelve disciples and a summary of Jesus' missional activity (Matt 4:23-24) Matthew's gospel focuses on five major sermons or discourses: (1) the nature of discipleship (chapters 5-7); (2) the mission of the twelve (chapter 10); (3) the parables of the kingdom (chapter 13); (4) the church practice (chapter 18); and (5) the end times (chapters 23-25). The most important of these for understanding the Great Commission is the first discourse, usually referred to as the Sermon on the Mount. This sermon, like no other, expresses the essence of Jesus' ethic and what it means to be a follower or disciple of Christ. Moreover, it describes a community ethic not just an individual or personal ethic.

When the risen Christ instructs his disciples to "make disciples" by "teaching them to observe all that I have commanded you" what he primarily has in mind are his teachings as summarized in this great sermon.[66] The word "therefore" (vs. 19) is of key importance in interpreting this passage. It connects the command to make disciples with the preceding verse where Christ states: "All authority in heaven and earth has been given to me." This verse denotes his divine authority to act and is most likely an allusion to Daniel 7:13-14, which is a prophecy that the "son of man" would be "given authority, glory, and sovereignty" forever.[67] This places the Great Commission in an eschatological and kingdom context. Matthew's concern, in other words, is not just with verbal proclamation of the gospel but also with "the manner of life which Jesus had offered the true Israel as the praxis of the reign of God."[68] As Gerhard Lofink summarizes this passage:

> The apostles are to take care that there emerge everywhere in the world communities of disciples in which Jesus' praxis of

the reign of God (or, as we might also say, the social order of the true Israel) is lived in radical faithfulness to Jesus. Matthew does develop a worldwide, universal concept. But he never loses sight of the concrete communities in which alone the "new justice" of the Sermon on the Mount (Matt 5:20) can be lived.[69]

Making Disciples—the Nature of Discipleship in Matthew

The Great Commission is often appealed to as the basis for commissioning individual "missionaries" to "go" and preach the gospel in distant lands. Such activity is indeed an important and necessary part of the church's mandate—but that is not the primary meaning of this passage. The word that is used here for "go" (*pareuthentes*) is the aorist participle of the verb *poreuo*, which means "to go, proceed, journey, travel, carry over, take one's way, set out, depart," and thus to "pass from one place to another" or cross all kinds of boundaries. But the emphasis of the aorist participle is not on the idea of going but on the quality of action. In other words, it reinforces the action of the main verb "to make disciples." To "go. . .and make disciples" then does not mean in this context to go somewhere, but to start immediately to make disciples.[70] Making disciples is the sole imperative and the central activity enjoined in the Great Commission.[71] Moreover, the verb is plural, meaning that this action is to be taken collectively. Jesus is sending a *community*, not just individuals, into the world for the specific purpose of making disciples. In fact, although Christ is clearly speaking to his disciples here, the force of the command suggests that it goes beyond those immediate followers of Christ.[72]

It is equally important that we understand the nature of discipleship that is enjoined here. In the beginning of his book on discipleship, Jim Peterson of Navigators makes the revealing statement: "Thirty years of discipleship programs and we are not discipled."[73] Why? Simply put, because discipleship is not a program! In most cases, discipleship in our churches and seminaries is equated with conveying a set body of information, such as the basics of Christianity or the spiritual disciplines, usually within a structured academic setting. Progress is usually measured in terms of completion of a course with a clearly defined beginning and end. Such teaching is, of course, important. But this method of discipleship is insufficient if it is divorced from the *relational dimensions* of making disciples. The term most commonly associated with discipleship in the New Testament (and especially in Matthew) is the verb *akolouthein*, which means "to follow (after)." The background of this terminology is the rabbinic teacher-student relationship in which the student learned the Torah from the rabbi.[74] But, as Bosch argues, according to Matthew "making disciples" involves far more than simply teaching what Jesus taught or being his messengers.[75]

Bosch suggests that there are three types of relationships that Matthew has in mind when he talks about discipleship. First, there is the relationship between Jesus and his disciples, which involved a solidarity and correspondence that was fundamentally different from the relationship between the Jewish rabbis and their students. The disciples' relation to Christ himself who is the embodiment of God's reign determines discipleship. The context is not the classroom but the world.[76] Secondly, there is relationship or link between the first disciples of Jesus and the disciples at the time of Matthew's community. As a prototype of the church, the first disciples replicated themselves in others. And in so doing, they established the essential continuity between the history of Jesus and his ministry and the era of the church.[77] Jesus' command to "make disciples" takes us back through Matthew's narrative to see how Jesus (and his disciples after him) made disciples. This pattern of discipleship involves a three-fold process of: (1) communicating the gospel of the kingdom; (2) embodying the gospel or being a faithful "re-presentation" of the message or truth we seek to convey; and (3) reproducing disciples who are like the first ones.[78] This, in fact, is the method Jesus and the first disciples used to establish and grow the church. The third relationship, which is implicit in Matthew's description of the Great Commission, is the relationship between disciples within the community itself. "Every disciple follows the master, but never alone; every disciple is a member of the fellowship of disciples, the body, or no disciple at all."[79] These three relational dimensions—(1) of Christ to his disciples; (2) of the first disciples to the church (*ekkesia*), and (3) of Jesus' followers to one another in community (or what we might term "discipleship in community")—are all foundational to understanding discipleship in Matthew's Gospel.

The following diagram of two square buildings with the corners touching each other helps to illustrate the relational aspects of disciplemaking.

Figure 16. The Relational Aspects of Disciplemaking

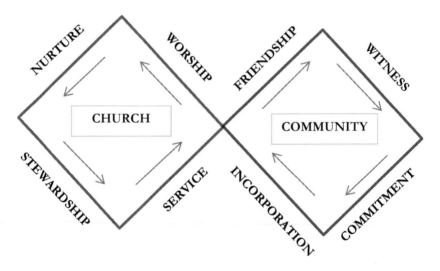

The disciple of Christ is involved in two spheres of life—the church (or body of Christ) and community. Within the church, the disciple grows through worship, nuture, stewardship, and service. But discipleship is incomplete if Christians are not also involved in the community, reproducing disciples through friendship, witness, challenge to commitment, and incorporation into the body of

Christ.[80]   This reminds us, again, that discipleship cannot be limited to the classroom. It must involve modeling, mentoring, and coaching in the process of actual ministry.

It is important to note that "making disciples" does not simply involve individual disciples reproducing themselves. It is, as I have emphasized, a corporate process involving a replication of *communities* which are faithful representations of God's kingdom. Or as Chris Wright observes, Jesus commissions his disciples "to go out and replicate themselves by creating communities of obedience among the nations."[81]

Making Disicples of all Nations by Baptizing and Teaching

We can now look in greater detail at the key three phrases that are connected with making disciples: (1) "of all nations;" (2) "baptizing them in the name of the father, son and Holy Sprit;" and (3) "teaching them to observe all that I have commanded you." For some, the reference to "nations" (*ethnos)* means that the objects of discipleship are entire societies or nations. Others think Matthew has in mind "people groups."[82]   However, since that later part of Matthew's Gospel is where the Gentile mission comes into focus, it is most likely that the emphasis is simply on the inclusion of Gentiles in God's plan of salvation.[83]   In the New Testament the word "ethnos" never refers to an individual.   The use of the masculine "them" in the following clauses ("baptizing them" and "teaching them") strongly suggests, however, that Jesus does not have in mind "corporate discipleship" or the discipling of entire nations but the winning of individual disciples *from* all nations.[84]   This further suggests that the task of making disciples must be global as well as local—moving from those who are closest to us (Jerusalem and Judea); to those "neighbors" with whom we do not have close affinity or even desire to be with (Samaria); and finally to all the nations, near and far (ends of the earth) (Acts 1:8).

The verbs "baptize" and "teach" further define what is involved in making disciples. The fact that Matthew refers to the baptismal formula first has led some missiologists to see these two events as sequential: first baptize converts, then teach them. But the absence of the coordinate conjuction "and" (*kai*) between the two verbs strongly suggests that "teaching" is associated with the "baptizing," not merely subsequent to it. These two activities are to be conducted *simulatneously, contemporaneously*, not successively.[85] Baptism is a symbol of God's grace and the reality of the forgiveness of sins. The reference to the baptismal formula ("in the name of the Father, Son and Holy Spirit") signifies that becoming a disciple involves a public profession of faith and identification with Christ. Through baptism the believer signifies his/her death to sin and resurrection to a new life in Christ (Rom. 6:3-9). Baptism also signifies that those who become disciples are incorporated into the eschatological community—the "church." This harmonizes with the whole tone of Matthew's gospel, with its emphasis on the forgiveness of sins (26:28) and the formation of the church (16:18).

However, it is clear from this passage that mission also entails nurturing converts into the full obedience of faith by teaching them to "observe" all that Christ commanded. In the context of Matthew's gospel this means following after righteousness as articulated in the teachings of Jesus.[86] The Greek *terein* ("observe, keep") that is used here is the counterpart of the Hebrew *shamar* ("to keep, guard, obey"), which is the verb most often used in connection with keeping the commandments.[87] But to emphasize only the ethical aspect, as Bosch points out, does not fit with Matthew's fierce polemic against legalism. Rather, the emphasis in Matthew's use of *dikaiosyne* (righteousness) is on *faith in action*—or doing God's will as summarized in the command to love God and one's neighbor (22:34-40). This, of course, harmonizes with the emphasis in the Old Testament covenant upon obedience as a *response* to God's gracious acts of deliverance.[88] We can conclude with Bosch that, for Matthew, it is unthinkable to separate the task of mission from commitment to justice and love, and obedience to the entire will of God.

> Mission involves, from the beginning and as matter of course, making new believers sensitive to the needs of others, open- ing their eyes and hearts to recognize injustice, suffering, op- pression, and the plight of those who have fallen by the way- side. It is unjustifiable to regard the "Great Commission" as being concerned primarily with "evangelism" and the "Great Commandment" (Matt. 22:37-40) as referring to "social in- volvement." [89]

Conclusion

What can we conclude about the connection between Jesus' announcement of his mission (Luke 4: 16-21) and his Great Commission (Matt. 28:18-20)? Some argue on the basis of John's version of the Great Commssion in John 20:21 ("As the Father has sent me, so I send you") that Jesus' mission is the *model* for our mission. The church's mission is simply an extension or continuation of Jesus' mission. Others argue, on the other hand, that Jesus' mission is entirely unique and unrepeatable. After all, Jesus was the Son of God, the Savior of the world. And we are not saviors. This debate, however, tends to be divorced from the larger theological context. As Russell Moore states, "Evangelical Protestants will talk tirelessly about the Great Commssion, but rarely do we grasp what it means in the cosmic purposes of God in forming a Kingdom for his messiah."[90]

The Old Testament prophets looked forward to the time there would be a dawning of the messianic age (Isaiah 11:1-12), the kingdom of God. Jesus' words in Luke 4:16-21 are an announcement of the fulfillment of those ancient promises and the creation of a new order of life. In parallel passages (Luke 14:12-23, 18:31-34, 22:14-30) Jesus also looks forward to the final vindication of his messianic claims and the ultimate authentication of his ministry through his death, resurrection, and glorification (Dan. 12:2-3; Ezek. 37:13-14). Similarly, the Great Commission points to cosmic restoration through faith in Christ and the forgiveness of sins. It is a "theology of cosmic warfare—a theology centering on the unveiling of the long-hidden mystery of Christ and his church."[91]   The Great Commission begins and ends with an allusion by the risen Lord to his resurrection as that which both establishes the power and authority that he delegates to the church and is a guarantee of his presence with the church through his Spirit. "In the church, the triumphant Warrior-King has established an outpost of the Kingdom—a colony of the reign that will one day engulf the world (Eph. 1:20-23)."[92]

Luke's version of the Great Commission is followed by a description of Jesus' ascension into heaven. For Luke (as well for Mark and John) this signifies that the resurrected Christ is being elevated to the Lord of the world.[93] In Luke's Gospel (24:50-53) and in the book of Acts (1:9) the ascension provides a connecting link between his account of Jesus' ministry and the his description of the coming of the Holy Spirit at Pentecost and the formation of the church (Acts 1:4-11, 2:1-47). The church is commissioned to both speak Jesus' message and live it out in righteousness, justice, peace, and unity. In so doing it heralds the coming kingdom of Christ, manifests a commonality in the Spirit of the risen Christ (Gal. 6:12-15), and is a witness to the world of Christ's ultimate triumph over evil forces which are opposed to his kingdom (Rom. 16:17-20).[94] This brings us to Luke's theology of mission in the book of Acts.

Notes

[1] I Howard Marshall, New Testament Theology: Many Witnesses, One Gospel (Downers Grove, IL: InterVarsity, 2004), pp. 34-5.
[2] Ibid., p. 37.
[3] Bosch, Transforming Mission, p. 55.

[4] N.T., Wright, *How God Became King: the Forgotten Story of the Gospels* (New York: HarperOne, 2012), pp. 3-10.

[5] Ibid., pp. 26-7.

[6] Ibid., p. 159.

[7] Ibid., pp. 158-59.

[8] Ibid., p. 161.

[9] Ibid., p. 162.

[10] Ibid., p. 178.

[11] Wright, *Knowing Jesus Through the Old Testament*, 1992), p. 141.

[12] Wright, *How God Became King*, p. 180.

[13] Goheen, *Light to the Nations*, p. 77.

[14] Mott, *Biblical Ethics and Social Change*, p. 92. We will further develop this argument in the following sections.

[15] See Glasser, *Announcing the Kingdom*, p. 188.

[16] Wright, *How God Became King*, pp. 184-96.

[17] Ibid., p. 187.

[18] See I Howard Marshall, *Luke: Historian and Theologian* (Grand Rapids, MI: Zondervan, 1970), p. 117.

[19] See Bosch, *Transforming Mission*, p. 91. At the conclusion of his gospel, Luke also emphasizes the ascension of Christ (Luke 24:50-53). As we I will argue later, this provides a connecting link between his account of Jesus' ministry in his gospel and the his description of the coming of the Holy Spirit at Pentecost and the formation of the church in Acts (Acts 1:4-11; 2:1-47).

[20] Wright, *How God Became King*, p. 196.

[21] Ibid., p. 197.

[22] Ibid., pp. 112-13.

[23] Allen Verhey, *The Great Reversal: Ethics and the New Testament* (Grand Rapids, MI: Eerdmans, 1984), p. 13.

[24] Wright, *How God Became King*, p. 204.

[25] Ibid., p. 203.

[26] Verhey, *The Great Reversal*, p. 31.

[27] Ibid., pp. 73-4.

[28] L. Schottroff and W. Stegemann, *Jesus and the Hope of the Poor* (Maryknoll, NY: Orbis, 1986), p. 91. Quoted in Bosch, *Transforming Mission*, pp. 101-2.

[29] See Gustavo Guteirrez, *A Theology of Liberation: History, Politics and Liberation* (Maryknoll, NY: Orbis, 1988), p. 97.

[30] Graham Cray, "A Theology of the Kingdom," in *Mission as Transformation: A Theology of the Whole Gospel* ed., Vinay Samuel and Chris Sugden (Carlisle, CA: Regnum, 1999), pp. 37-38. See also James F. Engel and William A. Dyrness, *Changing the Mind of Missions: Where Have We Gone Wrong?* (Downers Gove, IL: InterVarsity 2000), p. 80; and Thomas D. Hanks, *God So Loved the Third World: The Bible, the Reformation, and Liberation* (Maryknoll, NY: Orbis, 1983), p. 103.

[31] DeYoung and Gilbert, *What is the Mission of the Church?*, pp. 38-40. See also Kostenberger and O'Brien, *Salvation to the Ends of the Earth*, p 117.

[32] John Howard Yoder, *The Politics of Jesus* (Grand Rapids, MI: Eerdmans, 1972), p. 39.

[33] Michael Prior, *Jesus the Liberator: Nazareth Liberation Theology (Luke 4:16-30)*, (Sheffield, England: Sheffield Academic Press, 1995), p. 164.

[34] Ibid.

[35] Pilgrim, *Good News to the Poor*, p. 64.

[36] Bosch, *Transforming Mission*, p. 91.

[37] Ibid., p. 105

[38] See Goheen, *Light to the Nations*, p. 123.

[39] Ibid., p. 124.

[40] Ibid., pp. 93-4.

[41] Prior, *Jesus the Liberator*, p. 147.

[42] See Wright, *Old Testament Ethics for the People of God*, p. 206; and *The Mission of God*, p. 301.

[43] Bosch, *Transformation of Mission*, p. 101

[44] See Robert Willoughby, "The Concept of Jubilee and Luke 4:18-30," *Mission and Meaning: Essays Presented to Peter Cotterell*, ed. Antony Billington, Tony Lane and Max Turner (Carlisle: Paternoster Press, 1995), p. 46.

[45] See Prior, *Jesus the Liberator*, p. 195.

[46] Bosch, *Mission as Transformation*, pp. 109-10.

[47] Prior, *Jesus the Liberator*, pp., 139-50.

[48] Willoughby, "The Concept of Jubilee," p. 45.

[49] Wright, *The Mission of God's People*, pp. 106-7.

[50] Prior, *Jesus the Liberator*, p. 140.

[51] Pilgrim, *Good News to the Poor*, p. 57.

[52] See Verhey, *The Great Reversal*, p. 15.

[53] Wright, *The Mission of God's People*, p. 109.

[54] Pilgrim, *Good News to the Poor*, pp. 72-3.

[55] Mouw, *Political Evangelism*, p. 71.

[56] Prior, *Jesus the Liberator*, pp. 171-2.

[57] Pilgrim, *Good News to the Poor*, p. 77.

[58] Verhey, *The Great Reversal*, op. cit., p. 94.

[59] Larkin, "Mission in Luke," op. cit., p. 163.

[60] See Beale, *The Temple and the Church's Mission*, p. 175. Also, Tim Hegg, "The 'Great Commission': An Inquiry" p. 6

[61] Wright, *The Mission of God*," pp. 354-5.

[62] Ibid.

[63] Beale, *The Temple in the Church's Mission*, p. 172

[64] Ibid., p. 174

[65] Mott, *Biblical Ethics and Social Change*, p. 93

[66] See Bosch, *Transforming Mission*, .p. 69.

[67] Beale, *The Temple and the Church's Mission*, p. 175. See also R. T. France, *Jesus and the Old Testament* (Grand Rapids, MI: Baker, 1971), pp. 142-3.

[68] Gerhard Lohfink, *Jesus and Community; The Social Dimension of Christian Faith* (Philadelphia, PA: Fortress, 1982), p. 137.

[69] Ibid.

[70] William Banks, *In Search of the Great Commission: What Did Jesus Really Say?* (Chicago, Moody Press, 1991), p. 73.

[71] David J. Hesselgrave, *Planting Churches Cross-Culturally: North America and Beyond* (Grand Rapids, MI: Baker, 2000), pp. 20-21. See also Wright, *The Mission of God*, pp. 34-5.

[72] Banks, *In Search of the Great Commission*, p. 21. See also Goheen, *A Light to the World*, p. 114.

[73] Jim Peterson, *Lifestyle Discipleship: The Challenge of Following Jesus in Today's World* (Colorado Springs, CO: NavPress, 1993), p. 15.

[74] Lofink, *Jesus and Community*, p. 32.

[75] Bosch, *Transforming Mission*, p. 75.

[76] Ibid., p. 67.

[77] Ibid., p. 74.

[78] See Hirsch, *The Forgotten Ways*, pp. 114-20.

[79] Bosch, *Transforming Mission*, p. 74.

[80] See David W. Shenk and Ervin R. Stutzman, *Creating Communities of the Kingdom: New Testament Models of Church Planting* (Scottdale, PA: Herald Press, 1988), pp. 158-9.

[81] Wright, *The Mission of God.*, p. 391.

[82] John Piper, *Let the Nations be Glad! The Supremacy of God in Missions* (Grand Rapids, MI: Baker, 1993), p. 180.

[83] See Kostenberger and O'Brien, *Salvation to the Ends of the Earth*, p.104; Glasser, *Announcing the Kingdom*, p. 237; Bosch, *Transforming Mission*, p. 64.

[84] Glasser, *Announcing the Kingdom*, p. 237.

[85] See Bosch, *Transforming Mission*, p. 78; Banks, In *Search of the Great Commission*, ap. 78; George W. Peters, *A Biblical Theology of Missions* (Chicago: Moody Press, 1972), p. 183.

[86] Kostenberger and O'Brien, *Salvation to the Ends of the Earth*, pp. 104-5.

[87] Hegg, "The 'Great Commission': An Inquiry," p. 16.

[88] Bosch, *Transforming Mission*, pp. 71-2.

[89] Ibid., p. 81.

[90] Russell D. Moore, "Triumph of the Warrior King: A Theology of the Great Commission," http://www. russellmoore.com/documents/russellmoore/ Theology_of_the_Great_Commission.pdf, p. 1.

[91] Ibid. p. 2.

[92] Ibid., p. 17.

[93] In Luke's account, the ascended Jesus is worshipped by the disciples (Luke 24:52). In John the appearance of the risen Christ to Mary Magdalene and his assertion that "I am returning to my Father, to my God and your God" is followed by the exclamation "I have seen the Lord." At the end of the chapter, the parallel confession of Thomas is "My Lord and my God!" (John 20:18, 28). In Mark's account the ascended Christ is pictured as seated at the right hand of God. As has been pointed out, this is an image of Lordship.

[94] Moore, "Triumph of the Warrior King," pp. 17-9.

Chapter 11
Acts: The Church as a
Witness to the Kingdom

In the last chapter we saw how Jesus' Great Commission to his disciples focused on the creation of a community of believers as the true "people of God" who faithfully represent the reign of God in word and deed and reproduce themselves in others. After his resurrection and before his ascension into heaven Jesus gave another commission to the "emerging" church (Acts 1:8). Charles Van Engen points out that while this statement of Jesus has been overworked in missionary theory "few have looked at Jesus' promise as an image of the self-understanding of the Church."[1] But "could it not be that Jesus is telling his disciples that they are a certain kind of fellowship which in its essential nature is an ever-widening, mushrooming group of missionary witnesses?"[2] It is this essentially missionary nature of the church, which I think is highlighted in the book of Acts. A proper understanding of the mission of the apostolic church therefore requires that we rethink the nature of the local church. As Van Engen states, it entails developing a vision of local congregations as God's missionary people in a local context.[3] This will be the focus of the chapter.

Theological Narrative and Mission

The book of Acts belongs to that biblical genre called *theological narrative*. It has a story, with a plot, events, and main characters. Of course, it is not just any story. Unlike fictional accounts, a theological narrative conveys truths about God's interaction with humanity. Still, these truths are conveyed by means of a narrative framework. If we fail to understand the nature of this framework we will misunderstand the message that Luke intends to convey. Luke clearly wants his readers to see the continuity as well as development between the Gospel account and Acts. As Larkin points out, both works are set within a "promise and fulfillment" salvation history framework. But there is a difference in emphasis. In the gospel account Luke stresses salvation accomplished. In Acts, while this aspect of salvation is clearly present in the summary statements and speeches, what comes to the fore is mission—or salvation applied.[4] In other words, Luke's gospel tells us about *God's salvation through Christ.* The book of Acts, on the other hand, tells us about *God's mission through the church.*

How are we to understand this mission from the perspective of Acts? Usually what is described is the sending by the church in Antioch of Paul and Barnabas on their first missionary journey (Acts 13:1-3). This is thought to be the beginning of the missionary movement and therefore becomes the paradigm for the cross-cultural missionary work of evangelism and church planting. What is missing from this picture of mission in Acts is that it is often divorced from the larger context of Luke's theology. Recent studies of Acts have shown convincingly that the primary purpose of Luke's narrative in Acts is to persuade other Jews that Jesus is the messiah of Old Testament Scripture and that the church is a fulfillment of prophecies regarding the restoration of Israel. This self-understanding of the early church is crucial to understanding the nature of its mission.

When we speak of mission in Acts it is probably more appropriate, then, to describe it in terms of the purpose of God's people as witnesses to his kingdom. One of the ongoing debates in Christian mission, of course, has been whether our focus ought to be "church growth" or "kingdom growth." I believe that this debate is often misplaced. The paradigm of "witness" focuses the task of mission on evangelism and the multiplication of churches but fleshes this out in terms of the *multiplication of kingdom communities that manifest (however partially and imperfectly) the wholeness of God's redemptive purpose in the world.* Acts is clear that God's chosen vehicle for the expansion of his kingdom *is* the church.

The Three-Dimensional Focus of Acts 1:8

Luke portrays the maturation of the early church's identity and mission through successive stages, as it lived out the meaning of the gospel in light of Old Testament promises. This successive unfolding of the church's mission is conveyed in Jesus' statement:

> *But you will receive power when the Holy Spirit has come upon you; and you will be my witnesses in Jerusalem, in all Judea and Samaria, and to the ends of the earth. (vs. 1:8).*

This passage shows the connection between the witness of the first Christians and the expansion of the early Christian movement. Jesus' words also emphasize the role of the Holy Spirit in empowering his disciples to accomplish their mission. Prior to this commission Jesus instructs his disciples to remain in Jerusalem so that they might receive the baptism of the Holy Spirit (Acts 1:5) which he specifically connects with being "clothed with power from on high" (Luke 24:49). He is clear, then, that it is the Holy Spirit which empowers his disciples for witness to God's salvation which has come through his death and resurrection.

But what was the nature of the growth that would characterize the disciples' witness? Commentators have generally referred to these words of Jesus in Acts 1:8 as describing the geographic and physical growth of the church. This has provided the rationale among some missiologists for making quantitative and statistical projections or "goals" for church growth in a particular region or country—a practice that Eckhard Schnabel has criticized as foreign to the New Testament.[5] Who is right? There is no disputing the fact that the numerical increase of the church is an important theme in Luke's account of the early church. What is often missed, however, is the fact that there is a broader theological motive behind this "fondness for statistics."[6] As depicted in the figure below, there are three dimensions to Acts 1:8: (1) geographic; (2) theopolitical; and (3) eschatological. Each of these dimensions highlights three types of growth that characterized the early church's mission and would be achieved through the power of God's Spirit.

Figure 17. The Geographic, Theopolitical, and Eschatological Dimensions of Acts 1:8

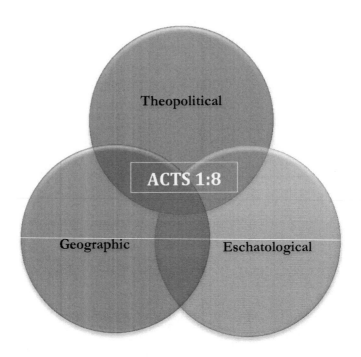

The Geographic Dimension

At one level, of course, Acts 1:8 is a summary account of how the early Christian witnesses to Jesus began their task in Jerusalem and then spread out into Judea and Samaria and ultimately the wider Gentile world. This *geographic* dimension corresponds with Luke's concern with the physical and numeric expansion of the church. As one reads this narrative it becomes apparent that numerical increase is an important element in the book of Acts. Luke uses it to describe the universal dimensions of the gospel and the fulfillment of Christ's mandate to proclaim the gospel of repentance and forgiveness of sins to all nations. (Luke 24:47; Acts 8: 12, 11:20-21, 13:47).[7] That God wants his church to grow numerically and multiply and gives that growth blessing undergirds and gives legitimacy to the role that "numerical growth" has played in the church growth movement. It also highlights the importance of urgent evangelism and discipleship.[8] However, if we look at Acts as simply giving an account of the geographic expansion of the church from one center we will miss the wider significance of this commission of Jesus to his disciples.

The Theopolitical Dimension

Acts 1:8 should be interpreted, not only geographically, but also *theopolicially* in terms of the reconstitution of Israel *through the church* as the true "people of God." The phrase "to the ends of the earth" in this verse is repeated in Acts 13:47. Both passages are a clear reference to Isa 49:6, which refers to the "restored Israel" as the agent of God's universal plan of salvation.[9] In Acts 1:8 Luke is outlining three stages in God's program of salvation in terms of: (1) the dawn of salvation on Jerusalem: (2) the reunification of the two kingdoms of Judah and Israel as a fulfillment of the ancient promise of the restoration of the whole house of Israel (e.g., Ezekiel 37:15-22); and (3) the inclusion of the Gentiles within the people of God.[10]

This relationship between the church and the theme of a restored Israel is indicated, in part, by the terms Luke uses to describe the three critical junctures in the growth of the church. These terms connect the story of the church with the redemptive-historical story of God from creation and throughout the history of Israel.[11] The chart below shows the relationship between these growth summaries and the overall structure of the Acts account:

Figure 18. Luke's Growth Summaries & the Basic Outline of Acts

Section in Acts	Geography	Theopolitical Significance	Growth Summary
Acts 1-7	Jerusalem	The dawn of salvation in Jerusalem	"So the word of God grew. The number of disciples in Jerusalem was greatly multiplied." (Acts 6:7)
Acts 8-12	Judea and Samaria	Reunification of Judah and Israel (Acts 9:31)	"So the church throughout Judea and Galilee, and Samaria. . . multiplied." (Acts 9:31) "But the word of God grew and multiplied " (Acts 12:24)
Acts 13-28	". . .the ends of the earth." (Gentile world)	The inclusion of Gentiles in the people of God (Acts 13:47)	"In this way the word of the Lord increased and grew in power." (Acts 19: 20; cf Acts 13:49)

The Greek words for "grow," "increase," and "multiply" that Luke uses in these summaries are connected with the power and conquest of "the word," a theme that is emphasized in the Exodus-Conquest and Isaianic traditions to underscore the eventual success of God's people. In these thematic emphases, then, Luke portrays the early Christian community as the continuation of the covenant people of the ancient Israelite traditions.[12] The connection of Acts 1:8 to Isaiah's eschatological vision of universal salvation places it within the worldwide context of the restoration of the kingdom.[13] The early church therefore saw itself as the people among whom God's reign had begun. Luke's theology of mission and church growth simply cannot be understood apart from this conception of the church as a messianic community and a continuation of God's plan to bless the nations.

The Eschatological Dimension

Luke's theology of mission and church growth is thus informed by a "kingdom vision" which sees the body of Christ as a community of God's reign. Growth is a result of God's blessing on his people who are corporately a "sign," however imperfectly, of the reality and promise of his future reign. This "kingdom growth" is specifically related to the *eschatological* dimension of the church's witness. Here, we need to begin by looking at the immediate context of Jesus' words in Acts 1:8. In the exchange between Jesus and his disciples immediately preceding this Great Commission (vss. 6-7) the disciples ask if this is the time when he would restore the kingdom to Israel. What they undoubtedly had in mind was the establishment of the Davidic kingdom, which the prophet Isaiah predicted would be characterized by righteousness and justice (Isa. 9:7), peace (9:6-7) and prosperity (11:6-9). Jesus' response to the disciples actually indicates that, while the *final and complete* fulfillment of the Old Testament promise belongs to an undetermined future (lit. "It is not for you to know the times or dates. . .") *the beginning of the process of the restoration of Israel has already begun.*[14] This is indicated by Jesus words: "But you shall receive power, when the Holy Spirit is come upon you. . ." This is a direct reference to Isaiah 32:15, which gives the picture of the outpouring of God's Spirit from on high *upon a restored Israel.* (cf. Isa. 44:3; Ezek. 36:27)

This "already" and "not yet" nature of the kingdom is featured in

Peter's speeches in chapters 2 and 3 of Acts, as illustrated by the figure below:

Figure 19. The Already and Not Yet of the Kingdom in Acts 1-3

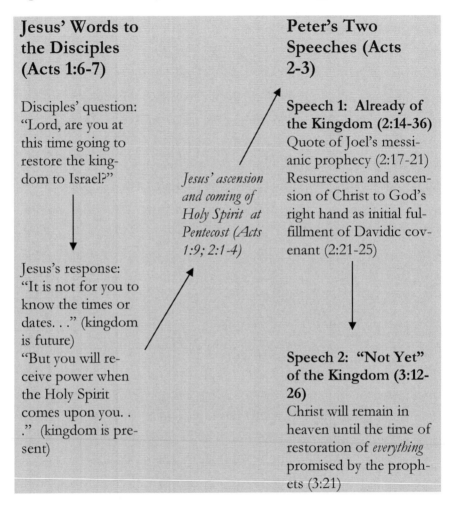

Jesus' Words to the Disciples (Acts 1:6-7)		Peter's Two Speeches (Acts 2-3)
Disciples' question: "Lord, are you at this time going to restore the kingdom to Israel?"	*Jesus' ascension and coming of Holy Spirit at Pentecost (Acts 1:9; 2:1-4)*	**Speech 1: Already of the Kingdom (2:14-36)** Quote of Joel's messianic prophecy (2:17-21) Resurrection and ascension of Christ to God's right hand as initial fulfillment of Davidic covenant (2:21-25)
Jesus's response: "It is not for you to know the times or dates. . ." (kingdom is future) "But you will receive power when the Holy Spirit comes upon you. . ." (kingdom is present)		**Speech 2: "Not Yet" of the Kingdom (3:12-26)** Christ will remain in heaven until the time of restoration of *everything* promised by the prophets (3:21)

Following the dramatic events of Pentecost Peter addresses the large group of Jews,[15] which Luke describes as "from every nation under heaven living in Jerusalem." This is a clear reference to Isaiah's prediction of the ingathering of the exiles as the reconstituted nation of Israel (Isa. 43:5-7).[16] Peter begins by quoting the messianic prophecy of Joel, which places the gift of the Spirit in the "last days" (2:17), a term used in the Old Testament to refer to the time of the eschatological kingdom of God when Israel would be blessed (Isa. 2:2; Hos. 3:4). To further make his point, Peter presents the resurrection and ascension of Christ to God's right hand as the initial fulfillment of the Davidic covenant promised in Psalm 110:1 (2:33-35).[17]

But while Peter's speech in Acts 2 highlights the present or "already" aspect of the kingdom his speech in Acts 3 brings out its future or "not yet" features. In his second speech Peter distinguishes between a current period of "refreshing" which people can enjoy if they repent and the *final* restoration of things promised by the Old Testament prophets. Perhaps recalling Jesus' words to the disciples prior to his ascension, Peter asserts unequivocally that Christ will remain in heaven until the time when there will be a restoration of *everything* promised by the prophets (3:11). Evidently, then, Peter sees the kingdom as coming in two phases. In the first phase the new community of believers gives a "preview" of the coming kingdom in which all people will be subject to Christ's rule of justice and righteousness. With the second phase, all of the promises to Israel *as a nation* will be completed when Christ returns and establishes his earthly kingdom.[18]

The Church as a Witness to the Kingdom

Peter's sermon is not the only instance in Acts where the "good news" of the gospel is portrayed in terms of "kingdom witness." This can be also seen in Luke's depiction of other critical junctures in the growth of the church. Philip "preached the good news of the kingdom of God and the name of Jesus" in Samaria (8:12). Paul and Barnabas instructed their disciples in Antioch about the kingdom of God. (14:21). In Ephesus, Paul entered the synagogue and argued persuasively about the kingdom of God for a period of three months (19:8). In Rome, Paul "explained and declared" the kingdom of God to large numbers of people (28: 23). For two whole years, "boldly and without hindrance he preached the kingdom of God and taught about the Lord Jesus Christ" (28:30).

Throughout his account Luke depicts the nature of this witness to the kingdom. These early Christian missionaries are described as messengers who follow the example of Jesus and are faithful to his direction to preach and to heal (Matt. 10:7-8) and make disciples. They preach the gospel, they heal sick people, and they establish communities of followers of Jesus that are characterized by selfless love and mutual care.[19] This witness should then be described in terms of the three aspects of *kerygma* (proclamation), *diakonia* (service/ministry), and *koinonia* (community).[20]

In virtually every instance in Acts where the words "witness" or "witnesses" are used they refer to the verbal preaching or proclaiming of the gospel forgiveness of sins through Jesus' death and resurrection. *Kerygma* is therefore absolutely essential to mission. Much of evangelistic proclamation by the early apostles and Paul took place in a variety of public forums—the temple, the marketplace, and other public meeting places. However, following the pattern of Jesus, this public proclamation of the gospel was often accompanied by the ministry of miraculous healings that demonstrated not only the power of Christ working through the Holy Spirit but also the holistic nature of the in-breaking of God's kingdom (cf. 3:10).

Luke wants to show the very close connection between "word ministry" and "deed ministry" in the spread of the gospel. For example, he deliberately connects the *power* of the apostles' "testimony to the resurrection of the Lord Jesus" with the community's economic sharing (Acts 4:32-35). "The testimony is credible because the evidence of God's power is palpable in the community's life."[21] Two chapters later, the ministry of the deacons (*diakonia*) is established to meet the needs of widows in the church and free the apostles for the "ministry of the word." Luke adds the phrase "so the word of God spread" to indicate the close connection between the preaching of the apostles ("service of the word") and the activity of those appointed to organize the distribution of food to the poor ("service of tables") in the spread of the gospel and growth of the church (6:7). The message of the apostles, then, was not disembodied. It was linked to the broader definition of the church as a witnessing community. As Darrel Guder states:

> The message is embedded in the empowered reality of a community of witnesses that has been present in the world since Pentecost. Out of the community emerges the message, and the proclamation of the message, empowered by the Spirit, leads to the response of faith, which in turn builds up and expands the community. In that sense, there is a cyclical relationship between *koinonia* and *kerygma*, community and its proclamation.[22]

It is particularly significant that Luke depicts the missionary expansion of the church in qualitative as well as quantitative terms. Luke describes the outward spread of the gospel in terms of an ever-widening circle of recipients from the nucleus of believers in Jerusalem: (a) devout Aramaic-speaking Jews (2:5); (b) Greek-speaking Jews (6:1); (c) those on the fringes of Judaism—the Samaritans (8:24) and the Ethiopian eunuch (8:26); and finally (d) Gentiles (10:1-11:18). He is clear that an important part of the missionary work of the early church was the attraction of the communities of believers who had fellowship in private homes, celebrated common meals, cared for each other financially, worshiped God together, and reached out to surrounding neighborhoods.[23] The significance of this "life-style evangelism" is evident from the response of unbelievers to the first Christians following Pentecost (Acts 2:42-47). It is easy to miss the importance of the phrase "enjoying the favor of all of the people" (vs. 47) in this passage. But this is the connecting link between the *daily practice* of the early believers (vss. 42-47) and their *evangelistic success* (vs. 47b). Note also that the attractiveness of the early church was not in its glitzy programs but in its *lifestyle*. As Rene Padilla states:

Acts 2:41-47 clearly shows that the result of the Pentecost experience is no ghetto-church, devoted to cultivating individualistic religion and an exclusive, separatist church. On the contrary, it is a community of the Spirit, a community that becomes a center of attraction, 'having the good will of all the people' (v. 47), because it incarnates the values of the Kingdom of God and affirms, by what it is, by what it does and by what it says that Jesus Christ has been exalted as Lord over every aspect of life. It is a missionary community that preaches reconciliation with God and the restoration of all creation by the power of the Spirit. It is a community that provides a glimpse of the birth of a new humanity, and in which can be seen, albeit 'in a mirror dimly' (I Corinthians 13:12), the fulfillment of God's plan for all mankind.[24]

The household structure of the first century provided the foundation for an extended network of relationships with people in the neighborhoods and workplaces. These natural contacts provided an opportunity for house (or "oikos") evangelism—the sharing of the transforming power of God's grace through Christ in the context of natural associations of family, friends, and business associates. This "oikos evangelism" was *holistic* in the sense that it addressed the needs of the entire person, and integrated whole-life discipleship, the multiplication of churches, and ministry. So, the *oikos* was the training ground, not just for missional outreach and evangelism but also for demonstrating the love of Christ to both fellow Christians and non-believers.[25]

Some have described the multiplication of the early church as a "renewal movement," to indicate that mission can never be divorced from church renewal and its resulting social impact.[26] Likewise, Viv Grigg utilizes the concept of "web movements" to describe the early Christian missionary expansion in terms of the transmission of the power of the Spirit and exponential spread of the gospel through webs of relational ties—first, in the Jerusalem Jewish community;

then into transitional Gentile communities (the Ethiopian eunuch, Samaritans, Cornelius the Roman, and Antioch); and finally in trade centers throughout the Roman empire with the missionary activity of Paul and his missionary companions and co-workers.[27] These movements of renewal and revival in Acts were generated by an outpouring of the Holy Spirit, private and public repentance, and divine empowerment for love, unity, and proclamation. And they usually consisted of the following phases: (1) personal transformation, then (2) small group renewal and structural change, followed by (3) social and cultural engagement.[28]

Luke therefore characterizes the witness of the community of believers in terms of verbal proclamation (the evangelistic preaching of the apostles), service or ministry in the church, and visible attraction (the social and economic equality of believers).[29] As the gospel advanced and new believing communities were established the early church surmounted barriers of religion, race, class, gender, and prejudice. It exhibited unity in instruction, prayer, worship, witness, and the meeting of needs through the power of the Holy Spirit. Evangelism and social concern were indissolubly united. All of this was the manifestation of a new reality in Christ that had a transforming effect upon the surrounding community. Luke's vision of church growth is that of the expansion of vital and dynamic "communities of the kingdom."[30]

Danger of Idealizing the Early Church

Having said all of this, we should be careful not to idealize the first-century church. Christians anxious to cull "lessons" or "principles" from the Acts account may do so in a way that naively romanticizes the early church, fails to account for cultural differences between the first and twenty-first centuries, and does not distinguish hermeneutically between what is descriptive and what is (possibly) prescriptive.[31] Some evangelical scholars have suggested a "narrative theological hermeneutic" that goes beyond a purely historically-oriented retelling of the story and an exclusively grammatical, lexical study of the text but also avoids a totally subjective approach that ascribes to the narrative whatever meaning we want to see. This approach studies the Bible as the narrative of the pilgrimage of God's people over time and it recognizes that Scripture portrays a deepening understanding from Israel to the church of God's self-revelation in the midst of human history. Thus, God's self-disclosure is seen as taking place in the midst of a faith-journey, or the walk of God's people with God. There must be an interaction between the self-definition of the early church and the self-definition of today's believers who wish to be inspired and guided by the early witnesses. [32] To illustrate this method, we will examine two issues which faced the early church: (1) the impoverishment of many Christians in the Jerusalem church; and (2) the inclusion of Gentile believers within the people of God.

Poverty and the Sharing of Possessions

The response of the church in Jerusalem to the first of these issues involved a sharing of possessions following the coming of the Holy Spirit at Pentecost (Acts 2:44-45, 4:32-37). A careful reading of these passages reveals that the statement in 4:23 that "there were no needy persons among them" is virtually an exact quotation of Deuteronomy 15:4, which specified that the purpose of the sabbatical year was that "there should be no poor among you." This law specified that every seven years slaves had to be liberated, debts were to be cancelled, and land should remain fallow for the benefit of the poor. Luke therefore portrays the church after Pentecost as a fulfillment of the Deuteronomic ideal of the covenant community.[33] Luke also wants to show the church's common life of economic sharing (along with spiritual rebirth and fellowship) as the "first fruits" of the mission announced by Jesus in Luke 4:16-21 to bring "good news" to the poor. The community's practice of distributing goods to meet the needs of the poor is portrayed as a response of obedience to Jesus' teaching throughout Luke's Gospel (cf. Luke 6:20-21, 12:13-21, 16:19-31). At a deeper theological level Luke wants to show that the eschatological era of the Spirit foretold by the Old Testament prophets has begun. The economic sharing is "sign" of a future hope. In the words of Chris Wright: "The church by its internal practice was erecting a sign-post to the reality of the future. The new age of life in the Messiah and in the Spirit is described in terms that echo the jubilee and its related sabbatical institutions."[34] The "glad and generous hearts" (Acts 2:46) of the Jerusalem community is evidence of the presence of God's spirit.

At the same time, the response of the early believers to the needs of the poor was not uniformly positive, as the story of Ananias and Sapphira clearly shows (Acts 5:1-11). Moreover, the sharing of possessions was not a long-term solution to the economic crisis facing the church in Jerusalem, which was caused by persecution and a general famine under the reign of Claudius. This is clear from on-going efforts by Paul and others to provide relief aid from the church in Antioch (Acts 11:27-30) and other churches in Asia Minor on behalf of the poor in Jerusalem. This means that there should not be a rigid application or imitation of the Jerusalem model today. Even within the early church, the methods of practical caring and sharing took on different forms. Rather, the account of the early Jerusalem community provides a "positive paradigm" for how the economic practices in our communities ought to powerfully bear witness to the resurrection and manifest sacrificial giving for those in economic need in a way that unsettles our "commonsense" view of economic reality.[35]

The Inclusion of Gentiles in the People of God

The second issue facing the church in Acts is reflected in Luke's account of the apostolic council in Acts 15. The basic question had to do with what criteria had to be met to belong to the elect church of God and at the same time maintain continuity with the people of God of the first covenant. The Jews regarded circumcision as a sign of God's covenant (cf. Gen. 17:11) and thus of membership in the people of God. Jewish food laws also regulated what one should eat and stipulated that there should be table fellowship only with one's own people. So, how do believers in Jesus come to participate in the covenant as God's people? To what extent should these traditional "boundary markers" of Jewish identity be applied to the emerging Gentile churches?[36]

It is not necessary at this point that we go into the details of the on-going dispute over these questions in the fledgling church. Luke's account indicates that there was a group of conservative Jewish Christians or "Christian Pharisees" (Acts 15:5) who insisted on the circumcision of Gentile believers and observance of Jewish purity laws. The apostle Paul and the majority of other leaders at the conference recognized, on the other hand, that the Gentile mission did not require circumcision (15:10-12). The resulting compromise called for approval of the Gentile mission based upon the observance of a minimum of ritual prescriptions and abstinence from sexual immorality (15:19-21, 28-29; 21:25). New Testament scholars have pointed out that this Jerusalem decree did not fully solve the question of how Jewish and Gentile Christians should live together, specifically as it related to communal fellowship. As we will see in the next chapter, subsequent developments in the Galatian church, for example, clearly show that conservative Jewish Christians who insisted on Gentile circumcision and observance of the law did not give up.[37]

What relevance does all of this have for us? Briefly, we can say that the Christian Judaizers were guilty of three errors. First, with their emphasis on the law they were splitting the church along racial and ethnic lines and requiring circumcision as a necessary supplement to faith in Christ. Paul was concerned that such a preoccupation with the Mosaic law was creating two denominations: a Jewish Christianity and a Gentile Christianity. As Scott McKnight states:

> Here is Paul's principal argument against Judaizing legalism: whatever practices detract from the all-sufficiency of Christ

and the enabling ministries of the Spirit must be opposed; whatever practices build walls between people who believe in Jesus Christ must be torn down; whatever practices seek to supplement trust in Christ and dependence on the Holy Spirit must be cleared away; whoever seeks to demand any such things must be countered. In effect, whatever message that is not Christ and the Spirit alone is a perversion and must be radically denounced.[38]

While there are no Christian groups today that explicitly require circumcision or place restrictions on table fellowship on the basis of Old Testament Levitical Law, the question then is whether there are analogous beliefs and practices today that deserve similar condemnation.

The second error of the Christian Judaizers involved an over-reliance on human tradition. Paul is probably alluding to this group in Philippians 3:2 (where they are described as "mutilators of the flesh") and in Phil 3:17-19. The phrase "whose god is their belly" (3:19) is a reference to their preoccupation with Jewish traditions, which required a ritual washing of hands and utensils before eating along with adherence to dietary laws as a precondition for membership in the covenant community. Beale points out that they revered this oral man-made tradition more than Scripture. "They were so committed to this old Jewish tradition, they were substituting it in place of God's Word and thus had made an idol of it. Paul can refer to such over exalting of these dietary laws as making your 'belly' into a 'god.'"[39] In similar fashion, churches today can be divided on the basis of adherence or non-adherence to certain traditions that take precedence over Scripture. When this happens the traditions become idolatrous. "Such idolatry can be subtle, since the church may not deny the truth of Scripture but effectively ignores it in the life and practice of the church."[40]

Finally, the Christian Judaizers had a misplaced emphasis on Jerusalem and the temple as the center of God's presence and activity. To fully understand this we need to return to events of Pentecost, which took place while the early believers were gathered in the temple courts (Acts 2:1-2, 46). In a detailed examination of the events and imagery of Pentecost, Beale has convincingly shown that Luke regarded Pentecost as the "temple of the new age."[41] Peter's subsequent depiction of Pentecost as fulfillment of Joel's prophecy of the destruction of the old world and the emergence of the new order and his reference to Christ as cornerstone of the new temple (Acts 4:1, 10) are further confirmation that Christ was building the true temple composed of himself and his people.[42] This is why Stephen regarded temple worship with its rejection of Christ as blasphemy. For God's presence and his salvation purposes could no longer be contained in houses built by man—i.e., the man-made temple in the old, temporal Jerusalem (Acts 7:48-49).[43]

Paul Barnett is right when he states: "Implicit in Stephen's criticism of the Temple was a rejection of the eschatological centrality of Jerusalem. For him the mission of God for the gathering of the nations was not centripetal (pulling in to the center) but centrifugal (driving out from the center)."[44] Philip the evangelist likewise saw that God's mission purposes were *outward from* Jerusalem, not *inward to* Jerusalem. Barnett continues: "The notion of Jerusalem as centrifugal and not centripetal in God's mission to the nations, which became so much associated with Paul, had its seeds in the vision of Stephen and the activities of Philip."[45] This represented a dramatic shift in thinking for Jewish Christians. To be sure, they rejoiced in the fact that God had granted even the Gentiles repentance unto life (Acts 11:18). But during the early years of its formation, the Christian church was generally regarded as a messianic sect within Judaism. Although they confessed faith in Christ, the early Christians in Palestine observed the law, worshiped in the temple, and participated in the religious and social life of the synagogue (Acts 3:1, 5:12, 10:14).[46] In all likelihood, the apostles remained in Jerusalem because they regarded the Holy City as the center of God's end-time universe.[47] As we have observed, what was particularly upsetting to the Christian Judaizers about the Gentile mission was that the new converts were not being circumcised or taught the Mosaic law—two key "markers" of God's covenant people. Paul counters this thinking by emphasizing that Christ is the end-time temple in whom God dwells (Col. 1:19)[48] and in whom both Jews and Gentiles could become members in true Israel, "not with a circumcision done by the hands of men but with the circumcision done by Christ [i.e., his death and resurrection]" (Col. 2:11).

To the extent that we limit the activity of God's Spirit to man-made buildings, budgets, and programs we are guilty of the same error as the Christian Judaizers. Bob Roberts remarks that we often equate the size of our churches with the level of our people's spirituality:

> The kingdom of God is bigger than any building, although most of us live our lives to build edifices in temporary settings. How foolish for the church, for Scripture tells us that we are to live for the eternal not the temporary. Instead, it's possible to live our lives in such a way to demonstrate that the kingdom is far bigger than we are."[49]

Conclusion

I have suggested that Luke's theology of mission as witness in the book of Acts is informed by a "kingdom vision" which sees the body of Christ as a community of God's reign. Theologically, this idea of kingdom witness (Acts 1:8) is rooted in a three-fold conception of the church as (1) expanding numerically and geographically; (2) fulfilling the Old Testament prophetic hope for a "reconstituted Israel;" and (3) manifesting the reality of God's future kingdom through *kerygma* (proclamation), *diakonia* (service/ministry), and *koinonia* (community).

The practice of the early church as recounted in Acts should not be idealized. But neither should it be dismissed as unimportant. The theology of mission as described in Acts provides a model for present-day mission. There must be a dynamic interaction between the self-understanding of the early church and the self-understanding of today's churches as they seek to find guidance and inspiration in the early Christian witness. The practice of mission in Acts therefore indicates that Christian mission cannot be limited to verbal witness— although neither, of course, can it be disengaged from a proclamation of the gospel. Furthermore, ministries of justice and mercy not only support the church's witness. They are *part of* the church's witness to the kingdom of God. The planting and multiplication of churches locally and overseas is therefore not an end itself but the means through which the body of Christ strives to be a visible expression of his reign in both word and deed.

Notes

[1] Van Engen, *God's Missionary People*, pp. 42.

[2] Ibid.

[3] Ibid., p. 27.

[4] William J. Larkin Jr., "Mission in Acts," in *Mission in the New Testament: An Evangelical Approach*, ed., William J. Larkin Jr. and Joel F. Williams (Maryknoll, NY: Orbis), p. 173.

[5] Eckhard J. Schnabel, *Early Christian Mission, Vol. II: Paul and the Early Church* (Downers Grove, IL: InterVarsity, 2004), pp. 1581-2.

[6] See John Mark Hicks, "Numerical Growth in the Theology of Acts: Part One," *Church Growth Magazine* 11 (April-June, 1996). Available at: http://www.4churchm growth.com

[7] Thomas Moore points out that the connection of the phrase "to the ends of the earth" in Acts 1:8 and 13:47 to Isaiah 49:6 denotes the announcement and/or extension of salvation to the limit of the inhabited world. See Thomas S. Moore, "'To the End of the Earth': The Geographical and Ethnic Universalism of Acts 1:8 in Light of the Isaianic Influence on Luke," *Journal of the Evangelical Theological Society* 40/3 (September 1997), p. 393.

[8] Hicks, "Numerical Growth in the Theology of Acts," op. cit.

[9] Pao, *Acts and the Isaianic New Exodus*, pp. 90-101; 227-24. Acts 13:47 describes the apostolic witness as "being a light to the Gentiles" so that salvation will be brought "to the ends of the earth." This verse is an exact quotation of Isaiah 49:6 which

depicts the restoration of Israel in terms of the universality of salvation. The call of the apostles to "be my witnesses" finds its closest parallel in Isa 43:10-12.

[10] Andreas J. Kostenberger and Peter T. O'Brien, *Salvation to the Ends of the Earth*, pp. 130-1; Pao, *Acts and the Isaianic New Exodus*, p. 95. Pao gives an extensive treatment of this argument. He shows convincingly that Acts thematically depicts the restoration of Israel in a number of ways. First the election of Mathias to complete the circle of the twelve (Acts 1:12-26) signals the beginning of the restoration of Israel since the twelve apostles are representative of the twelve tribes of Israel (cf. Luke 22:28-30; Acts 26:7). Second, the reference to "all Judea and Samaria" (Acts 1:8) and the emphasis given to Phillip's ministry in Samara and the conversion of the entire region (Acts 8:9-25) point to the reunification of the two kingdoms in fulfillment of the promised restoration of the whole house of Israel under one king (Ezek. 37:15-22). Third, the ingathering of Jews from all over the world at Pentecost (Acts 2:5) depicts the ingathering of exiles from the Jewish diaspora predicted in Isaiah 11:11. Fourth, the early Christian community is depicted as the eschatological community of the Spirit predicted by the prophets (Acts 2:17; cf. Isaiah 2:1; Joel 2:28-32). Fifth, a number of passages in Acts make reference to the rebuilding of the Davidic kingdom in fulfillment of ancient promises (Acts 13:34, 15:16-18; cf. Isa. 55:3; Amos 9:11-12). Sixth, the call to repentance is specifically connected with the program of restoration (Acts 3:19). Finally, the conversion of the Ethiopian eunuch (Acts 8:26-40) points to the place of outcastes in the reconstituted people of God (Isa 56:3-5). Ibid., pp. 111-46.

[11] Hicks, "Numerical Growth in the Theology of Acts: The Role of Pragmatism, Reason, and Rhetoric," Journal of the American Society for Church Growth 8 (Spring 1997), pp. 17-34.

[12] Pao, *Acts and the Isaianic New Exodus*, pp. 147-80

[13] Moore, "'To the End of the Earth': The Geographic and Ethnic Universalism of Acts 1:8," p. 394.

[14] Ibid. p. 95.

[15] The fact that Peter is speaking to Jews is indicated by the fact that he addresses his audience as "men of Israel" (2:22) and later describes them as "brothers" (vs. 29).

[16] David Pao argues that the phrase "devout Jews from every nation under heaven" (Acts 2:5) establishes both the universality of the regions represented and the particularity of the ethnic identity of the audience. The possibility that Gentiles are among the witnesses to the Pentecost event is ruled out both by the emphasis on the Jewish identity of the audience and the fact that the conversion of the Gentiles is not mentioned before the conversion story of Cornelius in Acts 10-11. The list of nations in 2:9-11 is again balanced by a reference to "both Jews and proselytes" in vs. 11. The best way to account for both the universal and particular aspects in Acts 2 is to see it as describing the ingathering of the exiles from the Jewish Diaspora predicted by Isaiah. The list of nations in this passage is similar to the list in Isaiah 11:11, which describes the return of exiles in the last days ("On that day the Lord will extend his hand yet a second time to recover the remnant that is left of this people, from Assyria, from Egypt, from Pathros, from Ethiopia, from Elam, from Shinar, from Hamath, and from the coastlands of the sea."). Thus, while the

universal mission may be implicit here, the focus is on Jews who are present. See Pao, *Acts and the Isaianic New Exodus*, pp. 130-31, See also Rebecca I. Denova, *The Things Accomplished Among Us: Prophetic Tradition in the Structural Pattern of Luke-Acts* (Shefield: Sheffield Academic Press, 1997), p. 173.

[17] The apostle Paul makes a similar argument regarding the rebuilding of the Davidic Kingdom (Acts 13:34).

[18] See Darrell L. Bock, "The Reign of the Lord Christ," in *Dispensationalism, Israel and the Church*, ed., Blaising and Bock, pp. 56-7.

[19] Schnabel, *The Early Christian Mission, Vol. I*, p. 444.

[20] Guder, *Be My Witnesses*, p. 49.

[21] Hays, *The Moral Vision of the New Testament*, pp. 123-25.

[22] Guder, *Be My Witnesses*, pp. 51-52.

[23] See Schnabel, *Early Christian Mission, Vol. I*, p. 420.

[24] C Rene Padilla, "Holistic Mission," in *Holistic Mission*, ed., Evvy Hay Campbell (Lausanne Occassional Paper 33. Lausanne Committee for World Evangelization, 2004). See http://www.lausanne.org/docs/2004forum/LOP33_ IG4.pdf

[25] See Roger Gehring, *House Church and Mission: The Importance of Household Structures in Early Christianity* (Peabody, MA: Hendrickson, 2004), pp. 180, 293.

[26] Howard Snyder, "Church Growth Must be Based on a Biblical Vision of the Church as the Vital Community of the Kingdom of God," in *Evaluating the Church Growth Movement: 5 Views*, ed., Gary McIntosh and Paul Engle, (Grand Rapids, MI: Zondervan, 2004), pp. 209-31.

[27] See Viv Grigg, "The Spirit of Christ and the Postmodern City: Transformative Revival Among Auckland's Evangelicals and Pentecostals." (http://www. urban-leaders.org/PhD.htm)

[28] These phases are evident, for example, in Acts 2:42-47, 6:1-7, 11:19-30, 16:11-40, and 19:1-41.

[29] Wright, *The Mission of God*, p. 303.

[30] See Glasser, *Announcing the Kingdom*, pp. 274-76. Also, Snyder, "Church Growth," p. 213.

[31] See Schnabel, *Early Christian Mission, Vol. II*, pp. 1569-70.

[32] See Dae Ryeong Kim, "Toward an Holistic Approach to Bible Interpretation" in *Toward A Missiological Approach to Hermeneutics for Gospel Proclamation in a Post-modern World*, (Unpublished Ph.D. dissertation, Fuller Theological Seminary, 2007). Website: http://members.fortunecity.com/dakim/holistic_herme.htm See also Grant Osborne, *The Hermeneutical Spiral, Revised and Expanded Version* (Downers Grove, IL: InterVarsity, 1993), pp. 220; 432-433.

[33] Richard B. Hays, *The Moral Vision of the New Testament*, p. 123.

[34] Wright, *The Mission of God*, pp. 302-303.

[35] Hays, *The Moral Vision of the New Testament*, pp. 302-3.

[36] See Udo Schnelle, *Apostle Paul: His Life and Theology* (Grand Rapids, MI: Baker Academic, 2003), p. 123-4.

[37] Schnabel, *Early Christian Mission, Vol. II*, p. 1019.

[38] Scott McKnight, *NIV Application Bible: Galatians* (Grand Rapids, MI: Zondervan, 1995), pp. 34-5.

[39] Beale, *We Become What We Worship*, pp. 187-88.

[40] Ibid., p. 302.
[41] See Beale, *The Temple and the Church's Mission*, pp. 201-18.
[42] Ibid., pp. 212-18.
[43] Ibid., pp. 218-23.
[44] Paul Barnett, *Paul: Missionary of Jesus* (Grand Rapids, MI: Eerdmans, 2008), p. 52.
[45] Ibid., p. 53.
[46] Glasser, *Announcing the Kingdom*, p. 271.
[47] Barnett, *Paul: Missionary of Jesus*, p. 52.
[48] A comparison of this verse with Ps 68:16-17 (cf. Ps. 67) shows that Paul is applying the psalmist's reference to God's dwelling in Israel's temple to God now dwelling in his Son. See Beale, *The Temple and the Church's Mission*, p. 267.
[49] Roberts, *Transformation*, pp. 23, 31.

Chapter 12
Ethics, the Church, and Mission in Paul's Theology

David Bosch and others have rightly argued that Paul's theology and his mission are integrally related—not as "theory" to "practice" in the sense that his mission flows from or is a practical outworking of his theology, but because his theology is a missionary theology.[1] Furthermore, it is clear from various passages that Paul spells out the goals of his apostleship in terms of the advancement of the gospel (I Cor. 9:19-23, 10:31-11:1; Rom. 1:1-5, 15:15-16, 16:25-27). But what did Paul mean by the gospel? For most evangelicals, the answer is obvious. It is the means by which individuals are saved through faith in Christ on the basis of his work on the cross. Contemporary mission practices are therefore often rooted in assumptions that Paul's own missionary activity was primarily limited to evangelistic proclamation and the incorporation of believers into churches (or community formation). As Michael Barram states:

> Although the subject of Paul's mission has been addressed by a number of scholars in recent years, that mission tends to be defined fairly narrowly in terms of what is known today as 'evangelism' (i.e., initiating efforts aimed at the conversion of

non-Christians and formation of communities). In effect, mission becomes nearly equated with initial evangelism.[2]

Yet, at the end of his letter to the church in Rome, Paul looks back on his apostolic activity in the East and summarizes it in terms of "leading the Gentiles to obey God by what I have said and done" (Rom. 15:17-19), thereby indicating that his instructions regarding behavior are integrally related to his comprehensive missional vocation.[3] It appears, then, that Paul's understanding of his mission (as well as his use of the word "gospel") may not be quite as clear-cut as we think.

In this chapter, my purpose will be to clarify this relationship between mission, the church, and ethics in Paul's thought. Since the "gospel of Jesus Christ" is at the heart of Paul's theology we will attempt to answer three key questions. (1) What is the meaning of the "gospel" in the context of Paul's missionary vocation and calling? (2) For Paul, does the "gospel" have a social dimension that has to do with relations between believers in the body of Christ? (3) Does Paul regard ministry to the poor (i.e., acts of social concern) both within and outside the body of Christ, to be an integral part of his apostolic mission to advance the gospel of Jesus Christ? But, first, we must look at two competing paradigms of Paul's theology among contemporary evangelicals.

Two Controlling Paradigms of Paul's Thought

Paul has been described as the missionary "par excellence." Bound up in this description of the apostle are three intertwining stories. First, there is the story of his direct encounter with the risen Christ on the road to Damascus (Acts 9:1-6) which resulted in his dramatic 180 degree conversion from "Saul," a zealous persecutor of the church, to "Paul" (lit. "little"), the "least of the apostles" whose only purpose in life was to know Christ and make him known (Phil. 3:5-10). Second, there is the story of his Gentile mission and his missionary journeys, which are recorded in the book of Acts but are also referred to numerous times in his letters. Included in this story are the various sub-stories of his converts and his relationship to the Gentile churches he founded. Finally there is, as Michael Bird points out, the grand narrative of redemptive history that Paul refers to in his letters and his descriptions of his missionary calling. "Story is the most characteristic expression of world view and identity. It defines who we are, where we come from, what the problem is and where we are going."[4] Therefore, understanding the stories embedded in his letters—especially the "story behind the story"—is crucial to understanding Paul properly.[5]

Unfortunately, there is considerable lack of agreement on the nature of this "meta-narrative" in Paul's theology. For the interpretative tradition derived from the Reformation (and especially from Luther) Paul's over-arching concern is with the transfer of the human being from the status of being condemned as a sinner to the status of being "just before God." This is rooted in Paul's Damascus Road experience. It is also historically rooted in the biblical narrative of God's unfolding purpose of salvation for all mankind through Abraham and his seed (Rom. 9:7-8). But, fundamentally, it is rooted in the death and resurrection of Christ whose righteousness is "imputed" to the believer. For some who adopt this interpretive framework the "dispensation of grace," which begins in the book of Acts, is most fully represented in the mission of Paul to the Gentiles. Paul's gospel of grace is therefore to be distinguished from Jesus' gospel of the kingdom.[6] But, even among those who do not come out of this tradition it is widely assumed that Paul did not exhibit a social consciousness and concern for the poor that characterized the ministry of Jesus and the practices of the Jerusalem-based church.[7] This view is reflected in William Loader's poignant observation that none of Paul's writings "would lead one to understand that good news for the poor was a central feature in the message of Jesus." The Jesus whom Paul claims had been revealed to him in a christophany (Gal. 1:16) and now lives "in me" (Gal. 2:20) must somehow be a different Jesus than the one who placed care for the poor at the forefront of his ministry.[8]

By now is it pretty much common knowledge at least among academics that there is another interpretive framework or paradigm for understanding Paul which is referred to as the "New Perspective." While supporters of the New Perspective do not all speak with one voice, its most well-known, able, and articulate spokesman is probably N.T. Wright. According to Wright, Paul sees Christ's death and resurrection as *the* eschatological event that marks the beginning of the new messianic age. It means fundamentally that the risen Christ is Lord. Furthermore, in his view, God's righteousness is not something that is imputed to the believer. Rather, it is God's faithfulness to the covenant through Christ. Justification therefore is not about one's status before God (the vertical) but a declaration that one belongs to the covenant "people of God" (the horizontal). The central question is not "Am I saved?" (an individualistic focus). Rather it is "Who is in the covenant?"—with a social or relational focus on embracing the Gentiles and regarding them as being on equal footing with the Jews. For Wright, Christ's Lordship also destroys the dichotomy that exists in people's minds between "preaching the gospel" on the one hand and social action or social justice on the other. For "there is no area of existence or life, including no area of human life, that does not come up for critique in the light of the sovereignty of the crucified and risen Jesus."[9] Finally, while it would be wrong to see Paul's mission as simply paralleling or repeating Jesus' mission (which was totally unique), there was "appropriate continuity" between two people living at different points in the eschatological timetable—much like the relationship between a composer and a conductor of his composition. Jesus' mission was to bring Israel's history to its climax. Paul's mission was to announce that "gospel" to the Gentile world.[10]

It is not possible, and it would take us too far afield, to go into all of the nuances of the debate between these two competing paradigms. But the theological differences between these two interpretive frameworks will serve as a backdrop for addressing the three questions posed above. Again, we will focus on some key programmatic texts in Paul's letters.

The Gospel in the Context of Paul's Mission

At important points in his letters Paul spells out the goals of his apostleship using various descriptive phrases.[11] Two expressions he uses to describe his mission are "obedience of faith" in Romans (Rom. 1:1-5, 15:15-18, 16:25-27) and "so that by all means I might save some" in Corinthians (I Cor. 9:19-23, cf. 10:31-11:1). Having a proper understanding of these phrases is therefore critical to understanding what he means by the "gospel" (*euangelion*). But let's first look briefly at the context of these two letters.

The gospel was probably brought to Rome by unknown missionaries who were engaged in business or commerce.[12] So, besides the church in Colossae, the church in Rome was the only recipient of Paul's letters that was not founded by him.[13] Originally, it was composed primarily of Jewish Christians. But because of Jewish disturbances, the emperor Claudius issued an edict in AD 49 expelling Jews from Rome. Although the edict was annulled when he died in AD 54 it had a decisive effect on the composition of the Christian congregations in that city. By the time Paul wrote his letter to the Roman church (around AD 65-66) Gentile Christians already formed a majority (cf. Rom. 1:5, 13-15; 10:1-3, 17-32; 15:15, 16, 18). At the same time, the letter indicates that there was a considerable and influential minority of Jewish Christians within the church (Rom. 9-11; 16:7, 11).[14] In the period between the edict of Claudius (AD 49) and Nero's persecution of the Christians (AD 64) the various house churches probably experienced considerable growth. But this growth did not come without increased pressure from Jewish and Gentile non-believers and perhaps even Roman authorities (Rom. 12:17-21, 13:1-6).[15] In this context, Paul urges the Roman Christians to exhibit the values of Jesus Christ (Rom. 12-13) and live in harmony with one another (Rom. 14-15).

At the time when Paul wrote his letters to the church in Corinth, the city was the capital of the Roman province of Achaia. As a commercial center between Asia and Rome/Greece it had a culturally diverse population and was a wealthy city that thrived on commerce, banking, and skilled trades. Paul founded the church there around AD 50 (Acts 18:5, 11). The majority of church members were converts from animistic religions (I Cor. 8:10, 10:27, 12:2). The church congregation therefore reflected the cultural, religious, and social pluralism of the city.[16] This helps to explain the many problems and issues that Paul addresses in I Corinthians—partisanship and internal divisions (1:10-4:21); immoral behavior (5:1-6:19); conflicts over eating meat offered to idols (8:1-13); abuses related to the Lord's Supper (11:17-34); and disputes over the use of spiritual gifts and order of worship (12:1-14:40). As Udo Schnelle states: "No other letter provides us such a window into the diversity with the Pauline churches as does I Corinthians, and shows how forcefully Paul's fundamental convictions and situationally conditioned arguments interact in his theology."[17]

The Obedience of Faith (Rom 1:1-5, 15:15-18, 16:25-27)

In the introduction (1:5) and concluding doxology (16:26) of his letter to the Romans Paul describes the purpose of the gospel and of his apostleship in terms of bringing about the "obedience of faith" among the Gentiles (or words to that effect). In repeating these words (which are also found in 15:18) Paul leaves no doubt that they are crucial to understanding his intentions in writing the letter. Dunn rightly states: "To clarify what faith is and its importance to the gospel is one of Paul's chief objectives in this letter."[18]

It is important to see that in each instance, Paul sets this phrase within a larger eschatological context. Romans 1:5 serves as a pivotal "hinge" between Paul's statement of his calling and his depiction of the gospel (vss. 1-4) and his description of the Roman Christians as being among those who are called to belong to Christ (vss. 6-7).[19] In verses 2-4 Paul succinctly summarizes the mission of Christ in terms of the "gospel of God:"

> The gospel he promised beforehand through his prophets in the Holy Scriptures regarding his Son, who as to his human nature was a descendant of David and who through the Spirit of holiness was declared with power to be the Son of God by his resurrection from the dead: Jesus Christ our Lord.

Here, Paul is probably quoting from a hymn or creed about Jesus that circulated widely among the first Christians.[20] While these verses are often glossed over, their significance for understanding his letter to the Romans cannot be overstated. Not only are they a statement about the Christ as human and divine. They also brim with allusions to Old Testament promises that squarely set the gospel within the covenant structure of the Old Testament. Paul is here describing the inauguration of the new age through Jesus' resurrection as a fulfillment of the promises made to Israel through Abraham and David (Gen. 17:6; II Sam. 7:12-16).[21] Jesus' resurrection as the "Son of God" fulfills the words of Psalm 2:7-8, which speaks of the coronation of the Davidic king who receives the nations as his inheritance.[22] Paul therefore sees his mission to preach the gospel as "the instrumentality by which the risen Christ in the fullness of time asserts his rule over the new people of God."[23]

In Romans 15:16 Paul further describes this mission as a "priestly duty" of "proclaiming the gospel of God *so that* the Gentiles might become an offering acceptable to God, sanctified by the Holy Spirit." This may be an allusion to Isaiah 66:18-21, which promises that God's emissaries will bring in both Jews and Gentiles as an "offering to the Lord" (vs. 20). Paul's Gentile mission is therefore set within the context of Old Testament prophecies regarding the eschatological ingathering of the nations, who will not only worship God and find salvation but also learn obedience to him (Rom. 15:18; cf. Isa. 2:3).[24] The reference to "signs and wonders" as a means by which this mission was being fulfilled (15:19) is significant, for this was a traditional way of speaking of the exodus miracles. In using this expression, Paul is not simply affirming his mark as a true apostle of God. He is at the same time asserting that Christ's working through him is part and parcel of God's redemptive activity that began with Moses at the exodus and continues through the ministry of Jesus and the apostles.[25]

Paul again places his mission within a salvation-historical framework when he states in the climax of his letter (16:26) that the "mystery" which has "now" been revealed in the preaching of the gospel is rooted in the Old Testament Scriptures ("through the prophetic writings") and the mission of God ("the eternal plan of God").[26] The adverb "now" (*nun*) continually appears in key Pauline passages which announce the arrival of the *eschaton* or new age (Rom. 3:21; 5:9; 7:6, 17; Eph. 2:12-13; Col. 1;26-27; II Tim. 1:9-10). Again, Paul asserts that the purpose of the proclamation of the gospel is that "all nations might believe and obey" God, whose glory is now revealed in Jesus Christ. "Paul's commission then is to be viewed as nothing less than the eschatological actualization of the eternal plan to create faith's obedience among the nations."[27]

We cannot grasp the full import of Paul's portrayal of the gospel and his mission in these passages without further examining the first-century context in which he wrote. The world of the eastern Mediterranean in which Paul lived and traveled was largely dominated by the imperial ideology of the Roman Empire. This imperial cult was the basis for unifying the diverse populations that had been brought under Roman rule. It promoted absolute loyalty and permeated every aspect of Greco-Roman society, including parades, dinner parties, festivals, religious rituals, athletic games, and gladiatorial contests.[28] The centerpiece of this imperial religion was the emperor-cult with its adoration and even worship of the Roman rulers who adopted titles such as Lord (*kyros*), Savior, and Son of God. In the East, where rulers and monarchs had long been regarded as divine, the "divinity" of the Roman emperor was accepted without question. In Rome itself the early emperors were careful not to claim such a high distinction. The title "Son of god" was sufficient.[29] Rome was regarded as the fountain-head of freedom, justice, peace, and salvation and the emperor was viewed as the guarantor of these ideals, which were often spoken of as *euangelion*, "good news," or "gospel."[30]

This was the social and political context in which Paul spoke of Christ as the "Son of God" and "Lord" to whom people from all nations were subject. He, of course, was not a political dissident as Romans 13 makes clear. But, contrary to the perceptions that most evangelicals have of Paul's theology, the "gospel" that he preached could not have been understood by its hearers as anything but "counter-imperial," and even politically subversive. Michael Bird puts it well: "Paul did not know of a neat separation between church and state and did not think faith in Jesus meant having a purely interiorized spirituality."[31] This is *not* to say that the gospel can simply be *reduced* to statements about Jesus' Lordship. There can be no gospel without an emphasis on the atonement for sins through Jesus' death and resurrection.[32] Nonetheless, N.T. Wright is correct in his description of Paul's ministry:

> His missionary work . . . must be conceived not simply in terms of a traveling evangelist offering people a new religious experience, but of an ambassador for a king-in-waiting, establishing cells of people loyal to this new king, and ordering their lives according to his story, his symbols, and his praxis, and their minds according to his truth. This could only be construed as deeply counter-imperial, as subversive to the whole edifice of the Roman Empire; and there is in fact plenty of evidence that Paul intended it to be so construed, and that when he ended up in prison as a result of his work he took it as a sign that he had been doing his job properly.[33]

It is in this context of the Lordship of the resurrected Christ that we must understand the phrase "obedience of faith." For while the believer is saved by faith in Christ, the Savior who is the object of our worship is also the King promised by the Old Testament prophets who will restore true justice and righteousness to the nations. Some argue that what Paul has in mind is obedience that is directed towards faith or "the obedience which is faith." And it is true that Paul sometimes speaks of people "obeying" the gospel (Rom. 10:16). But, as Douglas Moo points out, this does not do justice to the interplay between faith and obedience in Paul's theology. Rather, the two words "obedience" and "faith" are mutually interpreting—genuine faith always has obedience as its outcome and obedience that is pleasing to God is always accompanied by faith.[34] For Paul, faith in Jesus Christ is inseparably connected with obedience to God and the covenant, or "covenant faithfulness."[35]

This relationship between faith and obedience can be further clarified if we realize that Paul gives several meanings to the word "faith" (*pistis*) in Romans. At times, he emphasizes the *content* of faith and intellectual assent (Rom. 10:9; cf. I Thess. 4:14). At other times, as we have seen, he focuses on the *moral* or *ethical* aspect of faith by linking it with obedience (Rom. 1:5, 16:26). When he talks about Abraham, he also describes faith in terms of *trust* (Rom. 4:16-22).

Figure 20. The Three Dimensions of Faith in Paul's Theology

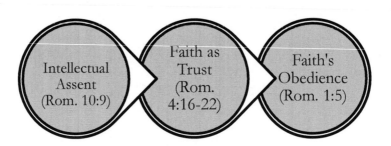

Each of these aspects of faith is best viewed as part of a continuum. Trust is rooted in the belief that what Scripture says about Christ as Savior and Lord is true. And real trust necessarily manifests itself in actions or the way one lives his/her life.[36] This is why, for Paul, the *gospel* is not only for unbelievers that they may be brought to faith in Christ. It is also for believers that they may grow and mature in the faith. Both activities of *gospel proclamation* and *gospel instruction* were part and parcel of his apostolic mission to form, multiply, and firmly establish obedient faith communities.[37]

In a number of respects, then, Paul's description of his mission to bring about the obedience of faith among all nations can be viewed as a paraphrase of Jesus' Great Commission. Both are concerned with a fulfillment of God's plan, rooted in Old Testament promises to Israel, to bring salvation to all nations. The church's mission is the announcement of God's saving power through Christ for the realization of God's purposes for all of humanity. But in neither the Great Commission nor Paul's mission is this simply about getting people to heaven. Rather, in both instances it is also about nurturing believers into full obedience of faith and incorporating them into a community of faithful obedience—or what Paul calls a "new creation" (II Cor. 5:17) that reflects God's character for his ultimate glory.

"So that by all means I might save some" (I Cor. 9:19-23; cf. 10:31-11:1)

In this key mission text Paul describes how he has given up his rights for the sake of the gospel. At the conclusion of this passage he sums up the method, which has characterized his whole missionary career:

> *I have become all things to all men so that by all possible means I might save some. I do all this for the sake of the gospel that I may share in its blessings. (I Cor. 9:22b-23)*

These words of Paul are often presented as a model for how to do evangelism. This is not wholly inappropriate. For it is true that this is a statement of Paul's cultural flexibility for the sake of his mission.

But the context of this passage clearly indicates that Paul's actions are not restricted to initial evangelism or his response to non-Christians.[38]   In the previous chapter of I Corinthians (I Cor. 8:1-9) Paul addresses the issue in the Corinthian church of eating meat offered to idols. And it is in this context that he talks about his own willingness to relinquish his own freedom and rights as an apostle for the sake of the gospel (9:12). "To the weak," he states, "I have become weak, to win the weak" (9:22). As Kostenberger and O'Brien elucidate, Paul is referring here to weak *Christians* whose consciences trouble them about matters that are not in themselves wrong (8:7-8, 11). His goal in "winning" the weak therefore is to bring them to full maturity in Christ. "'Win' or 'save' then speaks not only of the initial activity whereby a person comes to faith, but of the whole process by which a Jew, Gentile, or a weak Christian is converted and brought to glory."[39]

It is further significant that Paul presents himself as an *example* to the Corinthian church: "Follow my example as I follow the example of Christ." (I Cor. 11:1). Here, Paul's exhortation for believers in the Corinthian church (especially those who are strong) to imitate him by surrendering their rights and privileges for the "good of many" and God's glory (10:31-33) has strong missional overtones. He is concerned that the behavior of believers within the Corinthian church will not be a stumbling block but will instead result in the salvation of many—both Christians and non-Christians (vss. 32-33). In Paul's view of mission, then, the gospel simply cannot be divorced from ethical behavior within the church. For all actions taken by members of the Christian community are either a hindrance or serve to attract people to the good news of the gospel and the community it engenders.[40] In the words of Bosch: "Through their conduct, believers attract outsiders or put them off. Their lifestyle is either attractive or offensive. Where it is attractive, people are drawn to the church, even if the church does not actively 'go out' to evangelize them."[41]

Is There a Social Dimension to the Gospel?

Richard Stearns argues that most Christians in the West have what he refers to as a "Bingo Card" gospel. "More and more," he writes, "our view of the gospel has been narrowed to a simple transaction, marked by checking a box on a bingo card at some prayer breakfast, registering a decision for Christ, or coming forward during an alter call."[42] These words raise the fundamental question: "Is there a social dimension to the gospel?"

The significance of this question becomes apparent when we consider the story of Shivamma. She is the face of a grassroots revival of Christianity in India today.[43] Her home is a concrete storm sewer discarded by the factory where she and her husband work. Their family of four lives in an area of about 84 square feet, part of a "neighborhood" that consists of huge pipes lined up like mobile homes. Shivamma and her family are among the poor and illiterate caste in India called the *Dalit*, which literally means "broken people." Nearly 90 percent of all poor in India are Dalits. But to be a Dalit is worse than simply being poor. They are considered "polluted," much like the lepers in Jesus' day. As India's "untouchables" they are not allowed to drink from the same wells, attend the same temples, eat with or even wear shoes in the presence of members of other higher castes. Through the witness of another Dalit Christian, Shivamma came to faith in Christ. She is one of millions of Indians who are coming to Christ. By some estimates the church in India now comprises over 70 million members, making it the eighth largest Christian population in the world. Between 70-90 percent of India's Christians are Dalits. Christianity is thus stigmatized as a "Dalit religion" that is worthy of contempt from all other groups. This has contributed to discrimination among Christians as well, even between Dalit sub-castes. In the words of one Christian Dalit activist: "'All one in Christ' is theoretically correct, but practically it is not true. We are not all one in Christ."[44]

This is not to single out the church in India. For similar divisions exist within Christ's church as a whole. Not always as extreme perhaps. But they are present nonetheless. Recently, a small church in Kentucky became the epicenter of a debate over race relations and the gospel. Gulnare Freewill Baptist church banned an interracial couple from taking part in worship services or becoming members of the church. This ban was later withdrawn following a firestorm of criticism and the church adopted a new resolution welcoming "believers into our fellowship regardless of race, creed or color." [45]

It is commonly argued that the gospel has social *implications or results* but that there is not a *social dimension* to the gospel that is fundamental to its very nature. Kevin DeYoung and Greg Gilbert ask, for example, "Why does [Paul] never preach, 'The gospel is the good news that Jew and Gentile can be reconciled to one another through Jesus'? Why is the forgiveness of sins so readily called 'the gospel,' while no other particular blessing is?" [46] They go on to argue that this is because the broader blessings of gospel are attained only by means of forgiveness of sins through the cross. In their words, "we never see the promise of the new creation called 'the gospel.' Nor do we see reconciliation between humans called 'the gospel.' But we do see reconciliation between man and God called 'the gospel' precisely because it is the one blessing that leads to all the rest." [47] The implication of DeYoung's and Gilbert's argument is that divisions between Christians based on racial, ethnic, class or gender, prejudice or bigotry do not violate the *essence* of the gospel. In my view this diminishes the meaning of the "good news" of the gospel. The gospel as described by Paul means much more than a private transaction between God and us. But before explaining why this is the case we need to turn again to the debate over the "New Perspective" on Paul.

The "New Perspective" on Paul in Perspective

Imagine that you are a male Jew living in first century Palestine. From childhood you have been taught that God's covenant with Israel is foundational to your identity as a Jew. Moreover, you believe that Israel was chosen by God to be his covenant people solely on the basis of his grace but that the Law was given to regulate and maintain the covenant relationship. But you feel that your religion and your own identity as a Jew are under constant threat from the influence of the surrounding Greco-Roman culture. The particular observances of the Law such as food and Sabbath laws and circumcision have become increasingly important as "markers" of your Jewish identity. The rite of circumcision which in Mosaic Law was a sign of fidelity to the covenant (Gen. 17:9-14) is especially important as a "badge" of national and religious loyalty and as a way of distinguishing you as a Jew from people of other nations and cultures. In fact, some of your fellow countrymen in Judea have threatened to circumcise two Gentile refugees "if they wish to live among us."[48]

This, in a nutshell, is the picture that the New Perspective gives of the "law" as understood by the typical Jew in Paul's day. In the words of James Dunn, who first coined the term, by Paul's time "these works of the law had become identified as *indices of Jewishness*, as badges betokening race and nation – inevitably so when race and religion are so inextricably intertwined as they were, and are, in Judaism"[49] (Emphasis mine). In his view, then, it is incorrect to look at Paul through the lens of Luther who interpreted Paul's reference to "works of the law" (Gal. 2:16) as good works done to achieve righteousness before God, or "works righteousness." In Galatians in particular, Paul is responding to the issue of Gentile-Jewish relations within the Christian community. Among Jewish Christians, works of the law—especially circumcision and food and Sabbath laws— functioned sociologically as markers or indicators of membership in the covenant. And in this way the law fostered Jewish exclusiveness and pride (Gal. 2:11-21). What Paul is opposing, then, is a *racial* or *national* expression of faith and a use of the law that separates and therefore isolates groups from one another in the body of Christ.[50]

As we noted earlier in this chapter there are important differences in emphasis between the "old" and the "new" perspectives on the meaning of "justification by faith." In the traditional reformed perspective the central issue is how individuals despite their sin can be reckoned as righteous before God. The emphasis, in other words, is on the question "How can I be saved?" Proponents of the New Perspective argue that a preoccupation with this question has resulted in an overly individualistic understanding of justification by grace through faith that downplays the social dimension of justification. Rather, for them justification by faith is about inclusion of all Christians—Jew and Gentile—equally into God's covenant people on the basis of faith in Christ. Some of what they write gives the impression (rightly or wrongly) that they are almost exclusively concerned about church relationships and not about the salvation of individuals from sin.[51] Michael Bird has suggested that the questions asked by both perspectives are not mutually exclusive:

> I suggest that when you read Paul, don't just ask yourself the question, "What must I do to be saved?" as if that is the issue lurking behind every verse. Also ask yourself another question, "Who are the people of God?" With those two questions in our mind as we read Paul's letters it will hopefully lead us to a more comprehensive view of Paul's theology that integrates soteriology and ecclesiology.[52]

Bird further suggests that the way out of the impasse between traditional and revisionist interpretations of Paul is to be found in his statements about being "in Christ" (Rom. 8:1, 39; I Cor. 1:30; II Cor. 5:21; Gal. 2:17; Eph. 1:7, 11; Col. 1:14) and united to him through his death and resurrection (I Cor. 15:20-22). "Through faith believers are incorporated or identified with the risen and justified Messiah, and they are justified by virtue of their participation in him (cf. Col. 2:12; I Cor. 15:17)."[53] This union with Christ is the matrix for understanding justification as forensic, eschatological, effective, and covenantal (see diagram below).[54] First, justification is *forensic* because one is declared righteous by God solely by his grace and on the basis of Jesus' death which satisfies God's justice (Rom. 3:21-25, 8:1-3). Second, justification is *covenantal* because Christ's death and resurrection inaugurates the new covenant (I Cor. 11:25). The believer's status of being "in Christ" replaces Israel as the locus of participation in the covenant and faith replaces circumcision as the "badge" of membership in the covenantal people of God. Third, justification is *eschatological* because the verdict anticipated in the day of Judgment has been declared in the present (Rom. 8:31-34). And, finally, justification is *effective* because the verdict of acquittal logically entails that those who are in Christ have been delivered from the power of sin and death (Rom. 6:5-18). *"In sum, justification is the act whereby God creates a new people, with a new status, in a new covenant, as a foretaste of the new age."*[55]

Figure 21. Justification as Forensic, Eschatological, Effective, and Covenantal

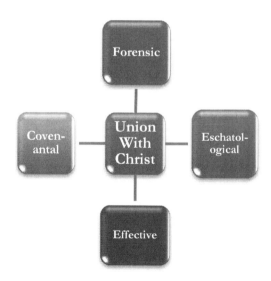

Justification and Unity in Christ

Returning to DeYoung's and Gilbert's argument, then, we might agree that the vertical category whereby God forgives sin and declares a person righteous is fundamental to Paul's description of justification. But to say that Paul does not call the horizontal reconciliation between Jew and Gentile "gospel" is to create a false and dangerous dichotomy. Indeed, any church which does not exhibit in practice the unity and equality of all in Christ implicitly communicates that membership in the people of God is not by faith and therefore in effect contradicts what Paul means by the "gospel." This, I believe, is evident from three Pauline texts that relate justification to unity in Christ: (a) Gal. 2:11-16; (b) Gal. 3:26-29; and (c) Eph. 2:11-3:6. We can better understand Paul's argument in the second chapter of Galatians if we look first at 3:26-29.

1. Oneness in Christ (Gal. 3:26-29).

This passage has been described as the "Magna Carta of the New Humanity."[56] But its full significance is often lost among evangelicals. Notice, first, that union with Christ is the *main focus* in each verse: faith *in* Christ (v. 26), baptized *into* Christ . . . clothed . . . *with* Christ (v. 27), one *in* Christ Jesus (vs. 28), *belong to* Christ (vs. 29). Paul, in other words, is using language that describes the justification of believers. The new relationships in Christ are both spiritual (vss. 26-27) *and* social (vss. 28-29).[57] Richard Longenecker suggests that both the structure and content of vss. 27-28 indicate that they were part of a confessional or liturgical formula in the early New Testament church. The same pairings are found in I Cor. 12:13 and Col. 3:11. The fact that all of these passages either explicitly or implicitly make reference to baptism indicates that Gal. 3:28 was originally part of a baptismal confession and that Paul is using this passage in support of his argument in verses 1-29 that we are justified by faith and not by the law (vss. 23-25).[58] The social as well as spiritual equality and unity of all in Christ is therefore not an optional addition or application of the gospel. It is part of the *essence* of the gospel. In the words of Walter Hansen, this "radical affirmation of unity and equality in Christ is a deliberate rejection of the attitude expressed by the synagogue prayer in which the worshiper thanks God for not making him a Gentile, a slave or a woman. Such an attitude of superiority contradicts the truth of the gospel, the good news that there is equality and unity of all believers in Christ."[59]

It is important to note further that these verses are connected with a picture of the church as a missional community that reflects a new eschatological reality. Paul uses the metaphor of a family and kinship language to express the new identity of those who have faith in Christ. They are all "sons of God" (vs. 26) and heirs according to the promise made to Abraham (vs. 29). In 4:1-11 Paul further frames the new collective identity of the church in terms of a contrast between what they were (slaves under the basic principles of the world) and what they have become (sons of God) through the Spirit of Christ. All believers therefore enjoy the full rights as children of God (vss. 4-7). External social and nationalistic differences of circumcision (Israel) vs. uncirumcision (Gentile) no longer have any significance; what counts is the "new creation" (6:15). Unfortunately, with our individualistic understanding of the gospel, we often miss the fact that Paul is here talking about the *church* as a new creation or a new humanity. Jacobus Kok draws out the missiological implications:

> The missionary impulse is thus not to be seen as a once off moment of a missionary preaching the gospel, but the *ongoing* process of *faith formation* and community building. The missionary process thus does not end in the act of proclamation but continues as the word of God and the message of salvation takes root and grows to perfection. It is certainly within the faith community itself that the new paradigm for life is lived, where life is shared and where the effects of the transformative missional message are particularized.[60]

It is significant that Paul describes the church as "the Israel of God" (6:17). In other words, the church is the true people of God.[61] Israel during the time of the Old Covenant was to be a reflection of God's peace, mercy, and justice in its social relationships —though, sadly, it failed in that regard. Under the New Covenant the church is to be the primary social structure for the expression of God's reign. As a prototype of God's future kingdom its presence in the world both exposes evil and draws people to Christ.[62] We will return to this point later when we discuss the issue of the poor in the context of Paul's mission.

2. Justification by Faith vs. the Law (Gal. 2:11-16).

Having looked at Gal. 3:28 and what Paul says at the end of his letter, I believe we are in better position to understand his argument in the first two chapters. Paul makes it clear at the beginning of his letter that certain members of the church in Galatia were not living up to their identity as sons of God. They were being duped by certain Judaizers who taught a "different gospel" and perverted the true gospel of Christ (1:7). What they taught was so serious that they were deserving of eternal condemnation (1:9). Paul is here expressing an absolute intolerance for those who deviated from his gospel.[63]

What were these Judaizers teaching that was so deserving of Paul's censure? This question has been the source of considerable debate— and acrimony. And it is not possible to address it in detail here. The entire context indicates that the problem that Paul was addressing was not simply theological. It was also social. Under the influence of Judaizers, Gentile believers were being excluded from fellowship with Jewish believers because they did not observe the Law.[64] In my opinion, based on Paul's general usage of the term (Rom. 3:20, 27, 28; Gal. 2:16-21; 3:2, 5, 10), it is not legitimate to limit "works of the law" to distinctive "boundary markers" (i.e., Sabbath keeping, food laws, and circumcision). It is more likely that it means the entire Mosaic Law code (which obviously *included* such distinctively Jewish practices). Earlier, Peter had separated himself from uncircumcised Gentiles in the church in Antioch for fear of offending the "circumcision group." As a consequence, Gentiles were not admitted to table fellowship with the Jews. The sharing of a common meal (which usually included a celebration of the Lord's Supper) was a visible and powerful symbol of the new reality that in Christ "there is neither Jew nor Greek, slave nor free, male and female," Hence, Paul's rhetorical question: "How is it that you force Gentiles to follow Jewish customs?" (2:14). The use of the Greek word for "force" (*anankazo*) in this context indicates that Peter was compelling Gentile believers to be circumcised (i.e., follow Jewish social laws).[65] Apparently, the circumcision faction in the Galatian church was insisting on a similar submission of Gentile believers to Jewish law as a condition for entering into the covenant community. The behavior of both Peter and the Christians in the Galatian church communicated a "gospel" that mixed conversion to Christ with conversion to nationalistic Judaism.[66] Therefore it contradicted the fundamental teaching of the true gospel that believers are justified (i.e., declared righteous before God) solely on the basis of faith in Christ and not the law (2:16).

How can we make contemporary applications? It is important that we avoid an over-emphasis on *either* the social or the theological aspects of the problem that Paul is addressing. On the one hand, Paul is opposing an emphasis on *any performance-based additions to the gospel* as a means of finding or maintaining acceptance with God.[67] Usually, what comes to mind in this context is a Catholic emphasis on works or "works righteousness." But, the gospel is similarly distorted when one's social, racial, or denominational affiliation or identity becomes more important than the simple fact that one is a Christian. When that happens people are made to feel that they must be part of a certain group to be "real Christians." Things which distinguish themselves personally or socially then, become "additions" to the gospel. Paul is also opposing a *cultural imperialism* which assumes the superiority of any one culture, race, or social group within the body of Christ. Unfortunately, throughout the history of the Christian church, differences of national, racial, and social identity have led to divisions and conflicts. Often, a distinction is made between the spiritual and social aspects of oneness in Christ. But it should be evident from what

Paul says that such a bifurcation between the spiritual and social is based on a false dichotomy. Divisions within the church and exclusions of other believers from fellowship or church membership on the basis of racial, social, or gender differences are in effect a denial of the gospel—the "good news" that acceptance into God's family, the covenantal people of God, is based solely on faith in Christ and his righteousness.

3. New Humanity in Christ (Gal. 2:11-3:6)

If there is any lingering doubt that reconciliation between Jew and Gentile is at the heart of the gospel it is erased by what Paul says in this passage. It is not possible in the space we have to give a full exposition of this text. But, first, it is crucial to realize that Ephesians as a whole expresses Paul's "missionary ecclesiology." As Charles Van Engen states "Paul saw the local church as an organism which should continually grow in the missional expression of its essential nature in the world."[68] This mission is rooted in God's election (1:4) and in union of believers with Christ (1:11-14) who is "head over everything *for the church*, which is his body" (1:22-23). In Eph. 2:8-10 Paul gives a ringing affirmation of salvation by grace through faith and not by works. But this is immediately followed by and connected to a description of the covenantal unity of Jews and Gentiles in one body (2:11-3:6). In verses 14-18, justification is described in terms of *both* horizontal reconciliation between Jew and Gentile (the "new humanity") and the reconciliation of all people to God through the blood of Christ. All ethnic and social distinctions have been abolished through the participation of believers in Christ's death and resurrection (vss. 16-18). This mystery of the gospel that Gentiles and Israel are "members together of one body and sharers together in the promise in Jesus Christ" (3:6) is to be made known through the church "to the rulers and authorities in the heavenly realms" (i.e., all creation) according to God's eternal purpose which he accomplished in Christ Jesus (3:10-11). Mission and unity are therefore wedded together in Paul's view of the church.[69]

Paul is further clear that the authenticity of the gospel is inextricably tied to the existence of a new community that embodies the life of Christ by maintaining the unity of the Spirit in the bond of peace (4:3). The church is the visible manifestation of Christ to the world. As it grows, the visible unity of believers is therefore crucial to the effective communication of the gospel (4:4-6). As Richard Hays argues:

> The New Testament makes a compelling case for the church to live as a community that transcends racial and ethnic differences. Insofar as the church lives out the reality of this vision, it has a powerful effect in society; insofar as it fails to live this reality, it compromises the truth of the gospel.[70]

This raises the question, "What about the church's relationship to those who are not part of the body of Christ?" Should Christians exhibit the same concern for addressing social, ethnic, and racial tensions with unbelievers as they do for eliminating ethnic divisions within the church? It is true that Paul shows special concern for relationships between believers. But the fact that the church is to embody "the ministry of reconciliation" and has been entrusted with communicating the message of reconciliation to an unredeemed world (II Cor. 5:19) means that such concerns cannot be limited to internal relationships. Hays concludes: "When the identity of the community is understood in these terms, participation in any form of ethnic division or hatred becomes unthinkable, and ethnic division within the church becomes nothing other than a denial of the truth of the gospel."[71]

Paul's Mission and the Poor

As mentioned at the beginning of this chapter, although Paul himself was many times "hungry and thirsty, often without food, cold and naked" (2 Cor. 11:27) concern for the poor is generally assumed to be low on his list of priorities. However, a closer examination of Paul's letters indicates that care for the poor and needy was more than simply a marginal concern and that, in fact, it was an important aspect of his ministry. To support this argument we will look at three sets of data: (1) Paul's general exhortations about "doing good" and share with those in need; (2) specific references to Paul's concern for the poor in descriptions of his ministry; and (3) Paul's appeals for churches to support his collection for the poor in Jerusalem. But, before elaborating on each of these points, we need to understand something of Paul's overall missionary strategy.

Paul's Missionary Strategy

There are three elements in Paul's missionary methodology that specifically relate to his concern for the poor. First, it was *two-pronged*. For almost two centuries mission has been defined almost exclusively by the "sending mode," which is patterned after the sending of Paul and Barnabas on their first missionary journey by the church in Antioch (Acts 13:1-3). In this mode certain individuals were set apart for itinerant ministry so that the faith would spread to key cities and areas of the Roman world. This certainly was an important component to Paul's goal of taking the gospel to the "ends of the earth" and planting churches in places where a witness was not present.[72] But this gives us only part of the picture. The "rest of the story" in Paul's missionary practice is what has been referred to as a "center mission" strategy—the establishment of young congregations that served as "centers" or bases of operation for missional outreach in the city and surrounding areas.[73] In this "organic mode" of mission the local congregations were called to be "new manifestations of God's eschatological people" that transcended and challenged their pagan cultural surroundings and were witnesses to God's kingdom. As they carried out God's mission in their own cultural context and embodied the good news of the gospel they grew organically.[74]

Second, Paul's missionary strategy was primarily *urban*, centering on cities in four major provinces of the Roman Empire: Galatia, Asia, Macedonia and Achaia. Most of the cities where Paul focused his efforts were centers of trade and contained vigorous Jewish communities.[75] Building on the work of Friesen, Bruce Longenecker shows that the urban settings of the Greco-Roman Empire in which Paul moved were characterized by a socio-economic (ES) continuum:

ES 1-3: Members of the governing elites (3%).

ES 4: Moderate surplus—some merchants, trade persons, freed persons and artisans (15%).

ES 5: Stable, near subsistence level—many merchants and traders, regular wage earners, artisans, large shop owners, freed persons, and some farm families (27%).

ES 6: Subsistence level, and often below the minimum level to sustain life—small farm families, artisans, wage earners, most merchants and traders, small shop owners (30%).

ES 7: Below subsistence level—i.e. unattached widows, orphans, beggars, disabled, unskilled day laborers, prisoners (25%).[76]

Assuming Longenecker's estimates are correct, poverty was "one of the realities of life that pressed down on vast swathes of the Greco-Roman population."[77] Nor was the early Jesus-movement immune from the "realities of poverty" that affected the majority of the imperial world.[78] While the communities that Paul addresses did include the more well-to-do members of urban society (ES 4) as well as those in the next two socio-economic categories (ES 5-6), they must also have included a fairly significant number of needy and destitute members.[79]

This leads us to the third element in Paul's apostolic strategy—namely, an emphasis on the practice of *hospitality*. In continuity with Jewish tradition, Paul highlights the practical importance of hospitality as a concrete expression of love—"love for sisters and brothers, love extended outward to strangers, prisoners, and exiles, love that attends to physical and social needs" (Rom. 12:13; Heb. 13:2).[80] It appears that the consistent objective of Paul upon entering a city was the conversion of God-fearers and Gentiles who were connected to the local synagogue. Many of them belonged to the more affluent social classes and owned homes that could be used for the assembly of believers and served as bases for local and regional mission.[81] The household was the basic unit within the city. To belong to a household was to be part of a larger network of relations—both within the household, which consisted of relations between patrons and subordinates (slaves, household laborers, etc.), and outside the household in the form of links of kinship, friendship, and business associations.[82] It was this institutional overlap of household and church that provided the environment for the unique fellowship and growth of the earliest churches. But as Christine Pohl points out, the church was more than the sum of individual households. It was "a new household, God's household, and believers became family to one another." Worship, care, and hospitality included believers from different political, ethnic, and socio-economic backgrounds. Thus the reconstituted household provided the setting for three dimensions of hospitality: "hospitality as an expression of respect and recognition—in welcoming persons of different status and background into a single place of often a shared meal; hospitality as a means of meeting the physical needs of strangers, traveling Christians and the local poor; and hospitality as the hosting of local assemblies of believers."[83]

We can see, then, how the hospitality that characterized the house churches established by Paul and his co-workers played a key role in missional outreach. In addition to providing lodging and a safe-haven for missionary travelers, the house churches opened the door to a whole network of relationships (friends, relatives, and business clientele) that served as the basis for evangelist contacts. Numerous passages indicate that households functioned as meeting places for believers and had an evangelistic impact through their personal confession of faith as well as through the attraction of their community life together (cf. Rom. 12:1-2; I Thess. 4:10-11; I Cor. 6:1-11; II Cor. 6:14-7:1; Phil. 2:12-16; Col. 4:2-6).[84] As Gehring states: "The message to love one another, which was anchored in Pauline doctrine of the justification of all through faith in Christ alone, did not remain mere theory but was experienced in practice and lived out in exemplary fashion in the house churches. . . Pauline house churches were both a training ground *in* brotherly love for Christians and a showcase *for* brotherly love to non-Christians."[85]

Paul's general exhortations to care for the poor

Paul does not devote large sections of his letters to the topic of care for the poor. But as the table below indicates, it was a common theme in his letters.

Figure 22. Paul's Exhortations to Care for the Poor

Passage	General exhortations
Rom. 12:13,16	". . . share with God's people who are in need. Practice hospitality. . . Do not be proud but be willing to associate with the lowly (i.e.., those of low position). . ."
Gal. 6:9-10	"Let us not become weary in doing good. . .Do good to all people, especially those who belong to the family of believers."
Eph. 4: 17, 28	"No longer live as the Gentiles live. . . he must work doing something with his hands that he may have something to share with those in need."
II Cor. 9:13	". . . men will praise God for the obedience that accompanies your confession of the Gospel of Christ and for your generosity in sharing with them and with everyone else."
I Thess. 5:14	". . . encourage the timid, help the weak. . . always be kind (lit. 'follow the good') to each other and to everyone else. . ."
II Thess. 3:13	"And as for you brothers, do not be weary in doing good."
I Tim. 5:3-16	". . . so that the church can help those widows who are truly in need."
I Tim. 6:18	"Command them (i.e., the rich) to do good, to be rich in good deeds and to be generous and willing to share."
Titus 3:8	"And I want you to stress these things, so that those who have trusted in God may be careful to devote themselves to doing what is good."

A careful analysis of each of these passages reveals that it was an important part of his "theological DNA."[86] I have argued that an integral part of Paul's apostolic call was to bring about the "obedience of faith" among the Gentiles, and that this theme figures prominently in his letter to the Romans. James Miller shows convincingly that in 12:1-15:6 Paul describes the nature of that obedience in terms of love and unity among Christians as the "eschatological people of God."[87] This communal concern is most evident in 12:3-13 and also in 14:1-15:6. Paul's ethical injunctions are set within the context of his description in 5:12-21 of the difference between the two "ages" of the reign of Adam, which is characterized by sin and death, and the reign of Christ, which is characterized by righteousness. Paul therefore calls for the Christians in Rome to offer themselves *collectively* to God as one "living sacrifice" (12:1) by not being conformed to the pattern of this world but being transformed by the renewing of their minds (vs. 2). He immediately follows this exhortation with a description of what relationships between believers within the body of Christ should look like. In addition to using their particular spiritual gifts (i.e., teaching, encouragement, generosity, mercy) for the up-building of the body (12:4-8), believers should "share with God's people who are in need" (12:13). Douglas Moo maintains that the "needs" referred to here "are material ones: food, clothing, and shelter." Furthermore, while some scholars think that Paul might be thinking specifically of Jewish Christians in Jerusalem (cf. 15:25-6) to whom he was bringing money collected from the Gentiles (cf. 15:30-33), "there is nothing to suggest that he has them particularly in mind here."[88] This appeal is set between two interlocking "essays" which encourage genuine love between believers (12:14-16) and Christian harmony (12:15-16)—including a willingness to associate with those of low position (vs. 16). "Accordingly, in a letter that outlines something of Paul's good news to Jesus-followers in Rome, care for the needy is given a prominent foothold at a significant structural junction in an essay on how 'love' is (to be) put into practical effect within communities of Jesus-followers."[89] It is further significant that Paul encourages a similar caring response to the needy *outside* of the church, even to those who actively oppose it (12:17-21).

In various letters, Paul's instructions to care for the needy are framed in terms of "doing good" on behalf of others (Gal. 6:9-10; 1 Thess. 5:15; 2 Thess. 3:13; 1 Tim. 6:18; Titus 3:8). This phrase, which is also prominent in Peter's instructions to churches scattered throughout Asia Minor (1 Pet. 2:12, 14-15, 20), includes the concept of supporting those in need with material aid.[90] According to Bruce Winter, the phrase "to do the good" was virtually technical terminology in the ancient Greco-Roman world for bestowing material benefits on others.[91] Paul's instructions in Gal. 6:9-10 are particularly significant. Richard Longenecker points out that the construction "then therefore" (*apa oun*) at the beginning of verse 10 is found frequently in Paul's letters. In this context, it signals the conclusion and main point of the discussion. The implication, then, is that what follows is to be seen as the *main point* not only of the directives given in 6:1-10 but also of all that has been said in 5:13-6:10: "In effect, the exhortation of 5:13, 'through love serve one another,' and 6:10, 'do good to all people,' function as an *inclusio* for all that Paul says against the negative tendencies among the believers of Galatia in 5:13-6:10.[92] At the conclusion of his first letter to the church in Thessalonica Paul similarly gives the charge to "encourage the faint hearted, help the weak, be patient with everyone" (1 Thess. 5:14). The term "the weak" here probably includes those who are economically vulnerable.[93] As in Gal. 6:10 the Christians are instructed to "pursue the good" in relation to both fellow believers who are in need within the community and the poor and needy within the broader society.[94]

Two other texts are significant in that they allude to the existence of common treasuries for the poor in churches founded by Paul.[95] It appears that the practice of a daily distribution from a money chest for the poor (including widows) which characterized the early Jerusalem church (Acts 2:46; 6:1-6) was adopted without modification by the church of I Timothy.[96] But it was being abused by some widows who should have not been eligible for support of this kind (5:3-16). Similar problems were occurring with the treasury in the church in Thessalonica where some idle members were receiving aid from other members. This violated Paul's teaching that all able-bodied Christians should work so that they were not a burden on the church and could themselves share with those in need (II Thess. 3:12; cf. Eph. 4:28). In both instances, however, Paul closes his letters with an emphasis on continued faithfulness in good works (I Tim. 6:18; II Thess. 3:13). Bruce Longenecker argues that Paul likely

> expected communal funds for the poor (or their equivalent) to be established within communities that he founded, with the urban destitute-beyond-the-confines-of-a-household probably having a strong presence within those communities, many of them having been attracted to such communities for whatever economic support might have been provided. This feature helps to explain, for instance, how Paul can laud communities like those in Thessalonica for their "work of faith and labor of love" that had been reported throughout the region of Macedonia and Achaia (as says Paul hyperbolically in I Thess. 1:3-10).[97]

Finally, Paul expresses the same concern for the general practice of corporate generosity in his second letter to the Corinthians. At the end of a long exhortation to give generously to the poor in Jerusalem he broadens his appeal by adding that the same generosity should be shown to "everyone else" (2 Cor. 9:13).[98] Evidently, Paul did not expect the collection for the poor in Jerusalem to disrupt all other forms of generosity that were to characterize the on-going corporate life of Christians "for all" of the needy.[99] He views such generosity as an expression of the "the obedience that accompanies your confession of the gospel" (9:13). This is particularly significant in view of the fact that in his previous letter to the Corinthian church he had expressed his indignation over the neglect of the poorer members of the community in the corporate practice of the Lord's Supper (1 Cor. 11:17-34).

It should be emphasized, again, that Paul's emphasis in almost all of these passages is on Christian *corporate* conduct. As Richard Hays argues, "Pauline ethics is fundamentally ecclesial in character and we . . . begin to grasp his moral vision only when we understand that he sees the church as inheriting the corporate vocation of God's covenant people, Israel."[100] Furthermore, his emphasis on the community is not just a matter of practical expediency. "Rather, Paul develops his account of the new community in Christ as a fundamental theological theme in his proclamation of the gospel."[101]

This raises the further question of the extent to which Paul regarded care for the poor as an integral part of the advancement of the gospel. Bruce Longenecker notes that, given the limited resources in the churches, efforts to address the needs of poor within the broader society necessarily took a back seat to meeting the significant needs within their own communities.[102] Still, as we gave seen, on at least three occasions (Rom. 12:13-16; Gal. 6:10; and 1 Thess. 5:15) Paul extols good works towards all people. This, again, needs to be viewed in relation to the larger context of Greco-Roman culture. Though not absent, charitable initiatives for people living in poverty were given relatively little attention within the Greco-Roman world. Generosity was valued, but it generally took the form of patronage designed to enhance the status of the giver and was often restricted to those within the giver's social circles.[103] This difference between the Christian communities and non-Christian Greco-Roman associations in this regard could not have gone unnoticed.[104] And there are clear indications that Paul regarded the uniqueness of Christian benevolence towards outsiders as well as love between believers as important to maintaining a positive witness in the face of social and political opposition and hostility. This is evident in Paul's exhortation in Rom. 12:13-16, which should probably be interpreted in conjunction with 13:3 where he states that those who do good will receive praise from the civil authorities.[105]

I have argued that the good news of the gospel preached by Paul would have been regarded as politically subversive and anti-imperial. The Roman imperial cult was a central feature of the urbanized settings where the church was spreading.[106] In Galatia, where the church was under pressure from the imperial cult, Jewish Christians wanted to make a good outward impression and avoid persecution by compelling the Gentile Christians to be circumcised (Gal. 6:12). In the eyes of authorities in Galatia they would all be Jewish and not a mixed association. Those Gentiles who observed the Jewish law would, as the Jewish converts, be exempt from observance of the imperial cult.[107] Paul responds that what is important is not circumcision but the "new creation." In other words, the "good deeds" that are part of the church's corporate witness to God's kingdom (6:10) demonstrate to Roman authorities that the followers of Christ are committed to the welfare of the city and its inhabitants. For Paul, as well as for Peter, good works are not only an eloquent defense against false accusations but also the means by which critics will become converts who praise God on the day of salvation (Rom. 12:17-21; II Cor. 9:13; cf. I Peter 2:12).[108]

Concern for the Poor in Paul's Descriptions of His Ministry

On two occasions Paul refers to care for the poor as being an important part of his apostolic calling: Acts 20:35 and Gal. 2:10. In Acts 20:18-35, Paul gives what are essentially his final words to the elders of the church he founded in Ephesus. In this farewell speech he emphasizes his faithfulness in completing the task of "testifying to the gospel of God's grace" and proclaiming the kingdom and "the whole will of God" (vss. 24-26). He also encourages the elders to be "shepherds of the church of God, which he bought with his own blood" (vs. 29). He concludes by holding up his own ministry as an example of how "we must help the weak, remembering the words of the Lord Jesus: 'It is more blessed to give than to receive'" (vs. 35).

There are several things that should be noted about this passage. First, the context makes it clear that the word "weak" here refers to those who are poor and economically vulnerable. The fact that Paul is speaking to Ephesian elders about their responsibilities as overseers (vs. 28) indicates that he has in mind the weak and vulnerable in their congregations as well as (by implication) the poor in other Gentile churches.[109] Second, it is also clear from the context that "helping the weak" does not simply mean praying for them or wishing them well. Paul's reference to Jesus' words ("It is more blessed to give than to receive") means that he has in view an economic sharing of resources to offset the needs of others who were unable to care for themselves.[110] Paul cites his own practice of hard work and sacrificial giving for the sake of his companions as an example of how his hearers were to serve others without concern for present material reward. "The Greco-Roman world was honeycombed by social networks grounded in the principle of reciprocity, of 'giving and receiving.' Paul's exhortation here is to break that cycle and serve and help those who can give nothing in return."[111] Finally, Paul preaches concern for the needy as an *essential part* of the "good news" of the gospel of God's grace "which is able to build you up and to give you an inheritance among all those who are sanctified" (vs. 32).[112] In holding himself up as an example for leaders of the church, he is also asserting that concern for the poor and vulnerable should be as much a part of their proclamation of the gospel as it was of his own ministry.

In Gal. 2:6-10 Paul describes how, at the *beginning* of his ministry, he had agreed with the leaders of the Jerusalem church (i.e., James, Peter, and John) that when taking the gospel to the Gentiles he "should continue to remember the poor." This was, he says, "the very thing I was eager to do." McKnight argues that while Paul's concern for the poor was no doubt motivated by compassion, these words also indicate that it is also "partly to be explained by his desire to demonstrate to Judea that his gospel and his churches were one with gospel and the churches of Judea." Concern for the poor was, in other words, part of his apostolic calling.[113] The standard interpretation among commentators is that Paul is referring here to the meeting at the counsel at Jerusalem (Acts 15), which took place around AD 48, and that Paul is recounting an agreement to continue with relief mission to the Christians in Judea who were suffering from the extensive famines that plagued that region in the late 40's. However, as Bruce Longenecker has extensively documented, this view does not emerge until the middle of the fourth century. Prior to that date, Christian interpreters understood Paul as referring to the "poor" in general without any geographic specificity.[114] Furthermore, in Romans 15:30-31 Paul expresses some concern that his collection for the poor in Jerusalem will be "accepted by the saints." David Downs maintains that "it is very difficult to explain Paul's trepidation about the possibility of Jerusalem's rejection of his efforts . . . if, in fact, he is doing nothing more than fulfilling an accord previously established with the Jerusalem leadership."[115] Paul may, then, simply be expressing his agreement with the leaders of the Jerusalem church that the Gentile churches will care for the poor and needy in their local contexts. As Bruce Longenecker puts it:

> James and other leaders of the Jerusalem church were sure that the Jews to whom Peter was to take the gospel of Christ would exhibit concern for the poor and needy, as stipulated in Jewish scripture and tradition. What those leaders wanted to ensure was that the Gentiles to whom Paul was taking the gospel of Christ would similarly be involved in caring for the poor and needy wherever they found them, in conformity with the will of God expressed in Jewish Scripture.[116]

It is not possible here to go into detail on the pros and cons of different interpretations. Whatever view one adopts of Paul's words in 6:10, they should not be regarded simply a parenthetical statement that is divorced from the rest of his argument in this letter (see chart

below). As we have seen, the Galatians were enthralled with circumcision as a means of observing the law. Paul responds that in Christ
"neither circumcision nor uncircumcision has any value. The only
thing that counts is faith expressing itself through love" (Gal. 5:6).
He goes on to contrast a selfish indulgence of the sinful nature with
serving one another in love and argues that the whole law is summed
up in the single commandment to "love your neighbor" (5:13-15).
Among the "fruits of the Spirit" that Paul enumerates is the act of
generous giving to those in need (*agathosune*, 5:22). As we have pointed out, Paul's exhortation to "doing good" in 6:9-10 is a summation
and the main emphasis of all that has been said from 5:13 up to that
point. Such good works are evidence of true saving faith in Christ
(5:7-9; cf. James 2:18).[117] This is an essential part of the "gospel" that
Paul had been commissioned to preach to the Gentiles (Gal. 2:6).
Thus, "the apostolic agreement about remembering the poor resonates throughout the theological echo-chamber that Paul establishes
in these later parts of his letter."[118]

Figure 23. Remembering the Poor in Galatians

Gal. 2:6.10	Gal. 5:13-15	Gal. 6:9-10
". . . they saw that I had been given the task of preaching the gospel to the Gentiles, just as Peter had been given the task of preaching the gospel to the Jew. . . All they asked was that we should continue to remember the poor, the very thing I was eager to do."	*"For you were called to freedom, brothers and sisters; only do not use your freedom as an opportunity for self-indulgence, but through love become slaves to one another. For the whole law is summed up in a single commandment, "You shall love your neighbor as yourself."*	*"Let us not become weary in doing good, for at the proper time we shall reap a harvest if we do not give up. Therefore, as we have opportunity, let us do good to all people, especially to those who belong to the family of believers."*

Paul's Collection for the Poor in Jerusalem

A major aspect of Paul's ministry was the collection for the poor in
the Jerusalem church from the Gentile churches (Rom. 15:25-30; I
Cor. 16:1-4; II Cor. 8:1-15, 9:1-15). Paul devoted much of his ener-

gies to this endeavor, particularly in the final years of his missionary career. A large number of monographs have been written on the subject of Paul's motivations for the collection—and, undoubtedly there were many, not the least of which was its symbolic significance as a validation of the Gentile mission.[119] Again, it is not possible to treat this issue in detail. Here, I will limit my discussion to two questions. First, is there a humanitarian element in the Pauline collection? Second, did Paul regard it as important to the fulfillment of his apostolic mission and the larger mission of the church?

Arguing that Paul emphasized the importance of relying on local resources to meet local needs, Christopher Little downplays the significance of humanitarian concern for the Jerusalem church as a reason for the collection. In his view, the description of the Jerusalem church as "poor" (*ptochos*) carries the connotation of "humble" or "pious poor" as a designation for the entire Jerusalem church and therefore does not have reference to a specific socio-economic group within the church.[120] However, as Stephen Joubert points out, the grammatical construction of the phrase "to make a contribution for the poor (*ptochos*) among the saints in Jerusalem" in Rom. 15:16 specifically points to the material poverty of believers in Jerusalem. Paul actually uses another term ("the saints," *tous ayious*) as a general designation of the Jerusalem believers (I Cor. 16;1; II Cor. 8:4, 9:1,12).[121] C.K. Barrett likewise argues, "By far the most important point, and the only one that he makes explicitly, is that the collection was an act of love for the benefit of those who were in material need."[122]

Most commentators have emphasized the point that Paul saw the collection as a way of expressing and fostering the unity of Jews and Gentiles in the body of Christ. It is particularly instructive that Paul employs three terms—grace (*charis*); fellowship (*koinonia*); and service (*diakonia*)—in reference to the collection (cf. 2 Cor. 8:1-6; 9:1, 12-14). Taken together, these terms specifically refer to Christian brotherly fellowship, which is expressed in the meeting of spiritual and material needs. Both *koinoia* and *diakonia* are closely associated with the celebration of the Lord's Supper, in which material provision for the needs of the poor played a prominent role. "It was simply a broadening of this function within a Christian community to extend to the charitable relief from one Christian community to another which resulted in the application of the term 'service' to a monetary collection."[123]

In II Corinthians 8 Paul makes it abundantly clear that God wants Christians who have sufficient material possessions to share with other Christians who are less fortunate. In II Corinthians 8:14 he expresses the principle of mutual sharing in the midst of crisis ("At the present time your plenty will supply what they need, so that in turn their plenty will supply what you need"). The Greek term ("this bounty" or "lavish gift") that is used to describe the collection in verse 20 suggests that the gift was intended to be quite substantial. The very fact that the congregations were prepared to send such a large sum of money testifies to the ideological and material value they attached to the collection.[124] As Meggit argues, "From the apostle's lengthy discussion of the subject of the collections . . . and the open and effective response that the churches made to its appeals, it is clear that Christian mutualism was indeed a prominent and distinct component of the lives of the Pauline communities." This theme of mutualism was inseparably bound up with Pauline corporate theology, which emphasized that Christians are bound together in love as brothers and sisters in Christ. In addition to its corporate significance in expressing Christian love and *koinonia*, there is reason to believe that economic mutualism as expressed in the Pauline collection was an important "survival strategy" that served to meet real material needs within the Early Church.[125] Particularly, "the money was to be used to give the Jerusalem Jewish community financial backing in its attempts to achieve a reasonable degree of economic security for its strenuous witness. . ."[126]

However, there is a deeper significance to the collection, as is evidenced by Paul's willingness to go to Jerusalem despite the risk of personal danger to himself. Paul suspects trouble, especially from non-believing Jews, when he writes to the Christians in Rome: "Pray that I may be rescued from the unbelievers in Judea and that my service in Jerusalem may be acceptable to the saints there" (Rom. 15:31). Why does Paul anticipate this reaction from unbelieving Jews? I have argued throughout this chapter that Paul sees the church as God's "reworked" chosen people.[127] Those who accept the gospel become part of God's redeemed humanity that exhibits kingdom righteousness by alleviating poverty and transcending ethnic, economic, racial, and social differences in the community of believers. The church thus testifies "to the regenerative power of the Spirit and to the global scope of the coming reign of Christ."[128] For Paul, then, the collection has symbolic and eschatological significance. This can be seen in II Corinthians 9:10 where Paul describes the collection in these terms:

Now he who supplies seed to the sower and bread for food will also supply and increase your store of seed and will enlarge the harvest of your righteousness.

These words are an allusion to Isaiah 55:10 and Hosea 10:12, both of which refer to the eternal covenant between God and Israel and to the miracle of Israel's returning home. The Jews, of course, looked forward to that day of restoration, which would also include the justice of God being exercised over the pagan nations. But God "had brought his covenant purpose for Israel to fruition in Israel's representative, the Messiah Jesus."[129] Throughout Romans, Paul's concern is to show that the blessings envisioned eschatologically for Gentiles are presently inaugurated and received by them through the gospel (Rom. 1:5, 15:9-19, 16:25-26).[130] This does not mean a displacement of God's promise to Israel. But it does mean a reversal of roles in that Israel's salvation and glorification is no longer the prerequisite for the salvation of the Gentiles.[131] For Paul, the collection symbolizes the success of his Gentile mission. The ultimate irony is that the Gentiles are beneficiaries of spiritual blessings through God's covenant with Israel without prior compliance with the requirement of proselytes, which is precisely why they should reciprocate in terms of material blessings (Rom. 15:27).[132] This could only have been a constant source of irritation to the majority of Jews of Paul's day who rejected the message of salvation preached by Paul. This, of course, was apparent to Paul. Which is why he hoped the Jews would be provoked to jealousy and accept Christ (Rom. 10:1, 11:11-24). Jewish expectations were, of course, that Jerusalem would be the center of God's final salvation and the ingathering of the nations. Paul's mission of bringing the collection to that city—a gift that was given not at the temple but to poor Jewish Christians by a delegation of non-circumcised Gentiles—was a symbolic act, much like the symbolic acts of the Old Testament prophets, which were designed to bring Israel to repentance.[133]

In all likelihood, then, the Pauline collection combined a variety of factors, including humanitarian concern, motivation from the love of God, concern for unity within the body of Christ, and a commitment to the world-wide mission of the church. Undergirding all of these concerns was a vision of the church as a new creation called into being by God and maintained by his grace alone.[134] While we tend to separate these factors, this was not the case with Paul. If Paul is to serve as a "model" for contemporary missionary practice perhaps, then, as Joubert remarks:

> Present-day churches should once again pay serious attention to the principles inherent in the Pauline collection. Analogous caritative projects could serve as powerful witnesses to the overflowing grace of God in our troubled world. What better way is there to make God's presence felt than through the generous and joyful bestowal of benefits on fellow believers in need? Such efforts to address the situation of the socially destitute could at the same time give concrete expression to the bond of fellowship between God's people.[135]

Conclusion

There is currently a deep divide within evangelicalism between those who emphasize Jesus and the gospels and those who emphasize Paul and his epistles. Scott McKnight observes: "I meet many young, thinking evangelicals whose 'first language' is Jesus and the kingdom. Yet despite the trend, perhaps in reaction to it, many look to Paul and justification by faith as their first language."[136] But this supposed disjunction between Jesus and Paul disappears if we realize that there is a deeper unity at the level of *gospel*—a term which operates at a deeper foundation than either "kingdom" or "justification."

A key text in which the apostle Paul defines "the gospel" is I Corinthians 15:1-8:

> *Now, brothers, I want to remind you of the gospel I preached to you, which you received and on which you have taken your stand. By this gospel you are saved, if you hold firmly to the word I preached to you. Otherwise, you have believed in vain. For what I received I passed on to you as of first importance: that Christ died for our sins according to Scripture, that he was buried, that he was raised on the third day according to the Scripture, and that he appeared to Peter, and then to the Twelve. After that, he appeared to more than five hundred brothers at the same time, most of whom are still living, though some have fallen asleep. Then he appeared to James, then to all the apostles, and last of all he appeared to me also, as to one abnormally born.*

Notice, here, that Paul does not mention the "kingdom." And, although he talks about Christ dying for our sins, he does not speak of "justification" per se. What he emphasizes is the story of Jesus (vss. 3-8) as a completion of Israel's story and fulfillment "according to the Scriptures" of its aspirations for the Messiah who would save people from their sins (vss. 1-3). "Behind or underneath both kingdom and justification is the gospel, and the gospel is the saving story of Jesus that completes Israel's story. 'To gospel' is to tell a story about Jesus as the Messiah, as the Lord, as the Son of God, as the Savior."[137] As has been discussed in chapter 10, in numerous passages in the Gospels Jesus similarly describes himself as the "one who was to come," the Anointed One in and through whom Israel's story of salvation would be fulfilled (cf. Luke 4:21, 7:20-23).

Returning to the views of N. T. Wright with which we began this chapter, the relationship between Jesus' vocation and Paul's now comes into better focus. Jesus' vocation was entirely unique, unrepeatable. If Paul had simply mimicked what Jesus said he would have been denying his role as a follower of Jesus and setting himself up as another Messiah. Rather, his vocation was to announce that Israel's history had been brought to a climax through Christ's death and resurrection and to implement that achievement by calling the world to allegiance to its rightful Lord.[138] In other words, the gospel that Paul preached and lived out was the good news that Jesus, Israel's Messiah, has defeated the evil powers of this age and inaugurated a new age through his death and resurrection, and is thus the Lord, the one true King of the world.[139]

I have argued that it is in this context that we must understand Paul's own description of his apostolic activity as one of "leading the Gentiles to obey God by what I have said and done" (Rom. 15:17-19). We have seen that in his use of two phrases to describe his apostolic mission ("obedience of faith" and "so that by all means I might save some") Paul is as concerned about bringing believers to full maturity as he is with "primary evangelism." Indeed, for Paul, if Christ's Lordship is to have any meaning for the believer there cannot be a dichotomy between "preaching the gospel" and demonstrating a new way of being human, a way characterized by self-giving love, justice, honesty, and breaking down traditional barriers that divide people and set them against each other.[140]

This is not to deny the central importance of the traditional doctrine of "justification by grace through faith." But the problem highlighted in Romans 1:18-32 (i.e., sin and God's wrath against mankind) finds its response not just in Romans 3:21-31 or 5:1-11 (i.e., the imputation of Christ's righteousness to the believer) but also in Romans 8:19-27 (i.e., the liberation of creation from the present state of bondage and decay). The Christian call to holiness is a matter of inaugurated eschatology, "of beginning to live in the present rule of what will be the case in the ultimate future."[141] Actually, Romans 8 is, as N.T. Wright argues, the deepest New Testament answer to the problem of evil and the question of God's love and justice. It invites Christians to live as God's "exodus people"—to live a renewed life in the Spirit, to oppose all the things that deface human life and are hostile to God, to seek righteousness, justice, and mercy (8:1-17, cf. 12:1-21).[142] These are signs of hope for a world that groans in the pains of childbirth, waiting for its promised liberation (Rom. 8:21-22).

Notes

[1] Bosch, *Transforming Mission*, p. 124; Kostenberger and O'Brien, *Salvation to the Ends of the Earth*, p. 164.

[2] Michael Barram, *Mission and Moral Reflection in Paul* (New York: Peter Lang, 2006), pp. 2-3.

[3] Ibid., p. 10.

[4] Michael F. Bird, *Introducing Paul: The Man, His Mission and His Message* (Downers Grove, IL: IVP Academic, 2008), p. 39

[5] Ibid., pp. 38-9.

[6] See Charles C. Ryrie, *Dispensationalism, Revised and Expanded* (Chicago: Moody Press, 1995), p. 45.

[7] Bruce W. Longenecker, *Remember the Poor: Paul, Poverty and the Greco-Roman World* (Grand Rapids, MI: Eerdmans, 2010), p. 138.

[8] Ibid., p. 139.

[9] N.T. Wright, *What Saint Paul Really Said: Was Paul of Tarsus the Real Founder of Christianity?* (Grand Rapids, MI: Eerdmans, 1997), p. 154.

[10] Ibid., pp. 180-81.

[11] Kostenberg and O'Brien, *Salvation to the Ends of the Earth*, p. 170.

[12] It is possible that the church in Rome was founded by those who are described in Acts as "visitors from Rome" on the day of Pentecost (Acts 2:10).

[13] It is not likely that Paul ever visited Colossae as this city is not mentioned in the record of his missionary journeys in Acts and Paul himself states that the believers in Colossae and Laodicea had not seen his face (Col. 2:1). It is more likely that the

gospel came to the region through two of Paul's converts—Epaphras, who taught them the gospel (Col. 1:7) and Philemon, in whose house the church met (Philemon 19). See Herbert M. Carson, *The Tyndale New Testament Commentaries: The Epistles of Paul to the Colossians and Philemon* (Grand Rapids, MI: Eerdmans, 1972), p. 11,

[14] Schnelle, *Apostle Paul*, pp. 303-4.

[15] Ibid., p. 306.

[16] Ibid., pp. 193-4.

[17] Ibid., p. 197.

[18] Quoted in D.B. Garlington, "The Obedience of Faith in the Letter to the Romans: Part I: The Meaning of hupakoe pisteos (Rom 1:5; 16;26)," *Westminster Theological Journal* 52 (1990), p. 201. See also James C. Miller, "The Jewish Context of Paul's Gentile Mission," *Tyndale Bulletin* 58.1 (2007), p. 102.

[19] Darlington, "The Obedience of Faith," p. 203.

[20] Douglas J. Moo, *Romans: The NIV Application Commentary; From Biblical Text to Contemporary Life* (Grand Rapids, MI: Zondervan, 2000), pp. 36, 39.

[21] Moore, *The Kingdom of Christ*, p. 57.

[22] Kostenberger and O'Brien, *Salvation to the Ends of the Earth*, p. 176.

[23] Darlington, "The Obedience of Faith," p. 203.

[24] Wright, *The Mission of God*, pp. 426-7,

[25] Kostenberger and O'Brien, *Salvation to the Ends of the Earth*, p. 169.

[26] Wright, *The Mission of God*, p. 527.

[27] Garlington, "The Obedience of Faith," p. 205.

[28] Michael F. Bird, *Introducing Paul*, pp. 84-5.

[29] N.T. Wright, *Paul in Fresh Perspective* (Mpls, MN: Fortress Press, 2005), pp. 64-65.

[30] Ibid.,

[31] Bird, *Introducing Paul*, p. 88.

[32] Michael Bird rightly points out that this is a deficiency in some of N.T. Wright's portrayals of the gospel. See Ibid., p. 83.

[33] N.T. Wright, "Paul's Gospel and Ceasar's Empire," p. 2. Available at: http://www.ntwrightpage.com/ Wright_ Paul_Caesar_Empire.pdf

[34] Moo, *Romans*, p. 38.

[35] See John H. Armstrong, "The Obedience of Faith," *Reformation and Revival Journal* 12/4 (Fall 2003), p. 18.

[36] Jouette M. Bassler, *Navigating Paul: An Introduction to Key Theological Concepts* (Louisville, KY: Westminster John Knox Press, 2007), p. 24.

[37] Kostenberger and O'Brien state that "Paul employs the *euangelion* word-group to cover the whole range of evangelisitic activities–from the initial proclamation of the gospel to the building up of believers and grounding them firmly in the faith. . . Proclaiming the gospel meant for Paul not simply an initial preaching or with it the reaping of converts; it includes also the whole range of nurturing activities which led to the firm establishment of congregations." *Salvation to the Ends of the Earth*, pp. 182-3.

[38] See Barram, *Mission and Moral Reflection in Paul*, p. 148.

[39] Kostenberg and O'Brien, *Salvation to the Ends of the Earth*, p. 181.

[40] Barram, *Mission and Moral Reflection in Paul*, p. 151,

[41] Bosch, *Transforming Mission*, p. 168.

[42] Stearns, *The Hole in Our Gospel*, pp. 16-17.

[43] Tim Stafford, "India's Grassroots Revival," *Christianity Today* (July 2011). Available at: http://www. christianitytoday. com/ct/2011/july/indiagrassroots.html? start=1

[44] Ibid.

[45] "All White Kentucky Church Reverses Ban on Interracial Couples," Christian Science Monitor (December 5, 2011). Available at: http://www.csmonitor.com /USA/Latest-News-Wires/2011/1205/All-white-Kentucky-church-reverses-ban-on-interracial-couples

[46] DeYoung and Gilbert, *What is the Mission of the Church?*, p. 107.

[47] Ibid., p. 109.

[48] Michael Bird, "When the Dust Finally Settles: Coming to a Post-New Perspective," *Criswell Theological Review* 2/2 (Spring 2005), pp. 64-6.

[49] James D.G. Dunn, "The New Perspective on Paul," *Bulletin of John Rylands Library* 65 (1983), pp. 95-122.

[50] Ibid., See also Bosch, *Transforming Mission*, p. 157.

[51] NT Wright states that "justification by faith" "has to do with the questions 'Who now belongs to God's people?' and 'How can you tell?' The answer is: all who believe in the gospel belong, and that is the only way you can tell—not by who their parents were, or how well they have obeyed the Torah (or any other moral code), or whether they have been circumcised. Justification, for Paul, is a subset of election, that is, it belongs as part of his doctrine of the People of God. . . And of course this does not mean, despite many efforts to push the conclusion this way, that it has nothing to do with sinners being saved from sin and death by the love and grace of God. The point of election always was that humans were sinful, that the world was lapsing back into chaos, and that God was going to mount a rescue operation. That is what the covenant was designed to do, and that is why 'belonging to the covenant' means, among other things, forgiven sinner'. . . . But the word 'call' itself, and the fact that 'justification' is not about how I get saved but 'how I am declared to be a member of God's people', must always have an eye to the larger purposes of the covenant." *Paul*, pp. 121-22.

[52] Michael F. Bird, "What is there Between Minneapolis and Durham?: A Third Way in the Piper-Wright Debate," *Journal of the Evangelical Theological Society* 54 (2011), pp. 299-309

[53] Michael F. Bird, "Incorporated Righteousness: A Response to Recent Evangelical Discussion Concerning the Imputation of Christ's Righteousness in Justification," *Journal of the Evangelical Theological Society* 47/2 (June 2004), p. 267. See also "Justification as Forensic Declaration and Covenant Membership: A Via Media between Reformed and Revisionist Readings of Paul," *Tyndale Bulletin* 57/1 (2006), p. 115.

[54] Bird, "Incorporated Righteousness," op. cit., p. 261. See also *Introducing Paul*, pp. 95-6.

[55] Ibid., p. 96.

[56] Richard N. Longenecker, *New Testament Social Ethics for Today* (Grand Rapids, MI: Eerdmans, 1984), p. 30.

[57] G. Walter Hansen, *Galatians* (Downers Grove, IL: InterVarsity 1994), p. 110-11.

[58] Longenecker, *New Testament Social Ethics*, pp. 31-2.

[59] Hansen, *Galatian*, pp. 112-13.

[60] Jacobus Kok, "Mission and Ethics in Galatians," *HTS Theological Studies* 67/1 (2011), p. 6.

[61] McKnight, *Galatian*, p. 303.

[62] Longenecker, *New Testament Social Ethics for Today*, p. 96.

[63] Hansen, *Galatians*, p. 38.

[64] Ibid., p. 25.

[65] This is the meaning in Gal. 2:3 and 6:12. See McKnight, *Galatians*, p. 107.

[66] Ibid., p. 100.

[67] Ibid., pp. 41, 133

[68] Van Engen, *God's Missionary People*, p. 47.

[69] Ibid., p. 51,

[70] Hays, *The Moral Vision of the New Testament*, p. 441.

[71] Ibid., p. 441.

[72] Goheen, *A Light to the Nations*, pp. 149-50.

[73] See Gehring, *House Church and Mission*, p. 181.

[74] Goheen, *A Light to the Nations*, p. 150. See also Wilbert R. Shenk, *Write the Vision: The Church Renewed* (Valley Forge, PA: Trinity Press International, 1995), pp. 92-3.

[75] Wayne A. Meeks, *The First Urban Christians: the Social World of the Apostle Paul* (New Haven, CT: Yale University Press, 2003), pp. 40-50.

[76] Longenecker, *Remember the Poor*, p. 53.

[77] Ibid., p. 57.

[78] For example, in I Cor. 1:26-29 Paul characterizes the believers as those who belong to the "weak," "lowly," and "despised" of this world. This indicates that the Corinthian congregation must have included many who were economically vulnerable. Ibid., p. 143.

[79] Longenecker estimates that at any given time about 25-30 percent of a typical urban group of Jesus followers may have been in dire economic situations and required economic support from the community's resources. (Ibid., pp. 294-96.) He argues that "the grain of New Testament data runs in the direction of signaling that those communities must have included a significant number of destitute members. This view is based not merely on the occasional reference to such people within Paul's letters (e.g., 'those who have nothing,' I Cor 11:22). It is based primarily on those texts that demonstrate that Paul expected communal funds for the poor (or their equivalent) to be established within those communities for whatever economic support might have been provided. This feature helps to explain, for instance, how Paul can laud communities like those in Thessalonica for their 'work of faith and labor of love' that had been reported throughout the region of Macedonia and Achaia (as Paul says hyperbolically in I Thess 1:3-10)." (Ibid., p. 232.) Rodney Stark has further shown that the typical city in which Pauline communities took root was characterized by chronic misery , chaos, fear, and brutality of life and that a primary reason for the rise of Christianity was that the early church provided support for the homeless, impoverished, strangers, orphans, and widows. (See Stark, *The Rise of Christianity*, pp. 147-62.) In a similar vein, Longenecker emphasizes the economic attractions of Pauline communities. "Arguably," he states, "the

early Jesus-movement offered a great deal to impoverished urbanites, especially those beyond the relative security of a household. If Jesus-groups set up communal funds for the poor and gathered to share food and drink in corporate dinners and other occasions, it is relatively easy to see what economic attraction such communities would have held for people in ES6 and ES7 who fell beyond the structures of a household. Moreover, this dimension might have distinguished early Jesus-groups from other urban associations, since Greco-Roman associations generally did not accumulate their membership from among ES6 and ES7 levels. . . While economic benefit is probably not a sufficient explanation for the attractions of Jesus-groups from among those in ES6 and ES7, it would nonetheless have served as a powerful means of attraction, alongside any other 'non-economic' factors that might be considered." (See Longenecker, *Remember the Poor*, pp. 259-61.)

[80] Pohl, *Making Room*, p. 31.

[81] Gehring, *House Church and Mission*, pp. 185-7.

[82] Meeks, *The First Urban Christians*, pp. 75-7.

[83] Pohl, *Making Room*, pp. 41-43.

[84] Gehring, *House Church and Mission*, p. 188.

[85] Ibid., pp. 189-90.

[86] Longenecker, *Remember the Poor*, p. 140.

[87] James C. Miller, "The Jewish Context of Paul's Gentile Mission," *Tyndale Bulletin* 58/1 (2007), pp. 102-115. This theme is treated in greater detail in his book, *The Obedience of Faith, the Eschatological People of God, and the Purpose of Romans* (Atlanta, GA: Society of Biblical Literature, 2000).

[88] Moo, *Romans*, pp. 779-80.

[89] Longenecker, *Remember the Poor*, p. 145.

[90] Ibid., p. 142.

[91] Ibid. Bruce Winter, *Seek the Welfare of the City: Christians as Benefactors and Citizens* (Grand Rapids, MI: Eerdmans, 1994), pp. 11-40, 58.

[92] Richard N. Longenecker, *Word Bible Commentary, vol. 41. Galatians* (Dallas, TX: Word Books, 1990), p. 282.

[93] Longenecker, *Remember the Poor*, p. 143. As we will see, the term is given an economic meaning in Acts 20:35.

[94] Ibid., p. 144.

[95] Bruce W. Longenecker, "Good News to the Poor: Jesus, Paul and Jerusalem," in *Jesus and Paul Reconnected: Fresh Pathways into an Old Debate*, ed. Todd D. Still (Grand Rapids, MI: Eerdmans, 2007), p. 49.

[96] Winter, *Seek the Welfare of the City*, pp. 66-7. Winter points out that the Jewish synagogues had established a program for the needy, with a weekly distribution every Friday from a money chest for the sojourners and resident poor, including widows. The Jerusalem church followed this practice, with the exception that the distribution occurred daily instead of weekly. See also David Batson, *The Treasure Chest of the Early Christians: Faith, Care and Community from the Apostolic Age to Constantine the Great* (Grand Rapids, MI: Eerdmans, 2001), pp. 44-5.

[97] Longenecker, *Remember the Poor*, p. 232. Batson argues that by the mid-century "the Chruch's practical caring work was becoming organized on a more consistent basis. . ." A letter by Cornelius (who became bishop of the church in Rome in AD

251) to Fabius, bishop of Antioch, states that the church provided financial support to 1,500 widows and other needy persons. See Batson, *The Treasure Chest of the Early Christians*, pp. 58, 93-4.

[98] The text literally reads "and towards all men" (*kai eis pantas*).

[99] Longenecker, *Remember the Poor*, p. 141.

[100] Richard B. Hays, "Ecclesiology and Ethics in I Corinthians." Available at: http://cpcnewhaven.org/ documents/Ecclesiology%20and%20ethics.pdf

[101] Ibid.

[102] Ibid., p. 292.

[103] Ibid., pp. 60-107.

[104] Wayne Meeks writes: "Perhaps. . . it was in certain of their social practices that the Christian groups most effectively distinguished themselves from other cult associations, clubs, or philosophical schools—(1) their special rituals of initiation and communion, (2) their practice of communal admonition and discipline, and (3) the organization of aid for widows, orphans, prisoners and other weaker member of the movement." *The Origins of Christian Morality: The First Two Centuries* (New Haven, CT: Yale University Press, 1993), p. 213.

[105] See Winter, *Seek the Welfare of the City*, p. 33.

[106] Longenecker, *Remember the Poor*, p. 168.

[107] Ibid., p. 137.

[108] This is Bruce Winter's understanding of I Peter 2:12 in *Seek the Welfare of the City*, p. 21.

[109] "Economic weakness in the sense of need, poverty is meant in Acts 20:35: the wealthy are to take care of the needy for, for it is more blessed to give than to receive." H.G., Link, "Weakness," in *The New International Dictionary of New Testament Theology, Vol. 3*, ed. Colin Brown (Grand Rapids, MI: Zondervan, 1971), p. 994. Some commentators see this as a reference to the poor in Jerusalem to which Paul was taking the collection (cf. 20:16). See Dean S. Gillialand, "For Missionaries and Leaders: Paul's Farewell to the Ephesian Elders, Acts 20:17-38," in *Mission in Acts: Ancient Narratives in Contemporary Context*, ed. Robert L. Gallagher and Paul Hertig (Maryknoll, NY: Orbis, 2004), p. 269. However, there is nothing in this passage which suggests that the reference to "the weak" should be so geographically limited.

[110] Longenecker, "Good News to the Poor," p. 50.

[111] Thomas Constable, *Notes on Acts*, p. 278. Available at: http://www.doc-txt.com/Commentary-on-Acts-20-35.pdf F.F. Bruce states that the meaning of Paul's words in vss. 34-35 is that "those to whom he was speaking [are to] likewise work hard and support not only themselves but others as well—the weak and the sick in particular." Frederick Fyvie Bruce, *The New International Commentary of the New Testament: The Book of Acts, Revised* (Grand Rapids, MI: Eerdmans, 1988), p. 395.

[112] Longenecker, *Remember the Poor*, p. 152.

[113] McKnight, *Galatians*, p. 87.

[114] Longenecker, *Remember the Poor*, pp. 157-82.

[115] Ibid., p. 186.

[116] Longenecker, "Good News to the Poor," p. 58

117 McKnight, *Galatians*, pp. 287-88.
118 Longenecker, *Remember the Poor*, p. 218.
119 Keith F. Nickle, *The Collection: A Study in Paul's Strategy* (Naperville, IL: Alec r. Allenson, 1966), p. 129.
120 Christopher R. Little, "Whatever Happened to the Apostle Paul? An Exposition of Paul's Teaching and Practice of Giving," *Mission Frontiers* (September 2001), p. 26.
121 Stephen Joubert, *Paul as Benefactor: Reciprocity, Strategy and Theological Reflection in Paul's Collection* (Toubingen: Mohr Siebeck, 2000), p. 90.
122 C.K. Barrett, *The Second Epistle to the Corinthians* (Peabody, MA: Hendrickson, 1993), p. 28.
123 Nickle, *The Collection*, p. 107.
124 Dieter Georgi, *Remembering the Poor: The History of Paul's Collection for Jerusalem* (Nashville, TN: Abingdon, 1992), p. 124.
125 Justin J. Meggit, *Paul, Poverty and Survival* (Edinburgh: T&T Clark, 1998), p. 175.
126 Georgi, *Remembering the Poor*, p. 157.
127 See N.T. *Wright*, Paul, p. 164.
128 Moore, *The Kingdom of Christ*, p. 169.
129 See N.T. Wright, "Romans and the Theology of Paul," in *Pauline Theology, Vol. III*, ed. David M. Hay and E. Elizabeth Johnson, (Mpls: Fortress, 1995), pp. 30-65. Available at: http://www.ntwrightpage.com/ Wright_Romans_Theology_ Paul.pdf
130 Bock, *Progressive Dispensationalism*, p. 270.
131 Georgi, *Remember the Poor*, p. 118.
132 Wright, "Romans and the Theology of Paul" p. 23.
133 Georgi, *Remember the Poor*, p. 118-20.
134 Ibid., p. 121.
135 Joubert, *Paul as Benefactor*, p. 219.
136 Scott McKnight, "Jesus vs. Paul," *Christianity Today* (December 3 2010). Available at http://www. christianitytoday. com/ct/2010/december/9.25.html?paging =off
137 Ibid.,
138 Wright, *What Paul Really Said*, p. 181.
139 Ibid., pp. 44-57. Writing from a reformed perspective, Kevin Vanhoozer describes this aspect of Wright's theological reconstruction of Paul as "important and exciting." See his "Wrighting the Wrongs of the Reformation?" in *Jesus, Paul, and the People of God: A Theological Dialogue with N.T. Wright*, ed. Nicholas Perrin and Richard B. Hays (Downers Grove, IL: InterVarsity Press, 2011), p. 241.
140 Wright, *What Paul Really Said*, p. 154.
141 N. T. Wright, *Evil and the Justice of God* (Downers Grove, IL: InterVarsity Press, 2006), p. 120.
142 Ibid., pp. 117-22.

Conclusion:
Four Characteristics
of the JustMissional Church

As a missionary, I have had the opportunity to visit numerous churches. One thing that stands out from these visits is how many ministries there are in our churches that could be relocated or duplicated within the local community and conducted for the benefit of the community. In other words, the church is turned "inside-out." My wife Kathi and I recently visited a large church in a suburb of Chicago. As we walked by an attractively furnished café, Kathi remarked, "What if, instead of (or in addition to) having the café *in* the church building it could be moved to some location in the town where Christians could rub shoulders with non-Christians. This would give more opportunities for witness. The café could even be used to employ people who are without a job."[1] Or consider the impact that a church with an education wing could have if it had a campus extension in an impoverished area of the city and provided mentoring for children of low-income families! One church that I recently visited has decided to build a community center in the heart of the downtown that can be used by families and groups in the community.

This concept of ministry is foreign to most churches in America today. The large majority of people who attend a typical worship service are passive recipients of religious goods and services. This "consumer driven" model is simply at odds with the call to discipleship as it is presented in Scripture. Moreover, most of the ministry people engage in is geared towards simply maintaining programs within the church, not in engaging in mission outside its four walls. In fact, the typical Christian sees little connection between his/her vocation and the church's mission to "make disciples." The Christian businessperson, for example, usually experiences a Sunday-Monday "gap." Beyond making money that he can give to support missionaries or church ministries, what he does in church on Sunday is not connected with what he does the other six days of the week.

Imperfect as it is, the church was meant to be God's social laboratory in the world, a prototype of the future kingdom with a career ladder shaped like a cross not that of a modern day corporation.[2] One way of depicting this role of the local church is to view it as a "connection center" between believers and the different domains of society (economics, family, government, education, etc.). JustMissional churches integrate mission and justice through kingdom witness. They also focus on training and mobilizing people in the pew about how to use their particular vocation as their "Jerusalem" in terms of ministry, and, from there, globally to the rest of the world.[3]

Fortunately, changes are happening in churches across the U.S. "There is," as Stephen Shields puts it, "a new Spirit breeze blowing through many churches—a missional renaissance."[4] The Leadership Network documents many compelling stories of churches that are seeking to expand the kingdom beyond their four walls. These "Rising Influence" churches identified by the Leadership Network tend to be more networked and creative. They also challenge their people to obedience both in reaching the lost and serving the marginalized in their communities, to demonstrate a clear vision, alignment, and sense of divine calling, and to focus on making disciples of Jesus

Christ.[5]   This new vision for the church (which I have referred to throughout this book as the "JustMissional" church) is depicted in the diagram below.

Figure 24. The JustMissional Church

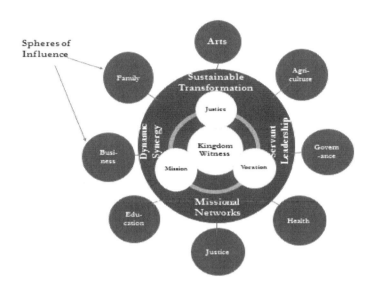

The following sections outline four "metrics of success" that ought to define the JustMissional church. First, it seeks *dynamic synergy* between the different vocations to further the mission of the church in a given community. Second, it places an emphasis on *servant leadership*.[6] Third, it works through *missional networks*, or global partnerships with those who share a church's mission. Finally, it seeks *sustainable transformation* as it addresses the spiritual, emotional, relational, and physical needs of individuals and communities.

Vocational Synergy & the Church's Mission

A concept of mission that has been around for a number of years is what has been termed a "synergistic" approach to mission. Instead of simply helping to support and fund missionary "professionals" to impact the world, local churches operating out of this mission model are more likely to adopt a multi-pronged approach that emphasizes partnerships and the active involvement of the congregation in ministry. The operative terms in the mission paradigm are *inter-dependence* and *leverage*. Synergistic churches recognize that they can accomplish more by working together with others than they could by ministering in isolation. They believe that the Great Commission applies to everyone. So they seek to involve their constituents not only as "goers and senders" but as active participants in ministry in the communities in which they reside. The focus is therefore on opportunity and empowering others to be involved in meaningful ways in outreach.[7]

One of the common objections to integral mission as I have described it in this book is that missionaries have personal limitations. Since they are finite with finite abilities, it is argued, they simply cannot do everything. Therefore, they should stick to what is most important—evangelism—and not try to spread their energies and time over a wide range of otherwise desirable objectives. This, however, presumes a view of mission that I have argued is not fully biblical. For God has called an entire "people" in all of their diversity of gifts to work out his mission purposes for the world.[8] As the slogan for the Lausanne movement states, mission is "the whole church taking the whole gospel to the whole world." A recent REVEAL survey of 1,000 churches found that the defining characteristic of High-Energy churches that rank high on the "spiritual vitality" index is that "Christianity is not a spectator sport." These churches: (1) get people moving by putting faith into action; (2) embed the Bible in everything they do; (3) create ownership by inspiring congregants to own the vision of the church; and (4) pastor the local community, that is, they are actively involved as a church body in addressing local community needs.[9] Having churches of this type requires that we rethink the concepts of "work," "vocation," and "calling" as they relate to the church and mission.

Seeing Work from a Kingdom Perspective

Work, Ben Witherington rightly points out, is "what weaves together the fabric of a called person's identity and fulfills it." It should then be seen as one's vocation—what one is equipped and experienced to do.[10] But what is work from a biblical perspective? If they are not retired, most people (including Christians) equate work with what they spend most of their time dong. Usually it is their job, but it may also involve being a stay-at-home mom, or a number of other activities. However, as Witherington argues, while this may be called one's *main* task it is not the Christian's *primary* task. Our primary task as believers is to fulfill the Great Commission to make disciples *and* obey the Great Commandment to love God with all of our hearts and our neighbor as ourselves.

> This is "job one." There are secondary callings that we may
> be called to in addition to this—being doctors, lawyers, busi-
> nesspeople, ministers, parents, etc. But they are indeed sec-
> ondary callings. Our primary task as persons re-created in the
> image of Christ is to do everything Christ come to earth to
> do—share the Good news of salvation, healing, the coming
> Kingdom. There are a variety of ways, venues, and avenues
> for accomplishing this primary task, and it can be accom-
> plished in tandem with and even by means of the secondary
> callings or tasks.[11]

The tendency in the church today is for Christians to make their *main* task (what is done five or six days of the week) *also* their *primary* task. This means that achieving a job promotion is often more important than fulfilling the Great Commission and "keeping up with the Joneses" often takes precedence over obeying the Great Command- ment to love our neighbor. These two commands then simply be- come elective "add-ons," directives we follow when we can find some "spare time" in our harried schedules. Of course, it is im- portant to be able to financially support ourselves so that we do not become dependent on family, friends—or the government. And a person's unique combination of talents, giftings, personality, and training should be factored into determining his/her calling or vocation. But the ultimate objective in all we do should be the advancement of God's kingdom and his glory. Work, from a biblical perspective, is then *"any necessary and meaningful task that God calls and gifts a person to do and which can be undertaken to the glory of God and for the edification and aid of human beings, being inspired by the Spirit and foreshadowing the new creation."*[12]

Understanding work from a kingdom perspective involves a new way of structuring social life and thus creating a new culture—a culture of conversion and a new creation in and through Christ. Whether one realizes it or not, every Christian is part of making culture—that is, an ethos or way of making something of the world. What we need to understand, then, is that whether we are at our job or worshipping in the church, we are at work constructing a culture that either advances or hinders the cause of the kingdom.[13] The new trend among evangelicals is to attempt to change society through politics rather than through changing culture. This approach comes at a time when many people acknowledge that politics cannot touch many of the deepest crises in society—crises that are cultural and "pre-political."[14] So, we must ask ourselves, are we seeking to change culture or is the dominant culture changing us? Does our agenda reflect more a liberal or conservative political agenda than the agenda of the kingdom of God? Are we more like the profile of a typical lawyer (or doctor or teacher) than of a follower of Christ?[15]

Calling and the People of God

In one of our small group Bible studies we were discussing a kingdom perspective on work. In the course of our discussion, one of the participants said, "I've always felt that I was meant to do more for God's kingdom than what I am doing. Deep down I feel that

God is calling me to be a philanthropist of some sort who would support ministry and give to people who are in need." Every person desires to make a difference. Os Guinness states that in his thirty years of ministry one of the most common questions he is asked is "How do I find and fulfill the central purpose of my life?"[16] Answering this question requires that we look more deeply at the concept of "call" in Scripture.

Let me begin with what I consider to be two unbiblical approaches. The first error is to create a division between "spiritual" and "secular" callings. "According to this mentality, it is best to leave the secular arena and go into the spiritual arena so we can be 'full-time Christian workers.'"[17] Implicit in this division is a hierarchy of religious importance or value. "Going into the Lord's work," means becoming a pastor or missionary.[18] This notion that only those who engage in "religious" tasks full-time are "called into ministry" is simply not biblical.[19] At times, it leads to *clericalism*, characterized by clergy domination, a professionalization of ministry (witness the large staffs in our mega-churches), and near disdain for laity as unreliable, incompetent, and unavailable. But the more common phenomenon in Protestant churches is an often uneasy *co-existence* of lay people and full-time "clergy" or ministers. Although each functions (ideally) in a complementary way, this co-existence still involves "two peoples" separated by education, ordination, function, and even culture.[20] "Lay" people are still defined as non-ordained, unpaid, and untrained. Generally, it is the laity who "receive" ministry while the clergy "give" it. To the extent that laity *are* involved in ministry, it is limited to helping the clergy and other paid professionals do the work of the church.[21] Both the *clerical* and the *co-existence* models run counter to the biblical model of *community* where all members supporting each other in a diversity of functions contribute to a rich social unity and are involved in service to God and others.[22]

The second error is to simply view an occupation as one's Christian vocation or calling. When one becomes a Christian one's occupation becomes *the* "calling" in which he/she serves God. This is *not* to say that one cannot serve God in and even *through* an occupation. But to simply equate one's occupation with God's call is, in my view, a mistake. Some historical context is important here. Apart from the general "call" to be a Christian, the medieval Catholic Church limited vocation to church occupations or the "call" to be a monk, nun, priest, or bishop. In reaction against this division of life into "sacred" and "secular," Martin Luther and the other Reformers rightly emphasized a whole-life faith in which service to God and others is related to life in the *world* not just the church or a monastery. The common interpretation of Luther is that he subsumed vocation under the "Orders of Creation."[23] Under the creation mandate, all work is both meaningful and has a part in advancing the purposes of God. Therefore, in this view, it is legitimate to view one's work or occupation as one's calling.[24] This view of work is often uncritically accepted by many Evangelicals. But it contains a dangerous half-truth. While it is true that we are to glorify God in all that we do and that all work is therefore intrinsically meaningful, the tendency to simply identify one's personal occupation with vocation or calling "flies in the face of the evidence of the Gospels, where Jesus calls disciples *away* from their nets, *away* from tax collecting, and in Jesus' own case away from carpentry."[25] Obviously, then, one's occupation or job does not automatically become one's calling and may in fact *conflict* with one's larger calling as a believer.

The Latin roots of the word "vocation" (*vocation* and *voco*) simply mean to "be called" or to "have a calling." This expresses the biblical truth that vocation starts with being called by God. It is not something we choose, like a career. There are three dimensions to the Christian doctrine of "call" or vocation—(1) the collective (general) vocation; (2) the individual (specific) vocation; and (3) the human (cultural) vocation.[26] These three dimensions are intersecting.

Figure 25. Three Dimensions of Calling

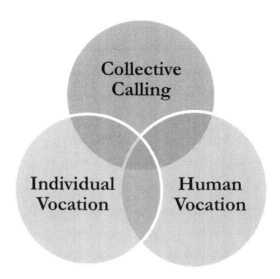

As I have previously argued, biblically, the concept of "call" or "calling" is rooted in the corporate identity of the church as the "called out" people of God who participate in his salvific work. The use of the verbal adjective *klētos* most often refers to the collective identity of Christians. In Romans 1:6-7 and I Corinthians 1:2, Paul addresses the *klētoi hagioi*, those called as saints. Paul also uses the word "call" to refer to God's summons of the individual to salvation, discipleship, and service. The individual calling is part of our personal response to God as unique individuals with specific gifts. This aspect of call is often emphasized in our culture. But, as Os Guinness rightly argues, individual callings should complement, not contradict, the corporate calling. This prevents calling from degenerating into excessive individualism.[27] Most Christians are surprised to learn, for example, that Philippians 2:12 ("work out your salvation with fear and trembling, for it is God who works in you to will and to do") is an exhortation to a group not individual believers. In the original Greek, the word "you" is in the plural. So, salvation in this context is a group project—as is work.[28]

The concept of "church unique" is useful in expressing this dialectical relationship between the individual and collective calling. Will Mancini has coined this concept in arguing that every local body of Christ has a unique identity or "kingdom concept"—or simple, clear "big idea" that defines how a local church will glorify God and make disciples.[29]   Local churches can identify their unique "kingdom concept" by examining the intersection of three areas that represent aspects of their church's God-given uniqueness: (1) their *local predicament*, or unique needs and opportunities of the community where God has placed them; (2) the *collective potential* or unique resources, capabilities, and giftings that God brings together in a local church body; and (3) the *apostolic esprit* or particular focus that energizes and animates the church's leadership. Again, this requires a collective vision, and an effort on the part of leaders to view the individual giftings within the church in light of the whole so that the church doesn't become a chaotic mess of everyone wanting to do his/her own thing.[30]

This leads to two questions. First, what distinction (if any) is there between the so-called "lay person" and those who engage in "full-time" Christian work, including pastors and cross-cultural missionaries? Is there a "special call" associated with ordained ministry or "missionary" service?   I would agree with Greg Ogden that there is not a call to leadership that is qualitatively different from that experienced by other members of the body of Christ. Rather, the New Testament conceives of the call to leadership as a particular call among other particular calls. "From within the body of Christ some have the function of helping the members of the body discover their ministry to upbuild the church and be deployed to the world. Any view of call that debilitates and devalues the ministry of the whole body of Christ is contrary to the New Testament conception of the church."[31] This will be discussed more fully in the next section on servant leadership.

The second, related, question is this: Are individuals "called" to specific occupations? Here, again, it is crucial that we distinguish between primary and secondary callings. As followers of Christ we are called by him, to him, and for him. This is our primary calling. The individual believer's secondary calling is what one *does* in using his/her gifts for God's glory. It is one's "life purpose," that which flows out of a response to God's sovereignty. This might include a call to homemaking, the practice of law, or teaching. But we must be sure that first things remain first and that the primary calling leads without fail to the secondary calling.[32]

Luther rightly understood that so-called "secular" work is valuable in God's sight and could be performed in service to him and one's neighbor. However, he wrongly interpreted Paul's injunction in I Cor. 7:17 ("each one should retain the place in life that the Lord assigned to him and to which God has called him") to mean that one ought to stay in one's "station in life" (i.e., occupation), seeing it as his/her calling from God. From this, he and other reformers developed the idea of a "worldly calling."[33] This has led to what Guinness calls the "Protestant distortion," where the secondary calling is elevated above the primary calling and work is made sacred. Individuals, including Christians, have come to invest ultimate significance in their occupations as their source of meaning and fulfillment.[34]

Correctly interpreted I Cor. 7:17 simply means that the call of God comes in a particular social setting or circumstance. Basically, then, Paul is saying that the situation in which the Christian finds himself is taken up in the call of God who is providentially involved in every aspect of one's life. Another way of putting this is that the call of God takes place within a particular sphere of life that varies from believer to believer. There is an inner core of giftedness, motivation, and experiences that is unique to each individual. But calling is comprehensive, and has multiple dimensions, including relationships, not just the interior makeup of one's giftedness. Moreover, an occupation or profession is only one of many "spheres" of our vocation or calling to service (Eph. 2:10). Christians should then integrate God's call into every area of their lives including their careers.

This brings us to the third dimension of calling—the human (cultural) vocation. In Genesis 1:27-30 Adam and Eve are given what is often referred to as the "cultural mandate." As imagers of God they are told to have dominion over all of the earth. John Walton suggests that this commission to Adam and Eve involves the mission of bringing order to their world just as God brought order to the cosmos. Their task of "taking care" of the Garden (Gen. 2:15) went beyond the physical task of "gardening" to managing it as a sacred place where God's presence dwelt, protecting it from forces of corruption, and extending the borders of the garden so the glorious presence of God would be expanded over all of the earth.[35] Psalm 8 suggests this role of Adam and Eve when it states that God made man "ruler over the works of [His] hands" (vs. 6) with the ultimate goal that the whole earth will be filled with God's glory or majesty (vss. 1, 9).[36]

This image of humans as "co-creators" with God in extending his glory throughout the earth means that all of our actions should be unified in obedience to Him. His sovereignty bears on every dimension of life. This again raises the issue of how Christians are to live *in* the world without simply being *of* the world and the surrounding culture. An appropriate view of the cultural dimension to the Christian's calling means resisting three current trends: (1) *privatization* or practicing faith only in the private sphere and avoiding the public square; (2) *politicization*, or trying to change people and culture through policy; and (3) "*pillarization*," that is building pillars or institutions that parallel secular institutions, sheltering ourselves in private groupings and not being salt and light in society.[37] Witherington maintains that the task of engaging culture and introducing culture change must begin with small groups. "It starts small and branches out like ripples on a pond from a small stone thrown into it." This is how Jesus set about to change the world—with an inner circle of three disciples (Peter, James and John), and a slightly larger circle of 12, then after Easter a group of 120 (Acts 1:15). This principle of "the 3. . . then12. . . then 120" for culture making and cultural change involves social networking. It is also about increasing the size of the body of Christ, so that more and more people will be in a right relationship with God and fulfill their destiny to love God and their neighbor wholeheartedly.[38]

Servant Leadership

Ministry in a JustMissional church also requires a "less-is-more" type of leadership. Dale Burke puts it this way: success in leadership is not defined by doing *more*, but *less*. As a church grows the temptation is for leaders to work harder and devote longer hours to ministry. But the key to success is to *lead* more and *manage* less.[39] This principle of servant leadership is modeled in Act 6:1-7. When the early church outgrew the apostle's ability to manage the care of poor widows, what did they do? They *mobilized* a team of seven other men who were known to be full of the Spirit and wisdom and entrusted *them* with the responsibility to oversee this ministry. This freed the apostles to continue unimpeded with their ministry of the Word of God. The result was that the church continued to grow.

Using the terms frequently employed by the leadership of the mission of the Evangelical Free Church of which I am a part, I would suggest that mobilization through "less-is-more" leadership involves a fourfold process of: (1) *casting* vision; (2) *developing* other leaders; (3) *empowering* people for ministry; and (4) *releasing* ministry teams.

Casting a vision or image of where God wants us to be in the future is necessary to get us out of the comfort zone of where we are in the present. Without a shared vision there is little understanding of where a congregation wants to go, why it is important, or how it will get there. A vision is not truly shared, however, unless the people are given a voice in its development. Vision helps leaders and the people pull together for a common purpose. It sets the broad outline for action while the details are worked out as God's Spirit works in and through members of the congregation.[40]

Figure 26. "Less-is-More" Leadership

The pastor and elders of the church, for example, can caste vision for reaching the community for Christ. They can urge people in the church to support efforts for church planting and multiplication. In addressing issues of justice and mercy such as poverty, A.I.D.S, or human trafficking the pastor-teacher(s) can instruct the people they lead in biblical principles of mercy, justice, and holistic ministry. To help raise awareness, they can make the church available for workshops or conferences on human trafficking and other forms of injustice. They can encourage the those in the congregation who are in the medical profession to treat those suffering from A.I.D.S or help children whose limbs have been blown off by land mines; those in agriculture to help farmers in poor countries with water treatment programs, crop rotation and livestock; or the businesspeople to use their expertise to help the poor through micro-finance and/or business development. But the specific form that various ministries take is as much bottom-up as it is top-down.

The pastor-teacher(s) should focus on developing other leaders not on managing the congregation. The principle of leadership multiplication is given in II Timothy 2:2: "The things which you have heard from me in the presence of other witnesses entrust to religious men who will also be qualified to teach others." Notice that Paul goes on to connect this charge to Timothy with success in battle or a sporting event (vss. 3-5). In other words, achievement of our goals in spiritual warfare is necessarily tied to leadership development. As Dale Burke states:

> To empower an organization forward, you need not only a compelling vision or goals that energize troops, you also need leaders to organize those troops and turn the vision into reality.[41]

The move towards mentoring in some churches reflects a growing awareness of the need for leadership development. Instead of using the academic model that focuses on imparting content, these pastors place an emphasis on relationships and on-the-job training as the context for developing leaders.[42]

The lay people in the church must also be empowered to do ministry. In Eph. 4:11-12 Paul describes the diverse gifts in the church (the apostles, prophets, evangelists, pastors, and teachers) as having the *common purpose* of equipping or preparing God's people for the "work of ministry" (4:11-12). The noun *diakonia* in verse 12 is variously translated as "ministry," "service" or "mission." The same word is used in Acts 6 to describe the function of "waiting on tables" (vss. 1-2) and the "ministry of the word" (vss. 1, 4). Both are ministries without qualitative distinction.[43] So, it is clear from this passage that Paul regards ministry as the work of the entire community of believers, not just of a specially designated class of spiritually gifted individuals. Servant leaders then, facilitate ministry in and through others. "They network individuals and teams through a shared vision of a preferred future."[44]

Finally, there must be a releasing of self-organizing ministry teams that are made up of people who operate out of their areas of spiritual giftedness. Ministry teams are different from committees in that committees are primarily decision-making bodies while teams are organized to achieve a specific mission or goal. These missional teams network with other teams to carry out the overall vision or ministry purpose of the church.[45] This concept of ministry teams is indicated in Paul's description of spiritual gifts in II Cor. 12:4-6. In this passage Paul connects the variety of "gifts" (vs. 4) with the variety of "ministries" (vs. 5) and the variety of "workings" or effects (vs. 6). In other words, individuals using their spiritual gifts and experiences in ministries they are passionate about have maximum impact— particularly when they work with other team members to carry out ministry.[46]

A handful of innovative churches are engaging marketplace professionals in ministry that is having a significant impact for the kingdom. These churches realize that the traditional hierarchical top-down leadership must be replaced by flatter structures where leadership is shared with more people empowered to get a vision, set direction and strategy, make decisions, and move forward together.[47] "Idea generation flows freely from leaders in the congregation to the church's paid staff and back again. The lines between 'clergy' and 'laity' are blurred when it comes to who creates all the good ministry ideas and who gets the job done."[48] One innovative approach to mobilizing lay leadership in the church is the "strategic church initiative" pioneered by an organization called Halftime.[49] This is a guided transformational year-long partnership between Halftime and a select group of churches that are looking to identify, equip, and unleash "high capacity" leaders that are already in their congregations. These "high capacity leaders" are people who are reaching mid-life. They have had some success and would like to utilize their capacities, talents, and treasure for kingdom work in the second half of their lives. Halftime hosts a vision casting summit that helps individuals in the church to see how they can use their market-place skills to advance Christ's kingdom.

One of the issues that many churches struggle with is the how to eliminate as much debt and overhead as possible so that more of their resources can be deployed in local and global ministry. Here, again, servant leadership can play a critical role. According to a recent survey of over 700 churches by Warren Bird and Matt Branaugh, the typical church spends 45-50 percent of its budget on staffing. Comparing these churches with churches that spend 35 percent or less of their budget on staffing costs, these researchers found that "lean staff budget" churches have significantly fewer staff per attendee than do other churches. While factors such as outsourcing more jobs and finding more sources of income (i.e., renting a portion of the property) help to explain why some churches spend less of their budget on staffing, volunteer development and lay leadership was the "common thread" that differentiated lean staff churches from other churches. These churches also spend a higher percentage of their budget on ministry *outside* their walls and are more engaged with poorer communities.[50]

Missional Networks

It is significant that virtually all of the expansion of the early Christianity took the form of a multiplication of house churches. These churches consisted of "webs of social relationships" which connected the people in the church to each other and to the neighborhood and workplace. Evangelism was relationally-driven. There was a compassionate response to needs among Christians and to those outside the church. Rodney Stark argues that one of the primary reasons for the spread of the early Christian church was its growth through social networks, or a structure of direct and intimate interpersonal attachments.[51] Instead of depending on government they created their own worlds of work and service through which they met the needs of the sick and impoverished, both Christian and non-Christian. The Christian church was in fact the primary source of philanthropy in the Roman Empire. The Roman Emperor Julian noted, "Nothing has contributed to the progress of the superstition of these Christians as their charity to strangers. The impious Galileans provide not only for their own poor, but for ours as well."[52] In comparing other religions in the Roman empire with Christian efforts he noted that Christians had created "a miniature welfare state in an empire which for the most part lacked social services."[53] Stark describes Christianity as a revitalization movement which revitalized life in Greco-Roman cities by providing "new norms and new kinds of social relationships able to cope with many urgent urban problems."[54] He continues:

> To cities filled with the homeless and impoverished, Christianity offered charity as well as hope. To cities filled with newcomers and strangers, Christianity offered an immediate basis for attachments. To cities filled with orphans and widows, Christianity provided a new and expanded sense of family. To cities torn by violent ethnic strife, Christianity offered a new basis for social solidarity. And to cities faced with epidemics, fires, and earthquakes, Christianity offered effective nursing services.[55]

One encouraging trend among churches in North America is the emergence of networks as a new paradigm of partnership. Ed Stetzer and David Putman observe that "networks have become a major part of church life in North America."[56] While some networks are connected with a certain group or denomination, most are trans-denominational—working with churches in and out of other denominations. Though they represent a major step forward, there are two weaknesses in these emerging networks. First, almost all are "affinity-based," meaning that few develop mission relationships with groups different from themselves. In many of these networks ethnic diversity is sorely lacking. Second, most networks are solely focused on church planting and growth. Few have the structures to support ministries of compassion such as orphanages and care for the poor or engage in international mission beyond the "we'll send you money because you know how to impress visitors" approach.[57]

One notable exception to this pattern is Saddleback Church's P.E.A.C.E plan. As Rick Warren explains "This is a simple strategy that every church can use to **P**lant churches, **E**quip leaders, **A**ssist the poor, **C**are for the sick, and **E**ducate the next generation. It is a *local church-based paradigm for missions* in the 21st century, and we believe God will use it to bring worldwide revival."[58] Warren goes on to state:

> The bottom line is that we intend to reinvent mission strategy in the 21st century. . . In the first century, mission strategy was always congregationally based . . . There were no mission societies, mission boards, or parachurch organizations . . . Today most local churches are sidelined and uninvolved when it comes to missions. The message from most mission and parachurch organizations to the local church is essentially "Pray, pay, and get out of the way." But in the 21st century, Kay and I intend to help thousands of other local churches to move back to the frontline in mission, in compassion, and in providing the social services that historically the church provided. I believe the proper role for all the great parachurch and relief organizations is to serve local churches in a supportive role, offering their expertise and knowledge, but allowing the local churches around the world to be the central focus and distribution centers.[59]

Notwithstanding the theological weaknesses of Warran's P.E.A.C.E. plan which were pointed out in an earlier chapter, Stetzer and Putman refer to this as a "major paradigm shift" with regard to networking of missions—one that will eventually be adopted by other North American churches. They encourage denominations and churches to further explore and develop innovative ways of creating missional networks for kingdom impact.[60]

A concept that is promoted by two experts on the development of individual and community networks is *networlding*.[61] This approach, which goes deeper than conventional networking, has a number defining characteristics:[62]

- It is "values driven," meaning that there is clear intentionality about forming relationships based on shared values, goals, and beliefs.

- Unlike conventional networking that focuses on achieving one goal, *networlding* is multidimensional. It is intent on forming relationships that encompass more than one factor. "It may be that your values demand you fulfill not one but a series of goals; you may have to search for people with both the disparate skills and shared beliefs necessary to achieve successive goals."[63]

- It focuses on identifying *bridgers* in your personal and professional life—individuals who bring together people from different groups to develop new opportunities.

- It divides relationships into primary, secondary, and tertiary circles. The primary circle is made up of people with whom you have the most frequent contact and who are most closely aligned with your goals and values. This circle usually consists of three to ten influential people. About 80% of your relationship-building time is spent here. But interactions between people in primary circles lead to supplementary relationships that make up the secondary and tertiary circles. Though less important than relationships in the primary circle, these relationships are non-the-less valuable in expanding information, broadening perspectives, enhancing influence, and making referrals.

- This concept of networking focuses on creating deep and meaning relationships with *influencers*—those who use their knowledge, skills, experience, reputation and connections to make things happen.
- It maximizes connectivity by relying on e-mail, web sites, and other electronic communication mediums as both relation-ship-building and maintenance tools.

The importance of this approach to networking from a Christian perspective is that it emphasizes the formation of relationships based on a common vision, trust, and values. It also stresses the fact that collaborations have a synergistic and exponential force which orbits around a primary circle and gains strength from the contributions of others. These authors lay out a seven-step *networlding* process:[64]

1) *Establish a Values-Rich Foundation*: Identify your values priorities, align your values with your actions and set goals.

2) *Make Connections for Your Primary Circle*: Identify the qualities you want in a partner and find individuals from existing connections based on traits and qualities you value.

3) *Expand Your Circles*: Fill your primary circle with influencers and envision and create your secondary circle.

4) *Initiate Exchange Relationships*: Establish relationships with mutual exchange as a foundation that provide emotional , informational, knowledge, and promotional support.

5) *Grow and Nurture Relationships*: Maximize the potential of networking interactions by nurturing relationships to achieve vibrant, collaborative exchanges.

6) *Co-create Opportunities*: Move from talk to action and collaborating on opportunities that enhance the possibilities for mutual success.

7) *Recreate Your Networld*: Since networlds and the relationships they contain are dynamic rather than static, they need continuous monitoring, assessment and reformulation. This involves reas-

sessing goals, mission, and values and designing creative strategies to ensure that exchanges are healthy and continue to evolve.

Through this seven-step process local churches can form missional networks that expand Christ's kingdom and lead to individual and community transformation. In many of our urban neighborhoods churches are creating networks of communication, financial support, and technical skills to influence cultural and social change.[65]

Sustainable Transformation

There are many ways in which churches can help to alleviate the wide range of social problems in societies where they are located. When a church genuinely cares for people in every aspect of life, the healing and wholeness that it produces in the lives of its members positively affects others in the wider community as well. In this way, it engages in "preventative social medicine" by diminishing the pressures on already overloaded social and welfare services.[66] Robert Wuthnow observes that "for centuries the Christian church has been the mainstay of community life in the West ... But now our society seems to be at a loss for community. The question that faces us, then, is whether it too is beginning to succumb to the impersonal answers that fragment our society."[67] In addition, the many social problems are multifaceted and complex. More than one ministry to the poor has foundered on the rocks of good intentions and ended up doing more harm than good.[68] This requires that we have a proper biblical understanding of what "sustainable transformation" looks like.

Moving Beyond Donor-Driven Relief and Development

A number of years ago I had a conversation with a representative of a large Christian relief organization. He expressed his frustration that while working among the poor in Africa he knew that development projects that enlisted the support and cooperation of people in the community would be most effective in the long-run. However, he was not allowed to pursue them because they often conflicted with the goals of major donors whom the relief organization relied upon for funding.

Unfortunately, much of the relief and development efforts in the West have been donor-driven. This is true of projects both at home and abroad. And it has had a number of negative consequences. To begin with, donor-driven projects are often characterized by standardized or "cookie-cutter" approaches to relief and development in which the non-poor make all of the decisions about the project and then do the project *for* and even *to* the economically poor. What Corbett and Fikkert call "McDevelopment," or the fast-food franchise approach to poverty alleviation is generally done in the name of efficiency. But it usually ends up being grossly ineffective because it is not embraced and "owned" by the local population and is not sensitive to the local culture.[69] In addition, it often leads to the "poison" of five types of paternalism:[70]

- *Resource paternalism*: viewing the solution to poverty largely in material terms.
- *Spiritual paternalism*: assuming that because of our material prosperity we have to "teach" the materially poor about God and that there is little or nothing that can be learned from them.
- *Knowledge paternalism*: assuming that we know best how to do things and what is best for the materially poor.
- *Labor paternalism*: doing *for* people what they could do themselves, thereby undermining their sense of stewardship of their own time and talents.
- *Managerial paternalism*: in an effort to "get things done quickly," the tendency to "take charge" by planning, directing, and managing initiatives in low-income communities.

These weaknesses are prevalent in the type of Short Term Missions (STMs) that is engaged in by the majority of American churches. For most STMs the focus is on the impact these trips will have on the teams and the churches that send them rather than their long-term impacts on the recipients. The typical STM project operates as a "charity," where the materially non-poor "give" something that the materially poor lack. This "material relief" model is often emphasized to the exclusion of true development, or the investment of resources in job creation, businesses, and other projects that continue to operate to the benefit of the community long after the STM team has left.[71] Moreover, in many cases work is done building homes, schools, hospitals, orphanages, and churches without the active involvement of the members of the poor communities or churches that are being helped. I have personally witnessed this in relief and development efforts following hurricane Katrina. This may be the appropriate and necessary STM response immediately following a disaster. But the goal should always be to transition from outside aid to local involvement and control as much as possible as there is movement from relief to development. At the most, as Corbett and Fikkert argue, the STM team needs to be viewed as an extension of local organizations rather than as independent, outside agents.[72]

Redefining Sustainability: Sustainable Impact vs. Sustainable Profit

In an effort to arrive at a more biblically-based understanding of "sustainable transformation" John Rowell suggests that the foundational biblical principle for mission practice should be "maximum investment, for the sake of the kingdom, in a way that will not create unhealthy dependency." [73] This principle *both* discourages perpetual handouts that result in over-dependency *and* a focus on Westernized definitions of "dependency" that justify a selfish and stingy withholding of resources that could support or subsidize much needed indigenous ministries around the world. In other words, we need to avoid *both* unhealthy dependency *and* selfish complacency; and we should seek true *interdepency* characterized by biblical principles of *generosity*, *reciprocity*, and *equality*. Rowell agrees with most relief and development professionals that, "sustainability must become the target of prolonged missionary attention if we are to do a better job of ministering redemptively among the poor."[74] But, he argues, the goal of being *maximally generous* while working towards *sustainable investments* on the mission field requires that we redefine what we mean by sustainability.

In Western donor-driven definitions of sustainability emphasis is usually placed on an input-output model of "sustainable profits" that is drawn from the business world. As Rowell describes this approach, "it presumes that financial inputs should always generate disproportionate financial outputs." Thus sustainability is tied to financial profitability:

> We associate inputs with outputs, and measure outputs in terms of dollars, because "cash return on investment" is the logical metric used to measure success. This is standard market place wisdom. Business experience teaches us that a profit stream is necessary if a venture is to continue indefinitely, if it is to be sustainable. Profit makes the world go round. That truism has largely been imported into the mission arena, and is accepted as a relief and development reality as well.[75]

This is not to say that monetary factors should not be taken into consideration in determining project viability. But to make this the only or even the primary benchmark of success often results in a premature departure and withdrawal of project sponsorship even when it is having positive results in other areas. In addition, a pre-occupation with profitability can actually lead to "mission drift," or loss of the original goals, which the project was conceived to achieve in the first place. Jim Collins, author of the best-selling book *Good to Great*, asserts that the value of social sector agendas cannot be measured by using a "pricing system." Therefore, the use of the "profit metric" to measure success in social sector enterprises is both unhelpful and unfair.[76] Commenting on designated gifts of donors that are often counterproductive, he goes so far as to argue that non-profit organizations should "reject resources that drive them away from the center of their [core competencies]."[77]

Rowell proposes that "sustainable impact" rather than "sustainable profit" should be used to measure the sustainability of projects aimed at helping the poor. The concept of "sustainable impact" has actually been the measure of success in medical missions in the past. A village clinic that treats hundreds of patients in a given year (using indigenous doctors and nurses) is generally considered a "success" even if it is losing money.

> This would mean helping to fund the effort and remaining dedicated to sharing the financial costs of the project, in cooperation with our national brothers and sisters, as long as the desired outcomes (in nonmonetary terms) are being achieved . . . If the local economy can support the ongoing effort in the end, that is well and good. But in many contexts poverty is so entrenched that quick fixes born of small investments over short periods of time are not going to turn the tide.[78]

What implications does this concept of "sustainable impact" have for business creation in a mission context, or what is normally referred to as "business as mission?" Again, while the goal of business is usually seen as maximizing profit, a more biblical approach is to view it as a means by which individuals can fulfill their purpose as God's image bearers and are brought into a right relationship with God, self, others, and the environment. Some recent descriptions of capitalism as "value driven" rather than "consumer driven" highlight the difference between business entrepreneurs and social entrepreneurs.[79] Business entrepreneurship focuses on market forces while social entrepreneurship draws upon and builds community support. Both involve creativity. But while business entrepreneurship uses creativity to enter new markets and achieve financial gain social entrepreneurship employs creativity to solve intractable social problems and serve the public good.[80] Moreover, consumer driven capitalism is often characterized by capital mobility, the separation of people from neighborhoods, and the trivialization of any notions of settled communities that endure over time.[81] By contrast, social entrepreneurship emphasizes the attachment of the individual to family, local institutions, and community.

Michael Cooper and Daniel Bryan suggest that "social entrepreneurship" can be an effective framework for Christians to address social issues of poverty and injustice in the current global climate. They define a distinctly Christian social entrepreneurship as:

> a venture that addresses issues of local and global concern by catalyzing enterprises that create sustainable change for improvement of social conditions, quality of life and dignity of people as created in the image of God. Such enterprises focus on the economic, social, environmental, and spiritual good of community.[82]

A Christian approach to social entrepreneurial ventures does not eschew making a profit. Indeed, a goal of most if not all Christian-based social entrepreneurial ventures would be to become financially self-sustaining and help indigenous ministries and local communities achieve financial independence. However, the primary measure of sustainability is not profitability as such, but whether the venture is achieving the desired outcomes of restored relationships with God, self, others, and the environment. In fact, the best way to ensure profitability over the long term is *not* to make it a primary goal but to see it as a byproduct of people's restoration to full humanness in all areas as God intended.

In this context, the key to long-term sustainability is "buy-in" from all the stakeholders into the project, particularly the indigenous population. When people in a poor community have full participation in all aspects of a project from the very beginning they are more likely to make the sacrifices necessary for success over the long haul. Also, utilization of the knowledge and skills of the materially poor themselves is vital to long-term success.[83] As Stuart Hart puts it, capitalist ventures that are truly indigenous seek to develop native capabilities by learning how to "coinvent and coevolve products and services so that they are appropriately embedded in the local ecosystem and culture from the start."[84]

One example of Christian-based social entrepreneurialism is the business model called *Timothy Center Ecoprises* (TCE) currently being developed by the Timothy Center for Sustainable Transformation. Using innovative technology that is especially designed for the developing world, the business is involved in three areas of development: (1) building construction; (2) recycling; and (3) clean water production. To fund projects, the Timothy Center seeks capital investments from investors and business partners. TCE has recently opened a branch in Haiti. Since a housing crisis still looms in Haiti, with 350,000 people living in tents in Port-au-Prince, the current focus is building construction. TCE has purchased equipment for creating compressed earth blocks that can be used to construct homes and other buildings strong enough to withstand earthquakes and hurricanes. It is currently pursuing partnerships with NGOs and the Haitian government to build 850 square foot housing units. Each house can be constructed in about a week. Since the goal is sustainability and job creation, the business will employ 24 Haitians to work in producing compressed earth blocks and erect walls for new homes, schools, orphanages and other buildings. Additionally, as part of TCE's sustainability goal, the Haiti branch has Haitian investors and seeks to contribute to Haitian ministries.[85]

Principles for Long-term Sustainability

What principles can we derive from Scripture and from cross-cultural experience that would help ensure the future success of a project aimed at addressing the spiritual, emotional, and physical needs of poor individuals and communities? The diagram below gives a suggested model for long-term sustainability.

Figure 24. Model for Long-Term Sustainability

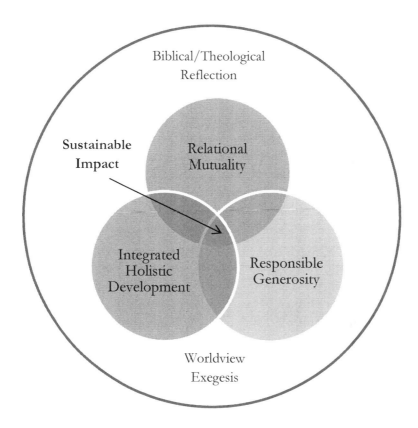

The outer circle represents the importance of: (1) *biblical and theological reflection* on the nature of God and his mission in the world and on humans as created in His image; and (2) a *"worldview exegesis"* of the society and culture of the proposed project. Both of these elements are indispensable in providing the proper foundation or context for long-term sustainable transformation. The three inner circles further define three characteristics of a project that are essential to achieving sustainable impact: (1) *relational mutuality*; (2) *responsible generosity*; and (3) *integrated holistic development.*

We have already addressed the element of "biblical/theological reflection" at some length in our development of a biblical framework for mission. It should go without saying that this is foundational to all that we do. As the extensive REVEAL survey by Hawkins and Parkinson shows, in High-Impact churches "God's word is the central axis around which every discussion, activity and decision revolves."[86] This means, first and foremost, that all of our actions must be Christ-centered and dependent on the direction and power of the Holy Spirit. As I write these words, the Chicago area where I live is experiencing one of the hottest and driest summers on record. Kathi, the one with the "green thumb" in our family, has a beautiful garden behind our house. But the flowers are beginning to wilt. What if, instead of watering the garden, she decided to paint the outside of the flower petals with a small brush to restore their original color and brilliance! We would think that something is definitely wrong with this picture. Yet, that is similar to what churches do when they simply develop external "programs" and neglect the continual inner nourishment of God's Word and his Spirit.

Making Christ central to the life of a congregation further means developing an "economics of discipleship" based on the metaphor of the church as a household or *oikos*.[87] In previous chapters I have discussed the integration of the house church of the New Testament into household (*oikos*) infrastructures and the significance that this had for the spiritual and material care of individuals both within and outside the church. Most scholars agree that the role played by the head of the household in missional outreach and congregational development and practice cannot be over-emphasized.[88] As a patron of the church, the householder was responsible for the well-being of all members in his care. Since the household was a socioeconomic unit there was a natural connection between business and ministry.[89]

Many householder patrons were themselves business people who had contacts with powerful individuals in urban government and society and were able to provide legal protection and a certain amount of social legitimacy for the faith community that met in their homes.[90] It is in this context that Paul gives his instructions that wealth creation must be tied to good works and the care of others within the church (I Tim. 6:18). In other words, the purpose of business and wealth creation is primarily relational.[91] However, this natural connection between business and the church as a socioeconomic unit was lost over time with the fragmentation of the family, the diversification of the economy, business and church, as well as the secularization of public institutions. It is essential that we return to economic practices, ideas, and relationships that are supportive of the proper ends and purposes of the church. Budde and Brimlow rightly argue:

> A church that takes itself and its own economics seriously will work to reemphasize place, will structure economic practices that make it easier for churches to stay together longer, and will encourage economic practices that allow congregants to enter one another's lives more deeply and completely.[92]

In addition to Christian social entrepreneurial enterprises this could include the creation of church-based credit unions, experiments in labor sharing in which people exchange their labor time and skills for those of other members of the church, and church-based consumer cooperatives, workshops, and appliance centers for both work and household needs. "If the church begins to enter into experiments with economic production, common consumption, and labor allocation/organization, it can offer some hope of ransoming some of its members from unemployment, work in immoral occupations . . . or work under exploitative or inhumane conditions."[93]

It is not possible here to give an extended description of "worldview exegesis." Basically, we can say that a "worldview" is a person's view of reality, or set of beliefs and values that one holds to be true and lives by. A key to sustainable development is "appreciative inquiry," or a positive understanding of the religious and moral beliefs, historical experiences, cultural practices, and ethnic identities that comprise the "worldview" of the people we are trying to help. Avoiding the persistent temptation to engage in a one-way charity of "doing for" that ultimately results in more dependency and a loss of dignity and engaging in development "with" the poor that is culturally sensitive requires true dialogue and mutual understanding. This takes time and a focus on relationship building. Worldview exegesis therefore involves asking questions such as: What are the practical issues and opportunities in the community? What is there in the community that can be a positive means to creating a more positive future? How does our ministry or business strengthen the fabric of the community and enhance its capacity to become more self-sufficient? This does not mean endorsing the humanist dictums that "truth is relative" and that humans are basically good. Sin infects cultures as well as individuals. It results in the distorted worldviews and fractured relationships with God, self, others, and the environment that are the root causes of poverty in this first place. The worldview provided by the gospel is the only ultimate solution to the world's ills. But sharing the good news of the gospel is more effective when we enter each other's worlds as friends and co-workers who both learn and give and receive help from each other.[94]

The following is a brief description of the three key ingredients for sustainable impact (relational mutuality, responsible generosity, and integrated holistic development) and a listing of further questions in each area that must be addressed in assessing the "sustainability quotient" of a given project. It should be noted that some of these questions are more applicable to certain situations than others.[95]

Relational Mutuality: Projects should be based on mutual friendship, responsibility, and accountability. We should work alongside each other as co-laborers in a spirit of mutuality, reciprocity, and equality.

- *Are we committed to incarnational ministry* that brings us into personal contact and a deep personal relationship with those we are trying to serve?

- Is there a *joint agreement* between U.S. churches, missionaries, and nationals on pursuing a common vision and goal?

- Does the ministry project focus on creating *structures that avoid unhealthy dependency and foster interdepence characterized by principles of reciprosity, generosity, and equality?*

- Is there a *rejection of all paternalism*, recognizing that our goal is to build the national church and the national agenda not our own ministries? Instead of giving money to individuals do we support national churches, which in turn can hire their own staff directly; and do we refrain from performing ministry roles that can and should be filled by nationals?

- In our relationship, *do the most contextually relevant parties take the lead* and is this done in a way that affirms their gifts, experience, calling, vision, passion, and credibility to their maximum potential?

- Does the project plan *attract, retain and/or develop indigenous leadership* in the community and through the local church?

- Does the *initiative for developing* new vocational workers, planning and implementing of new projects, and launching new programs for new facilities development *originate with national leaders rather than with expatriate missionaries?*

- Has there been a careful evaluation of the *national church's capacity to maintain, manage, and operate the ministries created by the proposed investment of funds?*

- Do we affirm that *mission ministry is the primary responsibility of the local church* and only secondarily the responsibility of mission agencies, relief workers, and parachurch organizations which come along-side of the local church rather than co-opt it or compete with it?

- Do all participants have a *goal of ministry excellence?* Are ministry projects and programs resourced and evaluated for excellence? Are there clearly defined measurements for success and leadership structures, and is there a clearly established evaluation process for all parties involved?

Responsible Generosity: While not everyone has equal capacity, there is equal responsibility. Giving should be generous without encouraging irresponsibility. At the same time, the avoidance of unhealthy dependency should not be used to justify self-indulgence, selfishness, or apathy.

- Are we all committed to *extravagent generosity*, with all parties to the agreement committing to give all possible resources (monetary and otherwise) to serve the mutually agreed upon agenda?
- *Is giving accompanied by efforts to help desperate people rebuild human relationships and re-establish affiliation with meaningful support systems?* Is it our goal to be in close enough contact with recipients of aid that we can assist them in reconnecting with neighbors, rebuilding fractured families and creating a community through the local church characterized by love, acceptance, and forgiveness?
- Are all parties in agreement that *all churches (whether Western or indigenous) are accountable for stewardship* of all human, material and monetary resources entrusted to our care?
- Do we have *appropriate systems* for testing the recipient's willingness to work, teaching social and employment skills, and evaluating personal reliability and accountability?
- Do we have *biblical discernment* in distinguishing between giving which is truly an act of love that blesses the weak and giving that is boondoggle benefitting the wayward?
- To achieve long-term sustainability is the *employment of all able-bodied heads of households a higher priority than offering aid?* Are

able-bodied recipients of aid required to work in service to the community in return for the help they get; and are they expected to work relief workers out of their role as temporary support providers by assuming responsible and rewarding jobs? Do relief workers avoid doing jobs that the able bodied persons in the community could do themselves?

- Do we have a *commitment to true freedom* that promotes justice and equity for the poor and opposes oppression, nepotism, favoritism, and inequities that keep them in poverty?

- Is our *primary motivation for giving God's grace*, which brings lasting change to both individuals and communities and enables unreached and impoverished people to find their true identity and destiny through Christ?

Integrated Holistic Development: As an extension of integral mission, development should seek to transform people from what they are to what they are meant to be in Christ. It is holistic because it addresses the entire person in his/her context and in all areas of life. And it is integrated because all aspects of ministry are tied together instead of being segregated.[96]

- Does the project plan involve a *commitment to holistic transformation of individuals and communities*, including spiritual, economic, and social dimensions? Does it involve a relational approach that seeks to restore people's dignity (relationship with self), community (relationships with others), stewardship (relationship with environment), and spiritual intimacy (relationship with God)?

- Does the plan *seek community viability and self-sufficiency*, as measured by the ability (where possible) to harness market forces and/or other mechanisms of socio-economic development?

- Does the project plan utilize an *asset-based approach* that builds upon the skills, intelligence, labor, discipline, savings, creativity and courage of the people it is intended to serve?

- Does the plan *integrate all dimensions of ministry*, including evangelism, discipleship, socio-economic projects, and church multiplication?

- Is the ministry project *church driven and church based?* Is it connected to a local church or an indigenous church planting effort? Whenever and wherever possible, is the ministry project a catalyst for new churches?

- Is the project *culturally relevant to the context in which it is implemented?* Is it driven by indigenous partners; guided by principles of health and cultural intelligence; and designed, implemented, monitored, and evaluated in concert with the local indigenous church and people in the community?

- Does the project have a goal of *intentionally sustainable disciple-making ministry?* Do the socio-economic projects serve as labs for discipleship and spiritual development and help the local church to be self-multiplying?

- Does the project plan help in the *promotion of the gospel message?* Is the ministry project planned in such a way that it opens doors for the sharing of the gospel and gathering people into communities of faith? Is it people-focused, balancing love and proclamation? Is it driven by the end product of changed lives and healthy church multiplication?

With this we come to the end of this book. For Christians and churches that have become accustomed to "business as usual" the vision I have proposed may seem overly idealistic and even imprudent. When it comes to money, occupations, church life, etc. our natural tendency is to tone down the radical nature of Jesus' call to discipleship. But more than one observer of the religious landscape in American today has warned that unless there is a willingness to make fundamental changes the church will become increasingly irrelevant and divorced from a desperately needy world. The church as God's New Israel is meant to be outwardly looking, reflecting his future kingdom, not self-absorbed. May he grant us the collective courage, imagination, and creativity to find twenty-first century applications of the first-century church that point to his ultimate purpose to create a new earth and a new humanity:

> *Then I saw a new heaven and a new earth, for the first heaven and the first earth had passed away, and there was no longer any sea. I saw the Holy City, the new Jerusalem, coming down out of heaven from God, prepared as a bride beautifully dressed for her husband. And I heard a loud voice from the throne saying, "Now the dwelling of God is with men, and he will live with them. They will be his people, and God himself will be with them and be their God. He will wipe every tear from their eyes. There will be no more death or mourning or crying or pain, for the old order of things has passed away." He who was seated on the throne said, "I am making everything new!" Then he said, "Write this down, for these words are trustworthy and true." (Rev. 21:1-5).*

Notes

[1] I am *not* saying that cafés in churches cannot have a positive purpose. Cafés on church premises can be used to create a warm and inviting atmosphere for visitors, including non-Christians, and can have an evangelistic focus. My experience is that in most cases, however, cafes are oriented around relationships between Christians. The same tendency is apparent in Bible studies which are almost always made up exclusively of Christians. There is, of course, a place for Christian fellowship. But an exclusively "internal" focus or "attractional" strategy for reaching people in a community is not, in my opinion, biblical. In the first place, it is based on the expectation that "outsiders" should "fit into" our particular culture. This runs counter to the incarnational principle that we should be like Christ, who leaving his home in heaven became flesh and walked among us (John 1:14; Phil. 1:3-11). Furthermore, an exclusively "come to us" strategy for church ministry has limited impact. As Eric Swanson and Rick Rusaw state, "You are not reaching all you could be reaching by a 'come to' strategy alone. You can also extend your reach into the community as far as you can through your 'go to' model—employing those in your church to go into the highways and hedges of your community. This is what window seat churches do. We find ourselves telling pastors wherever we go, 'the only thing more difficult that getting the church to go into the community is getting the community into the church.' It is actually far easier, through regular influence, to get the church into the community than through sporadic contact try to get the

community into the church." Eric Swanson and Rick Rusaw, *The Externally Focused Quest: Becoming the Best Church FOR the Community* (San Francisco, CA: Jossey-Bass, 2010), p. 30.

[2] See Michael L Budde and Robert W. Brimlow, *Christianity Incorporated: How Business is Buying the Church* (Grand Rapids, MI: Brazos, 2002), pp. 49-50, 156.

[3] See Roberts, *Glocalization*, p. 42.

[4] Stephen Shields, "Churches in Missional Renaissance: Facilitating the Transition to a Missional Mindset," (Leadership Network, 2008. www.leadnet.org).

[5] Warren Bird, "The Heartbeat of Rising Influence Churches," (Leadership Network, 2011. www.leadnet.org)

[6] The concept of "servant leadership" has been criticized for creating the perception in our culture that the leader is weak and indecisive. Furthermore, lay people might conclude that it is only the leader who must serve. Neither of these popular conceptions of "servant leadership" is based on a true biblical understanding of leadership. Jesus presented himself as a model for servant leadership (Matt. 20:26-28). But he was far from being weak and indecisive. Furthermore, every follower of Christ is called to good works (Eph. 2:10) and is commanded to look out for the interests of others (Phil. 2:4). In this sense, every Christian is a servant. As will be discussed below, the primary focal point of servant leadership in the church is "to prepare God's people for works of service, so that the body of Christ may be built up" (Eph. 4:12).

[7] See Bruce Camp, "Major paradigm Shifts in World Evangelization," pp. 135-36.

[8] See Wright, *The Mission of God*, p. 322.

[9] Greg Hawkins and Cally Parkinson, *MOVE: What 1,000 Churches Reveal About Spiritual Growth* (Grand Rapids, MI: Zondervan, 2011), pp. 207-8.

[10] Ben Witherington III, *Work: A Kingdom Perspective on Labor* (Grand Rapids, MI: Eerdmans, 2011), p. 13

[11] Ibid., p. 45. It should be emphasized that Witherington is not disparaging the value what we normally associate with "work" (i.e., occupation). Nor is he saying that "making disciples" cannot take place in the context of the workplace. His only point is that, for the believer, fulfilling the Great Commission and the Great Commandment is primary and should inform everything else that we do.

[12] Ibid., pp. xii, 35.

[13] Ibid, pp. 116-19.

[14] Guinness, *Fit Bodies, Fat Minds*, p. 17.

[15] Ibid., p. 141,

[16] Os Guinness, *The Call: Finding and Fulfilling the Central purpose of Your Life* (Nashville, TN: Thomas Nelson, 2003), p. 1.

[17] Miller, *Lifework*, p. 12

[18] R. Paul Stevens, *The Other Six Days: Vocation, Work, and Ministry in Biblical Perspective* (Grand Rapids, MI: Eerdmans, 1999), p. 6.

[19] Witherington, *Work*, p. 165.

[20] Stevens, *The Other Six Days*, pp. 52-3.

[21] Ibid., pp. 25-6.

[22] Ibid., p. 53.

[23] See Marc Kolden, "Luther on Vocation," http://lutheranentrepreneurs.com/uploads/Luther_on_ Vocation.pdf, p. 382

[24] See Tom Sine, *Mustard Seed vs. McWorld: Reinventing Life and Faith for the Future*, (Grand Rapids, MI, Baker Books, 1999), p. 161.

[25] Witherington, *Work*, p. 32

[26] See Stevens, *The Other Six Days*, pp. 72-73.

[27] Guinness, *The Call*, p. 48.

[28] Witherington, *Work*, p. 24.

[29] Will Mancini, *Church Unique: How Missional Leaders Cast Vision, Capture culture, and Create Movement* (San Francisco, CA: Jossey-Bass, 2008), p. 84.

[30] Ibid., p. 90. In my opinion, a weakness in Mancini's otherwise excellent book is that not enough attention is given to cooperation and collaboration between local church bodies. As has been discussed previously, when the apostle Paul addresses the "local church" he has in mind all Christians within in a geographic locality (i.e., city or town), not just a local congregation or assembly of believers. Mancini is nonetheless right in emphasizing that, to be effective, a local congregation must move from the myriad of things it "can do" to the one thing (or few things) it "must do" based on its unique DNA. (Ibid., p. 59) Even when there is cooperation between local congregations, it is important for each congregation to discern how its unique giftings relate to the larger whole.

[31] Greg Ogden, *The New Reformation: Returning the Ministry to the People of God* (Grand Rapids, MI: Zondervan, 1990), p. 211,

[32] Guinness, *The Call*, p. 31.

[33] Stevens, *The Other Six Days*, pp. 73-5.

[34] Guinness, *The Call*, p. 40.

[35] John H Walton, *Genesis: the NIV Application Bible Commentary* (Grand Rapids, MI: Zondervan, 2001), pp. 136, 180-86. See also Beale, *The Temple and the Church's Mission*, pp. 84-85.

[36] Ibid., p. 86.

[37] Guinness, *The Call*, pp. 153-62.

[38] Witherington, *Work*, pp. 124-26.

[39] H. Dale Burke, *How to Lead and Still Have a Life: The 8 Principles of Less is More Leadership* (Eugene, OR: Harvest House, 2004), pp. 19, 131.

[40] Bill Easum, *Sacred Cows Make Gourmet Burgers: Ministry Anytime, Anywhere, by Anybody* (Nashville, TN: Abingdon, 1995), pp. 82-3.

[41] Burke, *How to Lead*, p. 126.

[42] Pat Springle, "Developing Leaders in a Postmodern World: Current Principles and Practices in Selecting and Equipping Leaders," (Leadership Network, 2009. www.leadnet.org)

[43] Ogden, *The New Reformation*, p. 61.

[44] Easum *Sacred Cows*, p. 72.

[45] Ibid., p. 116.

[46] Team-based ministry works best in the context of "permission-giving" systems as opposed to "command-and-control" systems. Permission-giving systems have the following characteristics: (1) there is unity in essentials: vision, mission, values, and beliefs. (2) In non-essentials there is freedom (worship styles and types of minis-

tries). And (3) in all things there is love, trust, collaboration and networking. For a detailed discussion of the nature of team-based ministry see Bill Easum, *Team Based Ministry* (21st Century Strategies, 2009).

[47] See Sherry Surratt and Wayne Smith, "Team Collaboration: Broadening the Church Leadership Platform," (Leadership Network, 2011. www.leadnet.org)

[48] Andy Williams and Dennis Welch, "Permission Granted: Churches Giving Marketplace Leaders the Green Light for Kingdom Impact," (Leadership Network, 2006. www.leadnet.org).

[49] "Halftime" is term coined by Bob Buford to refer to that stage that many people reach (around mid-life) when they reassess where they are going and what they want to do with their lives. See www.Halftime.org. Also Bob Buford, *Half Time: Changing Your Game Plan From Success to Significance* (Grand Rapids, MI: Zondervan, 1994).

[50] See Warren Bird, "Lean Staffing: Churches That Handle Staffing Costs in Under 35% of Budget," (Leadership Network, 2010. www.leadnet.org.)

[51] Stark, *The Rise of Christianity,* p. 20.

[52] Ibid., pp. 83-4.

[53] Ibid, p. 84.

[54] Ibid., p. 161.

[55] Ibid.,

[56] Ed Stetzer and David Putman, *Breaking the Missional Code: Your Church Can Become a Missionary in Your Community* (Nashville, TN: Broadman and Homan, 2006), p. 171,

[57] Ibid., p. 172.

[58] Quoted in Ibid., p. 173,

[59] Ibid., pp. 173-4.

[60] Ibid., pp. 174-79.

[61] Melissa Giovagnoli and Jocelyn Carter-Miller, *Networlding: Building Relationships and Opportunities for Success* (San Francisco, CA: Jossey-Bass, 2000).

[62] Ibid., pp. 5-23.

[63] Ibid., p. 5.

[64] Ibid., pp. 37-190.

[65] See Nile Harper, *Urban Churches, Vital Signs: Beyond Charity Toward Justice* (Grand Rapids, MI: Eerdmans, 1999), p. 7.

[66] Robert and Julia Banks, *The Church Comes Home* (Peabody, MA: Hendrickson, 1998), pp. 237-38.

[67] Robert Wuthnow, *Christianity in the Twenty-First Century: Reflections on the Challenge Ahead* (New York, Oxford University Press, 1993), p. 33.

[68] See Steve Corbett and Brian Fikkert, *When Helping Hurts: How to Alleviate Poverty Without Hurting the Poor and Yourself* (Chicago, IL: Moody, 2009).

[69] Corbett and Fikkert, *When Helping Hurts,* p. 142.

[70] Ibid, pp. 115-19.

[71] See Roberts, *Glocalization,* pp. 86-87.

[72] Corbettt and Fikkert, *When Helping Hurts,* p. 167.

[73] John Rowell, *To Give or Not To Give? Rethinking Dependency, Restoring Generosity, and Redefining Sustainability* (Atlanta, GA: Authentic, 2006), p. 48.

[74] Ibid., p. 74

[75] Ibid., p. 224.

[76] Jim Collins, *Good to Great and the Social Sectors: A Monograph to Accompany Good to Great* (Boulder, CO: Jim Collins, 2005), pp. 18-19.

[77] Ibid., p. 23.

[78] Rowell, p. 228.

[79] See, for example, Stuart L. Hart, *Capitalism at the Crossroads: Aligning Business, Earth and Humanity* (Upper Saddle River, NJ: Wharton School Publishing, 2007) and Muhammad Yunus, *Creating a World Without Poverty: Social Business and the Future of Capitalism* (Philadelphia PA: Public Affairs, 2007).

[80] Shaw, E., & Carter, S. "Social entrepreneurship: Theoretical Antecedents and Empirical Analysis of Entrepreneurial Processes and Outcomes." *Journal of Management and Organization* 13 (2007), pp. 331-44.

[81] See Budde and Brimlow, *Christianity Incorporated*, op. cit., p. 170.

[82] Daniel Bryon and Michael T. Cooper, "A Christian Rationale for Social Enterprise." The Timothy Center (www.thetimothycenter.org), p. 5.

[83] Corbett and Fikkert, *When Help Hurts,* p. 144

[84] Hart, *Capitalism at the Crossroads*, p. 237.

[85] See: http://www.thetimothycenter.org.

[86] Hawkins and Parkinson, *MOVE*, p. 208.

[87] Budde and Brimlow, *Christianity Incorporated*, pp. 155f.

[88] See Gehring, *House Church and Mission*, p. 292.

[89] See Michael T. Cooper, "How Social Enterprises Fulfill a New Testament Model of Business and Can Contribute to Addressing Social Justice Issues," (The Timothy Center for Sustainable Transformation), p. 7.

[90] Gehring, *House Church and Mission*, p. 292.

[91] Cooper, "New Testament Model of Business," p. 10.

[92] Budde and Brimlow, *Christianity Incorporated*, p. 171.

[93] Ibid., pp. 171-72.

[94] See Lupton, *Compassion, Justice and the Christian Life*, pp. 67, 107.

[95] These questions have been borrowed from the following sources: 1. Rowell, *To Give or Not to Give*, op. cit., pp. 146-67; 2. Lupton, *Compassion, Justice and the Christian Life,* pp. 108-9; 3. Steve Corbett and Brian Fikkert, *When Helping Hurts*, pp. 190-91; 4. 'TouchGlobal Guiding Principles" (Unpublished article of EFCA TouchGlobal)

[96] See James Gustafson, "Integrated Holistic Development and the World Mission of the Church," (http:// www.thaicov.org/resources/documents/holistic.html, 1985).

Selected Bibliography

A Call to an Ancient Evangelical Future. "The Full Text of an Appeal to Live the Biblical Narrative." *Christianity Today* (9/1/2006), http://www.christianitytoday.com/ct/2006/september/11.57.html?start=1.

Anderson, Ray. *An Emergent Theology for Emerging Churches.* Downers Grove, IL: InterVarsity, 2006.

Baker, Ken. "Kingdom Mission," http://www.edsmither.com/ uploads/5/6/4/6/564614/ baker_ ems_2012.pdf

Banks, Robert. *Paul's Idea of Community, rev. ed.* Peabody, MA: Hendrickson, 1994.

Banks, Robert and Julia. *The Church Comes Home.* Peabody, MA: Hendrickson, 1998.

Banks, William. *In Search of the Great Commission: What Did Jesus Really Say?* Chicago, Moody Press, 1991.

Barker, Ash. *Make Poverty Personal: Taking the Poor as Seriously as the Bible Does.* Grand Rapids, MI: Baker Books, 2009.

Barker, Kenneth L. "The Scope and Center of Old and New Testament Theology and Hope." In *Dispensationalism, Israel and the Church: The Search for Definition*, edited by Craig A. Blaising and Darrell L. Bock, 293-328. Grand Rapids, MI: Zondervan, 1992.

Barnett, Paul. *Paul: Missionary of Jesus*. Grand Rapids, MI: Eerdmans, 2008.

Barram, Michael. *Mission and Moral Reflection in Paul*. New York: Peter Lang, 2006.

Bassler, Jouette M. *Navigating Paul: An Introduction to Key Theological Concepts*. Louisville, KY: Westminster John Knox Press, 2007.

Batson, David. *The Treasure Chest of the Early Christians: Faith, Care and Community from the Apostolic Age to Constantine the Great*. Grand Rapids, MI: Eerdmans, 2001.

Bauckham, Richard. *Bible and Mission: Christian Witness in a Postmodern World*. Grand Rapids, MI: Baker Academic, 2003.

Beale, G.K. *The Temple and the Church's Mission: A Biblical Theology of the Dwelling Place of God*. Downers Grove, IL: InterVarsity, 2004.

Berger, Peter. *The Noise of Solemn Assemblies: Christian Commitment and the Religious Establishment in America*. Garden City, New York: Doubleday, 1961

Bird, Michael f. *Introducing Paul: The Man, His Mission and His Message*. Downers Grove, IL: IVP Academic, 2008.

_____. "What is there Between Minneapolis and Durham?: A Third Way in the Piper-Wright Debate." *Journal of the Evangelical Theological Society* 54 (2011): 299-309.

Blaising, Craig A. and Darrell L. Bock. *Progressive Dispensationalism: An Up-To-Date Handbook of Contemporary Dispensational Thought*. Wheaton, IL: BridgePoint, 1993.

Billings, Todd. "What Makes a Church Missional?" *Christianity Today* (March 5 2008), http://www. christianitytoday.com/ct/2008/march/16.56.html

Bloesch, Donald G. *Freedom for Obedience: Evangelical Ethics for Contemporary Times.* San Francisco, CA: Harper and Row, 1987.

_____. *Crumbling Foundations: Death and Rebirth in an Age of Upheaval.* Grand Rapids, MI: Zondervan, 1984.

_____. *Essentials of Evangelical Theology, Vol. 2: Life, Ministry and Hope.* New York: Harper and Row, 1978.

Bock, Darrell L. "Hermeneutics of Progressive Dispensationalism," in *Three Central Issues in Dispensationalism: A Comparison of Traditional and Progressive Views,* edited by Herbert W. Bateman IV, 85-118. Grand Rapids, MI: Kregel, 1999.

Bosch, David. *Transforming Mission: Paradigm Shifts in the Theology of Mission.* Maryknoll, NY: Orbis, 1991.

Budde, Michael L. and Robert W. Brimlow, *Christianity Incorporated: How Business is Buying the Church* (Grand Rapids, MI: Brazos, 2002

Buford, Bob. *Half Time: Changing Your Game Plan From Success to Significance.* Grand Rapids, MI: Zondervan, 1994

Burke, H. Dale. *How to Lead and Still Have a Life: The 8 Principles of Less is More Leadership.* Eugene, OR: Harvest House, 2004.

Campbell, Evvy Hay, ed. *Holistic Mission.* Lausanne Occassional Paper 33. Lausanne Committee for World Evangelization, 2004.

Cannon, Mae Elise. *Social Justice Handbook: Small Steps for a Better World.* Downers Grove, IL: IVP Books, 2009.

Carson, D.A. *Becoming Conversant with the Emerging Church: Understanding a Movement and its Implications.* Grand Rapids, MI: Zondervan, 2005.

Collins, Jim. *Good to Great and the Social Sectors: A Monograph to Accompany Good to Great.* Boulder, CO: Jim Collins, 2005.

Conn, Harvie. *The Urban Face of Mission.* Phillipsburg, PA: P&R Publishing, 2002.

Conn, Harvie and Manuel Ortiz. *Urban Ministry: The Kingdom, the City and the People of God.* Downers Grove, IL: IVP Academic, 2010.

Corbett, Steve and Brian Fikkert. *When Helping Hurts: How to Alleviate Poverty Without Hurting the Poor and Yourself.* Chicago, IL: Moody, 2009

Costas, Orlando. *From the Periphery: Missiology in Context.* Maryknoll, NY: Orbis, 1982.

Dayton, Donald W. *Discovering an Evangelical Heritage.* NY: Harper and Row, 1976.

Denova, Rebecca I. *The Things Accomplished Among Us: Prophetic Tradition in the Structural Pattern of Luke-Acts.* Shefield: Sheffield Academic Press, 1997.

Dyrness, William A. *How Does America Hear the Gospel?* Grand Rapids, MI: Eerdmans, 1989.

Easum, Bill. *Sacred Cows Make Gourmet Burgers: Ministry Anytime, Anywhere, by Anybody.* Nashville, TN: Abingdon, 1995.

Engel, James F. and William A. Dyrness. *Changing the Mind of Missions: Where Have We Gone Wrong?* Downers Grove, IL: InterVarsity, 2000.

Estes, Douglas. *SimChurch: Being the Church in the Virtual World.* Grand Rapids, MI: Zondervan, 2009.

Field, Leslie Leyland. "The Gospel is More Than a Story: Rethinking Narrative and Testimony." *Christianity Today* (July/August 2012), http://www.christianitytoday.com/ct/2012/july-august/the-gospel-is-more-than-a-story.html

Robert L. Foster. "Understanding Justice in the New Testament, www.sbl-site.org/assets/ pdfs/TBv2i5_ Fosterjustice.pdf

Frankforter, A. Daniel. *Stones into Bread: A Critique of Contemporary Worship.* Louisville, KY: Westminster John Knox, 2001.

Frend, W.H.C. *The Rise of Christianity.* Philadelphia, PA: Fortresss, 1984

Fulford, Robert. *The Triumph of Narrative: Storytelling in the Age of Mass Culture.* New York, NY: Broadway Books, 1999.

Georgi, Dieter. *Remembering the Poor: The History of Paul's Collection for Jerusalem.* Nashville, TN: Abingdon, 1992.

Giles, Kevin. *What on Earth in the Church? An Exploration in New Testament Theology.* Downers Grove, IL: InterVarsity, 1995.

Giovagnoli, Melissa and Jocelyn Carter-Miller, *Networlding: Building Relationships and Opportunities for Success.* San Francisco, CA: Jossey-Bass, 2000.

Goheen, Michael W. "The Urgency of Reading the Bible as One Story," *Theology Today* (Vol. 64, 2008): 469-483.

_____. *A Light to the Nations: The Missional Church and the Biblical Story.* Grand Rapids, MI: Baker Academic, 2011.

_____. "Historical Perspectives on the Missional Church Movement: Probing Lesslie Newbigin's Formative Influence," *Trinity Journal for Theology and Ministry,* http://www.missionworldview. com/wp-content/uploads/2011/06/Historical-Perspectives-on-Missional-Church.pdf

Glasser, Arthur F. *Announcing the Kingdom: The Story of God's Mission in the Bible.* Grand Rapids, MI: Baker, 2003.

Gehring, Roger. *House Church and Mission: The Importance of Household Structures in Early Christianity.* Peabody, MA: Hendrickson, 2004.

Grant, George. *The Micah Mandate: Balancing the Christian Life.* Nashville, TN: Cumberland House, 1999.

Grenz, Stanley J. *Theology for the Community of God.* Grand Rapids, MI: Eerdmans, 2000

Guder Darrell L. *Be My Witnesses: The Church's Mission, Message and Messengers.* Grand Rapids, MI: Eerdmans, 1985.

_____. *The Continuing Conversion of the Church.* Grand Rapids, MI: Eerdmans, 2000.

_____. ed. *Missional Church: A Vision for the Sending of the Church in North America.* Grand Rapids, MI: Eerdmans, 1998.

Guinness, Os. *Fit Bodies, Fat Minds: Why Evangelicals Don't Think and What to Do About It.* Grand Rapids, MI: Baker Books, 1994.

_____. *The Call: Finding and Fulfilling the Central purpose of Your Life.* Nashville, TN: Thomas Nelson, 2003.

Guteirrez, Gustavo. *A Theology of Liberation: History, Politics and Liberation.* Maryknoll, NY: Orbis, 1988

Hanks, Thomas D. *God So Loved the Third World: The Bible, the Reformation, and Liberation.* Maryknoll, NY: Orbis, 1983.

Hansen, G. Walter *Galatians.* Downers Grove, IL: InterVarsity 1994.

Harper, Nile. *Urban Churches, Vital Signs: Beyond Charity Toward Justice.* Grand Rapids, MI: Eerdmans, 1999

Haugen, Gary. *Good News about Injustice: A Witness of Courage in a Hurting World* (Downers Grove, IL: InterVarsity, 1999.

Hawkins, Greg and Cally Parkinson, *MOVE: What 1,000 Churches Reveal About Spiritual Growth*. Grand Rapids, MI: Zondervan, 2011.

Hays, Richard B. *The Moral Vision of the New Testament: A Contemporary Introduction to New Testament Ethics*. San Francisco, CA: Harper Collins, 1996.

Hawthorne, Steve. "Response to Little's 'What Makes Mission Christian?'" *International Journal of Frontier Missiology* (Summer 2008): 77-8.

Hegemen, David. *Plowing in Hope: Toward a Biblical Theology of Culture*. Moscow, Idaho: Canon, 1999.

Heick, Otto W. *A History of Christian Thought, Vol. I*. Philadelphia, PA: Fortress, 1965.

Henry, Carl F. H. *The Uneasy Conscience of Modern Fundamentalism*. Grand Rapids, MI: Eerdmans, 1947.

_____. *A Plea for Evangelical Demonstration*. Grand Rapids, MI: Baker, 1971.

_____. *The Christian Mindset in a Secular Society: Promoting Evangelical Renewal and National Righteousness*. Portland, OR: Multnomah, 1984.

_____. *God, Revelation, and Authority, Vol. IV: The God Who Speaks and Shows*. (Wheaton,. IL: Crossway, 1999.

_____. "A Summons to Justice," *Christianity Today*, 36 (July 20, 1992): 40.

Hesselgrave, David J. *Planting Churches Cross-Culturally: North America and Beyond*. Grand Rapids, MI: Baker, 2000.

Hesselgrave, David J. and Ed Stetzer, eds. *MissionsShift:: Global Mission Issues in the Third Millenium*. Nashville, TN: B&H Publishing Group, 2010.

Hirsch, Alan. *The Forgotten Ways: Reactivating the Missional Church.* Grand Rapids, MI: Brazos Press, 2006.

Holm, Joel. *Church Centered Mission: Transforming the Church to Change the World.* Joel Holm Ministry Resources, 2004.

Horton, Michael. *The Gospel Commission: Recovering God's Strategy for Making Disciples* . Grand Rapids, MI: Baker Books, 2011.

_____. *Beyond Culture Wars: Is America a Mission Field or Battlefield?* Chicago, IL: Moody Press, 1994.

Hunter, James Davison. *To Change the World: The Irony, Tragedy, and Possibility of Christianity in the Late Modern World.* New York: Oxford University Press, 2010.

_____. "To Change the World." *Trinity Forum Briefing* (Vol. 3, No. 2, 2002), http://www.sallt. com/Websites/saltandlight/images/TO _CHANGE_THE_WORLD__HUNTER_.pdf

Hunter, Joel. *A New Kind of Conservative.* Ventura, CA: Regal, 2008.

Jethani, Skye. *The Divine Commodity: Discovering Faith Beyond Consumer Christianity.* Grand Rapids, MI: Zondervan, 2009.

Joubert, Stephen. *Paul as Benefactor: Reciprocity, Strategy and Theological Reflection in Paul's Collection.* Toubingen: Mohr Siebeck, 2000.

Kaiser, Walter C. *Mission in the Old Testament: Israel as a Light to the Nations.* Grand Rapids, MI: Baker, 2000.

Keller, Tim. *Generous Justice: How God's Grace Makes Us Just.* New York: Dutton, 2010.

_____."The Missional Church," http://www.shenango.org/PDF/ PMC/Tim%20Keller.pdf

_____. "The Gospel and the Poor," *Themelios* 33-3 (December 2008), http://s3.amazonaws. com/tgc-documents/journal-issues/33.3/ Themelios_33.3.pdf

Kostenberger, Andreas and Peter T. Obrien. *Salvation to the Ends of the Earth: A Biblical Theology of Mission.* Downers Grove, IL: InterVarsity, 2001.

Ladd, George Eldon. *The Presence of the Future: The Eschatology of Biblical Realism.* Grand Rapids, MI: Eerdmans, 1974.

Larkin, William J. Jr. and Joel F. Williams, eds. *Mission in the New Testament: An Evangelical Approach.* Maryknoll, NY: Orbis.

Lewis, Robert. *The Church of Irresistible Influence: Bridge-Building Stories to Help Reach Your Community.* Grand Rapids, MI: Zondervan, 2001.

Lewis. Lewis and Wayne Cordeiro. *Culture Shift: Transforming Your Church from the Inside Out.* San Francisco, CA: Jossey-Bass, 2005.

Linthicum, Robert. *Transforming Power: Biblical Strategies for Making a Difference in Your Community.* Downers Grove, IL: InterVarsity, 2003.

_____. *City of God, City of Satan: A Biblical Theology for the Urban Church.* Grand Rapids, MI: Zondervan, 1991.

Little, Christopher R. "What Makes Mission Christian?" *International Journal of Frontier Mission* (Summer 2008): 67-70.

Lohfink, Gerhard. *Jesus and Community; The Social Dimension of Christian Faith.* Philadelphia, PA: Fortress, 1982.

Longenecker, Bruce W. *Remember the Poor: Paul, Poverty and the Greco-Roman World.* Grand Rapids, MI: Eerdmans, 2010.

Longenecker, Richard N. *New Testament Social Ethics for Today.* Grand Rapids, MI: Eerdmans, 1984.

Lupton, Robert D. *Compassion, Justice and the Christian Life: Rethinking Ministry to the Poor.* Ventura, CA: Regal, 2007.

Mancini, Will. *Church Unique: How Missional Leaders Cast Vision, Capture culture, and Create Movement.* San Francisco, CA: Jossey-Bass, 2008.

Marsden, George M. *Fundamentalism and American Culture, New Edition.* New York, NY: Oxford University Press, 2006.

Marshall, I Howard. *New Testament Theology: Many Witnesses, One Gospel* (Downers Grove, IL: InterVarsity, 2004.

Marshall, Paul. *Thine is the Kingdom: A Biblical Perspective on the Nature of Government and Politics Today.* Grand Rapids, MI: Eerdmans, 1984.

Mathison, Keith A. *Postmillennialism: An Eschatology of Hope.* Phillipsburg, NJ: P&R Publishing, 1999.

McIntosh, Gary and Paul Engle, eds. *Evaluating the Church Growth Movement: 5 Views.* Grand Rapids, MI: Zondervan, 2004.

McLaren, Brian. *Finding Our Way: The Return of the Ancient Practices.* Nashville, TN: Thomas Nelson, 2005.

_____. *Generous Orthodoxy.* Grand Rapids, MI: Zondervan, 2004.

_____. *Everything Must Change: Jesus, Global Crises, and a Revolution of Hope.* Nashville: Thomas Nelson, 2007.

McNeal, Reggie. *The Present Future: Six Tough Questions for the Church.* San Francisco, CA: Jossey-Bass, 2003.

McKnight, Scott. *NIV Application Bible: Galatians.* Grand Rapids, MI: Zondervan, 1995.

Meeks, Wayne A. *The First Urban Christians: the Social World of the Apostle Paul.* New Haven, CT: Yale University Press, 2003.

_____. *The Origins of Christian Morality: The First Two Centuries.* New Haven, CT: Yale University Press, 1993.

Meggit, Justin J. *Paul, Poverty and Survival.* Edinburgh: T&T Clark, 1998.

Miles, Todd L. "A Kingdom without a King? Evaluating the Kingdom Ethic(s) of the Emerging Church," http://www.sbts.edu/ resources/files/2010/02/sbjt_121_miles.pdf

Miller, Darrow L. *Discipling Nations: The Power of Truth to Transform Cultures.* Seattle, WA: YWAM, 1998.

_____. *Life Work: A Biblical Theology For What You Do Every Day.* Seattle, WA: YWAM, 2009.

Miller, James C. *The Obedience of Faith, the Eschatological People of God, and the Purpose of Romans.* Atlanta, GA: Society of Biblical Literature, 2000.

_____. "The Jewish Context of Paul's Gentile Mission," *Tyndale Bulletin* 58/1 (2007): 102-115

Moo, Douglas J. *Romans: The NIV Application Commentary; From Biblical Text to Contemporary Life.* Grand Rapids, MI: Zondervan, 2000.

Moore, Russell D. *The Kingdom of Christ: The New Evangelical Perspective.* Wheaton, IL: Crossway, 2004.

_____. "Triumph of the Warrior King: A Theology of the Great Commission," http://www. russellmoore.com/documents/russell moore/Theology_of_the_Great_Commission.pdf

Mott, Stephen Charles. *Biblical Ethics and Social Change.* New York: Oxford University Press, 1982

Mouw, Richard. *Political Evangelism.* Grand Rapids, MI: Eerdmans, 1973.

Neill, Stephen. *Creative Tension*. London: Edinburgh Press, 1959.

Nickle, Keith F. *The Collection: A Study in Paul's Strategy*. Naperville, IL: Alec R. Allenson, 1966.

Noll, Mark A. *The Scandal of the Evangelical Mind*. Grand Rapids, MI: Eerdmans, 1994.

Ogden, Greg. *The New Reformation: Returning the Ministry to the People of God*. Grand Rapids, MI: Zondervan, 1990.

Osborne, Grant. *The Hermeneutical Spiral, Revised and Expanded Version*. Downers Grove, IL: InterVarsity, 1993.

Owens, Virginia Stem. *The Total Image, or Selling Jesus in the Modern Age*. Grand Rapids, MI: Eerdmans, 1980.

Padilla, C. Renee. *Mission Between the Times*. Grand Rapids, MI: Eerdmans, 1985.

_____. "What is Integral Mission?" http://lareddelcamino.net/en/images/Articles/what%20is% integral%20mission%20cr%20 padilla.pdf

Pao, David W. *Acts and the Isaianic New Exodus*. Grand Rapids, MI: Baker Academic, 2000.

Payne, Bishop Claude E and Hamilton Beazley. *Reclaiming the Great Commission: A Practical Model for Transforming Denominations and Congregations*. San Francisco, CA: Jossey-Bass, 2000.

Perkins, John M. *Restoring At-Risk Communities: Doing It Together and Doing It Right*. Grand Rapids, MI: Baker, 1995

Peterson, Jim. *Lifestyle Discipleship: The Challenge of Following Jesus in Today's World*. Colorado Springs, CO: NavPress, 1993.

Pilgrim, Walter E. *Good News for the Poor: Wealth and Poverty in Luke-Acts*. Mpls, MN: Augsburg, 1981.

Piper, John. *God's Passion for His Glory: Living the Vision of Jonathan Edwards*. Wheaton, IL: Crossway, 1998, 2006.

_____. *Let the Nations be Glad! The Supremacy of God in Missions*. Grand Rapids, MI: 1993.

Prior, Michael. *Jesus the Liberator: Nazareth Liberation Theology (Luke 4:16-30)*. Sheffield, England: Sheffield Academic Press, 1995.

Putman, Robert D. *Bowling Alone: The Collapse and Revival of American Community* (New York, NY: Touchstone, 2000.

Rauschenbusch, Walter. *Christianity and the Social Crisis*. London: Macmillan, 1907.

_____. *A Theology for the Social Gospel*. New York: Macmillan, 1917. Reprinted by Nashville, TN: Abingdon, 1981.

Roberts, Bob. *Glocalization: How Followers of Jesus Engage a Flat World*. Grand Rapids, MI: Zondervan, 2007.

_____. *Transformation: How Glocal Churches Transform Lives and the World*. Grand Rapids, MI: Zondervan, 2006.

Roberts, Vaughan. *God's Big Picture: Tracing the Storyline of the Bible*. Downers Grove, IL: IVP, 2002.

Rowell, John. *To Give or Not To Give? Rethinking Dependency, Restoring Generosity, and Redefining Sustainability*. Atlanta, GA: Authentic, 2006.

Charles C. Ryrie, Charles C. *Dispensationalism, Revised and Expanded*. Chicago: Moody Press, 1995.

Samuel, Vinay and Christ Sugden. *Mission as Transformation: A Theology of the Whole Gospel*. Carlisle, CA: Regnum, 1999.

Schnackenburg, Rudolf. *God's Rule and Kingdom*. New York: Herder and Herder, 1963.

Silvoso, Ed. *Anointed for Business; How Christians Can Use Their Influence in the Markeplace to Change the World*. Vetura, CA: Regal, 2002.

Scheffer, Steve. *Living in the Overlap: How Jesus' Kingdom Proclamation Can Transform Your World*. Enumclaw, WA: WinePress, 2010.

Schnabel, Eckhard J. *Early Christian Mission, Vol. I: Jesus and the Twelve*. Downers Grove, IL: InterVarsity, 2004.

_____. *Early Christian Mission, Vol. II: Paul and the Early Church*. Downers Grove, IL: InterVarsity, 2004.

Schnelle, Udo. *Apostle Paul: His Life and Theology*. Grand Rapids, MI: Baker Academic, 2003.

Schreiner, Thomas R. *Magnifying God in Christ: A Summary of New Testament Theology*. Grand Rapids, MI: Baker Academic, 2010.

Schultze, Quentin J. *High-Tech Worship? Using Presentational Technologies Wisely*. Grand Rapids, MI: Baker Books, 2004.

Schultze, Quentin J. and Robert Woods Jr. eds. *Understanding Evangelical Media: The Changing Face of Christian Communication*. Downers Grover, IL: InterVarsity Press, 2008.

Schottroff, L and W. Stegemann. *Jesus and the Hope of the Poor*. Maryknoll, NY: Orbis, 1986.

Scott, Waldron. *Bring Forth Justice: A Contemporary Perspective on Mission*. Grand Rapids, MI: Eerdmans, 1980.

Shenk David W and Ervin R. Stutzman. *Creating Communities of the Kingdom: New Testament Models of Church Planting*. Scottdale, PA: Herald Press, 1988

Sider, Ronald J. *Good New and Good Works: A Theology for the Whole Gospel*. Grand Rapids, MI: Baker Books, 1993.

_____. *Rich Christians in an Age of Hunger*. Dallas, TX: Word, 1990.

Sider, Ronald and James Parker III. "How Broad is Salvation in Scripture?" In *Word and Deed: Evangelism and Social Responsibility*, edited by Bruce J. Nicholls. Grand Rapids, MI: Eerdmans, 1985

Sine, Tom. *The New Conspirators: Creating the Future One Mustard Seed at a Time*. Downers Grove, IL: IVP Books, 2008.

_____. *Mustard Seed vs. McWorld: Reinventing Life and Faith for the Future*. Grand Rapids, MI: Baker, 1999.

Smith, Timothy L. *Revivalism and Social Reform in Mid-Nineteenth-Century America*. New York: Abingdon, 1957.

Snyder, Howard A. *Models of the Kingdom: Gospel, Culture and Mission in Biblical and Historical Perspective*. Eugene, OR: Wipf and Stock Publishers, 1991.

Stamoolis, James J. "A Brief history of Evangelical Involvement in Social Justice." in *Social Injustice: What Evangelicals Need to Know About the World*, edited by William J. Moulder and Michael T. Cooper, 4. Lake Forest, IL: Timothy Center Press, 2011.

Stark, Rodney. *The Rise of Christianity*. San Francisco, CA: HarperSanFrancisco, 1997.

Stearns, Richard. *The Hole in Our Gospel: What Does God Expect from Us?* Nashville, TN: Thomas Nelson, 2009.

Stetzer, Ed. *Planting Missional Churches: Planting a Church That's Biblically Sound and Reaching People in Culture*. Nashville, TN: B&H Academic, 2006.

Stetzer, Ed and David Putman. *Breaking the Missional Code: Your Church Can Become a Missionary in Your Community*. Nashville, TN: Broadman and Homan, 2006.

Stevens, R. Paul. *The Other Six Days: Vocation, Work, and Ministry in Biblical Perspective*. Grand Rapids, MI: Eerdmans, 1999.

Stevens, Tim and Tony Morgan. *Simply Strategic Growth: Attracting a Crowd to Your Church.* Loveland, CO: Group, 2005.

Stott, John, R.W. *Human Rights and Human Wrongs: Major Issues for a New Century.* Grand Rapids, MI: Baker,

_____. *Christian Mission in the Modern World.* Downers Grove, IL: InterVarsity, 1975.

Swanson, Eric and Rick Rusaw, *The Externally Focused Quest: Becoming the Best Church FOR the Community.* San Francisco, CA: Jossey-Bass, 2010

Tasker, R.V.B. *The Gospel According to St. John.* Grand Rapids, MI: Eerdmans, 1977.

Thomas, Cal and Ed Dobson. *Blinded by Might: Why the Christian Right Can't Save America.* Grand Rapids, MI: Zondervan, 1999.

VanDrunen, David. *Living in God's Two Kingdoms: A Biblical Vision for Christianity and Culture* Wheaton, IL: Crossway, 2010.

Van Engen, Charles. *God's Missionary People: Rethinking the Purpose of the Local Church.* Grand Rapids, MI: Baker, 1991.

Van Gelder, Craig and Dwight Zscheile. *The Missional Church in Perspective: Mapping Trends and Shaping the Conversation.* Grand Rapids, MI: Baker Academic, 2011

Vanhoozer, Kevin J. *The Drama of Doctrine: A Canonical Linguistic Approach to Theology.* Nashville, TN: Westminster John Knox, 2005.

_____ ed. *Everyday Theology: How to Read Cultural Texts and Interpret Trends.* Grand Rapids, MI: Baker Academic, 2007.

Verhey, Allen. *The Great Reversal: Ethics and the New Testament.* Grand Rapids, MI: Eerdmans, 1984.

Viola, Frank. *Rethinking the Wineskin: The Practice of the New Testament Church.* Present Testimony Ministry, 2001.

Wainwright, Geoffrey. *Eucharist and Eschatology.* New York: Oxford University Press, 1981.

Walton, John H. *Genesis: the NIV Application Bible Commentary.* Grand Rapids, MI: Zondervan, 2001.

Wax, Trevin. "The Gospel is More Than a Story: A Conversation with Leslie Leyland Fields," http://thegospelcoalition.org/

Wilson, William Julius. *The Truly Disadvantaged: The Inner City, the Underclass and Public Policy.* Chicago: University of Chicago Press, 1987.

Winter, Bruce. *Seek the Welfare of the City: Christians as Benefactors and Citizens.* Grand Rapids, MI: Eerdmans, 1994.

Witherington III, Ben. *Work: A Kingdom Perspective on Labor.* Grand Rapids, MI: Eerdmans, 2011.

Wolters, Albert. *Creation Regained: Biblical Basics for a Reformational Worldview.* Grand Rapids, MI: Eerdmans, 1985.

Wolterstorff, Nicholas. *Justice: Rights and Wrongs.* Princeton, NJ: Princeton University Press, 2010

Wright, Christopher J. H. *The Mission of God: Unlocking the Bible's Grand Narrative.* Downers Grove, IL: IVP Academic, 2006.

_____. *The Mission of God's People: A Biblical Theology of the Church's Mission.* Grand Rapids, MI: Zondervan, 2010.

_____. *Old Testament Ethics for the People of God.* Downers Grove, IL: Inter-Varsity, 2004.

_____. *Knowing Jesus Through the Old Testament.* Downers Grove, IL: Inter-Varsity, 1992.

Wright, N.T. *The New Testament and the People of God.* Mpls, MN: Fortress, 1992.

_____. *How God Became King: the Forgotten Story of the Gospels.* New York: HarperOne, 2012.

_____. *What Saint Paul Really Said: Was Paul of Tarsus the Real Founder of Christianity?* Grand Rapids, MI: Eerdmans, 1997.

_____. *Paul in Fresh Perspective.* Mpls, MN: Fortress Press, 2005.

_____. *Evil and the Justice of God.* Downers Grove, IL: InterVarsity Press, 2006.

Wuthnow, Robert. *Boundless Faith: The Global Outreach of American Churches.* Berkeley, CA: University of California Press, 2010.

_____. *Christianity in the Twenty-First Century: Reflections on the Challenge Ahead.* New York, Oxford University Press, 1993.

Yamamori, Tetsunao and C. Rene Padilla, eds. *The Local Church, Agent of Transformation,.* Buenos Aires: Kairos, 2004.

Yoder, John Howard. *The Politics of Jesus* (Grand Rapids, MI: Eerdmans, 1972.

12806531R00220

Made in the USA
San Bernardino, CA
27 June 2014